Dark Affinities, Dark Imaginaries

Dark Affinities, Dark Imaginaries

A MIND'S ODYSSEY

JOSEPH NATOLI

Cover image: Joseph Phillip Natoli, "Yellow Barque," oil on canvas, 15" × 18", 2014

Published by State University of New York Press, Albany

© 2017 Joseph Natoli

All rights reserved

Printed in the United States of America

For information, contact State University of New York Press, Albany, NY www.sunypress.edu

Production, Jenn Bennett
Marketing, Anne M. Valentine

Library of Congress Cataloging-in-Publication Data

Names: Natoli, Joseph P., 1943– author.
Title: Dark affinities, dark imaginaries : a mind's odyssey / Joseph Natoli.
Description: Albany : State University of New York Press, [2017] | Includes
  bibliographical references and index.
Identifiers: LCCN 2016021629 (print) | LCCN 2016036363 (ebook) | ISBN
  9781438463513 (hardcover : alk. paper) | ISBN 9781438463506 (pbk. : alk.
  paper) | ISBN 9781438463520 (e-book)
Classification: LCC AC8.5 .N38 2017 (print) | LCC AC8.5 (ebook) | DDC
  814/.6—dc23
LC record available at https://lccn.loc.gov/2016021629

10 9 8 7 6 5 4 3 2 1

Maybe the space of exile is one of the few spaces left in neoliberal societies where one can cultivate a sense of meaningful connections, solidarity and engaged citizenship. Exile may be the space where a kind of double consciousness can be cultivated that points beyond the structures of domination and repression to what the poet Claudia Rankine calls a new understanding of community, politics and citizenship in which the social contract is revived as a kind of truce in which we allow ourselves to be flawed together.

—Henry Giroux, "Academic Madness and the Politics of Exile," *Truthout,* November 18, 2014

Contents

Preface

You could say that the wily Odysseus's will to reach home could not be overcome by any arrangement of Chance or others—Sirens and Cyclops included. I would call this a millennial reading, one emerging from a readership encouraged by their own personal will and freedom to choose their own destiny. *The Odyssey* I read is rather different. It is one in which forces and conditions outside Odysseus's power to control, circumstances that Chance and others create that he must reckon with, shape both the choosing and the chooser. We become more than what we personally design ourselves to be, and that more very often means that we become less than we designed.

One of the wonders of cyberspace is that it offers us an alternative world within which we can pursue a politics that meets our own preferences, reduce society and the social dimension of life to friends we choose, pursue answers on Google to all our questions—but not very often to questions that exceed our own liking, interest, or erudition. Why wouldn't Odysseus now stand as an exemplar of that knowledge of *The Secret,* which tells us that if you will something strongly enough, the entire universe will conspire to fulfill your wishes?

My mind's odyssey over the past half century did not remain true to a charted course I had proposed long ago. What I call "my mind," at every stage reacted and reorganized itself according to what time, geography, and Chance put before it. There was no rudder pushing a personal will through all waters on an undeviating passage. My mind now is like a painter's palette that over time reveals where the brush has been, or like carved rock formations in tide pools, which are the shape they are because of wind, sun, rain, and the ebbing and flowing of the ocean's mighty force. When you scan the physiognomy of a mind, you see countless encounters with a culture within which that mind is embedded so that any retelling of the odyssey of that mind is, at the same time, a revelation of a culture.

In my case, that is US culture, which we arrogantly call "American," although the fact that I was raised in an Italian-American community in Brooklyn, a bilingual community in which neither English nor Italian were schooled, fashioned affiliations in many things, which were far from the American cultural norm.

My own father was born in the United States, but through odd circumstances—I call it the play of Chance—was educated in Sicily and returned to the United States as a teenager; and so the entire immigrant-family experience was mine, transmitted through my father. There is a certain subaltern psychology that develops, preconditioning the mind toward skepticism and even dissent. On a dark imaginary level, the Jewish Algerian Jacques Derrida was always deconstructing the French social order of things that marginalized him. The appearance of a Derrida at a certain moment is an exposition of a culture at a certain moment. The whole notion of a coherent, autonomous, and controlling subjectivity contends with the notion that we are variously positioned within the circumstances of our surround and no account of *my* mind can mean anything without reference to this.

The discipline to apply what brains I had came from the surround, as my father and my uncles encouraged me from early age to do well in school and grasp an opportunity denied to them. And so an intention-less intelligence was directed toward academic success. At Brooklyn College, I came under the influence of Jewish intellectuals who had escaped the Holocaust. History, politics, and economics were represented not as neutral social sciences but very much affected by socio-economic and political arrangements of power. So-called objective critique was always already interpreting within the interpretive frame of what was being critiqued. I was, early on, in every way, prepping for the skepticism of both Heidegger and Derrida, a skepticism that extended to the utopian view of Reaganite "supply side economics" as well as to both Marx's view of the inevitable course of history and the inevitability of a timeless communist utopia. And so I had an inevitable falling out with SDS (Students for a Democratic Society) in the late sixties and meandered my way toward a Max Stirner sort of anarchism, one I later saw as narcissistic and libertarian.

In the four books I wrote in the nineties, attempting to describe the American cultural imaginary as it moved in the nineties, I put myself forward only to access that imaginary, which a Frankfurt school type nay-saying had already done its work in conditioning my description, making the entire project fallible, flawed, and unreliable as documented social history. And yet, the play of one person's mind over a decade with a cultural imaginary, sometimes unchanging and sometimes changing swiftly, was for me something like a live performance—transitory and ephemeral like a sand painting but revealing an interplay of a mind and world, a mind not unwilling to put forward its own inclinations.

Dark Affinities, Dark Imaginaries is an extension of that nineties effort, extended to the whole range of my mind/culture encounter. I employ "I" and not "I-positioned-thusly" for brevity's sake. I also realize that within a long-abiding American imaginary—always defiantly free and independent, more so now in cyberspace—the odyssey of a mind too aware of outside influences and directives is decidedly analog and back-in-the-day. I reckon that the repetition of the word "dark" in my title owes something to my explorations into the American imaginary, along with much more that these selected writings might reveal.

I do not deny uniqueness to individual life but not resulting from some a priori qualities that remain resistant to time, place, and Chance or some ruling passion or force of will that renders the outside world inconsequential. I see uniqueness in the outside world's composition and arrangement of a stretch, long or short or in between, of encounters between its priorities and our own or what we call our own yet remain what all previous encounters have made of us. We are, indeed, never outside the world but always inside it; and so the arrangements of self that we presume to call our own are owned by and owed to those never-released imbrications of self and world.

The particular arrangement of my worldly encounters almost at once made an outsider of me, and so my odyssey discloses the American cultural imaginary from a certain perspective, one that is neither mainstream nor representative of any statistical norm. I believe that events such as the Occupy Wall Street protest and the 2008 Great Recession have made outsiders of a notable percentage of the American populace, mostly in the bottom 80 percent of wealth and income. That belief leads to my presuming that selections from the lifelong writings of a fellow outsider may give voice to what is kept at low volume. A democracy threatened by or already transformed into plutocracy has sent dissident minds into exile and drowned out dissident voices in a deluge of mindless chatter that has preempted effective social interrelationship.

In a working-class household, I could have been tempted by government jobs that required a college degree and that paid at the end a government pension that loomed large and inviting. It was quite a different climate some half century ago than it is now, both in regard to the attractions of the federal government and to pensions, which now do not have the appeal of personal speculation. I was offered a position in the Department of Health, Education and Welfare, Social Security division just as Medicare was about to be launched. While I did well in my three-month classroom preparation, I lasted only one week in my first post-grad assignment. I proved to be almost at once a "dissident bureaucrat," something like a vocal Bartleby, and I never clung to what Kafka called a "brotberuf." I held the actual 1935 Social Security Act as prior to the four thousand pages of bureaucratic directives, which had evolved; and so, in one week, I upset the order of things in that downtown Brooklyn office. I started on a Monday and resigned that Friday, deciding to go on to graduate school to study literature.

I could say that I was inclined toward literature and the arts because they interested me more than philosophy, classics, history, and anthropology—but such was not the case. My father's scorn of what was fictional and therefore false as opposed to the hard truth and reality of medicine, law, and business of any sort, pressed my oppositional buttons. And so I went off to earn a master's degree and a PhD in English, wandering away even from the mainstream of those studies and reading deeply in philosophy and psychology. My work on William Blake expressed both philosophical and psychological interests and so went outside an English department's disciplinary domain. Joint approval of a dissertation by more than one academic department was as radical as putting the Social Security manuals aside and applying the law as passed by Congress. In the end, I narrowed my work on Blake in order to remain within the authorizing province of the English department.

I would argue that experiences such as these did not turn out the way they did because I was before the event inclined in a fixed way, but rather my nature was slowly and incrementally shaped by these experiences. A great deal was already in place, the stage already set upon which I was thrown—whether it was the conditions and events that shaped my father or the federal government or academia or the overall societal marginalizing of the imagination in favor of a profit-making instrumental reason. But besides what time and place put before me, I saw the workings of Chance up close, and I concluded that, like global warming, we do not recognize its power because there is no profit in doing so. Nevertheless, it seems to me that it makes little sense to go on as if Chance is not a formidable player in whether we live or die, whether we live wealthy or poor. Not a determinist or a fatalist or a free-choice disciple, I keep an eye on what can move me outside my own will and choice, rather the way a sailor keeps a keen eye out for weather.

I was summoned to a draft physical in 1966; and after spending a week at St. Alban's Naval Hospital in Queens undergoing tests, I was released and given a temporary deferment from military service. That deferment was never rescinded. I was deferred because tests showed I was diabetic. Years later, I was told that an innocuous condition had been mistaken for diabetes, which I did not have. My draft physical was to have been simply a matter of form as I had already signed into Officer Candidate School, where had I become a second lieutenant. I would have most likely been serving during the Tet Offensive where the lifespan of a second lieutenant was seventeen seconds. I found out many years later that a Joseph Natoli, second lieutenant, was killed on July 29, 1967, due to a "mortar, rocket or artillery incident." I had not chosen to live nor am I sure had Lieutenant Natoli chosen to die. Choice was not even on the game board. If I were a Viking, I would say Odin or, as Ignatius J. Reilly would have it, the Goddess Fortuna had spun the wheel in my favor. If I had the odd faith that everything happened for a reason, I would yet be searching for the reason. And in the compassion-filled parlance of the day, I was a winner and Lieutenant Natoli, a loser.

My "I" and the odyssey of my mind have always remained so much like the huge projection of Oz on the screen in the *Wizard of Oz*, with an amplified voice booming godlike, while at the same time a small, crouching figure remains concealed behind a curtain. A philosophic turn of mind may lead us to this, but psychology is the tool of exploration and all the works of the imagination, high and low, the sites of disclosure.

I did not choose to be ousted in the early seventies from my tenure-track assistant professorship in English, but I did choose to help form a faculty union and that led to my termination. I joined a fight against willful and arbitrary terminations of radical faculty members under the phony flag of financial crisis. But, in truth, I was already disposed to fight. I never returned to the securities of academic life although I, like so many, have turned to poorly recompensed contractual adjunct teaching, work-for-hire contracts with no royalties paid no matter how many editions your writing appears in. Worse than that is the devolution of paid freelance writing into unpaid, online content provider. It did not surprise me when American universities tied themselves closely to corporate models, offered courses that would fuel globalized techno-capitalism, and constrained intellectual freedom in the classroom by putting the tether of limited-duration course providers on instructors.

I stored my PhD plaque and my doctoral gown in the granary on my farm in Oxley Hollow outside Athens, West Virginia, and until financial need forced me out, I worked from sunset to sundown with hands too calloused for pen or typewriter. I could no longer pursue my lifelong habit of reading for an hour or so at nighttime because I could not stay awake. I lived among people who learned how to read so they could read the Bible. I lived among those who would not fall out with me because I said I was raised Catholic or because I first drove down that Holl'er in a VW camper with a noisy muffler and New York State license plates. I lived among those who did not know that out there a zero-sum game was being played and that for one person to win, another had to lose. I gave what skills I had and what surplus of anything I had to others, and they, in turn, gave what enabled us to survive. I tell bits and pieces of that story in *Memory's Orbit* and here in this book in "Hearing the Ping of Poverty—or Not."

What Marx calls the "base" drove me to taking a night-shift job at a local college library. A new college president, a departing library director, and my PhD led to my being appointed acting library director. You can sort out where the "free to choose" made its play in all that. I did, however, choose to rebalance the black-and-white ratio of my library workers in this formerly all-black but now integrated college; and for that, I was cautioned to either back up or get out. NPR aired a program entitled "The Whitest Historically Black College in America" which details how an all-black institution became 90 percent white with only 6 percent black faculty. My reinstatement of former black managers led me to the door as surely as my union activities had done.

I moved to North Carolina where the PhD once again easily got me a job in a university library.

I had not been the first to retreat to the quiet corridors of a library and the peace created by silent words on pages replacing the world's commotion of voices. Eratosthenes had been the chief librarian at the great library of Alexandria; Mao had been assistant librarian at Peking University; J. Edgar Hoover had done some cataloguing at the Library of Congress; Casanova worked as a librarian for the Count of Waldstein in Dux, Bohemia; David Hume was a librarian at the Advocate's Library in Edinburgh; Lewis Carroll was a sub-librarian at Christ's Church, Oxford; Jorge Luis Borges was a municipal librarian in Argentina. No one knows if B. Traven ever worked in a library; but, as we are not even certain who he was, it does not seem reckless to conjecture that among all his various escapes from identity and society, he sought the anonymity of libraries.

I imagine Hoover's cataloguing experience had something to do with his lifelong penchant for files and lists of the nation's enemies. Mao probably spent time hiding in the book stacks reading Lenin, and I am sure Eratosthenes devoted some stolen time on the job to calculating the circumference of the Earth. We know Hume wrote his *History of England* while on the job, and Casanova spent more time writing the story of his adventuresome life than organizing the count's library. Libraries are not only the refuge of writers, as the British Museum was for Marx, but for those who choose to work in a surround so conducive to reading, reflection, and writing. It is an outlier's haven.

Libraries were to me a different kind of retreat from the world than southern Appalachia had been but still a retreat. Now I had the time and the opportunity to write as well as a growing number of experiences to write about. Naturally, I wrote not as someone who had found a "rug that tied the whole room" (i.e., the whole world), together, but as a traveller wandering on the outskirts of the camp, the camp of accepted norms, shared ambitions, and certain progress. I was looking at the world not from any Archimedean point from which I could presume to dominate, much less understand, all I could see, further presuming that what I did see was all there was. Before I read Gilles Deleuze's savvy words, "To interpret is to determine the force which gives sense to a thing," I was searching for the strategies and tactics that held the world to be a certain way within a certain order (*Nietzsche and Philosophy*, 54).

I borrowed time from the libraries I worked in, hoping to repay in the future with my own books on their shelves. I began with fiction because if I ever had a life's ambition it was to write novels. I never gave up the Blakean notion that reasoning and imagining were necessary contraries, and so I brought fictional techniques into all my writing and welcome with open arms the postmodern view that we live in stories and that calling some "fiction" and others "non-fiction" got us nowhere. It is not a story, of course, that water is H_2O but whether the Earth's waters are rising due to human-made global warming is either fiction or non-fiction, depending upon your politics.

When I returned to university teaching as a member of the flying-squad cadre of adjuncts that university administrators with Harvard Business School credentials had discovered were far more cost effective than tenured faculty with health and retirement benefits, I was something quite different than what students expected in a professor. Twenty-somethings are repeatedly like Shakespeare's young rebellious Prince Hal or a fiery Princess Leia. I appeared in the classroom like a disrespectful, anarchic force, a Falstaff, not fat or self-indulgent but lean, edgy, and angry. Although students were becoming increasingly business and career oriented, there yet remained a fringe of perpetual countercultural types, and to these I seemed to be an adult who, unlike their own fathers, had remained a rebel at heart.

When you speak the words of great fiery prophets against empire, such as Blake and Byron, who was "mad, bad *and* dangerous," teach courses in radical American thought, express the dissent of every anarchist from Stirner and Bakunin to Proudhomme and Kropotsky, confound Enlightenment notions of reason, reality, and truth with the words of Debord, Barthes, Derrida, Foucault, and Deleuze, show the films of David Lynch, the Coen brothers, and Quentin Tarantino, unravel the dark domination of subliminal fears and desires, turn the world, in short, on its head, you will find, as surely as Ishmael trailed funeral processions, a strong affiliation of students. After all, for a very short period in their lives, all students are outliers and outcasts from whatever place their society has made camp. It is this inherent drive to do things differently and unmask the Wizard behind the curtain that incited Occupy Wall Street (OWS) and the Vietnam protests, protests that launched a neoliberal campaign to turn the young from politics to Wall Street. OWS marks a major setback in that effort.

I drew on that inherent drive to found my "Is This a Postmodern World?" Europe travel program which lasted fifteen years and which expanded the classroom experience into the variant realities of everyday life in as many countries as we could rail to in a month and a half. I lived with the students in hostels, railed, ate and drank with them and so brought us beyond a two-party instructing and learning ambiance and toward the learning experience itself. We sought to learn something together in the foreign places we visited. Deconstructing my own privilege as instructor and tour leader came naturally, by which I mean all my experience led to this. Attendant with this, I introduced in my students an uneasy skepticism colliding with the many assurances that a country saturated in its own exceptionalism had created. Who you are and who you become were not a matter of a will to power, a will to win, but a matter of geography, genetics, and Chance, and, most importantly, an interpretive ability by which to comprehend the play of each and so proceed without illusion.

Dark Affinities, Dark Imaginaries is not a *bildung* revealing the formation of my character, nor a bildungsroman, nor a memoir revealing a life story, nor an apologia for a life, nor a work of narrative non-fiction with a theme. Nor is it merely selected essays, older to newer. But I've arranged that some of all that is here so that discursive joins non-discursive, critique

joins imagination, the affective joins the cognitive, experience joins interpretation, and, in the end, section by section, a certain personal psyche is
observed working toward a certain mass psyche, an individual imaginary
entwined within a cultural imaginary.

Acknowledgments

I have been fortunate throughout the years in my association with SUNY Press, beginning with Carola Sautter who aided and abetted my efforts in creating an academic press series, "Postmodern Culture," whose manifesto sought manuscripts sans foundational footnoting and resolvable arguments but Blakean imaginative, creative, journalistic, and careless of disciplinary borders. That series continued to prosper under the able guidance of James Peltz who has now gone along with my "mind's odyssey" and put that production in the hands of Jenn Bennett, production editor, who, as it happily turned out, is a fellow Blakean. And so, from beginning to end, the aura of William Blake resides here in this book, an aura, I hope, not lost in reproduction.

Introduction

As its subtitle indicates, this book is the odyssey of a mind, but it is also the odyssey of an American culture from the counterculture to the Tea Party era. I mean by *culture* what Raymond Williams meant—"a whole way of life," the ferment and furor out of which society, like the tip of an iceberg, is visible and when written about is called "social history." In my own books and continuing in my online essays, I seek to describe the movement of an American cultural imaginary, meaning always only the United States, following William Blake's focus on the imagination out of which what is now real emerges.

I was doing what one reviewer called "the history of the American mass psyche," pursuing an ongoing portrait of that psyche by focusing mainly on popular culture. Popular culture has played a big part in that pursuit but only a part. I saw in popular culture symptoms of what was being played out in headline events: the power of market priorities, the rising sea levels of ideological differences, and a steady progression from middle-class democracy to plutarchy. Conversely, what over the years I came to know about the American cultural imaginary became the horizon upon which I was able to see in popular culture the play of that imaginary, both its open display and its suppression. I could explore headline events as Livingstone explored the Nile, searching for the wellsprings within the cultural imaginary.

The more familiar I became with the terrain of the cultural imaginary, which was at once always in motion and at the same time transfixed and fixated, the more easily I could discern connections. I saw connections in everything from presidential elections, pre-emptive attacks, mesmerizing court trials, the affiliations of power and wealth, the collapse of anything 'enlightened' in self-interest, and the recurring psychotic episodes of a culture whose imaginary had grown dark. There is a definite pathology, for example, in a population that complains of political gridlock and yet in every election votes to ensure that gridlock. The fact that only a small portion of Americans has monumentally increased their well-being while huge numbers have experienced a decrease in theirs, and yet there is an equally divided tug of war between the two—is itself truly fascinating.

Dark Affinities, Dark Imaginaries is a culminating work, a stepping back and a study of the various installments made over the years in tracing this American cultural imaginary. I include its hierarchy of values, its rapidly changing disposition toward the past and its historical register, its enfolding the future within the ambitions and innovations of hi-tech, and its blindness to potentially cataclysmic threats in the present. And because I see this work as a continuance of what has been done before, a deepening of the portrait, I select, excerpt, revise, and supplement. I do not find what was originally published as now unworthy, but I do presume that a backward gaze enables me to more clearly see directions than I could on those prior excursions. I add never-before-published essays in order to fill gaps and add signposts to what I now see as the odyssey I have been making for so many years. I am in a search for what often years before was hidden or not highlighted, as in a painting that slowly reveals itself and so the artist subdues tones while heightening others, etches lines more deeply while fading others.

When you go back over the productions of many years, you look for a theme, a thread, and some pattern, a recurrence of focus and interest, some revelation of a mapping, primary and secondary roads. I first published in *The Journal of Phenomenological Psychology*. It is not surprising then that I feel I have always been doing a pathography of a culture. My dissertation was on William Blake so it is not surprising that I see a "fallen" imagination as a key feature in that pathography. I was enlightened by the Old Left, further enlightened in the years ahead by the many continental theorists I was exposed to at University of California, Irvine. None of this made me a ready and willing participant in Ronald Reagan's "new morning in America."

I began a life on the outside, disrespectful of all disciplinary boundaries perhaps because I have not been affiliated with academic disciplines, perhaps because my own views lie so far from the principles of market rule. I was terminated at the very start of an academic career for attempting to form the first faculty union in New England. When dissidence and all things antiestablishment are considered virtues, being labeled "an incorrigible and a troublemaker" seems not a problem. However, that sort of 'recommendation' prevented me from continuing an academic teaching career, one in which promotions, tenure, and affiliation within a field might have gone on. I began as what the poet Claudia Rankine calls "a flawed exile."

Blacklisted from teaching, I first considered accepting appointments offered in both Brazil and Columbia but was dissuaded when it was pointed out that my leftist leanings would clash dangerously with the politics of both countries at that time. I 'expatriated' by moving to Oxley Hollow in southern West Virginia—it was like moving to another planet for someone Brooklyn raised—and engaged in subsistence farming. It does not seem a surprise to me that I was, years later, much taken with the dissenting and disrupting work of Derrida, Foucault, Deleuze, and Lyotard and onward to postmodernity. I had, so to speak, the appropriate credentials. I set out to discover how I have made use of over the course of some forty years the incompatibles of phenomenological psychology, a quasi-Gramsci and Frankfurt School politics, literary theory and post-analytic continental thought, postmodernity, and the visionary politics of William Blake. My assumption is that the outlier paths I followed gave me a perspective on American culture that a persistent heterodox, mutinous spirit in that culture, had already historically sanctioned.

In 1991, I launched a book series for the State University of New York Press, which I called "Postmodern Culture." We published a great many books from 1991 to 2009; and I myself edited and published over a dozen with various publishers, including the SUNY Press. I taught as an adjunct lecturer and then began a fifteen-year Europe program called "Is This a Postmodern World?" In 2010, I retired from my part-time library work and my adjunct teaching, which was a neat trick since to retire or withdraw from something such as a career implies having been inside something, such as a career.

I never was inside either academe or the dominating market-driven values of the culture. And that I see as a kind of key to my perspective on the American cultural imaginary. The position of the observer is itself a key element in an attempt to parallel the odyssey of one mind with the odyssey of a culture. I do believe that my long run on the outside incites curiosity among those beginning careers at a time when such beginnings are difficult, especially careers that are not driven by profit, dividends, and the arcane workings of the American financial sector. Being launched in the countercultural sixties is a far cry from being launched in a Tea Party climate. However, I believe relevance persists in the odyssey of a mind continuing to encounter the mostly stochastic movements of a culture and often challenging the same without hiding behind the mask of an objective impartiality or wide-ranging intellectual credentials based on increasingly narrow and specialized study.

When I began to publish online, not blog but submit my work for editorial review, I became a content provider, with no ranking or titles or distinctions of any kind. What I wrote was an intermingling of journalism, gonzo and investigative, wandering Montaigne-type essays, memoir, film review, political rant, philosophical reflection, satire, and dark comedy. It was all thrown into the mosh pit that academic writing, cloistered in its readership and reviewers and certain as to what contributed to truth and what did not, agreed to leave alone, as it left the abyss alone.

A piece posted on Friday could have a thousand readers by Sunday, something astounding and exhilarating. Comments might run from savage, vitriolic attacks to testaments of enlightenment. I have no idea whether cyberspace comments reveal finally, what was in Pandora's box or whether they, like Twitter hashtag rounds, contribute to the public understanding of anything, or are no more than the best revelations of the darkness of our natures.

When a mind finds over a long period so very much that is affili-ated darkly rather than bathed in sweetness and light, that mind eventu-ally finds its way to politics. Politics, as Aristotle advised, was the place to be if one wished to make a fight for the "the virtuous life" of the citizenry, wished to replace darkness with the *eudaemonia* or well-being of a society. My odyssey has wound its way through dark affiliations and dark imaginaries—that, I cannot deny; although it has never seemed to me an option to achieve *eudaemonia* by camouflaging the obstacles in our path, the challenges of the journey. And perhaps it is true that Rankine's "flawed exile" may be, as Henry Giroux states, "the space where a kind of double consciousness can be cultivated that point beyond the structures of domination and repression" (Academic Madness and the Politics of Exile," *Truthout*, November 18, 2014).

Finally, what matters is what the reader can take from this odyssey of a culture from the varied perspectives of a varied identity. What Gary Hoppenstand referred to as a "way of knowing" and what Georges Sime-non's Maigret denied as having—namely, a method—is, I think, disclosed in this book—a method that is circular.

At the start, I assume some features of an American cultural imagi-nary in motion, openly admit a theoretical approach, bring both into electrifying headline issues, establish from these a horizon upon which to view popular culture, and so fix an image of the American cultural imaginary within that time and place, one that expands or contracts the imaginary with which I began.

The term *imaginary* is used to reflect my attempt to not remain on the level of what people say or what reasons they give—but delve into imaginative, emotional, and sensuous wellsprings, sometimes unconscious, that rule but are masked or unsayable.

Theoretical intentions and ideological perspectives are revealed because I do not presume my seeing is world-less, theory neutral, and value-free. The theories are like scaffolding in the building process: necessary at the beginning and then removed. However, I do not want to dismiss what has become very clear to me. My post-truth view provides a view and an entry that an empirical and purely rational approach cannot. And my politics follows those of William Blake who sought to both diminish and expose the usurpation of rationality in his own time by resurrecting the imagination as the instrument of rebellious overthrow.

I need to unpack this. In our own time, market rule has usurped every domain, even those that clearly have other and different goals than profit to shareholders. I take to hand the critical rod of liberal and leftist critique, though Liberals fail to mount what the Leftists would call a critique, and leftist critique has to be mounted in the United States in such a way as to distance itself from every variety of socialist critique. This is a neat trick and one yet to be done in the United States. The journal *Jacobin*, founded in 2012, presumes to be open about its socialist bent, after the Great Recession as well as Occupy Wall Street seemed to make it crystal clear that market rule, not the federal government, was the Orwellian Big Brother.

In similar fashion to Blake's observation that the worship of reason crossed all boundaries, I see that wealth and its dark priorities and dispositions cross liberal and neoliberal boundaries. In a politics of the imagination, then, we witness a divide in cultural imaginaries, prereflective and preempting the political ideology to which we attach ourselves. In the politics of the imagination, we do not know what politics rules our perceptions as well as our values. We probe for what the American cultural imaginary may be among those who reflect and reveal it—but in the way analysands reveal in their stories to a psychotherapist what they themselves cannot fathom.

Troubling issues revealed in the headlines are now themselves troubling as we do not all have the same cell-phone apps nor interface with the world on the same sites in cyberspace. The *New York Times* headlines are no longer reliable as to what the electrifying issues may be. Nevertheless,

I have no difficulty in proposing as magnetizing issues: the 9/11 cataclysmic event, presidential elections, preemptive warfare, global warming,
the wealth divide, ideological gridlock, the Great Recession, poverty and
gentrification, Occupy Wall Street, hi-tech and cyberspace, social media,
and so on. I realize, though, they may be less public than private issues
and, on that level, not issues at all.

I consult with popular culture because it needs to stay close to the
hot spots in the cultural imaginary and so reveals what is going on there.
We do not find answers and resolutions here; but rather what is unnerving, mesmerizing, haunting, and alien culturally is put into play. We see
troubling real-world events put into play in popular culture, very often
peripherally or masked because popular culture does not remain popular if
it unsettles its audience. But to ignore the hot spots that put the audience
on the edge of their seats, though they cannot know why, is as dangerous
to pop culture as to disconcert by putting into play unsettling difference.
And in real-world events, we often see played out what pop culture has
prepared us to see, what in fact may bring something in everyday life to
headline status. The transport between real world and imaginative worlds
is dynamic and without a starting point, not causal and not unchanging.

What really gives with these issues? How are we to interpret them
and therefore bring them to some understanding? These are questions
my way of knowing has tried to answer over the years. The American
cultural imaginary is in motion, and therefore we need to keep reading
it, finding where it is now so that the reality that the imagination surely
brings to pass does not become a reality to which we are foreign and
within which we are alienated or exploited. What matters finally is that
the reader enters the culture's odyssey and takes on the challenges of
disclosing the ongoing journey.

Chapter One

William Blake

Prophet against Empire

If my reading of thirty-four years of commentary has produced any one single effect, it is this: there is an overall unity of perception of Blake's work which extends to what it is and what it is worth to us, if not to what it means in purely rational terms.

—*Twentieth Century Blake Criticism: Northrop Frye to the Present*

I found in the work of William Blake the bottom of my wide-ranging interests over the years; and if there is no unifying vision in those interests, the idea of such vision, or the possibility of such, is what I owe to my lifelong meditation on Blake.

I was an inconvenient Max Stirner-type anarchist to the Students for a Democratic Society (SDS) in the sixties and an apostate to the Stirner creed years later when I observed the illusions of individual will and autonomy at work in the new millennium.

I was an absorbed and fascinated Jungian leading to my dissertation on Jung and Blake until I read the work of Jan van den Berg and observed how deftly the pathologies of mind could be revealed without referring to the hidden dimensions of an unconscious mind.

I was very much Heidegger-prone in the eyes of other theorists when 'theory' was the rage, attempting to place consciousness and culture as corridors outside the "prison house of language." Nevertheless, I was a full-blown deconstructionist, according to a British reader of a manuscript submitted to St. Martin's Press—a manuscript that attempted to show that Dickens experienced a *crise de quarante ans* in which he deconstructed his earlier Pickwickian conviviality.

With the publication of *A Postmodern Reader*, edited with Linda Hutcheon, followed by *A Primer to Postmodernity* for Blackwell and then the long run of the *Postmodern Culture* series for SUNY Press, I was labeled a "ludic" postmodernist to all, a defender of an -ism that, according to the Right undermined the Western tradition of realism and rationality. The Left did not approve of postmodernity's dismissive approach to the critical rod of reason by which the Left challenged capitalism. Everyone waited anxiously for the mad fad to disappear.

My turn to online writing, mostly in popular culture and politics, gave me a wider audience but one that placed Obama on the Far Left and Jesus on the Far Right. "Progressive" was meant to be a signifier Liberals could hide under but nevertheless in the American mass psyche the linkage was clear: "progressives = socialists = communists = left-wing radicals = anti-capitalists = un-American." Within my heartland affiliation, I became the last Marxist standing, a throwback relic in the view of the post-partisan crowd who, at heart, objected to politics simply because it was still going on after the millennium ushered in our new cyber-alternative universe. The presence of something so antediluvian as partisan politics when there are so many colorful apps to engage seems more annoying than comical. The Marxists recognized that I did not quite fit; and so after publishing with *Political Affairs*, an online publication of the American Communist Party, I was excommunicated, although my work still appears in their archives.

As a member of the editorial collection of *Bad Subjects: Politics in Everyday Life*, the oldest online political journal, I wrote a series of articles in which Liberals were critiqued as strongly as Neoliberals. And although *TruthOut* is a progressive online journal, it published an essay— "Dark Affinities: Liberal and Neoliberal"—which estimated ideological differences as insignificant compared to the deep affinities of wealth and lifestyle, the bond in which "le luxe est un droit."

In my early seventies now, I am called a "hippy who is still a hippy," although I failed to connect in any way with the California flower power/Timothy Leary bullshite nor with a New Left on the East Coast, which was as quickly and as easily absorbed into the capitalist machine as pot, tie-dyed tees, and bell bottoms. The reappearance of my essay on the Coen brothers' *The Big Lebowski* in Oliver Benjamin's collection *Lebowski 101* (Abide University Press, 2014) relocates my mind's journey with dudeism, which Benjamin calls "a new religion." However, I do roll more easily into thought than into other people's lives, and therefore dudeism is not "the rug that ties everything together" for me, and I do not abide there although the Dude's emergence on the screen in 1998 remains for me a wonderful, timely counterpoint to the Wall Street player heroes that obsessed the American cultural imaginary.

At every staging point of my mind's odyssey, the substance of how I imagine world and consciousness has remained Blakean.

I select these three excerpts because the first signals my looking at Blake through a phenomenological lens, the second, my use of Blake to pursue my own meditations on disorder in literature, and the third, introduces the politics of a phenomenal divide, a politics Blake well understood and took on with the tools of the imagination.

I humbly pursued that Blakean vision, grounded in the contraries Blake described in *The Marriage of Heaven and Hell* in both my master's thesis and in my dissertation, originally titled "Blake in the Twentieth Century," wherein I ranged widely with chapters on depth psychology, existentialism, the myth of the eternal return, the Death of God movement, the Beats, and more. That work was 'disciplined' to one chapter on Blake and Jung. Norman O. Brown's *Life Against Death: A Psychoanalytic Interpretation of History* had inspired me to go beyond disciplinary borders. The wide-ranging brilliance of that work set me, as well as so many who would move on to the accommodating theory wagon that began with the 1966 Johns Hopkins conference on structuralism, to jump departmental fences. With only two exceptions—the William Blake essay for the *Critical Survey of Poetry* series and *Twentieth Century Blake Criticism: Northrop Frye to the Present* for Garland in 1982—I left off writing in the field of Blake studies as they went from non-existent to grist for the academic mills. However, I never abandoned the idea that "what is now proved was once only imagined" ("Proverbs of Hell," in *The Marriage of Heaven and Hell*, 1790–1793). And regardless of how far I travelled, I took Blake with me.

My interest in the phenomenological psychologists' notion of *Lebenswelt,* the human life-world which encompassed an affective and imaginative manner by which we mediate the world, is no more than a Blakean pursuit that goes beyond "weights and measure" and reaches for how and what we envision imaginatively.

Deconstruction for me became an assault on those illusions fashioned in a Blakean fallen world whose formations Blake challenged, his visionary work always seeking to answer our question: "Then tell me, what is the material world, and is it dead?" (*Europe, a Prophecy*, 1794). The "Orb of Fire," our imaginations are obscured by minds and hearts bound in "slough" and rock. Reason's "Heart / In a fleshy slough formed four river / Obscuring the immense Orb of fire / Flowing down into night: till a

Form / Was completed, a Human Illusion/In darkness and deep clouds involv'd" (*The Book of Los*, 1795).

Blake's vision followed me through my work on literary theory, postmodernity, popular culture, and a cultural critique that ranged widely across education, politics, economics, literature, history, chaos theory, and headline events, both extraordinary and everyday. "I travel'd thro' a land of men, / A land of men and women too; / And heard and saw such dreadful things / As cold earth-wanderers never knew" ("The Mental Traveller"). I wrote about Rodney King and the Central Los Angeles Riots; the "Little Man" James wilding murder; the O.J. Simpson trial; the psychopath Jeffrey Dahmer; Susan Smith's murder of her two sons; Ted Kaczynski, the Unabomber; the death of Princess Di; the murder of Yusef Hawkins in Bensonhurst; the siege of David Koresh at Waco; Tim McVeigh and the Oklahoma City bombing; the September 11th attacks on the World Trade Centers; and the Occupy Wall Street protest. Closer to where I lived when I wrote these books were the unsolved murder of Brandon D'Annunzio and the Gunson Street riots in East Lansing, Michigan.

I took the spirit of Blake into a *Postmodern Culture* book series for SUNY Press that I created with the imaginatively free-spirited Carola Sautter, editor at SUNY Press, and continued under the ever-faithful directorship of James Peltz. We trespassed across the boundaries of high culture into everyday life, left behind foundational footnoting and arguments building to determinate closure, and brought the creative imagination of fiction into the high court of academic discourse. And when Blackwell Publishers asked me to put together an introduction to postmodernity, accessible to an inquiring general public, I employed characters from the TV sci-fi *Star Trek* to tell that story in a postmodern manner and wrote *A Primer to Postmodernity*. I began a Europe travel program in 1995 that continued for fifteen summers—"Is this a Postmodern World?—initiated by a theory that explored everyday life as expressions of imaginative phenomenal realities and history itself as the productions of imagination within contexts that might fade but never die.

Through popular culture, I sought to disclose an American cultural imaginary that was both immoveable and transient, and in *Speeding to the Millennium*, I combined my cultural critique with vignettes in an attempt to imaginatively supplement my critique. Years later, I wrote of a new Gulliver in *Travels of a New Gulliver*, relying now wholly on fictional satire to reach further than my cultural critique had in my explorations of the American cultural imaginary.

Throughout I attempted to follow Blake's own counsel: "I will not reason and compare: my business is to create." Though I have not abstained from reasoning, I have eschewed modernity pretenses and jumped back upon my own reasoning, positioning it and thus tagging a caveat lector to my writing. These are 'truth stories' or mediations of world and self at certain times and from within a certain culture. The quest to imagine more expansively is implicit in a postmodern view prompting us to refashion the productions of *this* time and place when countered by the productions of *another* time and place.

The infinity that Blake describes thusly: "If the doors of perceptions were cleansed, everything would appear to man as it is, infinite" has always meant to me endless attempts to imagine the world beyond the limitations of empirical proof and validation. Such reasoning "or the ratio of all we have already known," is an obstruction, a seeing with and not through the eye.

> This life's dim windows of the soul
> Distorts the heavens from pole to pole
> And leads you to believe a lie
> When you see with, not through, the eye.

Whether, however, we can through the imagination open "the eternal worlds" Blake found, or do no more than see through the presumptions of our truths and certainties is undecidable, as prophecy presumes a truth that theory can question but not assert. I have employed, admittedly, my imagination in interrogating and deconstructing rather than pointing to "the eternal worlds" that Blake was so sure would reveal themselves beyond "our senses five." But skepticism attends skepticism itself and the question Blake posed can never be answered:

> How do you know but ev'ry Bird that cuts the airy way
> Is an immense world of delight, clos'd by your senses five?

At the time I wrote my introduction to Blake criticism, I was a rebel from academe and the institutionalization of intellectual work. I saw classroom and course as disciplinary in a very un-Blakean mode. I conceived this bibliography of Blake criticism as a means of pursuing one's own understanding of Blake without any classroom mediation. Therefore, the endless amount of Blake commentary I covered were obstacles as well as aids in reaching into Blake. Some forty years later, I see all criticism not as the establishment of a monologue but a continuous battle of stories. A critical commentator of any work must go on in the hope of presenting a strong interpretation that a reader will adopt. It is strong in terms of how well it suits the disposition of both the times and the reader. But the reader is not a free-choosing agent here but already choosing within cultural priorities. In place of the imprisoned reader I imagined forty years ago, I now see a reader living within the illusions of personal freedom to choose, to design a Blake the way one designs one's own reality in cyberspace. Such liberation is liberation not only from what Blake means despite what you choose him to mean but also from the criticism itself. When I wrote this introduction, I hoped to detach the student of Blake from an academic reading of Blake. I could not imagine a cultural attitude in which reading itself would be superfluous in a world in which personal opinion rules. I could not imagine that criticism would vanish or be reduced to a continuous 'Like' feedback from friends or vitriolic comments from those who were not.

Introduction, *Twentieth-Century Blake Criticism: Northrop Frye to the Present*[1]

The Pragmatics of Reading Blake

There is a pragmatics of Blake study that involve time invested and profit extracted. In fact, it has been a key concern with a variety of Blake commentators for the entire thirty-four years this bibliography surveys. My own assumption is that students take from Blake according to their own needs, interests, and capacities and that a tabulation of debits and credits is purely an individual enterprise. I hope that a very early reward of Blake study would be a replacement of a cash-nexus mentality with something more humanly oriented.

The Blake that is comprehended by any individual reader is inevitably that individual's Blake. That comprehension is something very different from the quest made by the total corpus of Blake scholars and critics for a definitive introduction, a definitive biography, a definitive exegesis. The degree to which Blake's entire work can be reduced to uniform, systematic comprehensibility does not affect the degree to which his work has an effect upon any individual reader. The discursive cannot be substituted for the non-discursive. The quest for a common ground, for an objective Blake, for comprehensible, communicable themes, *is* the academic quest.

It is engaged as enthusiastically with poets as with philosophers, with painters as with physicists. And yet, there is no objectively understood Blake; there is only Blake understood by someone. The work will always have an effect. Effects, which are the results of not striving to locate and define Blake's work, may be productive by virtue of encountering a greater proportion of one's own mind than Blake's work. Since we are all, as individual readers, variously encountering our own minds, the only question pertains to how we make our reading of Blake's work efficient. Effects, which are the results of staying closely with Blake's work, reliable text and commentaries, are most efficient if one is indeed reading Blake. When we read Blake, we are committed to that reading. We are committed to reading what others have said, to locating a reliable text. We are committed to locating Blake's work as it exists outside our own minds. *We* intend to read *Blake*—a dialogue of reader and work to be read.

In this dialogue of Blake's work and the reader of Blake's work, the exegetist of the work goes on as if the individual reader did not have determining priorities. And it cannot be otherwise. Whether or not the priorities of the reader are acknowledged, the exegesis of the work goes on. It is only when an attempt is made to impose uniformly a supposed definitive, objective exegesis on the individual reader that the inviolability of an equal dialogue must be asserted. Unfortunately, Blake-in-the-classroom is too often a uniformly perceived Blake for the purpose of uniform evaluation of response. One of the purposes of this bibliography is to provide students with a guide to Blake studies so they can select in accordance with their interests. Thus, a bibliography such as this becomes a means by which to break through the circumference of a possibly too Urizenic, institutional presentation. It is hoped that, most often, it will complement Blake-in-the-classroom. Whether or not a student of Blake who comes to this bibliography is enrolled in a course that includes Blake, this bibliography can aid the student in coming to terms with Blake's work.

Neither the poetry nor the pictorial art *is* the commentary, and the failure to find a precise equation for the two should not exasperate the student nor lead to the conclusion that Blake's work is incomprehensible and therefore meaningless. The reader who intends to read Blake does not read with less of the imagination, emotion, and senses than of reason. There are really two instances when a reader's comprehension of Blake may go on in the absence of commentary or in opposition or partial opposition to commentary: when Blake's work is merely a vehicle by which one is transported back into one's own mind, and when an imaginative-emotional-sensuous-rational comprehension of Blake's work is achieved. In this latter instance, comprehension has gone beyond commentary. Only Blake's poetry and pictorial art represent such comprehension. But the commentary that does exist is an aid to locating Blake's work and therefore an aid to enabling a reader to achieve what Blake would call a "fourfold" understanding.

If my reading of thirty-four years of commentary has produced any one single effect, it is this: there is an overall unity of perception in Blake's work that extends to what it is and what it is worth to us, if not to what it means in purely rational terms.

The Politics of Blakean Criticism

In order to come fully to terms with a literary text, a student approaches commentary. It is doubtlessly true that when a student approaches Blake commentary, he or she feels at first compelled to seek commentary for the commentary. I think this is true because one has to learn the language of the myth in which Blake's work is housed. There are countless proper names in Blake, which any critic may call up in the interpretation of any one of Blake's works. A try at commentary on "The Fly" or "Laughing Song" may send the unsuspecting reader reeling. Characters and actions of the later works are often used to gloss the early and middle works. Before discussing the various ways Blake commentators divide themselves, I should like to comment on Blake's obscurity. Regardless of how accessible on the levels of imagination, emotions, and senses any individual may find Blake's work, it is true that his work is difficult to reduce to a lucid, discursive exegesis. It is difficult to decipher Blake, to work Blake out like a puzzle. Nor is Blake a puzzle read by a cabbalistic coterie of devotees, however puzzle-like his work may seem and however esoteric Blake commentary may seem. I maintain that Blake's work is difficult-to-reduce and that the faculties, which are called upon by his work, are not commonly exercised nor are they the basis of critical exposition.

In order to put Blake together on this strictly expository level, Blake commentators frequently present ingeniously subtle, ornate interpretations or exhaustively particularized exegeses in which both the reader and the writer assuredly lose sight of the whole. In regard to the whole, Bentley asserts that "the most interesting part . . . is effable and eluctable" (*Blake Books*, 37). I read this to mean that the whole of Blake is difficult to reduce, to make effable and eluctable; and, therefore, the most interesting part of Blake, for the interpreters, is the portion that can be interpreted, that can be reduced. I have serious problems with this view, although I firmly believe in the worthiness of clarifying Blake where he can be clarified. It seems indisputable to me, however, that in order to either illuminate or interpret Blake, various ineluctable, ineffable aspects of his work are bracketed out.

A student who approaches the commentary must realize that he or she is approaching not only something different from Blake's work but also less than Blake's work. As a last word on Blake's obscurity, I would say that just as there is no understanding of Blake without someone, some individual, understanding, there is no difficulty without some individual experiencing that difficulty. Who could disagree that Blake is the number-one choice in our own Urizenic time with whom people will have difficulty?

An artist who remolds, imaginatively, his own age and its traditions and then produces poetry and engravings and paintings within that recreated world is an artist who will attract a wide variety of commentators. Even that number is extended if we recall that Blake believed he was, in his work, laying down a string that his reader could follow to paradise, regeneration. The academics look down at the lunatic fringe, those hapless souls who believe in Blake's vision. There are also those, like N.O. Brown and Theodore Roszak, who apply Blake to the contemporary malaise like aspirin for fever. Allen Ginsberg invokes Ginsberg's Blake as a protector and founding father of uncircumscribed exuberance and spontaneity. Thomas Altizer finds Altizer's Blake to be a premature observer of God's absence. Kathleen Raine's Blake is a Blake who accepts the baton of the "perennial philosophy" and at the appropriate time passes it on. Northrop Frye's Blake is a hot, poetic crucible of archetypes inherited from literary ancestors and bequeathed to literary progeny. Harold Bloom's Blake deliberately misread everyone. T.S. Eliot's Blake did not read enough. Middleton Murry's Blake is a Christian-Marxist. English critics go about trying to fit Blake into their own eighteenth century while some American critics wrestle with Blake's message to America, and others turn to Blake as a worthy subject for their shiny new critical surgery. While Frye and Adams, among others, advocate a non-developmental view, Gillham and Paley are spokesmen for a developmental view. Bindman and W.J.T. Mitchell feel that Blake breaks with the tradition of *ut pictura poesis* while Hagstrum has argued he follows it. For Erdman, social and political forces are determining in Blake's work. For Frye, Blake's art need only be glossed by art. Blake is either easily explained by referring to Thomas Taylor, Boehme, the Antinomians, etc., or is completely different, transforming everything that came before into something totally unique. In the middle are those who find varying degrees of transformation of sources by Blake.

This variety of approaches and interpretations can be frustrating, exasperating. It means that Blake is the kind of artist who cannot be totally reduced to rational paraphrase but is nonetheless inspiring over a very wide range. The total canon of Blake commentary does not provide a single, unified view of Blake. It does not even come close to this, although there is a hard core of Blake scholars who mistake a rigorously constructed Trojan horse left outside the Blakean walls for a successful infiltration and victory over what lies within. We have a concordance, a dictionary, a descriptive bibliography (revised three times), any number of enumerative bibliographies, two Blake journals, biographies, letters, facsimiles (being produced by an English Blake Trust and an American Blake Foundation), two worthy editions of Blake's poetry and prose, all the illuminated work in one inexpensive volume, all the engravings in one volume, and a *catalogue raisonné* on the way.

I think these are useful tools. If I did not, I would not have put countless hours into the preparation of this particular bibliography. I think these are useful tools that enable one to come as close as possible to Blake's work. In the dialogue of a reader reading Blake, coming as close as possible to Blake is precisely one-half of making Blake one's own.

Excerpt from *Mots d'Ordre: Disorder in Literary Worlds*[2]

Blake's Marriage

In *The Marriage of Heaven and Hell,* William Blake gives us interplay of Reason, which "is the bound or outward circumference of Energy," and Energy, which "is Eternal Delight." Energy is the alien other since from it, evil actively springs; whereas Reason elicits the Good that contains, holds back, and orders Energy. Nevertheless, without these contraries, Blake boldly announces, there "is no progression." Both the Energy and the disorder springing from it and its bound or outward circumference of order "are necessary to Human existence." The question arises, however, concerning how much order is necessary? In the "Proverbs of Hell" Blake tells us "You never know what is enough unless you know what is more than enough." Because the *Marriage* conveys to us a strong rhetorical preference for what is *not* bounded, and because it portrays man as having "closed himself up, till he sees all things thro' narrow chinks of his cavern," it is clear that in regard to boundaries that, like a cistern, contain the overflowing fountain, humankind is faced with "more than enough" order.

"The Argument": The Play of Disorder

The "Argument" argues in "a year of dearth," a year in which "number weight and measure" have been brought out, in which we do not know what is enough in regard to exuberance, desire, wrath, excess, "the roaring of lions, the howling of wolves, the raging of the stormy sea, and the destructive sword" because we clearly do not know what is "more than enough." Excess is "too great for the eye of man" although it comprises "The Bible of Hell," which Blake possesses, and "the world shall have whether they will nor no." Thus, Blake declares that limitations in perception, in a "bounded perception," prevent mankind from seeing beyond the "narrow chinks of his cavern," beyond what he has concocted as the boundaries of his own body and his own world.

All this is a redeemable condition in Blake's view. A reaching toward what we cannot say or see, a reaching toward what exceeds our sense of reason and our sense of what is enough, what breaks the boundaries of an ordering circumference that over restrains us and generates pestilence and damns us with its braces—all this is fundamentally "necessary to Human existence."

We also learn that the Devil of Energy and the Angel of Order mutually impose upon each other. They each concoct a narrative that stands forth as a monologue, one that gives the other no room to interject his or her monologue. Despite Blake's rhetorical preference for the energy of disorder, his contraries point to a necessary interplay of order and disorder, mutually exclusive categories that paradoxically interanimate each other. Blake's own work crafts that interanimation, although he never leaves off trying to represent it within a system of signs, within meaning that can be semantically processed.

You might say that the myth he creates both represents within an eighteenth-century regime of *mots d'ordre* and produces away from that regime. Order and disorder remain semantically conceivable only in terms of his response to the ways in which order in the eighteenth-century empirical world exceeded his own structuring of it, and to the ways disorder was structured by that world as unavailable. Blake's total staging of order and disorder is therefore a response to what the eighteenth-century "ways of world making" have left out, a staging of what in Wolfgang Iser's words "refers to things that are suppressed, unconscious, inconceivable, and perhaps even incommensurable" ("Changing Functions of Literature," in *Prospecting* [Baltimore, MD: Johns Hopkins, 1989], 231). What "disorder" means in Blake is finally conceivable only in terms of his own staging, his own mise-en-scène, of what a prevailing conceptualization had discarded as inconceivable. Blake performs the eighteenth century's own "unconscious." He actually brings to conceivability in his work what appears as inconceivability within the eighteenth-century socius.

Even though Blake's work is an impetus to my own meditations on disorder and literature, I cannot recreate the Blakean drama of order and disorder nor can I ground my meditating in a meaning that emerges only through the suppression of the incommensurable. I cannot do the latter because it is precisely Blake's "play of the incommensurable" that interests me. I would also be 'absolutizing' as a perdurable presence what Blake's *Marriage* does not presence but rather transmits within a dynamic, continuous exploit. And finally, "[o]ur intentional acts of understanding will always result in an unavoidable reduction of the potential contained in the literary text, and this holds true for one reason in particular: these very acts are semantically oriented." In Iser's view, such an orientation inevitably goes on within an established theoretical frame, as do my own meditations, in spite of the fact that meditating immediately acknowledges the inaccessibility of the *topos* meditated upon. Blake's contesting drama then *is* a magnificent drama within literary worlds that "explode into . . . multifariousness" any attempt on anyone's part to establish an origin by defining "disorder." Any mapping of disorder as a *topos,* by reifying it within a frame that by definition has no way of reifying it, would lead very shortly to a fatal implosion. Disorder would always exceed the meaning I gave to it while my semantically oriented act would prove too confining. That immuring would preserve what we have already identified as "enough," and at the same time because we were kept within that identifying web, the unidentifiable and inaccessible of literature—the "more than enough"—would escape us.

The political divide in the United States between Liberals and Neoliberals paralleled the deep wealth divide, both constructing phenomenal realities that were being treated as rational conditions responsive to resolving platforms, legislation and Supreme Court decisions. I perceived it all as going on in conflicting imaginaries or, in Blakean terms, fallen imaginaries in which perceptions could not range beyond such tragic constrictions. What each side held to so vehemently was only the offspring of a failure of imagination. To rouse us from this collapse, a politics was needed which disclosed the strategies of power, greed, and what Spinoza called "the ordinary human sentiments," all dark, to erode our mutual bonds of love and affection, not only for each other but the creatures who shared this planet with us.

Why Are We Not Roused to Action?

> After losing some ground in 2008, the top one percent has since seen their incomes soar, capturing . . . 95% of all gains from economic growth between 2009 and 2012, a period when incomes for the bottom 99 percent have hardly budged. . . . But if people are angry about so much wealth going to so few, they are keeping quiet about it nearly everywhere. (Paul Starr, "A Different Road to a Fair Society," review of *The Society of Equals*, by Pierre Rosanvallon, *New York Review of Books*, May 22, 2014)

According to Charles M. Blow's *New York Times* article, "Poverty is Not a State of Mind," over 5 percent of Republicans believe that rich people work harder than poor people, that rich people don't have more advantages than poor people, that poor people should blame their own lack of effort for their poverty, and that no circumstances are beyond poor people's control. The figures tell us no more than what we already know: there is a deep divide between Republicans and Democrats in regard to what anything means and how anything is to be valued. It is as if there existed a Holy Grail of reality and truth that both sides claim, neither ever able to summon the facts and statistics, the 'smoking gun' that would convince the other.

There is also a kind of evidence that shows we live increasingly in a Humpty Dumpty world, which to my mind is always a world where we are told what is what, a world that is perceived to be what somebody wants it to be. Right now, we are living within two dominating perceptual domains that we call "Liberal" and "Neoliberal," neither locked into anything more than the phenomenal realities they work as busily as bees to construct.

Quoting statistics has as little chance of reaching phenomenal realties as convincing with scientific fact and evidence a climate-change denier or a creationist that he or she is wrong. You cannot storm the walls of phenomenal reality as if they were real walls; you do not treat a nightmare with an aspirin, fight fear with a gun, or obliterate xenophobia with dollars. Our phenomenal realities are a dark combination of what power perceives the world to be and what our own self-enclosed perceptions tell us the world is. Humpty Dumpty brands the world to be what he wants it to be, pushing aside poor Alice's own view of things. But Alice is not innocent, by which I mean she is also inevitably branding the world in her own light.

How lost can we be in our own perceptual worlds? How far down the rabbit hole can we go? In an essay in *Twilight in Italy and Other Essays*, D.H. Lawrence perspicaciously reveals in an encounter with a woman spinning a state of perception that is impenetrable, without doubt, and never challenged:

> She was the substance of the knowledge, whether she had the knowledge in her mind or not. There was nothing which was not herself, ultimately. . . . And she, the old spinning-woman, was the apple, eternal, unchangeable, whole even in her partiality. It was this which gave the wonderful clear unconsciousness to her eye. How could she be conscious of herself, when all was herself? . . . She went on talking as if she were talking to her own world in me. (Cambridge, MA: Cambridge University Press, 1994)

This is a blindingly tragic condition when what we hear others say is only what we ourselves would say—that what challenges our own perceptions never reaches us. William Blake writes:

> I see Every thing I paint In This World, but Every body does not see alike. To the Eyes of a Miser a Guinea is more beautiful than the Sun & a bag worn with the use of Money has more beautiful proportions than a Vine filled with Grapes. The tree which moves some to tears of joy is in the Eyes of others only a Green thing that stands in the way. ("Letter to Dr. Trusler," 23 August 1799)

Unless we consider a politics of phenomenal divide, one in which perception does not rest on measurement and arguments summoned to support our reasoning, we will continue to ignore interpretation that offers a chance at success. Unless we give up the idea that an opponent, an antagonist needs more and clearer proof that they are wrong, we will continue to dig our partisan divide deeper and deeper without hope of an eureka moment.

How then do we change phenomenal realities? This is not a question with which political game theory or econometrics can deal. Marketing and branding, however, connecting product and services with personal identity have fully established themselves in a post-truth world. The way we do politics is, in this marketing and branding way, by assembling voters like consumers and spinning factional worlds. At the same time, politics proceeds as if this was all adventitious, a fluff that lengthy debates on PBS *Newshour* or in even more presidential TV debates or conclusive Pew polls would see through, exposing the bedrock of 'real matter.' As long as politics remains mired in an Age of Enlightenment truth, one side or the other at any moment about to prove their uncontestable truth, while all the apparatus that fabricates phenomenal realities in a post-truth world runs the show, nothing will get done that does not bring profit to shareholders or in any small way obstructs that enterprise. We need to brand on the side of our threatened eco-system and the 80 percent of the world's population not benefiting from our profit-making ways. But as to what effect these words have on our phenomenal realities is not a matter of calculation or, more precisely, a matter determined from within those phenomenal realities.

Let us say, however, that the Humpty Dumpty of market rule can be challenged, that it can be knocked off the wall and cracked, that a phenomenal regime can give way to the exigencies of the real world. Let's say that a culture, like a person going to a therapist, can and have his/her blinders taken off and begin to see beyond the boundaries of what he or she has been branded to see. The therapist relies on societal norms as reference points, as benchmarks that aberrant perceptions can be calibrated. When van den Berg writes, "[S]omething that is unnoticed by anyone, and, when suggested, is denied by everyone, appears to be a reality to the patient," common sense tells us that this person is wrong, that he or she is a victim of a misunderstanding self-created (*A Different Existence: Principles of Phenomenological Psychopathology*, [Pittsburgh, PA: Duquesne University Press, 1972]). The therapist observes that a phenomenal construction of the world has seriously distanced itself from common observation. The diagnosis is not at all clear if you extend this individual approach to an entire culture, especially one in which two different observations of the world claim the common or normal Archimedean point, the standard by which the 'other' view must be weighed and measured. When sound minds are involved and power is evenly divided between factions and, most importantly, there is an understanding that all factions are representing the world as it appears to them, then contesting observations can lead to a mutual supplementation. What is absent in one phenomenal world is recognized as present in another.

But phenomenal realities in the United States are not so clearly divided nor does our politics share, to repeat, the post-truth realizations of marketing and branding strategies. What we face is an asymmetric display of wealth and power as well as a stubborn faith that the methods of science hold fast in politics. We hold onto the illusions of determining evidence as well as illusions of our own imminent rise to wealth and power. Those without both wealth and power may yet live within a phenomenal framing of such, imminent because Americans live very deeply in the phenomenal reality of a freedom to choose a destiny of wealth and power. We are not roused to any action against the obscene inequities of wealth and power because in our phenomenal worlds we are destined to wealth and power. Our societal norms are housed here, no more than the constructions of wealth and power. Without the corrective of recognized norms or, more disastrously, only a recognition of illusions held as norms, phenomenal-reality bubbles cannot be burst.

The wealthy live in a phenomenal reality quite different from the phenomenal reality of the economically anxious and hard pressed. There is no puzzle on the wealthy side. The phenomenal reality is explicable: the world of the wealthy is defined by its exclusion of all other ways of being in the world. Not knowing anything about not being wealthy is a sine qua non of being wealthy. The puzzle in the United States is entirely on the side of the have-less-each-day, those living on either one or the other path of an illusionary phenomenal reality. On one path, already mentioned, a will to power and wealth depends only on willing such strongly enough. The other path is as illusionary but sadder, the one in which Americans survive on the fumes of former middle-class well-being. Right now, we have made a god of an economic system that confirms the passage of wealth to even more wealth while denying any passage from working class to middle class to wealth.

If you are not positioned with a sizeable stock portfolio but depend on wages and savings from wages, your destiny on the American ship of state is to reside in steerage, something that 90 percent of the European population did until the French Revolution. But unlike the Jacobins of yore, we continue to hold our *nouveau regime* of wealth and power not as dangerous and destructive but as to what we need to aspire. This phenomenal depiction defies all 'the conditions on the ground' yet holds fast. You cannot stage a revolt against plutarchy when you identify with the plutarch and share this fear of the revolutionary. This sharing of phenomenal realities nullifies revolt and vilifies protest. It is a dark and tragic state of affairs.

There's increasing danger in this pathology whereby we disconnect conditions on the ground or the experiences of everyday life, and what we take from them, what we perceive them to be. Perceptions are not emerging from or meshing with the world but only with a state of mind constructing what the world *looks like*. Facts and figures can never be free of our intentions and observations and, therefore, are not an antidote to incongruities of perception and reality. However, they establish a bit of 'world,' not ever as universally acknowledged or observation-free as implied. The established conditions of the physical universe, from planet to galaxies, can in the future and have in the past burst the bubbles of all personal and social mediations, of all phenomenal realities. This is not the party of market rule or the party of a Vichy France-like liberalism. This is a presence and not a party, a discourse *res ipsa loquitur*, a politics where "the thing itself speaks."

No one is outside a phenomenal frame and can assert an authority based on direct access to things in themselves, but we are capable of being aware of others, of hearing them and responding to them because we share what Lucretius called "the nature of things." This does not mean that we at some point fail to live in the world as it appears to us but rather that we are all creating in the same workshop and with the same materiel. And when that workshop and its materiel changes, we all experience the change, regardless of how we then go on to narrate the change. This voiceless voice sounds a politics by which we can measure our phenomenal fabrications.

We are now living very deeply in rival fabrications that sometimes misconstrue "the nature of things" and other times remain heedless. It is frightening to recall D.H. Lawrence's observations of the spinning woman who does not talk to you but only her own world in you. It is also frightening to think that we accept an economic regime that is not heedless of its impact on the human and natural life-worlds. The threatening and endangering aspects of this regime have become a vital part of a perverse phenomenal reality. The more imminent the danger and the greater the risk, the greater the chance of winning, of establishing superiority. We cannot dissolve or resolve the haunting vision of you as no more than an extension of another's reality or the equally haunting vision of a psychopathology ruling our economics and politics. Yet history reveals that it does become clear when pathological perceptions threaten us and efforts are made to dissolve such threats. We arise out of both the web of branded illusions as well as our own. Stories clash, phenomenal worlds run into each other, and though none may claim a truthfulness superior to another's, what burdens the many and denies the full humanity of each is gradually brought to disclosure. Such has been the case with African slavery and women's suffrage. But even more clearly, history shows us that we bend or break when our illusions confront "the nature of things."

Notes

1. Revised from the original. Joseph P. Natoli, *Twentieth-Century Blake Criticism: Northrop Frye to the Present,* New York: Garland, 1992, xxi–xxvi. Reprinted in Routledge Library Editions: *William Blake,* 2016.

2. Reprinted from Joseph Natoli, *Mots D'Ordre: Disorder in Literary Worlds,* New York: State University of New York Press, 1992, 16–18.

Chapter Two

A Patient Appears at the Psychiatrist's Office

The Turn to Phenomenological Psychopathology

I was led from the depth psychology of Carl Jung, whose work I used as analog to Blake in my dissertation, to the phenomenologists, most directly the work of J.H. van den Berg who asks us to "set aside the hypothesis of the unconscious and look into the discrepancies between the patient's story and the `facts of reality'" (*A Different Existence*, 30). Similar to Blake, postmodernity and Marxism, phenomenological psychology, and especially the work of van den Berg on the notion of the *Lebenswelt*, or human life-world, remained a major player in all my writing.

My postmodern bent may set up the idea that we live in multiple realities, all shaped within the sociocultural conditions that we ourselves bring into being; and my leftist view holds that some dominating, equally fabricated realities have led to the usurpation of what Lyotard in *The Postmodern Condition*, 1979, calls "petits recits." However, it has been phenomenological psychology that guides me to the imaginative makeup of both imposing and powerless ways of being in the world. And the assumption that pathologies lie deep within us, construe our imaginaries, and too often get the better of our "Glad Day" imaginaries is all Blake, whose visionary work dramatically displays the fall and resurrection of the human imagination.

In a follow-up piece to my "Dark Affinities: Liberal and Neoliberal" in which I employed my phenomenological approach, Michael Johnson wrote:

> Natoli shows how this culture-driven mass of personal trag-
> edies works itself out specifically issue by issue—education
> "reform," immigration, taxation, etc. The sheer clarity of his

specific understandings of how this unconscious common core
overwhelms our rational thinking cuts to the heart of our political darkness. ("Transforming Our Dark Affinities," *Truthout*,
February 1, 2014)

I thus carried my interest in dimensions of consciousness from literature
to politics. In my online political writing, I probed the nether regions
of the American mass psyche, assuming that I was dealing with a psychopathology and applying the approach of pathography, what van den
Berg calls "a description of the pathological physiognomy of objects" as
well as one's relationship to self, others, and time. The attempt here is to
draw a portrait of the American mass psyche as it altered and disclosed
itself in headline events, pop culture, and everyday life. For example, this
approach led me to what I called the "dark affiliations" of liberal and
neoliberal views—dark because they were forged by wealth and power,
neither ideology representing those without wealth or power, the mass
of the populace. Pathography reveals that greed and rapaciousness cross
ideological boundaries while fear, distrust, suspicion, indifference, and animosity more powerfully guide one's relationship with others than the
biblical counsel "to love thy neighbor as thyself."

How the world appears to us seemed to me to directly relate to
Blake's focus on perception and the discrepancy between our phenomenal
realities, our one-fold perceptions, and a four-fold perception through
which we were able to see "a World in a Grain of Sand / And a Heaven
in a Wild Flower, / Hold Infinity in the palm of your hand / And Eternity
in an hour" ("Auguries of Innocence"). Certainly, Blake's visionary 'facts
of reality' would present as monumental discrepancies in a pathography.
But Blake, too, is an examiner of consciousness, a therapist of both a
consciousness fallen into "Newton's sleep" and an apocalyptic consciousness achieved through the work of the imagination.

What phenomenological psychology offered me was a casebook
approach to describing phenomenal realities, an approach I applied to
literature because here I felt were the richest observations and details of
human consciousness. Here were literary worlds that were transparently
phenomenal worlds with characters embedded in their own intentional
configurations of what a reader or an audience measured from within
their own unquestioned compact with the facts of reality.

The psychotherapist would not ascribe a pathology to all human
consciousness and would therefore limit pathography to the mentally
ill. The most illustrious creators of literary worlds, however, pose one
phenomenal reality alongside another and explore beyond categories of

morality, rationality, functionality, and sanity. Whether all consciousness was fallen and made sick by Blake's "invisible worm / That flies in the night / In the howling storm" or only sometimes wandering away from the 'facts of reality,' it seemed to remain true that all consciousness was literature's métier.

My interest in psychological approaches to literature resulted in *Psychological Perspectives on Literature: Freudian Dissidents and Non-Freudians* (Archon, 1984), which included essays on Jacques Lacan, R.D. Laing, cognitive psychology, Wilhelm Reich, Karen Horney, Roy Schafer, Normal Holland, Carl Jung, Alfred Adler, Erich Fromm, and my own on phenomenological psychology, which included interpretations of Blake's "The Sick Rose," *Hamlet*, and Joan Didion's *Play It As It Lays*. In 1986, I published "Dimensions of Consciousness in *Hamlet*" for *Mosaic*, extending my interpretation of *Hamlet* as I read more deeply into the case studies of Ludwig Binswanger. However, I chose "Phenomenological Psychology and Literary Interpretation" as the first selection in this section because it reveals the approach overall, both theory and praxis.

That same year, 1984, Frederik L. Rusch and I compiled *Psychocriticism: An Annotated Bibliography*. "This bibliography," we wrote, "will be of use to students of literature interested in the application of the tenets of formal psychology to literature. It should also be of use to psychologists interested in literature as a non-discursive source of human behavior, perceptions, and intentions." There were indeed dark affinities and dark imaginaries in literature, the very domain that psychology set out to explore. But it was necessary to ignore borders between the two and within the two. For instance, both *Psychological Perspectives* and *Psychocriticism* ignore the notion of orthodox or unorthodox psychological approaches, as well as ignoring the proscription against applying extra-literary analogues to literature itself. There was inviolability to what C.P. Snow called "the two cultures" that one preserved and hesitated to violate. We violated them nevertheless.

Psychocritism was my second and last book-length bibliographic work and like the Blake bibliography, it represented my taking advantage of my tenure in various well-stocked academic libraries. I worked at the University of California, Irvine library at a time when the School of Theory and Criticism was in residence; and I used all available time then to read and talk theory, to seek out graduate students and visiting luminaries, questioning, reformatting thoughts, and moving rapidly toward editing *Tracing Literary Theory* for the University of Illinois Press.

I continued in my online writing to employ variations on the phenomenological approach to politics and present in this section "The Code of Crisis and Disaster" as an example.

I begin this section with a piece, "Voyaging in the Waters of the Father," I wrote forty-two years after my Jung/Blake dissertation and thirty-one years after my writing for the *Journal of Phenomenological Psychology*. I drew on my background in psychology as well as literary theory and postmodernity in my attempt to come to terms with my own father, irretrievably blended with the father of Blakean Nobodaddy power.

Dark Affinities: The Father

I understood the following sequence after it was disclosed in a dream, always for me the messenger of affinities we cannot confront, the messenger employed by a dark imaginary.

The sequence of events: I spend a summer painting and regardless of what I intend to paint, I wind up painting boats sailing in impossible places. Boats, big and small, with sails, sailing in the middle of what looks like woods or up in the sky or surrounded by splashes of line and color, formal not representational. Except for the boats.

Days I paint; nights I dream. I have a dream that I am helping my father across a darkened unfamiliar street; he's huddled against me, bent over, old as in the last times I saw him alive, and then I realize we can't get across. We are on a futile mission. Something is drastically wrong. But he looks up at me and tells me we can do it. I can do it. And the thought comes to me that he is dead and he cannot be there; thus the futility and the wrongness, the unreality.

None of that makes any difference. None of it prevents the dream from reoccurring. There is a potency here that won't be dispelled by lucidity. My father, the Father is trying to tell me something. Maybe I think almost immediately beyond my father to the Father, an archetypal figure from a collective imaginary, because I spent years, many years ago, reading Carl Jung's work as it came out in the Bollingen Series. I gave up my own Jungian analysis of myself after I descended in a dream down so many stairs till I reached a dark, dank, low-ceilinged place where I flashed a light on bones in the dark clay. Dread went through me in the frightening way it can happen only in dream. I delved no further. I then recalled that this was Jung's dream I had read in *Memories, Dreams and Reflections*. I had made it my own. It wasn't plagiarism. You cannot plagiarize an archetypal dream. I descended into the primordial dust of death. Yeats nailed it:

Now that my ladder's gone,
I must lie down where all the ladders start
In the foul rag and bone shop of the heart. ("The Circus
    Animals' Desertion")

In another dream, I am standing with my father on the pier in San Pedro, California, and he is pointing out a ship at anchor at the dock and explaining how he can tell by how she rests in the water something about the weight of cargo. He walks over to a bollard and runs a hand over the thickly painted, black surface. In my dream the bollard looks like some primitive totem. We are both absorbed in looking at it as if the object had something to reveal. I think of the word I can never pronounce: *autochthonous,* "native to the soil." Roget's lists "ancestral, patriarchal, preadamite."

And I know, as in a Joycean epiphany, that my father is entwined in a dark primitivism and ignorance I set myself against, a barrier I erect between him and me. Nothing is gone and is irretrievable in hidden places in my mind where matter is made to matter. I need to delve into the darkness of our relationship. I need to delve into a place I already am.

I am a student of psychology, of thought and creativity, popular and elite, of all manner high and low of cultural interpretation, of the politics and pragmatics of everyday life, of politics itself. I am never free of second-order observing. It is what I have learned to do. I have also learned through the English Romantic poets to seek to unlearn, to imagine beyond what I can say, to understand beyond what I can interpret. "Our meddling intellect," Wordsworth writes, "Mis-shapes the beauteous forms of things / We murder to dissect" ("The Tables Turned").

My consciousness works both in concert with my dark affinities and dark imaginaries and also counter to them, as if too much let in will destroy the house of reason and purpose. So in one way I know that an eureka moment in a dream is really an intrusion of conscious cogitating in a landscape of startling, non-sequitur moments. A masquerading, wonderland world suddenly has a hole in it, and you see both into it and outside it. A penetrating disclosure. A clever thief has entered the darkest imaginary.

My paintings are mindscapes with boats whose mysterious development, disclosed as if hidden and suddenly seen, were my masked renderings of my father, my attempts at resolving in paint his place in my life. My father was a dock boss on the Brooklyn "finger piers," now gone, and loading and unloading ships (my "boats") was what he did his whole life. I am repeatedly painting my father into my paintings, each boat a symbolic presence of his absence in my life. They are therefore my mindscapes. I cannot part with them without losing a long labor of the psyche.

In a dream, my father had stood there pointing to a bollard covered and recovered with black paint since the beginning of time, the bollard of what was hardened and long hidden, dark and enigmatic in my own unconscious.

He was showing me death surely, his and someday mine. But he was also touching a prereflective, terrible way of being in the world, which was his, now passed on to me. And which I have spent a lifetime refusing. Nonetheless, my refusal irrelevant, there has been a mystery working inside me that I needed to see into; and he was directing my gaze to that hard, dark nub of impenetrability.

In my earlier dream, I was holding him up, half carrying him across the street, nothing illuminated, all opaque. I did not know where we were going. He was wrapped in my arms so tightly that we could not walk. We shuffled. But that closeness had never been true. Neither of us had been embracingly close.

My father's father had died in WWI when my father was three, and so he had never known his own father. By my father's bedside in the nursing home was an old, brown photo of his young father in uniform, standing beside my grandmother. My father was in his late nineties when that photo suddenly reappeared by his bed. Long unseen by me, it was now there where he lay his head. What his dreams of his unknown father were as he himself approached the century milestone, I cannot imagine; but I believe he wanted to be told by his absent father what he himself told me that last time I saw him: "I'm proud of you, Joe." That never had any hope of realization in my father's case. Those words would be, for him, endlessly deferred.

Perhaps I was painting my father as a boat sailing, voyaging to where that deferment would come to rest. These dreams may be about many things, but they are most certainly mememto mori dreams. It is my father who is guiding my own voyage to a final port.

I inherit a yearning from my father for the Father, for what can never be fulfilled. I am on a quest for a fulfillment that can never be reached. My memory of him has sails, and he is the ship. The subtitle of this book is "A Mind's Odyssey," a long voyage to places where I have, in the real world and in my imagination, "come into port," and where full disclosure of this long being in the world has not escaped shipwreck. Imagine the entire *Odyssey* not as Odysseus's voyage but that of Telemachus, whose father is both absent and always about to return.

My father is a sailboat I paint repeatedly, always differently, always in a new scape. They are pictured on this book's cover, as if opening the book was a launch. I know I am working out in paint a relationship absent on my own mindscape, just as I feel my own daughters are caught within a similar psychic drama. My relationship with my daughters, to me a deep love for them always deferred from full expression, has been the most immediate trigger of my dreams of the Father. This is a drama in which a never fully retrievable absence gains what Jung called "mana" potency, a subliminal magnetism that far exceeds the dimensions our conscious mind is able to give it.

The Father lies deep within layers that far exceed our personal dramas, descending into a collective unconscious that has grown on the landscape of our human history. In my dissertation research on William Blake through the lens of Jungian psychology, I traced the various archetypes, primordial and mysterious, throughout Blake's work, especially in the later prophecies. Nobodaddy was the usurper god of a rational consciousness who was also "Nobody," the absent daddy, the Father who withheld the dangers of the senses, the emotions and the imagination, held them bound within the constraints of his suppressive and repressive order of things.

"At bottom God is nothing more than an exalted father," Freud tells us and so opens the door to Jung's staging the Father onto-theologically and mythically. The Father dwells in a shadow landscape of the psyche where he has deep mana value because he is at the origin of self. The Creator Father is him to whom we trace our own being and because that beginning is more absence than presence, more words than reality, more signifiers than a determinate signified, we are forever unappeased and unfulfilled. Pater Noster who may be in heaven but is not here, who himself does not show up but sends a prophet or a son, a son who is driven to cry out "Why have you forsaken me?"

Is not the son, like the daughter, deeply anguished by both father and mythic Father that can never provide the firm determinacy of real presence? Mater Noster is not simply a feminist hailing of a patriarchal attention but a need to transform the unreachable Nobodaddy of law and restraint into the Magna Mater, the Jungian archetype of a loving, nurturing, always-present Mother. We are on this deep onto-theological and mythical level seeking to end the Father's campaign to put the ego where id is. We are on a journey to revive what is absent in the Father, that absence shaped by the absence of a capacity to feel, to imagine, to sense in ways that create affinities and affiliations on the deepest layers of being. I see all this in Blake's mockery of his Nobodaddy.

In the view of the phenomenological psychiatrist, "there are no layers, there is just one layer (which we must not call a layer at all) of life
as such. There, in that life is the depth of life" (van den Berg, *A Different
Existence*). My relationship or lack thereof, or my daughters' or lack thereof
is, in this view, not repressed but always present. It is a consciousness of
something I hold off, like a dentist appointment, until the weak state of
that relationship brings it to center stage. Dream then, in this phenomenological view, does not sneak by the gates of the conscious mind and
disclose what is deeply buried but rather is a nighttime residue of what
has been too much now in mind. But while I can recognize a viable
pathography of simply what we reveal in our consciousness of others,
time, objects, and ourselves, I judge a Jungian archetype such as the Wise
Old Man (i.e., the Father), to be disassociated from our consciousness
but nevertheless shadowing it, so that I am aware that my awareness is
overwhelmed by what I cannot fully represent.

We do indeed mark our consciousness with our deeds and desires,
and there may be no need to recognize a storage chamber in our own
psyche that we lose connection to, we lose the key to; but nevertheless,
our being in the world may itself be multiplex. Within varying reality
frames, varying hierarchies of meaning and value exist. This is not dis-
sociative identity disorder or what Freud called "schizophrenia" but rather
a normal state of being in the world. It becomes pathological if we give
names and identities to the different reality frames through which we
travel. We are aware of how each framing differs from the other. We keep
track, aware of the differing valences we assign, aware of what could be
resolvable and what remains in Rudolph Otto's term, "numinous."

In Oscar Wilde's novel *The Picture of Dorian Gray*, all that Dorian does
is not revealed in his face and figure but in a portrait hidden away in an attic
room. As Dorian plunges deeper into moral decadence, the portrait bears
the ugly signs of this degeneration while he remains a handsome youth. The
portrait is locked away but not inaccessible to Dorian; his debauchery is
not hidden away in deep levels of the unconscious but is what he chooses
to keep out of sight. I think then that my relationship with my father, its
disturbing absence, has itself never been absent, never repressed but always
present. What is unavailable to a conscious mind must be absent in our
conscious life—otherwise it would be available to our observation. If it were
not absent but present in our conscious life, we would have no need of a
depth psychologist to reveal what is there for us to see.

Whether the indirections of dream 'out' what we ignore or bury,
whether we bury beyond the recognition of consciousness or live on the

edge in our consciousness of a disturbing knowing, whether we bury deeply all signs of what troubles or what is troubling, it seems undeniable that we duplex and multiplex our existence and bear the record like the picture of Dorian Gray. The imprint of the father/Father on that shadow palimpsest of the psyche, one either barely visible to the conscious mind or present as a persistent trace in all our thoughts, possesses this mana power that remains different from any other mark the world makes on us. I think this is so because it has both psychological and onto-theological dimensions.

The father is always troubling because, as a signifier, it is psychologically and onto-theologically loaded but also culturally positioned to be removed and gone from the family setting but also central and directing. A movement toward equalizing that positioning between both mother and father and also two mothers or two fathers or only one mother or one father has yet a small imprint on an onto-theological structuring at play before Genesis. This overloaded Father signifier connects, first, to what Derrida calls "metaphysics of presence," a futile pursuit in words, signifiers, of a presence that such words assume to reflect in a knowable way. But as the Father, it connects with a transcendental signified, a presence that all the words of every sacred text seek to reflect in an absolute and reliable way but that, nonetheless, remains remote and ungraspable.

This is an absence most disturbing because this is the originating presence: "In the beginning was the Word, and the Word was with God, and the Word was God. The same was in the beginning with God. All things were made by him" (John 1:1, King James Version). Conflating God the Father with Word does not however conflate our words with that transcending presence. John the Apostle is then the first to self-authorize through his own testament the presence of Jesus, who "was in the beginning with God," whom "no one has ever seen" (1:2–4; 1:18). The Father then floats between being there and being absent, revealing full meaning and withholding it, standing as a firm foundation upon which all meaning rests and destabilizing any foundation of meaning by virtue of its own unreliability.

Whether repressed in the unconscious or disclosed as what we are conscious of, the father/Father plays a catalyst role in human self-development. Absence here sets progeny on a lifetime path of seeking what was lacking at an irretrievable stage. Comparable to an anxiety of influence and, I think, of greater import is an angered confusion against an absent father/Father.

Blake finds himself compelled to create a mythos/system or otherwise be enslaved by another man's. Whether he had his illiterate father in mind, or the tyranny of Newton, Reynolds, and Locke in the eighteenth-century Age of Reason, or "the Creator of this World is a very Cruel Being," Blake portrays characters such as Orc and Los pitted against the tyranny of Nobodaddy.

Melville's Ahab expresses the same rage against the whale, the mask behind which an absent and infuriating creator lies: "I see in him outrageous strength, with an inscrutable malice sinewing it. That inscrutable thing is chiefly what I hate; and be the white whale agent, or be the white whale principal, I will wreak that hate upon him" (*Moby Dick*, "The Quarter Deck").

Hamlet's pathography is rich and interesting, but an absent father of the same name is the ghostly presence that triggers his revenge, a revenge he defers for reasons never fulfilling but always deferred. It may be that the grounding for this lies in the replacement of king/father, an authoritative presence, by a ghost/father, a victim father easily and unceremoniously replaced, allowing then the rotten state of Denmark to which Hamlet returns. All action then remains unsanctioned in any righteous way and is released into some version of a postmodern world, a world without foundations. Hamlet is not prepared to play on a Derridean bottomless chessboard but rather asks a version of the question that a character voices in Dostoevsky's *The Possessed*; namely, "If there is not God, how can I be a captain?" With Hamlet, the question becomes, "If the father's presence dissolves suddenly into absence, regardless of the means, upon what grounds are any actions to be deemed good or evil?"

The personal father interaction does not in itself produce anger and an ontological collapse. Dickens is full of happy father/child relationships, although there is an empty space reserved for father that Dickens seems pathologically compelled to fill. It is not the shame of a few days in a blacking factory but a father on the border of everything—society, solvency, success, reliable and authoritative presence, that seems to play out in the novels. The here-again gone-again father, like a magical sleight of hand presence, the father as not real and reliable but a conjuror, sets Dickens's imagination in pursuit of the reliable father. That Dickens himself was a talented conjurer is, in a subliminal way, a recognition of the ease at which he could conjure in his novels absent fathers as present.

Dickens writes the needed plots of what remains out of reach: the waif who grows in the absence of the father; the multitude of characters whose seemingly endless proliferation displays an obsessed energy, which overwhelms author and reader. Male characters either clearly represent Jung's Wise Old Man archetype, filled with kindness and wisdom, a well-meaning guide and mentor; or they are lost, suffering, mistreated, or, at worst, twisted, ruined, dysfunctional in contemporary terminology. Mr. Jarndyce, Mr. Brownlow, Joe Gargery, Magwitch, Daniel Peggotty, and the Cheerybly brothers represent the former. Dysfunctional sons abound in Dickens, from Richard Carstone, Smike, Steerforth, Herbert Pocket, Newman Noggs, Dick Swiveller, as do dysfunctional fathers such as Vincent Crummles, Daniel Doyce, and Micawber. Dark and twisted males with brutalizing power over the young abound: Murdstone, Gradgrind, Ralph Nickleby, Pecksniff, Wackford Squeers, and Quilp, more deeply and dramatically represented than the ingénues they afflict. There is in Dickens a compelling urge to try out or replace the father whose image cannot hold in any firm way in Dickens's mind. Because the efforts here—creating a new creation in which the father is firm—are attempts doomed to failure, attempts than cannot succeed, the efforts go on and on. The creativity can end only in death.

The father/Father's impact is as observable I think in politics as in art and literature.

Consider the last three presidents: Bill Clinton, George W. Bush, and Barack Obama. Clinton's father, a salesman, was killed in a car accident three months before Bill was born as William Jefferson Blythe. Clinton's stepfather was an alcoholic who "sometimes beat" Clinton's mother. The couple divorced and then remarried when Bill was fifteen. He then changed his name from Blythe to Clinton "as a gesture" of a willingness to accept what he could easily reject. You could say that Clinton's "triangulation" politics, his leaning into his nemesis was born with that gesture.

Bill Clinton is a Lincoln heir in the humbleness of his origins. Lincoln condensed his origins as being no more than "the short and simple annals of the poor" preferring not to dwell on his relationship with his father, which, by all accounts, was a distant relationship. Both Bill Clinton and Lincoln never ceased campaigning not only to forge their own destiny but to become a father to themselves, to become what they had been denied, to become both father and son. There can be no fulfillment by the son if there is no father of origin.

Clarke Roundtree, in a biography of George W. Bush, describes young George as a profligate ne'er-do-well, suffering under the success of his own father, and unlike Clinton who forged onward without self-deprecation, George W. almost sinks within his own self-image as a failed son. At some mysterious point, the father, George H.W. Bush ascends from disappointed father to the Father, the Father of the country, a now-sacred figure the son will not disappoint. This fixation not to disappoint the father but to rise from listlessness and ineffectiveness shapes a man who will wage unending war, who will not fall back into doing nothing, who will do what needs to be done, thus reclaiming his worth in the eyes of his father.

Barack Obama's Kenyan father divorced Obama's mother when Barack was two, and he saw him only once again. "Obama formed an image of his absent father from stories told by his mother and her parents" (Wikipedia). But the absent father haunts the future president, resulting in *Dreams from My Father: A Story of Race and Inheritance* (1995). It seems that from the start Obama sees himself as that triangulated point which represents successful compromise, a successful blending, which he personifies. Such a driving, personal mythos leads him to misperceive the real neoliberal antagonism facing him in his first term as president. The real difference of his African father, the essential otherness of this father, is not realized by Obama but transmuted into an approachable, assimilable difference. The real absence of this father allows such an idealistic, naïve assumption to fill the missing space, as the seeking son would have it. He himself has the force to reunite an absent father and a dead mother, to reunite a union of difference that had fallen apart. He is then like Lincoln, the Great Unifier.

My own father's complicated childhood—his being called "the American" in the tiny Sicilian village in which he grew up, his difference prominent because of his US birth, and subsequently in his return to the United States at the age of seventeen, subject to all the bigotry awaiting Italian immigrants who couldn't speak English—set him on a lifelong voyage to find an identity. He seized on a vision of 'American.' He employed the word "American" as a corrective rod and as a goal I should pursue, to become American in every way.

I rankled under that rod, and turned my critical mind to taking down that icon in my father's mind. I turned to the margins, the very edge of the American Dream as energetically as my father sought entrance into the mainstream, into what, ironically, he himself had only a view of from the margins. He knew of the nasty bigotry, the arbitrary, arrogant, and controlling power of the native WASP, and the inhumanity of a capitalist dog-eat-dog world and, in fact, experienced very little of that golden realm of Americana he held on to. He found for himself a dream identity that his own sharp mind deconstructed and yet he held on to it, holding it out to me as a life raft. There was so much that I had to accede to in order to succeed so that I could fulfill what remained in him a liminal identity.

I abjured every bit of that. My antinomianism is set deeply against the laws of a fraudulent, fabricated order of things that sets profit as a god, a false order that my father bent a knee to but at the same time did not spare his sarcasm. My rebellion is like the fiery Orc's, whose declamation in Blake's *America: a Prophecy* (1793) so moved me that in 1967, on the verge of writing my master's thesis, Blake became my mentor/father.

> I am Orc, wreath'd round the accursed tree;
> The times are ended: shadows pass, the morning 'gins to break,
> The fiery joy that Urizen perverted to ten commandments,
>
> What night he led the starry hosts thro' the wide wilderness,
> That stony law I stamp to dust. (8:1–5)

It was many years before that spirit, so accommodated by the countercultural spirit of the moment, gave way to a deeper understanding of the imagination, in life, politics, and art; and so I moved closer to Blake's Los, the transforming force in Blake's later prophecies. And so I began to imagine in a more empathetic way my father as well as my own questioning of all authority that masks an absence that both my father and I felt, an absence that burdens all of humanity, the absent Logos. The disorientation and turmoil that we associate with the postmodern lies in this turn away from any search for an absent presence and a hard-to-comprehend *jouissance* that results from so doing. But I hold that the mythos here is intractable and does not dissolve into the endless play of differing and deferring signifiers that Derrida describes. The Father resonates with a mana value that has no linguistic reduction. There may be neither Logocentric presence nor any father whose absence can be brought to presence, but we voyage in the waters of a Father/ father relationship that only death brings to an end.

We are embedded in dark affinities that are themselves entangled in dark imaginaries, dark only in the sense of opaque, which imagination itself breaches and discloses in what we write, what we dream, what we paint.

Phenomenological Psychology and Literary Interpretation[1]

At the core of any psychological approach to literature is people—author, reader, or character. As I later discuss, a phenomenological approach to literature considers all three. But it begins with characters. Once the assumption is made that characters in literature are reflective of people in real life, it remains only to find a psychology that enables us to probe deeply into a character. Phenomenology's emphasis upon a person's own perceptions closely corresponds to the phenomenal experiences generated in literature.

The novelist, for example, is concerned with particularity and action, with description, with the world of appearance and the spontaneity of lived experience. We need a method to trace action and description back to thought (and vice versa), a method that does not accept consciousness as a black box but acknowledges the interconnection of consciousness and world through intentionality. A phenomenological perspective takes us out of the armchair of the psychoanalyst, attending only to the words a character speaks, and enables us to reconstruct the phenomenal reality of a character by attending to that character's varied interactions with the world. It is not simply a matter of a character's stream of consciousness but what that consciousness tends toward, the inextricable link between consciousness and world.

For instance, a character may say he loves his Brooklyn neighborhood, but the way in which he transfers to us the actual physiognomy of that neighborhood—the objects and people that comprise that neighborhood—tells us a story different from what he has told us, the simple statement that he loves his Brooklyn neighborhood. If it is true—and I believe it is—that literature is essential to our discovery of "the experiential foundation of our world," (Maurice Merleau-Ponty, *Phenomenology of Perception* [New York: Humanities Press, 1962], xx) then that discovery is made only when we have an approach that confronts consciousness interacting with the world, with human experiences themselves, and not thoughts, feelings, senses, or intuitions extracted from those experiences. Writers do not simply present characters who dramatically pour out their hearts and souls and are right in what they say about their hearts and souls. What we find, rather, in the richest literary works are characters deeply embedded in their own phenomenal worlds, their perceptions not commentary upon their actions but inextricably tied to their actions. We must find the physiognomy of their thoughts in the physiognomy of objects and people outside themselves with whom and with which they interact. In any literary text—novel, play, or poem—we find ourselves as readers not outside but inside literary worlds richly brocaded with a variety of interconnecting intentional universes: characters', author's, and our own. What everyone says or does not, what everyone does or does not, how everything is described or is not, how time passes or does not—are all unavoidable components of a literary world. We look to a psychology of a phenomenological bent in order to approach such a world without being seriously reductionist.

We first observe what is in a literary world by observing one character, by trying to describe the Lebenswelt of one character. That Lebenswelt is meticulously built up from a character's perceptions of self, others, objects, and time. Therefore, an intrinsic component of a phenomenological analysis is a scrutiny of the total literary world in which the character has his or her being. In answering the question, "What is the nature of a character's being within a certain literary world?" we must use what we know of that literary world, determined by other characters and the author, to know that character. And, we must use what we know of that character to know that literary world. We begin with one character and then through that character touch other characters, the physical setting of the work, the time frame—all of which are used to reveal that one character's Lebenswelt while simultaneously providing us with an entrance to the entire work. It is phenomenological psychology's recognition of an objectified consciousness, a consciousness interacting with the outside world that prevents us from becoming imprisoned permanently within any one mind. We range outward into the whole literary world, our mode of travel the intentional nature of consciousness.

The characterization of Hamlet has been the subject of numerous interpretations, and yet Hamlet's life-world remains elusive; the man behind the thoughts and the actions has been variously described. Any attempt at responding to the heart of the question as to why Hamlet procrastinates invariably leads to an exposure of a critical approach's strengths and weaknesses. It is in the hope of revealing most dramatically the phenomenological approach to drama that Hamlet has been chosen for discussion.

There is, Hamlet tells Rosencrantz, "nothing either good or bad but thinking makes it so." And indeed, Hamlet's thinking makes it so, makes the play, and makes the action and inaction of the play. What is Hamlet's thinking? Can we describe Hamlet's life-world, his Lebenswelt? And is that world and the good or bad it imposes upon time, others, self, and objects substantially different from the 'real world,' the good and bad evaluations in the play that are not Hamlet's? How great is the discrepancy between Hamlet's phenomenal reality and the phenomenal realities of other characters? Is there implicit in this play a normative reality that we can call Shakespeare's? We know at the start that this is the tragic history of Hamlet, Prince of Denmark. If the tragedy is with him, is it in his perceptions? Is there any way that it cannot be in his perceptions? If the tragedy is with him—is his tragedy—where is the non-tragedy in this play? Are there, in other words, non-tragic perceptions in this play? Where is the non-tragic counterpart that enables us to see Hamlet's tragedy? Is it explicit, implicit in the play? Is it in us and nowhere in the play? If there is a Shakespearean normative view of things implicit here, perhaps the non-tragic counterpart of the play is within it. Perhaps the tragic counterpart is not in Hamlet after all but in the world of Elsinore, and the play is his tragic history only insofar as he has the misfortune of being in such a world. If we cannot really be sure of the location of a tragic and non-tragic dimension, we can be sure of a dimension that is opened by a phenomenological method—Hamlet's world and outside Hamlet's world.

When we describe Hamlet's being-in-the-world, his Lebenswelt, we approach the world outside his mind through his mind, specifically through his perceptions of self, others, objects, and time. This is all of which he is conscious. If we wish to connect Hamlet the character to the play *Hamlet*, we must consider not only Hamlet's being in the world but also simply being in the world of Elsinore. The passage between Hamlet's mental landscape and the world of Elsinore is partially through what he himself is not conscious of and therefore does not possess. The play as it exists outside Hamlet's mind—T.S. Eliot's "facts of the play"—is not all known to Hamlet; some of the facts of the play lie in the consciousness of other characters. What has traditionally been found in the unconscious of Hamlet is in a phenomenological view found in the world around him.

In the phenomenological view, there are no layers to life. Life may be rich, deep, mysterious, but what is not conscious for one lies accessible in others. Such is the case in Hamlet. Within what Claudius, Horatio, Laertes, and everyone else in the play reveal to us on the conscious level is what Hamlet is unaware of, cannot perceive. Some of what they know comprises his unconscious, not hidden within him at all but out there and not perceived by him, available to us as observers-readers. By attending to the world of the play, the conscious themes of *Hamlet*, we discover what is not in Hamlet's Lebenswelt. We find the passage between Hamlet's Lebenswelt and the play that is *Hamlet*. Thus, a complete phenomenological study of *Hamlet* would go beyond the Lebenswelt of the character Hamlet and consider the phenomenal worlds of other characters. My discussion here is limited to Hamlet's being-in-the-world.

Once we have described Hamlet's being-in-the-world, we can attempt at answering questions this play raises, particularly the question of why Hamlet procrastinates. In order to describe Hamlet's Lebenswelt, we automatically range into the play, making our encounters through Hamlet's eyes, noting where and when the 'facts of the play' support or negate his perceptions. We, as readers, are not part of Hamlet's tragedy, though we realize very quickly that all of Shakespeare's art is unleashed to make us so, to make Hamlet's tragedy "speak loudly for him" (V, ii, 403). It is the compelling force of the tale in the telling that both enables us to view the depths of Hamlet's Lebenswelt and threatens to submerge us within the tragedy itself.

There are two dimensions of reality that we have defined in Hamlet via his own perceptions: one, the external dimension of the play, a dimension that we have gained through Hamlet's eyes and that has been corroborated in the play itself; and the other, the phenomenal reality that is Hamlet's. The first involves murder, Gertrude's precipitous marriage to her recently dead husband's murderer, and a vow of revenge by Hamlet to his father's ghost. The second involves a reality in which we are "arrant knaves all," in which even the great become bunghole stoppers. The dilemma here is for Hamlet to move from a phenomenal reality to an external reality, to put aside his own perceptions and assume perceptions outside himself.

Hamlet obviously agrees with Rosencrantz's estimate of the importance of that "spirit upon whose weal depends and rests / The lives of many" (Ill, iii, 14–15). Something is "rotten in the state of Denmark," the state outside Hamlet's mind; and it is he who, as prince, is born to set it right, to kill the usurper and thus avenge his father. It is important to reiterate at this point that Hamlet does not know all the 'facts' of the play. The external world he has constituted for himself, the world he perceives, has for us, as readers, its full dimensions only when we free ourselves of Hamlet's Lebenswelt and probe other characters. A full view of the world of Elsinore as it is constituted outside Hamlet's mind is essential to our full phenomenological description of the play. However, in considering Hamlet's Lebenswelt, we describe and analyze from the perspective of that Lebenswelt, in terms of that Lebenswelt. We get to see it all from Hamlet's view and then analyze what we have before turning elsewhere in the play.

Hamlet's external state as he perceives it does not determine his personal acts. This external state includes the requirements of revenge, of the "lives of many," of princely duties. And yet for Hamlet, a personal act, as the murder of Claudius, is dependent upon personal perceptions, upon a human life-world personally constructed. Hamlet's phenomenal reality must sanction the murder. In other words, for Hamlet to act as the situation constituted outside him demands he act, he would first have to become someone else.

The force by which Hamlet is bound to perceptions that keep him from acting creates the tension in Hamlet and may be viewed as Hamlet's true antagonist. This is not to say that Hamlet's view of what must be done, what actions should be taken, resolves the rottenness in Denmark. We cannot trust his sense of what 'normal behavior' would be under the circumstances abiding in the play as a whole. It is possible that action on anyone's part in this play resolves nothing. Or that Hamlet's own Lebenswelt, as difficult as it makes things for Hamlet, is the only human life-world in the play. In other words, to be in any other dilemma in this play except the one Hamlet is in would imply a lessening of one's humanity, a step backward into the evil that permeates the play. But from having described Hamlet's Lebenswelt, we know that if he is able to resolve the force by which he is bound to his perceptions, he is, in a sense, free to act as the external situation demands. This is the dilemma he has described for himself, and we know that regardless of whether his internal or external views can be verified, they remain real for Hamlet. Unfortunately, he moves further and further away from resolving his dilemma and plunges deeper into his own human life-world, from whose perspective he can consider only too curiously the world about him.

The tragedy we see in Hamlet is the tragedy of all whose own human life-world becomes deeply at variance with the world around them. The coinage of Hamlet's brain is no longer even a passable counterfeit for the coinage of the world. Hamlet has been caught within a world of intentions that give meaning to the world in a way antithetical to the fulfillment of his vows to revenge his father's murder. The struggle Hamlet makes in the course of this play is a struggle to give up personally constructed meaning and take on societally constructed meaning. This struggle ensues throughout the play: a mind is continually in the throes of freeing itself of a task it cannot perform while contemporaneously trying to free itself of a life-world that makes that task, the act of revenge, impossible. Hamlet's hesitancy is thus defined in this way in the phenomenological view.

If Hamlet's Lebenswelt were not malleable, he would make no struggle to act. But he does struggle. He is not the man so bound by pathological determinants that he sees nothing of his situation in the way other people see it. Hamlet sees the necessity for revenge at the same time that he considers suicide, at the same time that he considers the futility of all human life. But suicide and cynicism are the true products of his Lebenswelt, and they do not collapse but grow in strength as the play progresses. Hamlet's own Lebenswelt—the view we have described of his perceptions of others, self, objects, and time—wins the day, and thus Hamlet loses the struggle.

Claudius really arranges his own death. Hamlet, in the play's final scene, is simply an actor without internal motivation, without intentions. At the moment of his death, Hamlet is further away from acting in accord with the demands of a reality constituted outside his own mind than ever before in the play. His feigned madness is indeed a feigned madness, but one in the service of a mind struggling to put aside its own intentions and perceptions and take on the world's. That feigned madness is then a dissimulation in the service of a mind struggling toward societal perceptions. Had that feigned madness been constructed by a mind not convinced that the world and its creator were mad, a mind not constructing according to an intentional system at odds with society's, it could have been an effective, though roundabout, means of Hamlet taking revenge.

But feigned madness comes to naught because Hamlet's own dissociation from conventional perceptions and actions increases. He cannot function in the 'real world' except according to his own Lebenswelt, and from that perspective, murder serves no purpose. Only death mercifully saves Hamlet, resolves his dilemma. We have thus developed a view of Hamlet as a man who toils mightily for five acts to bridge the gap between his own Lebenswelt and the demands of an outside world. And it is his tragedy to fail.

Because Hamlet's tragedy is at the core of the play, a great deal of the play is revealed through our description and analysis of Hamlet's Lebenswelt. Through description, we have achieved some understanding of Hamlet's plight. If we move back from the play, from our close-up of Hamlet, we try to take in other characters as they are and not as they are perceived by Hamlet. We add this descriptive detail to our Hamlet description and modify it accordingly. If we move back still further, we perceive the play as a gestalt, as a dramatic interweaving of perceptions. Finally, what is not in the consciousness of any one character is in our consciousness. We become aware of the richness of Shakespeare's design as we probe deeper into the variety of phenomenal realities in the play. We become aware of the consciousness that has not only created Hamlet's consciousness and those of every other character in the play, but has guided our own consciousness toward an understanding of the play.

The Code of Crisis and Disaster[2]

Like Clotaire Rapaille, a child psychologist turned marketing strategist, I, in former times, observed a kind of protective and conciliatory façade—claimed as rational—in what people said which needed to be penetrated in order to get to what they really felt. "I don't care what you're going to tell me intellectually," Rapaille tells us. "I don't care. Give me the reptilian. Why? Because the reptilian always wins" (Frontline's *Merchants of Cool*, 2001). In Rapaille's view, once you understand the code, you understand why people do what they do, and that code involves emotional attachments that are prerational and prereflective but shape our behavior.

If you extend this approach to the idea that these bedrock emotions are wired to what we, as socially adapted, conscionable individuals, need to conceal, that we must be somewhere else than these low places in our minds, you enter a world of alibis and defenses you need to get around, that you need to see through. If you find the concealed code, you break through but this is no easy task when events are always political and the political discourse divide is unaccommodating.

In a millennial clime of a self-designed cognitive will to success, it is difficult to accept the view that our ideologies are no more than fronts for instinctive attachments. We now feel that we empower our own cognition and laugh at the notion that anything could trump our own self-empowerment and our rational choice directives. This itself is a defending alibi.

If it were the cortex and not the reptilian brain shaping our behavior, we would not now be facing the crisis and disaster reported in the news of the first week in April 2014. Consider the revelations of this one week: a Paris climate conference (UN's Intergovernmental Panel on Climate Change) gave yet another frightening report, pithily expressed in a *Slate* article: "New U.N. Report: Climate Change Risks Destabilizing Human Society." A Supreme Court decision further entrenched the 1976 decision to treat money as speech by abolishing a cap on total contributions any individual can make in a two-year election cycle. Paul D. Ryan, a likely Republican Party presidential candidate in 2016, proposed a budget that "lowers the top tax rate to 25 percent for the wealthiest taxpayers . . . while raising taxes on middle-class families with children by an average of $2,000." (*New York Times*, April 2, 2014). The bottom 40 percent of the population is not overlooked by Mr. Ryan, as he asserts that his proposed budget "empowers recipients to get off the aid rolls and back on the payrolls."

None of these occurrences is inconsequential. Our own survival and the survival of other species on this planet, the integrity of democratic elections, and the planned immiseration of many—all amount to crises moments, disasters looming. On a Saturn moon where water was found the same week, we can postulate possible life and that life observing us.

Saturn headlines: "Dire Climate Change, Bought Elections, and Budget Armageddon on Goldilocks Planet!"

To find the code of crisis and disaster that operates in American culture, we need to begin with what we say intellectually, our rational presentations, or our 'cortex' discourse. I begin with my own.

There is a ranking order to our crises and disaster, call it a "disaster order of things." Radical climate change, whether caused by a meteorite or humans, could go way beyond "destabilizing human society." Think of the lower orders. Read Elizabeth Kolbert's *The Sixth Extinction: An Unnatural History* to see the effects here on those with whom we share the planet. If you are looking for a disaster limited to us humans and specifically to democracy in the United States, consider the connection between wealth and power and the effect both, unrestricted, may have on our elections. If you assume that a serious wealth divide does not have dire consequences for a democratic society, you need to read Thomas Piketty's *Capital in the Twenty-First Century*. What oligarchs do is preserve the order of oligarchy. They can do so when wealth purchases the best brainwashing techniques marketers and advertisers have to offer. And lastly, covering the week's news, Paul Ryan's proposed republican budget gives us a few clues as to what would happen if Republicans win the Senate and hold on to the House in 2014. We can expect a feudal order of things.

All of this is, at best, arguably rational, if you accept certain premises, which are themselves grounded in certain ways of perceiving. In other words, there are other and different ways of being arguably rational about this chosen week's events. So we need to argue in this rational way on the other side. I admit that my purpose here is to weaken the rational domain and expose the ways we are 'arguably rational' as working both sides of the street, referring here to Nietzsche's reason as a strumpet easily bought. Following this pursuit of the other side of the street, the opposing rational façade, I probe the underbelly, searching for what inclines us toward our truth stories. In short, once the cortex discourse is out of the way, I follow the code to the reptilian brain.

And so the counter-reasoning, the cortex working the other side of the street.

Radical climate change, first, may not be that radical. There is nothing more variable and uncertain than the weather. The science, as they say, "isn't all in." It is premature to sink our economy intentionally when there is only a questionable justification for doing so. And, as we do not have a very deep historical record of weather change, it is very possible that what we see now has occurred before in cycles of which we are not aware. Whether humans are the single cause here or one of many variables or not a significant variable at all is unknown. What some perceive as disaster others see as opportunity. A new configuration of the planet's land and water represents a new marketing frontier, an opportunity to grow the economy, put people to work, and a maximize profit to shareholders. Whatever Mother Nature throws at us, we have the technological genius to withstand. We have a history of dominating Nature, not succumbing to it. Our adaptations will not be humble concessions but engineered in our own best interests.

Money plays an obviously vital role in a capitalist society, as do those who possess the skill set to amass fortunes within a competitive capitalist arena. You can call them "oligarchs," but these captains of industry and finance grow the economy, create jobs, and enable the United States to be competitive in the global arena. Money is the instrument employed in this crafting of a vibrant economy. And just as a writer's words, the expressive medium of his or her profession, are protected by the First Amendment, so too is money, the expressive medium of every American citizen. You cannot limit either speech or money by arguing that within this democratic free-for-all some are more adept than others in making use of money or speech. There exists no reason to level by governmental interference either forms of expression so that every citizen possesses an equal share of money and an equal facility with speech. The question of undue influence of money in politics is like questioning the undue influence of words on thought.

Many clear-thinking Americans will welcome Paul Ryan's budget proposal because it acknowledges that our economic growth is retarded by our welfare and entitlement governmental expenditures. These only serve to coddle an uncompetitive, unproductive, and dependent class. The United States is not a country wherein we will all equally queue up on a bread line, a country in which we will all be poor together. We are a country of opportunities for all to be rich, a country in which those opportunities will not be restricted. The psychology that drives winners to win is as forceful as the psychology that drives the dependent toward greater and greater dependency.

What we have in these point/counter-point stories, from both Left and Right, are alibis defending us and shielding us like a brick wall from any probing into what lies behind the wall. We must always be, as the Latin word *alibi* describes, "somewhere else, in or at another place," never where we actually are. Whatever impeccable logic and moral purpose we propose becomes a front concealing our desire to have the world the way we want it

There is clearly something about the inevitability of the climate change threat that challenges our own supremacy and presumes to override our own will. Earth First! advocates assume we would oblige and bend to a pantheist notion that we share with rocks, trees, and brooks the same underlying spirit, as if our individual human nature had no claim to superiority. Our technological innovativeness has not inclined us to respect interconnectedness with inanimate and animate but insentient Nature. Americans have become less and less inclined to a mutuality of life view that offends our zero-sum game, economics game in which others lose so we can win. No outside force stands long against our own ambitions, our own awareness, and consciousness. What we have continually dominated will not stand against us. There is thus within us, inside the walls of our alibis, no place for accommodation to Nature, either in the recuperating way Wordsworth imagines it or the destructive ways we are coming to know more repeatedly and tragically in the last quarter century.

There is an intolerable presumptuousness to Nature's challenge to our narcissism. Dig deeper and we unearth solipsism, a sense that if anything outside our own will exists, it does so because we empower it personally to exist. What encourages such solipsism is our uncontested rule in cyberspace, a space unlike Nature's, which awaits our design, which is given shape by our choices. We transfer our easy control of cyberspace to an equally easy control of Nature. More directly, cyberspace has replaced in our order of attachments the great outdoors of the real space of Nature, itself now a predigital kind of archaism. What no longer has place on a level of real desire and will cannot be allowed a recognizable force.

Affront and outrage become then our reptilian brain's response to the disasters resulting from human-caused climate change. We are thusly not inclined to either change our behavior or believe we cannot put Nature in her place.

The further extension of our First Amendment rights in Citizens United and in our chosen week's *McCutheon v. Federal Election Commission* Supreme Court case translates as a further extension of our individual freedom to choose to do what we want without restraint. The joy felt in this liberation is a childhood joy, the joy that we feel when our free play is not restrained. Once again, in a realm where total autonomy is the order of the day, we remain impervious to all influences. The rich man who buys political influence is never buying influence that will affect us personally; therefore, there is no influence. And, further, we are at any moment about to king ourselves and in that role, we abhor any infringement upon the uses we make of our wealth. The oligarch is always in this situation the person who has complete freedom, and we are always that person. All politics is evil and all politicians are corrupt not because an oligarchic arrangement of economic interests has no need of politics or any need of anyone 'doing politics,' but because we personally have no need of politics. Politics is not social because there is no society. Politics is personal and what we personally choose trumps in every instance what is reported as politics. We do our politics on Facebook within our own designed society.

Conceit and the "monarchal pride" of Milton's Satan render whatever dire relationship exits between money and politics small, undignified matter, or more tragically, totally absent.

Paul Ryan's budget proposal touches the most atavist impulses, but here our alibis or cortex thinking lies very close to what is imprinted much deeper. Our alibis do not really say we are someplace else than where we really are. We occupy both spaces at once, or are liminal, at the threshold of each. We do not begrudge the winners their winnings or question their lavish excesses or their Machiavellian ways but rather denounce the losers for their own misfortunes, their sly deceit, and thievery, and their parasitism of us. If not for these parasites, our own design of success would not be impeded. Those who already have what we seek and represent the fulfillment of our American Dream remain untarnished in this liminal space because we do not blame for our woes that to which we aspire. What pulls us downward is what we can identify as the occupants of the downward place. Ryan proposes to kill that bottom life and so destroy a middle class's fear that this is where they are heading. They cannot wind up in a place that no longer exists. Ryan becomes their champion, a champion who, with ironic fatality, is engaged in preparing oblivion for their eventual arrival.

A suicidal imprint is etched strongly here, an end to a Kierkegaard-like "fear and trembling, sickness unto death." This is a coding that the American middle class responds to in all its compliances with the war for extinction waged against the losers, a so-called creative destruction.

At the very beginning, I stated that in former times some deep digging was needed to disclose what Rapaille called the "code" behind our behavior, a code not disclosed by what we consciously might say. In the present American cultural climate, much that formerly needed to be hidden no longer needs to be hidden. There was need, say a quarter of a century ago, to never say where we actually were in our minds. Political correctness (PC) emerged as a kind of gatekeeper between cortex and reptilian thinking, a Miss Manners of the reptilian brain. It did not expunge the code, and it did not stand as an alibi. What it did do was expose the psychic dynamic. It admitted what we did not want to admit. Therefore, we indicted PC as an infringement on our individual freedom to choose, the most telling alibi in the American cultural imaginary. To possess total individual freedom of choice now involved no suppressive gatekeepers. We did not have to dig for the code because it was openly expressed in public discourse.

In short, the demons of our dark side no longer needed to hide. They had become part of a social, political, and economic discourse, part of a political party platform. Self-interest no longer has to pretend to be altruistic because our expression of an enlightened self-interest overwrites that conflict and does so in our own interest. There is no need of an alibi for our disinterest in a social moral sense because now our social networking fulfills all societal demands upon us. We can fall into as deep a pit of narcissism as we wish and feel no need to say we are elsewhere. An entire discourse opened a dark pit of human emotions and made them a part of a political platform. Think tanks were erected to produce alibis that would bring the reptilian brain into the rational discourse of the cortex. And the alibis that would work were the ones that lay closest to the underlying codes, which like keys, unlock all barriers between.

A politics that aligns itself quite closely to where we are in subterranean depths of mind has more appeal than one that pretends that we are really someplace else, that insists that our alibis are true and real. Emotions that we denied ever visiting can now be openly acknowledged. A politics that asks us to confirm in the voting booth what is already magnetically attractive because that politics has cracked the code to our subliminal emotional attachments is a winning politics. This attraction has proven to be more powerful than the crises it feeds and the looming disasters it ignores.

Nevertheless, neither history nor politics confirm the stability or perseverance of any cultural coding. However, a prolonged period of congressional gridlock, like a prolonged period of drought in Texas, seems to indicate that the reptilian brain is being tapped with enough success to keep a bottom 80 percent of Americans from recognizing the difference between their own interests and that of the oligarchs. What seems clear is that the apparent easy victory of a coalition of obliging rationality and unbridled instinct has been forestalled in different ways at different times and in different cultures. Recognition of what and where the battle lines are—not in what we say but what we feel—is always, in every age, a necessary means to resolve crises, itself a necessary step in the avoidance of looming disaster.

Notes

1. Selections from "Phenomenological Psychology and Literary Interpretation," *Psychological Perspectives on Literature: Freudian Dissidents and Non-Freudians* Hamden, CT: Archon Books (1984), 198–225 passim.

2. *Truthout*, April 14, 2014.

Chapter Three

The World Is a Book

"The world is a book and those who do not travel read only one page," attributed to St. Augustine, is the complete quotation; but before I travelled extensively to read the world's book, I worked in college and university libraries here and there in the United States. I spent precomputer days reading antiquarian book catalogs and making trans-Atlantic phone calls before 11 a.m. to antiquarian book dealers to dicker price and secure catalog items I wanted. I measured the dimensions of rare eighteenth-century books and worked through descriptive cataloguing details for a nationwide project. I compiled and published two annotated bibliographies, did a class at University of California, Irvine, on bibliography and research methods, wrote grants as acting director of the Bluefield State Library, and as head of reference at the Z. Smith Reynolds Library at Wake Forest University led a staff who could Google and Wikipedia *avant que ordinateur*. I used the back-in-the-day West system of legal research and Index Medicus for medical research. In short, my world was a world of books. Until I was able to outlive my blacklisted past as a union organizer, I made my living working in libraries. I bought, read, wrote books. And I wrote about them.

I suppose if the past is where you are wounded, you escape the forgiving nostalgia that visits where you were young, even Bensonhurst, Brooklyn. But I'm not addled, and I recall that I was not too happy about going for an MLS degree which would be my union card for university library employment, the only employment that kept me in the academic world where a PhD in English didn't necessarily have to be hidden. My work in libraries paid the bills for many years, and though I never really fit in that world, I had plenty of opportunities to read. And write. I was not the first flawed, from a societal point of view, exile who had retreated to the quiet sanctums of a library.

In both "Textual Studies and the Selection of Editions" and in "Meditating on a Postmodern Strategy of Reading," I attach phenomenology to my idea of the postmodern.

I brought my phenomenological approach into my work as a bibliographer and at the request of the Association of College and Research libraries brought that approach to bear on the seminal question regarding establishing the definitive edition of a particular work. An author's intention guided the selection among variant printings and different editions, overriding a collector's hunger for first editions. And as the idea of an intentional consciousness was the backbone of Husserl's phenomenology, I brought that as well as the idea of the human life-world or Lebenswelt into an enterprise that has traditionally been marked by very thorough methodological rigor. In a note discussing the established William James volumes, the editors refer to fully recorded documentary evidence which "attempts to reconstruct the author's true and fullest intention" though it is admitted that the "restoration of intention from imperfect sources is conjectural and subject to differing opinion" (William James, *Psychology: Briefer Course*, ed. Michael M. Sokal [Cambridge: Harvard University Press, 1985]).

The authority for intentions often rests on supplementing the text in question with biography, letters, and other outside sources, themselves open to the same questions as the text itself. It seemed to me that if we tied definitive edition to author's intention, we were tying a rock to something vastly more unreachable, not a ghost in the machine but certainly less material that words on paper. While I was prepared to use a literary text to reveal the life-world of characters, I saw little chance of describing a bridge from literary world to an author's mind. It also seemed to me that the intentions of readers, an audience that could and does change over time, had final say in which rendering of an author's work they preferred. In other words, the life-world of the author, from which intentions emerge, would change over time, and the life-worlds of readers would change over time. And both author and reader are mutually affected so that an author's intentions may change based on audience reception and that audience's intentions may change based on the author's work.

The second selection, "Meditating on a Postmodern Strategy of Reading," continues my interests in the vagaries of intentionality, here focused on the reader and the act of reading and not the author and the act of creation. However, the reader reads as a creator, repeating the act of rewriting in the act of reading. In this essay, however, I depart from the notion that the intentional consciousness of the reader creates subjective meaning in the same manner I rejected the idea that a writer's intentions regarding meaning are transparent in the work. The reader becomes attached to text in a game of deferment and difference obstructing any meaning, objective or subjective, into which the text itself draws the reader. Additionally, the effect of other texts gloss the reading of one particular text as words cannot be held within one particular context but are, as James Joyce asserted, "portmanteau." Words bear within them a trunk full of their past iterations, their past journeys, so that a reader is caught within a swirl of linkages and associations a text brings to life. And neither the context of a present reader or the context of a reader's consciousness, a reader's Lebenswelt, can subdue this textual play but are caught up within it, as part of it, in every act of reading.

The third selection, "Endless Deferment: The Inequitable Melee of Events and Words" is not about deconstruction but about our new millennial culture where everyone knows everything and everyone knows it differently. I surmise this is so because we have ceased to read texts in common, especially those that fail the formatting requirements of a tweet or a smartphone display. Thus, in our devotion to personal and not common interests and the inbred, insular confinement of thought that results, our level of public discourse as well as the sophistication of our strategies of reading have plunged. However, as we now confine public discourse to our many Facebook friends who think as we do, and we opt for the display of photos and videos as dialogue, we no longer seem equipped to assess what is enriching and what is a hollowing out.

Textual Studies and the Selection of Editions[1]

Classicist, intentionalist, and collaborative views of the text are actually grounded in the issue, "Where is the text?" This question places literary theory secondary to textual criticism and bibliography, a proposition lately reaffirmed by Herschel Parker (*Flawed Texts and Verbal Icons: Literary Authority in American Fiction* [Evanston: Northwest University Press, 1984], xiv). Bowers's approach is an amalgam of two very different responses to the problem. On one hand, he adheres to Shelley's notion that the poem in the mind loses power in actualization, that the poet's unspoken, unprinted intentions are the locus of meaning. But to this Shelleyan-Crocean tenet, Bowers adds the pseudoscientism of the New Criticism with its belief that objective methods can establish subjective intentions. In contrast, such collaborationists as Thorpe, Gaskell, and McGann relate to the hermeneutics of Hans-Georg Gadamer. Here the discernment of the best text lies in the convergence of the author's intentions, the institutions of publishing, and the reader. Since all three change over time, the notion of best is completely relative. The idea of "definitive" thus approximates the concept of "classic" in Gadamer's hermeneutics: it is that edition which enables a reader in the present to make real connections with the work. This concept that creation proceeds dually, both from the author's dialogue with the work and the reader's dialogue with the work is grounded in the contention that the text, like meaning, exists temporally in the world.

The identity of a collection derives from the texts it contains, but these dwell in the realm of consciousness, their essence residing not in physicality but in the interchange between words and the reader who seeks meaning contextualized within a present world. The literature collection is only superficially related to its physical presence, and to develop it as if it were a purely physical enterprise is to violate its nature. It follows that conscious cultivation of a collection demands the active, persistent intercession of the bibliographer as a knowledgeable agent searching for literary meaning. To comprehend and locate that meaning within both the academic institution of letters and the local collection are what is involved in the apparently simple matter of selecting an edition. In the view of Blake, enough here is synonymous with too much.

Meditating on a Postmodern Strategy of Reading[2]

When identity forges itself by repeating its own image, it draws a line in the sand of innumerable grains of sand. You cannot have identity by following the paths of every particle that you touch. Identity is constructed out of certain, selected particles—the rest denied, paths not taken. There is no one identity, no one reality, no one time, in Borges's garden of forking paths. But if the reader has always been in this garden, has always moved laterally into and across other narrative paths, even though the reader identifies on only one path, then clearly the strategy of literary life-worlds is to represent how word and world are linked on *other* paths. These other paths are, first narrative paths on which the whole culture, if not the reader, has been. However, *how* the world can be brought into existence on this other path has not yet been performed. Or, it has in the past but the culture has severed those lines of transmission in the present. The culture is always in a garden of forking paths, but it has put up and taken down road-closed signs in order to preserve its cultural identity, to delineate itself so as to establish an order of things.

....

What . . . do I observe of our strategies of reading? What . . . are the strategies of reading that readers will take? Today we are of two cultures when it comes to reading: we read either in fear of detachment or wary and weary of attachment. We read either to find the substratum of connectedness or to fork off from those connections into that from which we have been disconnected. Our strategy may be to bind fast our own life-world to persistent notions of world, self, and time that make up our Western cultural heritage. Our Western canonical works reiterate and reconfirm essential cultural values; if we cannot hook up with them, we yet feel obliged to. Education is the record of our effort. Eternal truths are hard; we study and memorize them.

....

Classic Realist readers read as long as they can make identical to what they already are what is represented to them in a literary life-world. . . . The other culture—wary and weary of attachments—produces a different attitude; it involves a certain weariness with the incessant rounding up of all the usual suspects that Western culture wants to continually erect. There is also an attendant wariness of the suspects that do show up repeatedly. Are these the only links that can be made, the only testimonies that are worth hearing? And who is making them? What framing of the real, what world did these stories come from? What are the polarities here?

The postmodern reader tends to ask the same question of a literary life-world as he or she does in a restaurant: what is good here? What is the narrative of truth and goodness, beauty and harmony, justice and civility that is concocted here? Which one of my senses is being hailed here and which are being shown the door? And finally, what is left out here? How much overspills the framing of the real here? Is indeed my own fractured self being put together for me in a way that marginalizes almost all my energies? And is what is left out, *my* sin, *my* neurosis, *my* error, *my* primitivism, *my* barbarism, *my* ignorance, *my* fault?

How can continuity be maintained here, when the vertical path goes lateral, when every path forks off? Length gives way to width. The postmodern reader's strategy enjoys the forking of paths outward, the lateralized motion. The novel spreads itself into and out of narratives that intersect but do not cohere. Everything is played in seventh chords: no dominants. And in the end, we find all the endings far apart because we have been stretched laterally and cannot bring the ends together to tie them. Without a desire for such closure, the very reading process has to go on differently. We began at a beginning that is trying to concoct itself as a beginning. I am at the middle interminably because I can only advance to an ending if I have already acknowledged a determinate beginning. And how can I be at the middle when there is nothing in my beginning that anticipates it?

Endless Deferment:
The Inequitable Melee of Events and Words[3]

In traditional analog media, the PBS *NewsHour* wonders—as if newly arrived on the planet Earth—what may be the cause and meaning of a Baltimore riot or uprising? Here on the *NewsHour* every occurrence takes us by surprise and is treated in a kind of isolation chamber. Something is happening here, a series of blacks killed by police?! Sudden violence, looting, mayhem. What is that all about? This is our United States. TV in depth and wide breadth coverage of the news, steering carefully between the Scylla of the liberal rocks and the Charybdis of the neoliberal ones. For those with a lengthy attention span this is supposedly the long, thoughtful essay rather than the tweet.

Every headline event is a source of wonderment. After surprise, wonder, and amazement, we go on to hear both sides of an issue after which we are told that the conversation remains open and will continue in the future, a future in which every conclusion will be balanced by an opposing conclusion, Koch Industries and the Center for American Progress locked in an eternal struggle. We are then free to make a personal choice. We are to add our opinion in a culture where everyone knows everything and each knows it differently.

But what exactly is being balanced here? We are seeking a balance on a ship already tilted heavily to starboard. One side has the mass of the population, the other side the mass of the wealth, rather like the present state of South Africa where minority-white wealth and economic power mocks the democratic power of the masses. In the US voter turnout, both sides have run about equal except, for instance, when Barack Obama was able to draw more of the masses to the polling booth. The populace responded to an election in which a man so melded with popular-culture celebrity status that he brought the populace out to vote.

Although the in-depth reportage of PBS seems in search of reasons as to why violence breaks out, any viewing of the conditions on the ground in the United States at this point should produce reasons galore. There are a myriad number of places where, what PBS *NewsHour* calls a "melee" can break out, each one, I am sure, bewildering to a news media grounded on the false and dangerous assumption that a disinterested reportage can emerge in a seriously lopsided society.

Our public broadcasting voice cannot represent the public in any just and logical way because it sustains the imbalances already in place. Like Hillary Clinton, it must lean into the wealth minority. It must probe for answers in a way that converts what is transparently clear into a muddle of indecisiveness. This is done by structuring equal presentation of voices on both sides, as if the matter were being treated objectively and rationally, concluding without prejudice to either view and leaving the whole matter for the viewer to personally choose where he or she stands.

Carrying on such balanced discussion of anything in a society already seriously bent in one direction is just a mockery, and at worse, a front behind which the biases of that society can go on as if they were guided by a rational discourse, by relentless, penetrating interpretation set on revealing lies and bullshit, set on deconstructing edifices of truth, which can only always and only be the truth by which the status quo, bent as it is, perseveres. Our media coverage is either a chaos of mindless venting, a deluge of 'information' whose only gatekeeper is Google's PageRank, the insulated de-friending domains of Facebook communication, or the disingenuousness of both balanced and biased reportage. In this way, our communication is in one way or another serving to maintain our inequitable order of things. Our media stands like the Baltimore police as servants of that order, protecting it from exposure, which is what the media is now doing, and from collapse, as what the police are paid to do as they protect and serve.

How to proceed then? We need to get as close to the context and surround out of which all events arise. This is a descriptive enterprise, one that, for instance, the PBS *NewsHour* should provide as a preface because it possesses the archival memory of the culture, both in the events it has covered and the resources it has tapped. The commentators, however, proceed *ab ovo* with every story and question as if they themselves have not paid any attention to what they themselves have been reporting for decades. Stories now stand apart, disconnected, without any attempt at disclosing interrelationships. The pieces of the puzzle are at hand, but it is as if each were picked up, looked at, and put aside as a mystery to be solved on another occasion when it is picked up, observed, and put aside. Endless deferment. The pieces form no picture. It is this sort of deferring activity that complicates, that muddies the waters of commonsensical observation. And it suits the corrupted deformation of our democracy because the picture that should be forthcoming, the puzzle not difficult to complete, is denied us.

Our media is either befuddling both events and our understanding, or, as in the case of Fox News working steadily on the worst devils of our human nature, from racism, bigotry, xenophobia, and homophobia to indifference, hatred, contempt, neglect. Coverage maintaining and protecting our bent society is always accompanied by a full portrait, a thorough contextualizing that is imprinted in our minds in such a complete way that nothing seems to be left out. So before we establish a context within which to consider an event, we need to wipe out the misleading spins. This means that we cannot begin with description of a societal surround but with dismantling the bogus arrangements already in our heads.

Once the bogus mythologies are confronted, a description of the surround out of which these events, whatever they may be, emerge. I am neither naïve nor utopian in my expectations that this can be easily done. Because the charge of "bogus" emerges from all directions, what we face is a battle of spins. We now exist in a post-truth world in which rational and empirical arguments universally persuasive or consensually validated have given way to narratives that yield to no external authority. The expansion of communication made possible by cybertech has expanded this arena of unleashed, contesting narratives. All transmissions now enter a mosh pit of narratives so overwhelming that one must narrow the receptivity band or tune out altogether.

Those whose bandwidth is limited to *Huffington Post* or *Truthout* are not those who receive the *Cato Institute* and *The Heritage Foundation* transmissions. If you follow *Fox News,* you do not follow PBS *NewsHour.* If you heed Rush Limbaugh, you probably do not heed Rachel Maddow. I maintain, however, that if reportage makes a beginning in any platform to contextualize a headline event—that is, provide an historical frame of contributing factors, events, and conclusions, no issue will remain as vulnerable as now to madcap spins and canny deceptions. If any reportage, for instance, of the Baltimore riots/uprising would begin with the statistics and demographic details presented in *ThinkProgress*'s overview of "The Economic Devastation Fueling the Anger in Baltimore" (Bryce Covert, April 28, 2015), a more informed context of reception could be created. This is not a free-for-all narrating but one fixed by undeniable conditions in the same way that the Earth is subject to gravity, the sun prompts photosynthesis, and trees breathe in carbon dioxide and breathe out oxygen.

Rather that fix the objective conditions and demography of an event, the PBS *NewsHour* presents this sort of informative horizon, this vital staging that must be known, as a matter itself to be debated in a balanced way. This manner of reportage clearly indicates that any determinate representation of a background story is itself incendiary, itself a threat to a lopsided order of things, an order that has the power to influence not only by ownership as in Fox but indirectly as in PBS which has lived in the shadow of a conservative threat to cancel its funding. This threat to cancel PBS news is, however, unlikely to be enacted because the objective posturing of that news service preempts and defuses a critique not restrained by presumptions of balance in an already out-of-balanced society.

We have been leaving headlines issues hanging in space and asking an audience to provide the background of their choice, a disastrous plan when statistics continue to tell us that Americans rank low in any understanding of history, civics, politics, and geography. If offenses become lost pieces, we cannot bring any puzzle to completion. If we are already disposed to living in a fragmented world in which we eagerly await the new fragment and forgo pondering a pattern or a connection to what went before, we are in no position to either recognize the bent nature of our society or do anything about it.

We do not ponder the loss of sustained focus, our cultural ADD (Attention Deficit Disorder) because the remedy to that problem is preempted by the problem itself. The context we need in order to achieve any understanding evaporates. Ironically, we believe we have lost what we have chosen to lose. Perhaps nothing maintains the out-of-balance nature of our society more significantly than a personal-choice determination oblivious to an actual existing context that in no way is bound by anyone's personal choice.

What should proceed after a review of the horizon out of which an event emerges is a presentation of the particulars of the event in reference to the surround out of which these events emerge—namely, the hierarchy of values and meanings at play or in residence within the society.

Our society has made victims of the innocent before, victims of unspeakable violence. Black Africans were enslaved without compunction by white Christians because they were inferior to a white humanity. Native Americans were exterminated by white Christians because they too had no souls. We have now more than a quarter of a century of reducing the humanity of the so-called losers, the poor who choose not to work and win, the ungentrified, the threatening homeless, the dropouts, all those who are in public view, walking, hanging out, not living in gated compounds, without private security, the displaced, flawed exiles from a stock-portfolio world, the ones we call "wretched" but without the understanding and empathy of Frantz Fanon, the ones in public housing, waiting for public transportation, those walking late at night or riding old bicycles or pulling shopping carts, the aliens and immigrants, vast numbers that strike fear in those few living in a privileged, feudal way in a democracy once aspiring to be egalitarian.

Blacks are not being subjected to a brutality that the rich are not solely and primarily because they are the victims of class warfare. Racism, the same kind that has been a factor in Obama's presidency, puts blacks at the vanguard of a quarter-of-a-century-long denigration and dismissal of have-nots and have-less-each-day, some 80 percent of the US population. The fall of our former working-class heroes into a class scheduled for extinction has not been engineered but has risen axiomatically from our economic system of choice and the insidious social creed of winners and losers, of ludicrous beliefs that the unfortunate choose their fate while the fortunate owe nothing to anyone, least of all to the society that nurtured them. The few fear the many not because the few are all elitists and racists but in a similar axiomatic way, in the way someone with possessions eyes warily those without, especially wary when they too take note of how seriously bent US society has become and how our public interpretation, meaning, and understanding are being endlessly deferred.

Notes

1. Excerpts from *English and American Literature: Sources and Strategies for Collection Development* #45 1987 ACRL Publications in Librarianship.

2. Revised and excerpted from "Strategies of Reading: Dickens and After," *Yearbook of English Studies 1996*.

3. *Truthout,* May 16, 2015.

Chapter Four

Looking for Disorder in Literary Worlds

It is implicit in Blake's view of our fallen state that the infinite is absent, and everything that is present to us in our limited one-fold vision is shadowed by that absence. "If the doors of perception were cleansed," Blake declares in *The Marriage of Heaven and Hell*, "everything would appear to man as it is, infinite." We live, however, in a fallen world that constructs an order of things, which masks that absence, which creates a "regime of order-words," Gilles Deleuze's *mots d'ordre*. Blake saw this as Urizen's rule, the rule of a reason that had usurped power and excluded an imagination that would forge a shape to absence and challenge that rule. Blake believed that what was absent was bound and hidden within a collapsed humanity, and therefore a resurrecting apocalypse was a task to which he set himself.

What I saw in Derrida's notion of words promising a meaning they could not fulfill was a version of a Blakean duplicitous world. Words affirmed a presence that was, in turn, affirmed by words, a compact that gave legitimacy to both, a compact that kept what was necessarily excluded absent. Meaning and order were grounded in the exclusion of what words could not bring to presence and a presence that always over-spilled and exceeded words. Words promising to reveal the meaning of what was present to our eyes were in play with other words making the same promise. That act, in Derrida's view, fails to bring presence to full meaning or full meaning to presence, and "it is evident that writing can be nothing but black, a shadow-writing, writing for protection" (*Spurs: Nietzsche's Styles* [Chicago: University of Chicago Press, 1979], 21).

Every text then is fallen away from full disclosure of the world and engages in a defense against and a walling out of a challenging absence. Absence is set up, like a dupe, to affirm a desired presence. A hierarchy of hyped presence rests on a demonized absence, the one inflated and festooned like an Emperor Jones with all the pomp of tradition and the order of civilization and the other always only vaguely and darkly affiliated, darkly imagined. As death is the absence of life, although without our mortality, as Keats reminds us, life would have no impact and become itself an absence.

It is always possible that what is absent goes as far as what Blake envisioned was absent. What seems more reachable is the way Blake went about disclosing what was absent. We had to imagine outside the gates of our regime of order. Such imagination is not confined to the shareholders' need for innovation, nor to a problem-solving outside-the-box Think Fest confined to client and consumer satisfaction. When we imagine in a Blakean way, we break through, find the moment of disclosure:

> There is a Moment in each Day that Satan cannot find Nor can his Watch Fiends find it, but the Industrious find This Moment & it multiply. & when it once is found It renovates every Moment of the Day if rightly placed. (Milton, Plate 35: 42–43)

Paul Feyerabend, the iconoclastic philosopher and scientist, urges the same approach: "We need a dream world in order to discover the features of the real world we think we inhabit" (*Against Method: An Outline of an Anarchistic Theory of Knowledge*, rev. ed. [London: Verso, 1988], 22–23). In *Mots d'Ordre*, I associated that dream world with literary worlds and approached those as literary life-worlds. What novelists, poets, and playwrights did was employ the imagination to exceed the regime of order words and disclose what was absent, what was inconceivable to us and yet might be imaginatively represented. A disclosed absence might possibly go beyond a dualistic opposition that confined absence to the shadows. I conjectured that literary worlds could possibly display a conflict between an order of things and a rejected disorder, a realm of absence that had no path to full representation, a threatening absence, like a terrorist denied a passport for obvious reasons. And the battle, like the psychic battles van den Berg described going on in his patients, was a true psychomachia, one that could be followed only if no regime of sense was imposed but the world as imagined, senseless, and disordered, or not, ruled, as in a dream.

In pursuit of our shadowed absence, all that we bagged under the word "disorder," a something denied its own substance but only represented in terms of what we clearly understood, I was *un rêveur sans frontiers*, crossing the borders of history, politics, science, philosophy to find my passage into the literary world. If the world was assessed, was measured, and weighed, as far less than it could be, which was Blake's view, a search for what was left out, ignored, inconceivable, and designed as absence seemed to me to be a worthwhile pursuit. An attempt to get off the perilous path was required. The clarity that our regimes of order brought to the world was purchased at the price of excluding what dissolved the determinate meanings of our order words. Derrida deconstructed that clarity and moved us toward an encounter with indeterminacy and over determinacy that no regime of order could incorporate and remain empowered. *Les mots d'imagination* of literary worlds could challenge the regimes of mots d'ordre.

I select excerpts from chapter 11, "Mapping the Inconceivable: Disordering Taxonomies," in which I briefly set out to uncover the literary worlds that have escaped us because their dreams remain inconceivable to us. The fact that I cite a few, of course means that we have caught up to them. And we have done so at a time when what others disclose remain absent. So the task is ongoing; and it seems to me that the quicker we respond to literary worlds that exceed our order of identifying and knowing, the more inclusive of the world we can be.

Mapping the Inconceivable: Disordering Taxonomies[1]

I think it transparent that most of what I say in the following excerpts emerges as much from my own experiences writing fiction and dealing with publishers as from various narrative theories. I owe much to the work of Jacques Derrida, Paul Feyerabend, Gilles Deleuze, and Wolfgang Iser. The feeling that we live in a fictitious rendering of order and that without imagination the world remains inconceivable to us is, of course, all Blake.

We are doubtlessly entertained and not unsettled by what matches our own life-worlds although circulating within our own limited realities—all those we friend in cyberspace—pose dangers to individual self-development as well as societal growth. I here pursue the impossible: a mapping of the inconceivable.

Literary worlds whose excesses lie on the opposite end of thesis and formula, literary worlds lost in an ocean of mutually incompatible (and perhaps even incommensurable alternatives) offer perhaps too much of a good thing, rather than too little. I am referring to a play of the text that thrusts us beyond our supplementing capabilities. I say such a situation is a good thing because I agree with Feyerabend that a deflection engineered by a dream-world from the present course of our legitimized ordering and reasoning, by what that order perceives as disorder, is a good thing. Novelists often praised and/or much read in our contemporary world, whose literary worlds parallel our own with scrupulous, photographic accuracy, employ and evoke a readiness of language and consciousness response on the part of their audience, while failing to engage the moment of creativity in its anarchic guise. "Our understanding of current literature," Nemoianu writes, "is blurred by forgetting that in any age the most visible and the best rewarded are the progressive conformists" (*A Theory of the Secondary* [Baltimore: Johns Hopkins, 1989]). This does not omit literary texts in which we find a certain carrying forth of what is in the present into a future that amends, or is at very least sensitive to, the deficits of the present.

Novelists who work assiduously to keep the noise down do indeed pocket the royalties or mount the prize, and leave us confirmed in the realities of our own preferred course. A steady diet of reconfirmations of what is already wholeheartedly confirmed for identical profit motives throughout our culture makes it more and more difficult for us to see beyond our epistemological prescriptions, to attend to that noise through which we are able to reorganize ourselves along continuously more inclusive lines.

. . . .

Literary worlds that display no hint of disorder, whose jangle rings harmoniously in communal ears, also happen to meet the first requirement of the mass-market best seller—accessibility to the majority of readers. There is a neat and harmonious mesh between such literary worlds and the existing outside world. The social order seems not so much interacted with as in lockstep with. Such novels remain fully with us and us with them, an affair of both heart and mind that marks best sellers as compellingly page turning. If there is a battle between what is already fully with us and what is not perceived as ours, that battle does not materialize within the encompassing order of the no-hint-of disorder literary world. Nothing disrupts the smooth course of our reading.

. . . .

For us to setup an active imagination that disturbs, we must imagine away from the existing worldly order. We must be brought into the struggle of disorder and order within a literary world. We must be confronted by literary worlds that are not extended photo albums of our own making. Contesting regimes of signs bring us into the agon of order and

disorder. The pictures in our mind blur because rivaling orders of picturing, of transforming the world, are at work. What we know ultimately
interpenetrates what we do not know. A security of place interpenetrates
a line of flight from that security. We are at a loss; we are far from home
and in a struggle of combatants who enforce opposing regimes of clarity
and blur. In the literary worlds, there is a decree of slippage, a disjunction
between us in the act of reading and us before the act of reading. Our
identity is shaken. We ourselves blur, as we get lost in an interchange that
extends to a metamorphosis of our world and ourselves.

....

Novels that replace prescriptive epistemology with the lineaments of
a dreamworld need not be works of fantasy or science fiction. Thomas
Savage's *The Power of the Dog* is a novel of stark realism, tightly constructed without a fissure of disorder and without a dreamworld in sight.
And yet this is a work of patent strangeness that mirrors no realness we
can put our finger on, a strangeness that exceeds the novel's own well-
made closure. There are no fissures to map, yet everything in this novel
proves fractal, open beyond what seem to be prescribed borders and lurks
elsewhere. It may seem as if I am writing about a novel of suspense, of
mystery, of unexpected chills, and unexpected happenings, or about a
novel of explicit strangeness such as Bulgakov's *The Master and Margarita*
or, more clearly, Kafka's work. Stephen King is supposed master of the
strange, and yet his strangeness is simply unexpected rather than unrecog-
nizable. John Irving's aleatory narration, replete with unexpected detours
into real catastrophe, catches the steady realistic flow of his own narrative
unaware, throws the literary world we are building out of joint. Savage's
use of making the world strange and unknown exceeds such narrative
innovation. His strangeness is not a result of technique; it is there despite
and outside of technique's efforts. The same can be said, for example of
the novels of Wyndham Lewis, William Gerhardi, Rosamund Lehmann,
James Purdy, Tommaso Landolfi, Manuel Puig, Italo Calvino, B. Traven,
Carlo Gaddi, James Street, and Louis Ferdinand Céline. The lineaments of
a dreamworld intersecting our everyday world are here, and yet we are
not in the genres of fantasy or sci-fi.

....

All our classics exhibit or have exhibited the paradoxical nature of
the order/disorder performance. . . . On one hand, a classic discloses a
disorder not wholly a function of its own culture, not completely trans-
mittable along the channels a culture may set up. The classic's perennial
attraction for us stems from the fact that a culture cannot fully grasp

literature's disorder although it feels compelled to do so. Disorder in this case is not ours. I mean it is not relative to us. On the other hand, classics are those works whose disorder has long since been exhausted but they continue to serve as a sort of cultural bulwark, a sort of cultural legacy, a resource for a cultural literacy that links all of us within the defined structure of our own culture. Disorder here is ours, and we endure in terms of our subsuming or vanquishing this disorder. In the former case, classics are classic because they possess a tantalizing disorder always just out of reach, and in the latter, classics are classic because the noise of their disorder has been eliminated, and that victory of order stands forth as always observable in the classic work. Classics are acting on both sides of the street; therefore, it is not surprising that they provoke reactions from all side. This ferment, too, is a sign of the classic.

....

What makes any work of art a failure is the absence of an identifying frame through which its particular drama of order and disorder can reach our already-formed consciousness. In a similar fashion, the canonical privileging of literary life-worlds, which depict in a clear and enviable fashion the ways a particular culture sees itself in its best moment, stands steadfastly as touchstones of the consciousness we wish to preserve. These touchstones thereafter stand for the coastline of literary order, and thus clearly represent what lies outside the pale. That these touchstones are not touching truth and beauty 'out there' as external reference points but are in fact *mots d'ordre* transmitting the semiotic coordinates of "privilege, power, domination, exclusion and so" is only a statement we can make. A detour of a touchstone order into a line of flight from that order is an exclusive accomplishment of the play of the text.

....

The aleatory alone does not make up the play of the text. Or as Kathy Acker puts it, "[N]onsense, since it depended on sense, simply pointed back to the normalizing institutions." Literary worlds purposely written to evoke disorder reveal no more than their enabling discourses say they will reveal. Disorder is not so much performed as celebrated as a confounding of the established order. What order already perceives as its enemy, already de-privileges, renders as the low other, is made the métier of such aesthetics. Such literary worlds are recognizable to a prevailing truth. In fact, they attempt to identify the play of the text with a replica of meaning erected by the prevailing truth. They are just as readily identifiable as those texts that mirror such a truth's own ordering.

....

The metafictional world is in fact an impossibility. In practice, meta-fiction ascribes to its own prior image of what it means, and to this, we can address ourselves. The literary world of totally denied referentiality and representation, totally antirealist/anti-mimetic intentions, is like the literary world of the Dadaists—its disorder exists purely in terms of its mimetic opposition to reference, representation, realism, mimeticism. The literary world of denied referentiality fashions a disorder as seen through the eyes of order. The situation is similar to what goes on at the quantum level: it is not that metaphysical idealism holds sway, that our saying has nothing to do with what is there, but rather that it has too much to do with it. The language of the anti-mimeticist is already implicated in redundancy, which is itself implicated in the order of any system. "[M]aking use of language," [Henri] Atlan writes, "is making use of the kind of order always implicit in the use of language. Talking about order, complexity and so on is *doing* something *in language* which has to do with what order, complexity, etc., are supposed to be" (in Alan Wilde, *Middle Grounds* [Philadelphia: University of Pennsylvania, 1987], 20).

Metafiction's intent to talk against and outside order is doing something in language which has to do with what order, complexity, etc., are supposed to be. A self-reflexivity unmodulated by any reference to the world is a chimera. Its language is the language of redundancy. The language of redundancy can never mount an Archimedean point to 'say' its own, different 'really there' because it is always already constrained only to say the things in heaven and earth that are in Horatio's philosophy. Metafiction does not escape this.

Note

1. Excerpts revised from "Mapping the Inconceivable: Disordering Taxonomies," in *Mots D'Ordre: Disorder in Literary Worlds*. New York: SUNY Press (1992), 175–209, passim.

Chapter Five

Postmodernity Is a Hoot

In 1993, Linda Hutcheon and I edited *A Postmodern Reader* for SUNY Press; in 1997, I published *A Primer to Postmodernity* with Blackwell; and ten years later, Hans Bertens and I edited *Postmodernism: The Key Figures* with Blackwell. *A Primer* was translated into Chinese; *Key Figures* was translated into Japanese, Turkish, and Czech; while *A Postmodern Reader* was shanghaied by a Chinese scholar and published without our permission, although the author wrote and apologized for his thievery but reminded us that we could do nothing about it. The issue was on his conscience so he wrote to us and confessed. I hope the *Reader* earned him some royalties; it sold a little over ten thousand copies in our English-language edition. Perhaps there are millions of copies of Chinese translations, but I only think if the Chinese character for the signifier "postmodern" was so removed from the English that it seemed fresh and alive, au courant—for "postmodern," once a ubiquitous buzz word is now entombed alongside all those neologisms that have offended so many: from "paradigm" and "narrativity" to "intertextuality," "phallogocentricism," and "neodialectic neosublimation." "Narrative," however, is in its political heyday. Politicians need to assert their narrative before their opponent does it for them, or this politician's narrative is strong and that one weak, and so on. What were previously arguments or briefs, positions, or cases are now all narratives. There is a tectonic shift in thinking here, whether acknowledged or not.

Although graduate students found the *Reader* accessible, my undergraduates required more supplementation, which was background on classical/scholastic, Enlightenment, and twentieth-century modernist traditions. An outline of philosophical explorations into approaches to truth and reality were also needed. Our introductions to each classic postmodern piece entered in the ongoing debates and confusions but could not reach back as far as was needed. And that background of cultural erudition or at least acquaintance had been displaced in US higher education by a career-oriented curriculum. The background required to follow the postmodern swerve had been replaced by a guess as to what the market's needs might be in regard to background. I therefore set out to write a primer. *A Primer to Postmodernity* turned out to be a primer turned against the concept of primer—"a scholarly text posing as a funzine," one critic wrote—not pretending to be a grounding text that would mark clear boundaries, establish basic definitions and key concepts, and thus create a foundation upon which intermediate, advanced, and post-doctoral work could be erected. Nonetheless, this anti-*Primer* was at once picked up by a Chinese publisher and translated. This time legitimately.

"The first line of chapter 1 is a hoot considering Natoli's own critical alliances with postmodernism. Becark says 'I don't know if I should object to being called a postmodernist or not, Mr. Warp,' to which Mr. Warp replies, 'The word was clearly being used as an insult, Captain.'" (Amy Elias, "And the Beat Goes On: Defining Postmodernism and Its Other," *Contemporary Literature* 40:1, 1999.)

I did not object to being called a postmodernist, just as I did not object to being called a Blakean or a Leftist or a Jungian or a phenomenologist or a deconstructionist, or, in the days I was a graduate student of British Romanticism, a Romanticist. I have been labeled a "1960s campus radical who is still fighting corporate capitalism," a Marxist, and "an academic who has been marginalized in the profession and fought back with his mind," and, in my union-organizing days, "an incorrigible and a troublemaker." There was a stigma to all but like all tags, what they revealed floated not only in the changing ether but also in changing minds.

Being called a "deconstructionist" was an accusation, rather like the "Are you now or have you ever been?" sort. "Marxist" and "postmodernist" became signifying equivalents of the Walkman, dial phones, snail mail, and cassette tapes. They were dead and gone, mockingly "back in the day." Nevertheless, it is becoming increasingly clear after the 2007 Great Recession that an out-of-control financial sector is operating within the mandate of a market rule that needs taming. A critique from the Left, only timidly borrowing from Marxist critique at this point, is being resurrected. In other words, we return to what at another time we dismissed. We may have moved on from the signifier "postmodern," but it becomes increasingly clear that our millennial times are fully loaded with the undecidability, indeterminism, and over-determinism of our truth stories. We are fully enmeshed in a postmodernized world that politicians and marketers are fully aware of and make clever use. As Liberals call themselves "Progressives," running from the "Liberal" signifier, postmodernists refer to a "post-truth" age.

Although it is commonly believed that the now-dead and buried postmodern silliness unleashed the anything-goes and things-are-whatever-they-mean-to-me attitudes, it in theory constrained personal autonomy within the dispositions of the surrounding culture. At every place and in every time, we are born into bubbles of thought out of which we parrot talk that we call our own. Anything goes, then, within an always already-existing hierarchy of talk, of stories, of truisms. This is nothing like the liberation that we promise ourselves fashioned by a personal freedom to choose which we personally choose to believe in. This is much like choosing to fly off a roof because we choose to believe we can fly. The surround thwarts us. We allow ourselves a freedom the world is not obliged to recognize, a freedom Chance and power override, and therefore no freedom at all, or at least one in which the signifier "freedom" needs work.

Things are whatever they mean to me; but as that "me" is already a fabrication of what things we are born into already are, this too is not the liberation for which we hope. However, none of these qualifications or codicils on our personal freedom has taken root in our post-truth age because we are astoundingly attached to the illusions of individual autonomy and personal freedom. We defend ourselves against those truisms that oppose our own by merely asserting the authority of our own personal determination. Others may have opposing opinions that bind them as if they were truths, but they cannot affect in any way the supremacy of our own personal freedom to design and live within a reality we like confirmed by the truisms supporting that reality. Personal preference is all we now think and so set ourselves up for rude awakenings.

We tweet boldly our preferences. What was open dialogue ready to accommodate an infinity of interpretations is now reduced to an absolute disinterest in another's opinions as long as they do not impose themselves in any way on our own, and a nasty assault on whatever invades our bubble of preferences. Both responding modes can be witnessed on Twitter most clearly, on Facebook and other social media, and in the interaction or comment sections of websites. This interpretation of contemporary dialogue explains, like a good theory, why an avowed post-racist millennial consciousness is as real as our political post-partisanship, something President Obama shared with the young who voted for him in 2008. We are post-everything we have no personal interest in, which means of course that we remain not only ignorant but indifferent to that ignorance and disinterested in informing ourselves. We are, therefore, clearly not going beyond but going backward; but as hi-tech defines what progress is, we cannot see ourselves running backward. However, if you study the reading, critical thinking, and sustained focus of the young, you observe we are running backward at a four-minute mile pace. Fragmented attentiveness and focus seem to oblige capitalism's need for a multi-tasking, easily distracted workforce. But when asked how he was able to think so far beyond his peers, Einstein humbly replied, "It's not that I'm so smart, it's just that I stay with problems longer" (*Ideas and Opinions* [New York: Random House, 1954).

The question arises regarding how we should go about informing ourselves, correcting our ignorance, and working ourselves out of our bubbles of personal preferences. We have worked ourselves into a world of narratives fighting narratives, one in which "those with the most power are accused of imposing their version of reality—the 'dominant paradigm'— on the rest, leaving the weaker to fight back with formulations of their own" (George Johnson, "The Widening World of Hand-Picked Truths," *New York Times,* August 24, 2015).

We could avoid all this if we had held on to a universally accepted universal form of judgment, which of course never existed except in our own minds. "Thinking makes it so" Hamlet tells Rosencrantz, but so much of Hamlet's torment comes from a belief that actions in themselves are good or bad, that there is bedrock or foundational moral order independent of our thinking. He cannot be sure and that uncertainty is itself postmodern because though we are confined to what we say and represent, that confinement does not deny the presence of what we cannot fully speak of or represent. Our human worlding encompasses much and is capable of encompassing so much more, from other creatures and their independence from our human worlding of this planet we share to the vast oceans of unthought out of which our own thinking emerges. We cannot expect that the islands of predictability that our sciences discover encompass the ocean of unpredictability in which we swim.

When the so-called science wars, also called "The Sokal Affair" of the mid-nineties went beyond academic walls and made newspaper headlines, I was asked as the series editor of "Postmodern Culture," a monograph series publishing works exhibiting the postmodern mindset, to jump in and defend that postmodern view. I declined.

I had postmodern reasons. The fury of contesting truth stories meant to me only that different ways of looking at the world had run into each other, and neither side was prepared to recognize the same neutral, disinterested arbiter. You could throw wood on the fire in one oven or the other, but you could not step forward as a mutually recognized judge in the matter at hand. While one side threw the facts at you, the other side traced those facts to a hierarchy of values that wrested 'fact' from a world smothered in facts but rising to identity at the call of values. Values that did not change for longer than memory could recall had a certain authoritative cachet, rather like the way the flat earth and Ptolemaic views persisted—until they didn't. It did seem that things changed as time passed and that the way we saw greatly depended upon the context or surround of our seeing. We saw the world relative to when and where. That sort of relativism always runs into a moral relativism, something that has no legs in the American cultural imaginary, which is more determined than a European imaginary to hold on to a firm moral basis for its own self-proclaimed moral superiority. Perhaps that need becomes stronger as a very dehumanizing form of rapacious capitalism displays a face to the world that Americans prefer not to see.

I thought back then that postmodernity's questioning of truth and its relationship with power as well as postmodernity's confounding notions of good and evil as boldly as William Blake was doomed to a very bad press and a very bad end. Our order of things was built not by reason, Blake's Urizen, but by a deeply entrenched economic system that had already turned any hope of an egalitarian order to plutocracy. Those entrenched in nifty locations of power and wealth do not easily allow a questioning of their raison d'être. So, I anticipated a venomous attack.

However, I did not envision the use that same system made of the postmodern attitude, although my understanding of capitalism's commodification of not only labor but of all cultural productions extended from Marx to the Frankfurt School. Marcuse's notion of a "repressive tolerance" was at work in conflating postmodernity's observance that no emperor was clothed with postmodernism's new and faddish hold on the arts. That conflation did much to erode postmodernity's deconstructive force. I did not think through to the ways market rule would use the revelations of postmodernity to create a world in which personal determination does not look for a universally accepted universal arbiter of truth. Rather postmodernity's apparent confirmation of subjective supremacy led to the belief that an ontological being-in-the-world had all to do with 'being you' and nothing to do with the world. Postmodernity came through as meaning one thing: personal choices, freely made in a world that could always be trumped, established the YOUniverse.

Market rule was prepared to provide those choices in a culture in which no truth determination could offset a personal relationship with the truth that ingenious branding of mind and product forged. An absurd but working situation developed, one within which we now live. Notions of the cultural link between truth and how we reason our way to the truth, between the social and cultural conditions out of which our personal choice emerge and much more turbulence churned up by the postmodern view were pronounced "dead." Even the scientific method fell before the advance of personal revelation. All methodologies that attempted to abrogate the power of self-design, of a personal will that ruled all, became faddish, arcane, perverse, destructive modes of thought, dead and buried.

We now live within a world in which everyone has a view of everything, and each is different. And that difference is sacred while former ideals of community and commonality, of mutual interdependence seem hopelessly back in the day, vestiges of a dying analog world. Here then is a world where truth is still held sacred because it is your truth, and nothing is more sacred than the personal. What capitalism has done is absorb the revelations of the new postmodern awareness, using alibi fronts such as multiculturalism and diversity, the displacement of identity with difference, the absence of any judgments that cannot be contested, and the narrative construction of life-worlds to develop marketing and political strategies, and then demonize the source (i.e., postmodernity). Regardless of such demonization, the postmodern view does itself appear profane because it questions illusions of personal autonomy and the foundations of sacred truths.

The former is the real offense in an age of expressive individualism. The power to present your truth in cyberspace and to be interactive with the views of others means, in effect, that you can interject your truth on any platform without recognizing the superiority, on whatever basis— scientific, philosophical, historical, or magical—of anyone else's beliefs. "The widening gyre of beliefs," George Johnson writes "is accelerated by the otherwise liberating Internet. At the same time it expands the reach of every mind, it channels debate into clashing memes, often no longer than 140 characters, that force people to extremes and trap them in self-reinforcing bubbles of thought" ("The Widening World of Hand-Picked Truths," *New York Times*, August 14, 2015).

Scientists, understandably, are most upset by this turn from empirically or at least consensually validated truths to "I've got my version, you've got yours." What we have in the scientific view in regard to issues such as global warming, evolution, and vaccination are clear instances of retrogression, of devolution, of a collapse into a subjectivity that the objective intentions of the scientific methods work hard to diminish. But that method is not populist, whereas the liberation into endless choices at your personal disposal is very populist. And while some scientists and historians and philosophers of science rave against a loss of respect for fact and evidence, for experimentation and verification, and the reappearance of magical ways of thinking, those committed to pursuing the path of technology leading to profit are busy supplying the market with a barrage of new hi-tech choices.

One can argue that there is no harm if individuals pursue in cyber-space the choices that enable them to design their own reality and the truths that nurture it. And it does seem as if an economy that thrives on such a populist dispersal of truth generates more profit than a monologist truth that may not satisfy everyone and, in fact, never does. "One Law for ox and lion is oppression," Blake writes, hoping to unbind an entire century from the rule of reason and make a path for the imagination, which would liberate us from contraction into divided selves and return us to an expanded oneness of humanity. Now, we interpret his word to mean anyone else's opinion oppresses us, if we personally choose to allow it. And no one law can hold itself superior to our own. The harm then is to our solidarity as humans who are interdependent, not only economically but also thought-wise. There is in Blake's view both a contraction into the self and an expansion outward into a "Universal Man," a communion of others in a dynamic of self-annihilation and communion with others. And the imagination inspires that dynamic just as in the postmodern view it inspires a representation of what counters our own narratives.

In many years of teaching and talking about the postmodern view, I was invariably asked if I had given up the search for truth. How could I tell what the truth might be, and aren't we all free to believe what we want is the truth? To the first, I replied that I was in a continuous interpreting mode, interpretation to my mind being the opposite of opin-ing. And I followed the advice of Gilles Deleuze in this: "To interpret is to determine the force which gives sense to a thing" (*Nietzsche and Philosophy* [Columbia: Columbia University Press, 1985], 54). Something in the culture is allocating sense and nonsense to either ideas or events, to words, images, dreams, history. Something in the culture is also allocat-ing right and wrong, sane and insane, sacred and profane, real and unreal, true and false, winning and losing, and much more. Whatever is held as unimpeachable, as an eternal verity, as doubtlessly the case seems to mean to me only that certain conditions—objective, historical, material—exist of overwhelming supportive and sustaining power. I seek to find their birthplace. I seek to find the continuing source of sustenance. I also seek to find what is left out, what is diminished thereby, and also who benefits. In a devoted capitalist society, you follow the thing to the force—money and the power it brings. It's not the force of Blake's' spiritual world that gives sense to our world, nor the force of Wordsworth's healing spirit of Nature, nor the force of any ideological will to power, of which the world has seen much.

I seek to hold on to stories of truth that hold on despite the forces of profit maximization set against them. I am seeking what the truth might be under conditions of here and now, of this time and this place, what the truth may be to this framing of reality. But to do this I need to know the changing hierarchy of forces, though perhaps drastically different, within which humans everywhere are held. The forces of globalized, cybertech-enabled techno-capitalism do not multiply the conditions within which we live but rather are solidifying them so that whether you drive through the eastern United States or the western, you observe the corralling efforts of an incorporating capitalism. If surrounding conditions become monolithic, it makes no sense to believe that individual differences are expanding. So, to the previous mantra that everyone knows everything in our new millennial world and each knows it differently, I append the corollary that there is less and less difference to know and that in fact the American cultural imaginary has a very bound imagination. We think we see, know, and design within the infinity of algorithms but in actuality we are contracting into the space of *Brave New World*.

Those who imagine winning at any cost are not met with any equally opposing imagination but rather by a confused, uneasy, and feeble hope that there is something other than winning at any cost. Call that the Liberal party. And that quasi-opposition is itself impotent compared to the illusions and delusions, a kind of imagining, of personal autonomy and individual sovereignty. There is a tragic sadness to this because there is less warrant for such imagining than at any time since Catholicism ruled minds, hearts, and souls.

The uses that both capitalism and consumers made of a collapse in Enlightenment pretenses and a turn from the anxieties of twentieth-century modernism have not been good. These uses range from the international scene and the futile wars waged even more nonsensically than Vietnam to the national scene where Tea Party nativists engage in a politics of confrontation and not compromise, school massacres proliferate as young minds spin into a frightening madness, gentrification creates a Praetorian Guard in invaded neighborhoods, inflated celebrity egos become presidential election frontrunners. You cannot lay all that to a radical change in mindset, a reality-framing change that broke the frame, and yet the dark complexities of our world go deep into our reality-making ways. There is no superficiality here; an ontological revolution occurred. And back then, when I wrote *A Primer*, I got more than a glimpse of it.

A Primer to Postmodernity (1997) was written in response to a query by Susan Rabinowitz at Blackwell Publishers regarding whether I could write an introductory text about postmodernism for undergraduates. I decided to rely on popular culture, namely the popular TV series *Star Trek*, to tell the tale in a postmodern way. The Brits thought it was a "stitch" and Amy Elias wrote in *Contemporary Literature* (40, 1999):

> It is a fascinating text for a number of reasons. First of all, it's fun and innovative. Second, it is deceptive, a scholarly text posing as a funzine; examined closely, the discussion reveals itself to be crammed with information and central points of debate about postmodernism as a critical theory, as a cultural moment, and as an epistemology.

The use of characters, different narrative voices, and story frames was my on-going attempt to bring fictional techniques into academic discourse, to rely on both my own imagination and that of the reader to grasp what can never be reduced to empirical and rational methodologies. We see the world through story frames and hear through other voices. In our own society, popular culture's stories, images and voices become pathways upon which we interact with the world, mediums through which we filter the disparate chaos of ourselves and the world.

In short, in *A Primer,* I attempted to shape an imaginary world within which all senses of the reader could roam. . . . My intent was to replace explanation, evidence, and proof, to interrupt repeatedly the conventional primer-like exposition with a carnivalesque canvas that drew a reader into it. I added "ten viewpoints held by postmodernists in the late Twentieth Century on the planet Earth" in response to a request by the publisher to give the reader some basic principles to hold onto. I decided on giving ten because ten was a sacred number. In truth, all ten raised more questions than they answered and so did no harm to what I was about in bringing the postmodern story to readers.

"You, the reader," was my introductory address, "are not a construct in the way Becark or Deja are constructs, but the way they are constructs is already shaped by the way you are real, and your reality in turn will be in the future shapes by the way they are constructed." This primer was an interactive performance, one that made it difficult for the reader to find a place to rest or an Archimedean point of observation and command. You understood it because you lived through it.

In the end, I want to lead a sort of prison break out of the notion that we're all living in the same, one reality and not in innumerable stories about reality that we share to various degrees and in various ways. None of these stories can validate themselves as reality and disprove all others. Or, to put it another way, they can all validate themselves in a thoroughly rational and/or empirical way and they can all invalidate each other. Reason and its minions, logic and statistic, work all sides equally well. It all depends on time and place. (7)

After a spring semester in 1995, rehearsing my postmodern happening on a study-abroad program in England, I launched "Is This a Postmodern World?" a rail/bus/ferry/bike/hostel /backpack program in Europe, which was repeated for fifteen years.

The chapter on Orson Welles's *Citizen Kane,* a film I present as being on the very edge of the playful postmodern world and yet at the same time being a brilliant example of the dark anxieties of twentieth-century modernism, also demonstrates how popular culture's captivating imaginative qualities make possible a fun voyage through "the troubled waters of postmodern discourse."

Go to *Citizen Kane* to Find Twentieth-Century Modernism: On the Edge of Postmodernity[1]

Centreless labyrinth.

—Jorge Luis Borges on *Citizen Kane*

I choose Orson Welles's *Citizen Kane* because it reveals the aspirations of twentieth-century modernism while at the same time tottering on the edge of postmodernity, which, as we see in the next chapter of *A Primer,* turns out to be a surface that has no edges. Postmodernity does not surpass or replace twentieth-century modernism, an approach to reality and truth masterfully represented by Welles. But our shifting toward postmodernity has made a difference: when we employ a twentieth-century-modernist way of attending to the world, we do so less unnerved by the failure of that approach. We take Thompson the reporter's investigative trek now not in the hope of everything finally adding up. Rather, we do it in the hope that all those divergent lives that cross our path will open up even further, reveal more of their divergence from our mission to 'crack' the signifier "rosebud." Even though Enlightenment optimism has darkened in the twentieth-century, we yet hold onto to the hope that we can connect word and world, "rosebud" and "Kane" and thus reveal the truth of a man's life.

What was unproblematic within Enlightenment modernity's framing of reality and truth, has become unnerving in twentieth-century modernism. The darkness and angst of twentieth-century modernism's tragic vision has all to do with its own rounding up of suspects that were not suspects previously: reason and its minions, of course, head the list (from "objectivity" to "inescapable logics"), language (words seemed to have become unglued from world), and self (desiring to discover but caught in a labyrinth of constructing). Welles's focus is on these suspects, so intense a focus that they begin to fracture and break up, in spite of a lens that was to provide in a typically modernist way "a momentary stay against confusion," a momentary glimpse of one commonly shared reality and the truths lying within it. The dark and difficult passage into the truth of one man's existence was to finally shed some light, provide a glimpse of what we were seeking. If only we could talk to everyone, put aside their biases as well as our own, cut through appearances to reality, distinguish narrative from fact, and clearly see what is reasonable from what is nonsense, and so on. If only time could have a stop; if only the "I" could be distanced from the flux, observing, dominating, and discovering the truth.

Rather than try to slip by all the hauntings of modernism, Welles uses a head-on, let's-see-the-very-worst-and-I'll-handle-it style. It is an exuberant, commanding, artistically superb, rash rush into the darkness that fell upon the world when Enlightenment modernity's own presumption flagged. I want to focus on the unnerving parts in *Kane,* the parts that seem to make any final recuperation, the resolution of closure, impossible. Rather than provide an ending to our search for the truth, they open up that search beyond the scope of Welles's camera to contain but not beyond the scope of his camera to make conceivable. The postmodern way of attending is rendered conceivable here; and it is that conceivability, that shifting of focus or transfer of one lens to another, that marks not only the greatness of Welles's film but a journey from one way of seeing the world toward another. But it is a crisscrossing journey, postmodern in itself, because while we are journeying away from Enlightenment modernity into the heart of the twentieth-century version and then are brought to the very beginning of a postmodern journey, the film imbricates all three modes.

Here is a 1965 plot synopsis of the film done clearly at a time when answers could be given. One has only to see the film to see how much this innocent plot summary leaves out as well as imposes:

> Charles Foster Kane dies at the age of seventy-six in his im-
> mense castle, Xanadu; his dying word is "Rosebud." In the
> projection room of a newsreel firm, a group of reporters note
> that Kane's public life—wealth, political and social events—
> does not contain the answer to the enigmatic "Rosebud." A
> reporter sets out to find the solution and, after reading the
> details of Kane's ruptured childhood, interviews four leading
> figures in the magnate's life: Bernstein, Leland (both associates
> of Kane at the height of his fame); his second wife, Susan
> Alexander, who Kane had forced to become an opera singer
> against her will and who is now drunk in a dingy nightclub;
> and Raymond, Kane's butler in the concluding stages of his
> life at Xanadu. All these are most forthcoming; some even give
> different versions of the same events; but none can explain
> the word "Rosebud" to Thompson, the reporter. The answer
> is given to the audience at the end: as Kane's belongings are
> packed up and removed from Xanadu, a workman tosses an
> old sledge into a fire. Painted on it is the word "Rosebud."
> It is the dim memory of his childhood toy that has haunted
> Kane throughout his life and on his deathbed. (Peter Cowie,
> *The Cinema of Orson Welles,* New York: Da Capa Press, 1965)

Bernstein's words have always haunted me: "It's funny what you remember. I remember seeing a girl in a white dress on the Staten Island Ferry. I only saw her for a couple of seconds but I guess a month hasn't gone by in the past thirty years that I haven't thought about her."

Then Thompson the investigative reporter—or we in the audience— asks this man with this sort of pattern of interaction with the world, with this sort of oddly selective memory, the big question: "You wouldn't know who Rosebud was would you?" It is the nut that the film sets out to crack, the signifier that we have to attach to a signified, word to world, so that we can connect it with Kane's chain of signification. It is our key—this signifier—into Kane's world, his mode of being, and his human life-world. And if we can talk to everybody who knew him, get all the takes on Rosebud, and then add them up, why then we would be bringing the old modernist project back to working order.

You have to remember it's 1941 and there's a terrible world war going on, with hints of genocide. It is a world that will get even darker with the Japanese bombing of Pearl Harbor. Reason has lost its hold on the world, or the world has gone mad despite reason's best efforts. And, most frighteningly, the Third Reich is claiming reason is on its side. Everything they are doing is eminently rational to them. Ditto the Japanese. It would have been irrational for them to do otherwise. Reason is constructing the nightmare world of 1941. And it is not going to get any better for a long time. This is the horizon of the film, the world outside the film that is resonating out there.

And we are going to this man, Bernstein, this mentality, this memory for answers? For the truth? This is scary. I get the twentieth-century modernism frissons. I feel deep, dark disillusionment coming on. Fear and trembling. Sickness unto death. Kane through a glass darkly, through Bernstein's mind, that is. Oh, what a tragic vision is this to view the world so arbitrarily, for mind and memory to be caught up in a viewing that meant nothing. Except he hooked up with it forever. A random crossing of paths leads to a lifelong forking off the golden road to the truth.

Can such a mind ever find that road? I mean if it is always forking off without rhyme or reason? And what a selective memory. Does he remember anything else that happened that day? We cannot register everything. We can't observe and mark everything in the world, but couldn't Bernstein have observed something that was going to stay with him his whole life that was more significant, that made some kind of sense in terms of his life? Because while his mind was indelibly marking the girl in a white dress, it was blind to everything else. Our attention, our focus is not only oddly selective, but it seems to hook up with things unconsciously. Unless our attention is brought into line as it is in *A Clockwork Orange* or *1984*.

Subjectivity is not focused; it wanders off. It connects with the world in strange ways; its connections remain part of us without apparent rhyme or reason. No pattern to our attentiveness. What shapes our attentiveness to the world? How can a wandering gaze picking up disconnected images that do not fade for unfathomable reasons establish common, reliable linkages to the world? Recall the scene toward the very end of the film when Kane walks past mirrors and his image is reflected several times. The unity of the subject breaks up into many selves. It fractures.

Who is the real Charles Foster Kane? The puzzle of the film. Disconnected, arbitrary, incommensurable memories, linkages in the mind surely imply that from this chain of signification one framing of the world cannot be forged? And if our notion of self is but a story fabricated by these word—world linkages—wouldn't we then be a different self for every framing?

Charles Foster Kane is not one but multiple. We cannot add up everybody's view and get the real Kane. Each perspective is a different framing, a different attentiveness. He remains multiple. And so is Bernstein. There is a Bernstein that is somehow tied to that girl on the ferry, but he is not the Bernstein to whom we are talking. That Bernstein's linkages of word and world are on a back burner. This Bernstein cannot even connect with them. "It's funny," he tells us, "how the mind works."

Enlightenment modernity assumed that an observer could put on disinterestedness, like a hat. To do that, of course, one had to assume first a coherent, unified, continuous subject. That was taken for granted. Twentieth-century modernism no longer takes that for granted. And it is on the threshold of announcing that subjectivity is caught within not-always-comprehensible perceptual frames. And if this is not enough, different frames narrate the subject differently. The controlling self we know we are is just the latest, most persuasive story of self within which we are ensnared. What gives the show away is the fact that other stories we've lived in, that have narrated our identities to us, have left us with traces of the linkages of word and world that they have made. Bernstein's is an example.

Freud was aware of these other displaced stories and the selves they created as leaving residue images in our memories. Words and images could evoke them. "Tell me the first thing that comes to your mind." Or, "What do you see in these ink blots?"

Needless to say, you cannot complete the modernist project, add foundational pieces to the Western Rationalist and Realist Tradition, keep on the road to progress, the ascent of man and so on, if we are essentially unknown to ourselves. We are the ghost in the machine; or more precisely, the ghosts of former stories we have lived in haunt our minds and memories. We're us but also somebody we've forgotten or a lot of somebodies we've partially forgotten. The ways they attended to the world pop up, sometimes in dream, triggered by what the world shows us now that it has showed us before in another time and another place. Déjà vu may very well be the result of a temporal discrepancy between right- and left-brain cognition. But what if déjà vu is but a palimpsest of other selves we have been, other stories that we have lived in? Multiple selves coming out of multiple narratives? How is anything else possible? How could we hold ourselves within one privileged story of the self? Or presume that the self was prior to stories, was not born into stories, was not the real self unless it could rise above all the stories it lived in? The story-less self is unborn to the world. To be born into the world is to be born into its many stories.

Every other unnerving in *Citizen Kane* comes out of this decentering of the self. And of course, Welles makes a valiant modernist effort to put the self back together with the Freudian early-trauma metanarrative. But it does not wrap Bernstein's story up, or the entire twentieth-century modernist dream of adding up everyone's perspective and finally reaching the truth. Everyone's perspective remains caught in the Bernstein way of attending to the world. We have been told "girl on the ferry" stories. Or maybe not. Or maybe sometimes. Sometimes we focused on Kane. But through someone's own eyes, in his or her own way, through a glass darkly.

Our gaze, like Kane's at the opera house he has built, cannot dominate what we see. Rather, that gaze wanders, attaching itself to the world from within all manner of stories that we live within. We are dominated by stories that we have created, some peculiarly our own, others part of the culture that enframes us. And it is this overlapping of stories in us and outside ourselves that, always already, makes us a part of that independently existing reality we wish to observe in a disinterested way and, finally, wish to dominate. Once the truth is not out there to be grasped but caught up in this web of stories, which we and the world are caught up in, then the truth can no longer be grasped the way the Enlightenment dreamed (told us a powerful story about how) it could be grasped.

That stalwart, independent observer takes a fall and gets cracked in *Citizen Kane*. He falls into the world. And all the king's horses and all the king's men couldn't put him together again.

It is interesting that the Enlightenment way of putting him back together is after the first eighteen minutes of the film rejected. The *News on the March* documentary of Kane's life is patently insufficient. It clearly cannot stand as a representation for the man's whole life. His real identity slips past that chronicle. And yet there are the facts on the screen. There is the film footage, the interviews, the verbatim text, the chronology, the surrounding social and political context.

Why can't this do? Why can't this objective, impartial unearthing of the facts of the man's life capture that life? And if it did, if we were able to work diligently, methodically, analytically, disinterestedly, wouldn't we be affirming our own capacity to capture the real and the true? And by doing that wouldn't we be affirming our own self-domination, our own coherence, our own control of our gaze, of the way we attend to the world, of our memories? Wouldn't there be proof here that the subject wasn't living in stories of self and world but was outside those stories as well as objectively distanced from the world? And because we were sitting in the catbird seat, outside the flux of things, we could keep both flux and stories from penetrating our subjectivities. We could stay pure, whole, unified, together, unfractured.

Welles discards all this Enlightenment posturing almost at once. Why? Well, he picks the straw that breaks the camel's back. He picks Kane's dying word, "rosebud." "Words," the editor says. Rose. Bud. As if perhaps Kane was calling on two people: Rose and Bud. At the end of the film, we see the sled and it has a bud of a rose tattooed on it. One word. But even at the end, we have to struggle to attach that word to the multiple Kanes we have met. Now, at the very beginning of the film, "rosebud" is an inscrutable signifier, so difficult almost immediately to connect to the man's life, to some meaning that would explain the man's life. Last words, the editor tells us, always mean something important. If we cannot get from what we say to what really is, then we are lost in a darkness we cannot penetrate, cannot illuminate.

The newsreel has nothing to say here. The signifier unravels the newsreel. We hear it flapping as we hear the men comment on it, in shadows. The newsreel has not enlightened us. We have a dark passage ahead of us. The whole film. And we end with the dark smoke funneling upward: "Those dark satanic mills of Blake," D.H. Lawrence writes. "How much darker they seem, now." Crack the signifier, find the man's life, find a fixed, determinate meaning, identify his identity. But the identity cracks, subjectivity cracks, and not the signifier.

In the postmodern world, the signifier floats; it is groundless; it is not anchored to anything, certainly not reality. If we were naïve realists, we would say words are not floating and they are not anchored; they are merely transparent. We see reality through them, as through a clear pane of glass. A word is like a window: pick the right window and you see what you are supposed to see. If we were Enlightenment modernists, we would say words were anchored to reality by the use of reason. A reasonable person would find the precise correspondence between word and world; the empirical investigator would support his or her account with the facts. Words are an unproblematic medium for the reasonable; they present difficulties only to those who are too stupid or too ignorant to grasp their meaning. If we were twentieth-century modernists, we would say words make ambiguous connections to reality because language-users always already have inescapable affective connections to reality and because objective reality itself is always already inescapably overlayered by the whole panoply of human culture. At best, we could, by means of a multi-perspective approach, represent that ambiguity and complexity and in doing that reveal the nature of a reality that has itself become ambiguous and complex because it is always filtered through a variety of cultural perspectives. Not only has reality constructed a no-trespassing sign in the twentieth century, but also we cannot find two people who read the sign the same way at the same time. In fact, people are wearing no-trespassing signs too, and they cannot read themselves any better than they can read someone else. It is just as hard to figure out who we really are as we search for who Charles Foster Kane really is.

Nothing is welcoming in the dark vision of twentieth-century modernism. The facts of Kane's life as revealed in that eighteen-minute *News on the March* account turn out to be images and words that are themselves in need of other images and words which, in turn, would be in need of further supplementation. While postmodernity sees this as an endless chain of deferment on the level of the signifier that never crosses over into reality, Welles's modernism makes a pilgrimage to reality through a canvassing of all the relevant word-world connections. The hope is that in the end we can add up the perspectives and get a glimpse of who Kane really is. It is a journey that we take along with Thompson, the reporter. It's a journey in which different takes on Kane's life turn out not only to be irreconcilably different—sort of like adding apples and bananas and getting strawberries—but they add up differently depending upon who is doing the adding up. The sorting through and adding up of accounts becomes clearly relative to the frame of the one doing the sorting and the adding up. And, most frighteningly, there seems to be nothing in Welles's own representation of this journey that provides a fixed center of reference and determination. Indeed, Welles's own take—rather like a headline banner from the *Enquirer:* "Freudian Childhood Trauma Theory Explains All"—is immediately followed by a return to Xanadu's fence, the barricade between us and Kane, and the sign—"No Trespassing." We haven't gotten over.

Along with Thompson, we put all our faith in reaching the people who knew Kane, listening to them and piecing together the puzzle of Kane's life. If we can piece that puzzle together, we can piece the puzzle of the film together. And if we can do all that, we have before us a film that shows us a way to piece reality together, a vindication of art's capacity to touch even a moving reality whose "center cannot hold." There are innumerable ways of setting up the camera so that all perspectives on things can be accounted for. Welles's technical mastery of representation, however, does not conceal the impossibility of its mission. This is a self-reflexive genius, one that doubles back on his own takes and pokes some holes in his own presumption.

Notice how we are repulsed three times at the very beginning of our search for truth: the first time when the camera closes on the "No Trespassing" sign; the second time, our alter-ego Thompson tells his editor whom he's going to interview—"everybody who knew him, everybody who's still alive that is": and the third time, when Thompson sits down next to Susan Alexander and she tells him "who told you to sit down?" She is drunk and she will not talk to him. To us. She won't tell what she knows. And even if she had decided to give us her account then, we would wonder how much of a booze-filtered account it was. The "No Trespassing" sign is unambiguous: we cannot get from where we are over to where reality is. The sign does not say "Open Only between the Hours of Nine and Five" or "Open to Members Only." And yet we are going to ignore the sign and we are going to try and trespass. The second setback is just as lethal: we cannot talk to everyone. Kane's first wife, Emily Norton Kane, and their son have been killed in a car accident. Her absence in particular haunts our journey to the truth: it is as if doing a puzzle that you know has a missing piece, a key piece. A lurking absence that all historians face.

When we next set off to get the story of Kane's guardian, Thatcher, we have to settle for a fixed number of pages in the man's diary because Thatcher too is dead. How able are we to resurrect the truth of the past when the principals are dead? But the text lies open before us, the Thatcher diary. Words. Can we connect these words to a past reality and truth? As Thompson looks down at a page and the camera draws in close and moves along so that we can read the text, Welles opens the scenes for us, the living reality behind the words. But it is Thatcher's voice now that is reading the words and Welles, after all, is only supplying for us those scenes as perceived, felt, understood by Thatcher. The words then do not transparently reveal an unfiltered, unmediated reality; the word-and-world connections we get are those made by Thatcher. Other characters in the film, as well as Thatcher's own diary, reveal what sort of observer he might be. "I would have liked to have been everything that you despise," Thatcher remembers Kane telling him. This is about as damaging to our modernist project to search out the truth as Bernstein's revelation of the totally quirky and unreliable nature of memory.

Our journey to the truth runs into this haunting obstacle: the consciousness of the observer who does the saying, the writing, who uses the words that we depend upon in order to solve the puzzle of Charles Foster Kane. One of the things Enlightenment modernity was able to do—or get away with for a time—was lift consciousness out of the how-to-discover-reality-and-truth formula. With that messy baggage fixed in a theory-neutral and value-free outside observing booth, hand at the Archimedean fulcrum, facts, empirical evidence, irrefutable logics, and supposedly blind testing, and so on, could secure reality and truth for us. Consciousness could project a rationality that would reach back and objectify itself. Welles's twentieth-century modernism returns us to the refracting surfaces and reverberating recesses of consciousness. Deep labyrinthine corridors of impenetrable darkness whose only access is the sort of memory that Bernstein has talked about. Welles's way out is through the camera's focus on as many lives as he can reach; every framing is modulated by other framings; no one take on things gets an uncontested ride. Rather than setting up Thompson as an external sorter of stories, Welles presents him as merely in the story of a journey to truth.

At first, the most disturbing thing about Jed Leland's story is that it is an embittered one, a story told by a man to whom Kane was once a god but now has totally lost faith. But this bitterness is so present, it so fills the frame of Leland's account that a hope lingers that maybe we can extract it, like a bad tooth or a tumor, and leave only the good stuff—the truth. Maybe, we think, it is what Gadamer refers to as an "enabling prejudice," one that gives us entrance to something and at some point is removable by us, the viewers, the observers. The film feeds on this hope, as does the whole twentieth-century modernist mind-set. It's the wind that fills the sails of our journey: we can listen to everyone, sort through and pick out truth from falsehood, add up all the truth bits, and wind up with the big picture of the truth: This and not That is the real Charles Foster Kane.

But there is a new unnerving that Leland presents: his story is cigar riddled. When we find him in a wheelchair in a sanitarium, the first thing he wants from us is a cigar. He tells cigar stories about his present surroundings; he appraises his young doctor by employing cigar criteria. He turns the story of who Kane was back to his search for a cigar. He has, in short, a cigar focus; he attends to the world in a cigar-attentive way. He lives in a cigar-modulated present. And, as we already know from

Bernstein's account of the way the present is perforated by the past, we now see that the past is also perforated by the present. We have, in short, a present focus—say, a cigar focus—that has nothing to do with the past we hope to retrieve, and yet that focus is our focus on that past. The cigar becomes the horizon upon which Leland emplots his story of Kane. This is different from a prejudicial lens—the bad blood between Kane and Leland—because the cigar attentiveness hints at the possibility of both rational and irrational dimensions of present focus. I mean that although Leland's cigar attentiveness signifies as some sort of senility, latent or full flowering, present focus can signify in a very positive way cogent, rational, clear-sighted memory of details.

Welles's revelation here remains disturbing: present focus, however we value it, dominates our so-called cognitive, affective, perceptual pursuit of what really went on in the past, although it is of the present and not of the past. It may then be more difficult to account for the variables of present focus than to account for prejudices, which by very definition are never mistaken for their opposite or lack of prejudices. What frighteningly remains, however, is the fact that present focus and attentiveness are in themselves lethal to our truth pursuit. Welles's doubles the fright by putting before us an aged Leland whose very consciousness has cross-wired and short-circuited; it keeps taking him back to cigars: a consciousness grounded in cigars. What if the ghost in the machine has never at any moment in human history been quite up to the task of facing reality and discovering truth? Can we assume anything but a normative definition of sanity? Would the Martians whom Welles announced in his famous radio broadcast be able to give us an outside judgment on the quality and stability of our human consciousness? Are we all, in different fashions, grounded in modes of real-izing as ludicrous as Leland's?

What is most unnerving and irreconcilable in Susan Alexander's narrative? The lens is most clouded here: Kane has brought her to an attempted suicide and now in the present she's a drunk. At first, she won't speak to us and then in the end she does. In spite of all the reasons, she has for hating Kane, we yet get the sense that perhaps she gets Kane right. At the moment she leaves him she recognizes that she has never existed for him as a subject but only as an object. Independent of his own consciousness, she has no existence. He is lost in some self-enclosed world of his own in which there is no room for other people. A little glass ball in which a cold, snowy world is enclosed falls from the dying Kane's hand at the film's beginning; and in the scene when Susan leaves him, he destroys everything in the room but that glass ball. That enclosed glass world does not have Susan in it. And somehow, Kane has a fetishist attachment to it. Only in the end of the film does Welles connect it to the snow-filled world of Kane's youth in Colorado, the childhood from which he was dragged away. Time passes but Kane remains fixed within that enclosed world. "Don't you think I feel sorry for him?" Susan tells Thompson. It is this capacity to take herself out of her own life-world into another's that makes Susan a very compelling witness. After all, Kane has led her to a suicide attempt, to her own death, and yet she feels some sympathy for a man who is himself dead-in-life.

Xanadu is a world he builds so that he can be the master, but it is also the tomb that he builds, the tomb in the world that parallels the tomb within which his own life has been enclosed. And Susan has an affective awareness of all this; she has never been part of the search for meaning we are on. She simply has been caught within the fireworks, no hope of assuming an outside perspective and thus some mastery of what is going on. Everything eventually becomes conceivable to her, but nothing becomes either representational or controllable. Understanding then is detached from lived-experiences, from the flux of life; it is not only difficult to shape a real understanding of what is going on in the world, but also life goes on regardless of what understandings we may or may not reach. Understanding what is real and what is true—which is what we have joined up with Thompson to do—now encounter Susan's life, which now adds one more horror to a dark journey to truth. Our understanding not only is mysteriously and unreliably attached to what anybody says is reality and truth, but it is beside the point. Life goes on: pain and suffering, delusion and confusion take their toll. We can never attend to the world as it is and that attending can never rise to a level of understanding that controls what the world does to us. Susan, then, shows us the hopelessness of our quest; she tells us a story of a life lived on the other side of the "No Trespassing" sign, a place where understanding cannot go and yet everything that humans can experience still goes on.

We have seen and spoken to everyone, everyone who is still alive. A difficult journey, a dark passage perhaps to the truth? And that truth and reality must emerge from the frame-by-frame sequencing of the film as Bernstein's account parodies and counters Thatcher's, and Leland's account parodies and counters Bernstein's, and Susan's parodies and counters the others, and they all counter Raymond the butler's account. Until finally Thompson, instead of winding up with truth and reality at the end of this differing and deferring, renders the 'undecidable' verdict. No one word can reveal a man's life, he tells us; but he has heard a lot of words from a number of different people. It is not just the failure to find a determinate meaning to the word "rosebud." What is haunting is the fact that the twentieth-century modernist journey to the truth was undertaken, and it ended up where it began: inscrutable darkness, "No Trespassing." At the very end, as the sled is thrown into the furnace and the camera zooms in to reveal the melting letters "Rosebud" painted on the sled, Welles cracks the signifier for us.

But does he? Or, are we back to all those overdetermined accounts of all the people to whom we have listened? Note Welles's hookup: "rosebud" = early childhood trauma = who Charles Foster Kane really is. The trauma triggered the man; the man was the trauma; he never moved in time; he felt he lost his mother's love and then went in search of it, but only as a man who felt he did not even deserve the love of his mother. He would not know what love was or is. "Rosebud" isn't the crucial signifier then; it's "love." In order to find love, Kane has to use his power to create a world in which he has sole power in connecting word and world, word and meaning. The only question that one has to resolve regarding what words mean is the question that Humpty Dumpty raises in *Through the Looking Glass*: "Which is to be master?" So through this rosebud narrative we can draw a portrait of the real Charles Foster Kane. He would create the meaning of "love" on his own terms. Freud would say there was only a childhood-induced trauma at work here; love comes to be tied to meaning in the world through multiple connections that are not even tied to the present. "Love" implies engagement, interaction, a crisscrossing of lives and emotions. In the same fashion, the signifier "rosebud" is not solely within Welles's power to define. We have already heard the accounts of others, crossed into the lives of others who have themselves intersected the life of Kane. Their representations of who he really was can only be made to bend to Welles's rosebud narrative if he imposes that submission, plots that resolution, leads us to that closure.

He has, in fact, done the opposite; we have been on a Borgesian forking-path journey and not a progressive journey to an all-encompassing master narrative. Welles's rosebud story falls in line as just another story. Can we add them up? We always and inevitably make this attempt. We draw a line and add up all the narratives, and then for a moment, perhaps, we see into an otherwise elusive reality and truth. Or, is that truth and reality momentary and elusive because another and different narrative of truth and reality has come on the scene and we are drawn back to that horror of postmodern construction—undecidability?

We add all the perspectives up and the sky is still filled with dark smoke and the sign still tells us "No Trespassing." We have to go back and see it again. Try again. Never give up trying. The film is a hair's breadth away from saying that each perspective comes out of a framing of the world and of the self, and all notions of reality and truth come out of such framings. And therefore there are not only multiple realities that we have encountered, but also Kane is a multiple self. Neither he nor his observers can legitimate their own realizing as the real truth, as the representation of Kane that is identical to the life itself.

The film never takes that step but asks us to redo the puzzle, try again. The dark tragedy of the modern quest for the truth lies in this, that like Sisyphus with his stone, we must go back and try to fit the pieces into a precise mirroring of reality, knowing that our efforts are doomed to failure, that our gaze is selective, that our memories are forking paths, that while we intend to find out who Charles Foster Kane is, we are drawn to the memory of a girl in white on a ferry, a memory we can make no sense of. How we attach ourselves to the world confounds us. There is no light here. No trespassing.

We are on the edge of postmodernity.

....

I include an essay I wrote for the film magazine *Senses of Cinema* because the issue of whether or not there is a moral sense or dimension to postmodernity, an ethics to be derived, has probably contributed as much to the rush from postmodernity as the need of the young to post postmodernity. I selected Quentin Tarantino's *Inglourious Basterds* because he was charged with an undeserved moral indifference or obtuseness, a moral insensibility attending his explosive view of reality. As in the work of the Coen brothers, Tarantino's films have displayed the influence of David Lynch, whose own films and TV series *Twin Peaks* can be pointed to when someone asks, "What does a postmodern world look like?" What Lynch shows us are moral responses emerging from differing reality frames while at the same time existing within a moral fabric attempting to bind together a regime of order. The moral worth of the postmodern view lies in its display and clash of stories in a world without privilege beyond a self-privileging, a world in which righteousness proclaims itself authorized by its superiority to what it proclaims to be without righteousness. What can emerge then is only a parody of moral pretense, a mockery of self-authorizing moral superiority. We are not as bad as the Third Reich is therefore we are good, or know goodness. What we have in a postmodern world are rivals for truth resting on alleged foundations of reality out of which moral affirmations are made. Recognizing the social construction and entanglement of reality, truth and morality are certainly not an affirmation of what remains unconstructed and un-entangled, but it is a disclosure of an ongoing struggle to create a human moral dimension and the moral worth of that lies in its honesty.

The Deep Morals of *Inglourious Basterds*[2]

Tarantino has become an embarrassment: his virtuosity as a maker of images has been overwhelmed by his inanity as an idiot de la cinematheque.

—David Denby, *New Yorker*, August 24, 2009

Earlier in 2009, before David Denby, a film reviewer for the *New Yorker*, had referred to Quentin Tarantino as an "idiot de la cinematheque," he had written this about the film *District 9*: "There's plenty of violent spectacle, but it's part of a politically resonant fable" ("District 9," *The New Yorker*, September, 2009). The locale is Johannesburg so Soweto comes to mind, but as an American, I think of District 9 as Gitmo and Prawns as Muslim terrorists. But this link does not resonate in any way. The director, Neill Blomkamp, is not interested in this Gitmo connection. So what is the political dimension here that is so powerful that the video-game pyrotechnics of most of the movie—the rest being *Nerd Loves* and *Pines for Wife*—are drowned out? What is the political resonance here? Nothing more, I think, than an extension to real aliens (they look like shrimp on two legs) of our globalized multicultural passion. Except Nigerians. The Nigerians are, it seems, *too* alien. They are gangsters in the District making a buck on the Prawns; nasty gangster capitalists who sell and eat Prawn flesh for its supposed—according to Nigerian superstitious belief—immortalizing qualities.

Apartheid has made us aware of a moral resonance. Because, however, it resonates on behalf of our multicultural globalized Prime Moral Directive, I view it as moral pandering. In a world driven by a multicultural ambition, Blomkamp kicks up the intensity and rides the moral righteousness of multiculturalism, behind which I see a globalized free market's drive to eliminate all barriers, from trade to national and cultural identity. Blomkamp asks us to feel for difference, no matter how alien it may be.

Now Quentin Tarantino's new film, *Inglourious Basterds*, which came out at the same time as *District 9*, displays what David Denby calls a "moral callousness." It does not resonate morally at all. Tarantino doesn't have a moral compass in a decade when, I recall hearing on entertainment-news cable TV, Brittney Spears satisfies her own moral compass and that is what counts, right? Bill Clinton, according to the Cato Institute, did not have a moral compass, or, did not back when he was president. No one has said that George W. Bush lacks a moral compass, though the record of his eight years would demonstrate an obliviousness that goes across the board from political to moral. Perhaps the most telling illustration of our deeply engrained, across-the-culture moral callousness is the hardball, bottom-line rules, the-guy-with-the-most-toys-at-the-end-wins savagery demonstrated by our market players. Bernie Made-Off-With-Everyone's-Money is not the only slime ball out there but only the one who got caught.

We here in the United States exist in a Wild West of winner-take-all competitiveness that mouths a sanctimonious Pecksniffian morality on every public occasion while in practice leaving any moral concern—from malaria and AIDS in Africa to environmental degradation—to the losers. A loser is, in fact, defined as someone who places moral issues before short-term return on investment. Le ROI is "return on investment" and Jesus is not his son. If this is too general and too tired a sweep, I refer you to the on-going health-care reform debate going on here at the end of the decade. The moral argument that most European nations made regarding health care, (i.e., universal coverage is something morally demanded of a wealthy country), receives little or no play in the American debate. The fact that some forty-five million Americans do not have health care is not a fact greeted as a moral matter but rather as evidence in the case that has been building against the losers since Reagan. All these people have to do is get out there and become entrepreneurial or at least get a job that provides them with health care. They have chosen by their actions not to want health care so why should the winners step up and through taxation pay their health-care premiums? Moral concern is clearly submerged within the greater concerns, interests and values of "free"-market capitalism grounded in "free" choice.

Most of this moral callousness is masked by the mantras of "family values" and "tough love," "Just Say No," and a variety of American moral-exceptionalism fantasies. Such mantras of a whole-scale Christian born-again hullabaloo make Jesus—biblically a non-competitive loser—their "personal Saviour," despite the clear indication that the biblical Jesus was a social Saviour. But this is mom and dad's moral callousness. The millennials—those born after 1980—display a different moral callousness, what I have previously described as "you and you alone are the arbiter of all moral concerns." In this view, the great outdoors (the world outside yourself) is a YOUniverse made up of your own personal choices, which you have freely made, mostly on Facebook. You may, for instance, choose to see all elections as uninteresting and unrelated to you. You do not then feel any moral callousness on your part if you never vote, for the matter involved is one you have chosen not to include in your YOUniverse. The personal choices here are endless—from whether we should change our ways because of global warming to whether we should buy sweatshop garments. There is remarkable flexibility here. And no moral burden unless you personally decide that one thing or another is a matter for moral review. There is remarkable tolerance here. Whatever anyone does or does not do is related to his or her own moral compass, which may not be yours but it does not matter. This is a kind of "whatever" tolerance, a moral concern that does not stretch beyond your own skin and therefore, ironically, not moral at all.

I think this view explains why there is so much clash and venom, so much vindictiveness, coldness and harshness, so many tangles begun with a war cry of "Bitch!" on reality TV shows. What clearly happens is a YOUniverse moral sense, one that is tolerant to the point of uncaring regarding what others do or do not do, is clearly destined to be trespassed by the moral callousness, which you share, of those around you. Each person living within his or her own world of choices and the moral concerns ensuing runs into others living within their own world of choices that are happily unconcerned with yours. You have a lot to say about their trespassing on your world; but as you are made up of only self-concerns, you have no social facility, no interpersonal ways of responding. No one on these reality TV shows is capable of stepping into the world outside his or her own fabrications to see and hear another. This too is ironic since these unscripted shows are full of blab and blather, every participant has reams of words and sentences to throw at us and at each other—each participant a social philosopher—but as language is intrinsically social and there is no social facility in the YOUniverse, there is no hope of connection. Each millennial is "whatever" about the other, and that sort of moral callousness is not personal and private but culturally systemic, a pandemic among the young.

All this is prologue or a stage setting; call it the moral surround, of Tarantino's film *Inglourious Basterds* that I find—with a certain powerful reservation I save until the end—morally honest, candid, and refreshing considering that surround. I do not say it takes a moral stand but rather repeatedly, in scene after scene, opens what transpires to a moral review yet unresolved instead of immediately closing it down. There is no pretense that we were a culture that had a commonly shared moral sense or one that was not a front for our moral callousness. Our deeply divided moral views as well as a moral apathy are not concealed. I do not argue that Tarantino is a thoughtful moralist or any sort of moralist at all but only that a great part of his talent as a director is to repeat and reflect what we are rather than at once imposing some ordering or resolving, whether it be moral or philosophical or psychological or political. This restraint or perhaps naïveté is also refreshing in our age of spin and sputter, blog and Twitter.

Colonel Hans Landa, the Jew hunter, is as ingratiating a devil as Walter Huston's Nick Beal was in *The Devil and Daniel Webster,* more appealing, more human than Conrad Veidt as Colonel Strasser in *Casablanca,* less odious than Ralph Fiennes as the Nazi Commandant in *Schindler's List.* As he drinks another glass of fresh milk he so clearly relishes, we expect such neighborly warmth to explode into blood. And it does. This is a stock scene, a classic re-enactment, but it possesses a spellbinding freshness. The audience has grown used to digital/graphic novel narrative timing, and this is classic analogue. Tarantino is a master of "shooting and editing . . . with classical rigor," of narrative unfolding that is slow and paced and yet always ahead of the viewer's expectations. In our postmodern world where films can no longer give the feel of direct experience but seem always to be sampling and quoting this is no mean feat. Although Tarantino is referred to as "a famously derivative filmmaker" and one would think his work illustrates Umberto Eco's announcement that in our postmodern world we can no longer say "I love you" but only "I love you the way a Barbara Cartland character loves" (*Reflections on "The Name of the Rose"* [London: Martin Secker & Warburg, 1985]), there is no we've-already-been-here-and-this-is-imitation quality to Tarantino's narrating. Tarantino's characters sample the film's past but manage not to leave us with a sense of déjà vu. *Duplicity,* another 2009 film, cannot escape certain staleness. We are removed, watching a film trying hard to be reality and not a film. This is a huckster, guy-and-gal rivalry, but it's pale compared to Hepburn and Tracy sparring, or Cary Grant and Rosalind Russell. George Clooney does Cary Grant in *Intolerable Cruelty,* but it remains within a "this is the way Cary Grant would do it" box. Tom Hanks and Meg Ryan, who redo Cary Grant and Deborah Kerr in *An Affair to Remember,* are literally in the shadow of that movie, sucking its blood to sustain our interest in romance redone. We have escaped to computerized hijinks and animation to avoid this. Tarantino does not.

The closer we are to what we feel is real and the further we are from what we think is reel, the greater the impact upon us. In this first scene, Colonel Landa explains his mission, his dedication to his mission, his understanding of the rat-like psychology of those he pursues, the choice the French farmer has to make in order to save his family. He then exterminates the Jews hiding under the floorboards but allows one of them to escape. We do not know whether he honors the promise he has made to the farmer to spare his family. This "refusal to show us how events play out comes across as sheer negligence, or indifference," the reviewer writes (David Denby, "American in Paris," *The New Yorker,* August 24, 2009). Moral callousness at work. But consider how Tarantino has worked our fascination for the evil Colonel Landa against us, how our complicity in his rationality (I say this because we, like the farmer, acquiesce to each point of Colonel Landa's discourse) weakens the same rationality we would use against him.

Follow the rationality interest a bit further to the scene when some of the American Jewish Nazi hunters, under the command of Aldo the Apache, join with a British intelligence officer at a meeting with a German actress who is a spy working for the Allies. An SS officer unexpectedly joins them and the tension at the table is palatable. Tarantino unfolds it steadily, always ahead of us, alternating between a pedestrian, everyday slowness and sudden nervous-making escalation. We are held on the precipice of violence but don't know when or how; and, meanwhile, typical of Tarantino, we attend a discourse on nothing less than how a really intelligent mind works as the SS officer pursues through a series of questions an identity pasted on his forehead but unknown to him. "King Kong." His mind moves so deftly as he gathers more and more information and slowly puts together the puzzle that we are awed. I mean we are aware that this SS officer who first approaches the spies with some doubt as to whether one of them is German or pretending to be German will very soon know that everyone at the table is a spy. His mind is too probing and too good at detecting. He is altogether too clever for these spies. And yet, he is the evil SS. Once again, it is clear that reason sides with the enemy as well as with ourselves, and perhaps, is more deftly used by the Nazis than the American Jewish Nazi hunters. Which side, the good or the bad, reasons its way to the correct moral stand?

When Colonel Landa also unexpectedly appears at the premier of Goebbels's film, he also confronts American Jewish Nazi hunters pretending to be Italian filmmakers. But Landa speaks a fluent Italian while Aldo the Apache and his cohorts pronounce their own names differently each time Landa asks them to repeat what they have said. So we have witnessed Landa speaking fluent English, French, and Italian as well as his own German. What do we note regarding the American Jewish Nazi hunters? The "Bear Jew" comes out of a cave and smashes with a baseball bat the head of a German soldier who dies, quite clearly, quite bravely, regardless of how evil he may be as a German soldier. Aldo the Apache cuts a swastika on Landa's head at the end of the film and declares it his masterpiece.

What is the opening to moral review here? I think that the American Jewish Nazi hunters are Barbarians of the Good, by which I mean that everything is morally permitted—stupidity, ignorance, savagery (Aldo the Apache sticks his finger in the German actress's bullet hole to get the truth out of her)—because goodness can never commit an evil in its battle with evil. You can take this attitude right up to Defense Secretary Rumsfeld and Vice President Cheney's advocacy of torture at Gitmo: we're the good guys; we can't do anything wrong. If we have reasoned our way to this view, then perhaps we have reasoned as Colonel Landa and the SS officer reason. If we come to this view on purely moral grounds, then we fail to apply the same moral evaluative criteria to ourselves, which means our moral base is no more than our own self-interest and the preservation of our own order of things with the help of the needed moral justification, the needed moral front, and the needed moral alibi. The need, in short.

Consider further how Colonel Landa's last-second choice to spare the fleeing girl and his pleasure in asserting his own freedom to choose, mimics what we all take to be the sign of our humanity: our freedom to choose. By not choosing to show what happens to the farmer and his family, we are left with a Colonel Landa whose evil has not the certainty that, say, for instance, George W. Bush conferred immediately upon bin Laden. No doubt our American cultural surround at this first decade of the twenty-first century requires, in the way an addict needs heroin, its evil tightly and firmly packaged without any what ifs, messy preemptive challenges, or moral reviews such as I am making here. We have progressed far indeed from the confounding rewriting of Milton's *Paradise Lost* that Blake presented in his prophecy *Milton* wherein Satan fascinates us with his energy and intent while surrounded by a pale, inert, and unimaginative goodness.

Now let me say at once that I do not think the moral opening here is to any Nietzschean or Blakean or relativist notion of evil. The opening is simpler and more easily observed. Our entrepreneurial drive to innovate the new and drive the old into obsolescence, to compete vigorously and creatively destroy our competition, to overthrow the opposition presented by tradition, religious and ethnic identity, and imagined community, and allow market values to rule in their place, to connect a rational choice to self-interest in every domain—all this smacks of Satanic energy and purpose, of, in fact, a Nazi-like credo to dominate.

Whether we are all Nazis now or whether we are Barbarians of Goodness who escape moral condemnation is a dilemma that presents the ultimate opening to a moral review that I believe Tarantino's film makes.

But he also, I believe, pre-empts such a review by converting an historical moment to a Tarantino blood farce. And the historical moment is one that has defined moral evil in the twentieth century. This muddling and degradation of a moral model is not refreshing.

Although we seem not to be able to summon any rational ethics upon which our moral notions are based, at least not one that is both universal and universally accepted, we do construct a moral sense, a moral compass, if you will, based on the case, or our historical experience. There's a transcultural recognition here, for instance, that genocide is a moral evil, though depending upon your cultural position—whether your are Native American, Armenian, Turkish, Palestinian, Jewish, German, African and so on—you may deny the event or reassign the villainy. Husbands beating wives and restricting their public appearances, child abuse and pornography, slavery and terrorism are some instances of clear-cut moral models. Women seeking abortions, states executing the condemned, corporations polluting the planet for profit, health-insurance companies denying legitimate claims, corporate executives raining down huge bonuses on each other while accepting taxpayer bailout money, the selling of automatic weapons, lobbyist control of Congress are, however, examples of much-argued cases and therefore the moral compass swings wildly. Although many would like to place the Nazi's systematic extermination of Jews as an unarguable instance of moral evil, we have witnessed both a questioning and a denial of the event itself. We have 'rational' arguments presented that interpret history not conclusively but persuasively enough to generate debate, to muddy the clarity of a moral position. This has been an effective strategy in our postmodern climate where reason is under suspicion and history itself collapses into a narrative told from a certain perspective. I am thinking of the Intelligent Design/Darwinian theory debate as well as the global warming: true or false debate. I am also thinking as well of the questioning of the civil rights movement as having an encouraging or deleterious effect on blacks, or, more recently, whether a president who wants to improve health care is really looking to put your grandmother and grandfather to death.

Inglourious Basterds affects the power of the Holocaust as a clear case of moral evil not by such tactically summoned arguments or wild irrationalism but by fantasizing a revenge drama that is itself, as I have shown, full of moral ambiguities. The Holocaust does not have the cast of Barbarians of the Good, Nazi super-intellects, and, most surely, the clear and satisfying closure of Tarantino's film. How deeply is evil defined by that very failure of the Jews to do no more than fall victim to the butchery of the Nazis? If we learn what moral good and evil are by what we ourselves have done, then the absolutely stunned and passive innocence of the Jews in the face of brutal and irrational attack is at the heart of the lesson, of the moral meaning. Whether or not present-day Jews live in a dream of revenge, retribution, and retaliation and would therefore find themselves drawn to Tarantino's on-screen revenge is yet another matter for moral review. It is a matter that has nothing to do with Tarantino's positioning of the Holocaust in a violently vengeful screenscape, a positioning that seems to not only resolve and cleanse what historically remains an open wound but rob the Holocaust of what I call its historical "cold-file" status. It is a tragedy whose tragic ending lingers and does not end.

Much effort has been made in film to maintain this lingering shadow of the Holocaust and Tarantino's film opens on the heels of such a film, *Defiance*, a 'true story' of Belorussian Jews who resisted the Nazis. This is a film that reawakens memory whereas Tarantino's film risks canceling that memory, a great risk when one considers the perilous state of historical memory in our "that was so five seconds ago" new millennium. When a startling clear case of moral evil remains on our historical register, we are as close to knowing and developing our moral sense as we humans can be. What David Denby calls Tarantino's "mucking about with a tragic moment of history," I define then as a muddling of that moral sense by translating historical tragedy into pulp fiction.

Jeffrey Goldberg in an *Atlantic* article "Hollywood's Jewish Avenger" (http://www.theatlantic.com/magazine/archive/2009/09/hollywoods-jewish-avenger/307619/.) finds Tarantino's "first movie to reference real historical events . . . disconcerting." Perhaps we can see this confusing and collapsing-into-fantasy script of the moral impact of a historical event as yet another opening to a moral review: The collapse of history itself into a twittering moment where only the present moment is sacred may eventually leave us without anything to which a moral compass can point.

But if we are comfortable in our role as Barbarians of the Good, perhaps this will not matter. I find myself morally opposed to this possibility.

Notes

1. "Go to *Citizen Kane* to Find Twentieth-Century Modernism: On the Edge of Postmodernity," in *A Primer to Postmodernity* (Oxford: Blackwell, 1997), 47–61.

2. "The Deep Morals of *Inglourious Basterds*," *Senses of Cinema*, September 2009. The essay was also translated into Portuguese and included in the Quentin Tarantino Retrospective Catalogue of the Centro Cultural Banco do Brasil, Quentin Tarantino Film Festival in Rio, http://www.bb.com.br/docs/pub/inst/dwn/tarantino.pdf.

Chapter Six

At the Theory Carnival

I was drawn to the boundary-free adventures of literary theory that in time became just theory, not simply a surrogate for what American analytical philosophy had given up, because I was attracted to its ventures into linguistics, semiotics, literature, politics, history, science, psychology, and popular culture. What discipline was this? Where was the department? For someone long ago released from both, I saw literary theory as an imaginative campaign into a postmodern world it was helping create. In response to a comment made by J. Hillis Miller regarding the need for a kind of interconnecting of all the various theory voices, I set to find that imaginative thread. I found it in the work of Mikhail Bakhtin and his concepts of dialogism and heteroglossia.

Bakhtin's vision was to me like a Blakean redemption of a world fallen into the single vision of Newton's sleep by imagination, not an apocalyptic but a literary imagination itself. "I imagine the whole," Bakhtin writes, "to be something like an immense novel, multi-generic, multi-styled, mercilessly critical, soberly mocking, reflecting in all its fullness the heteroglossia and multiple voices of a given culture, people and epoch" ("From the Prehistory of Novelistic Discourse" in *The Dialogic Imagination* [Austin: University of Texas Press, 1981], 60)). The universe is Borges's library:

> The universe (which others call the Library) is composed of an indefinite and perhaps infinite number of hexagonal galleries, with vast air shafts between, surrounded by very low railings. From any of the hexagons one can see, interminably, the upper and lower floors. The distribution of the galleries is invariable. ("Library of Babel," in *Collected Fictions* [New York: Penguin, 1994])

Through Bakhtin, I connected literary theory with literary worlds, each depending upon the other to reveal the world in full imaginative form. "Literature expands theory and theory in turn enables us to hear more of what has been unheard in literature" (Joseph Natoli, "Tracing the Beginning through Past Theory Voices," in *Tracing Literary Theory* [Urbana: University of Illinois Press, 1987], 23). And I had already come to the belief that literary worlds could disclose and represent what previously was inconceivable to us. The project of theory then was yet another revelation of dark affinities and dark imaginaries that blocked one being able to see interminably.

Bakhtin's notion of a carnival of voices described in his work on Rabelais was transferred in *Tracing* to a "theory carnival," disparate voices interacting though not dissolving one into the other or submitting to resolution within one Master Voice. These were the narrating voices in a postmodern world, each taking up issues that had been ignored, preemptively resolved, denied and negated, uninterrogated, and marked absent. Attempts at deconstructing truisms and illusions of a fallen world are moral attempts, the action of politics. "The good of man must be the end of the science of politics," Aristotle affirms in *The Nicomachean Ethics*. In time, I would turn more and more to a direct confrontation with politics, employing a cultural critique based on postmodern theory that I had described in the last chapter of *A Primer to Postmodernity*. I would in time conjoin a Blakean politics and prophecies against empire, literary world's capacity to revolutionize the imagination, and literary theory's extension of political performance beyond the borders of politics per se. But the political direction is already apparent in the theory volumes:

> Natoli perceives theory politically, either emancipating or imprisoning, and his anthologies as liberating. Throughout his introduction in *Tracing*, he contrasts Stalinist monologism to Bakhtin's dialogism, in affirming the "continual counterpoint, counter harmony provided by each voice," since both theory and literature "are composed of voices" that cannot be "sounded in monologue." Heteroglossia and carnival, to remain with Natoli's Bakhtinian terms, produce not chaos but are "the ground" from which meanings are explored. (James R. Bennett, *Style*, Spring 1990)

But Derrida's deconstruction, although then and increasingly now considered a "dark imaginary" of an outlier mind, underwrites the give-and-take of dialogism by undermining the modernist dialectic, the progression toward expanding universal truth.

Preface to *Tracing Literary Theory*[1]

Literary theory emerges from two conditions or modes at the heart of Mikhail Bakhtin's theorizing: heteroglossia and dialogism. Heteroglossia describes a basic condition governing the operation of meaning in any utterance. At any given time, in any given place, there will be a set of conditions—social, historical, meteorological, physiological—that will insure that a word uttered in that place and at that time will have a meaning different than it would have under any other conditions; all utterances are heteroglot in that they are functions of a matrix of forces practically impossible to recoup, and therefore impossible to resolve.

A world dominated by heteroglossia expresses itself in the epistemological mode of dialogism. "Everything means, is understood, as a part of a greater whole—there is a constant interaction between meanings, all of which have the potential of conditioning others" (Michael Holquist, "Glossary," in M. Bakhtin, *The Dialogic Imagination*, 428). This dialogic heteroglossia creates a universe of voices or perspectives with which we interweave our own voice, our word with the alien word. Theory is therefore in a state of being 'always already,' so that to enter it is really to be already into it and therefore beginnings have a suspect validity. To achieve an ending, a sense of closure, is an equally suspect task. And in the very midst of saying something about theory, we are equally in the midst of a still-operant theorizing. Thus, theory itself inevitably discloses a fissure, an opening in any attempt to create a smooth, polished narrative surface for theory, one with an unproblematic origin, middle, and ending.

....

Perhaps our fascination at this moment for critical theory is also a fascination that threatens us. It chokes us but at the same time fascinates us, draws us further and further into it. But it is part and parcel of this fascination of which we are dangerously filled to the brim to yet remain self-reflexive, to remain scrupulously observant within the carnival while yet adding our own voices to it.

....

This collection forms a first-order narrative—a narrative that, according to Jean-François Lyotard, gives up all claim to a metanarrative or higher order of knowledge—of contemporary literary theory in its interrelationship with other discourses, discourses which have interpenetrated literature and established a dialogue with it. The "tracing" of this body thus involves a number of narratives, none of which eschews facts or meaning. Jane Tompkins has pointed out "facts and meanings have not disappeared with the advent of poststructuralism, it is just that we no longer regard them as absolute but as dependent upon the interpretative codes that fill our consciousness" ("Graff Against Himself," *Modern Language Notes* 96 [1981]: 1095). And John Searle has argued that we do indeed proceed in the absence of firm metaphysical foundations. Especially in the case of this present historical survey of theory, we proceed in the absence of firm external points of reference in both history and source. "The only foundation," Searle writes, "that language has or needs is that people are biologically, psychologically, and socially constituted so that they succeed in using it to state truths, to give and obey orders, to express their feelings and attitudes, to thank, apologize, warn, congratulate" ("The World Turned Upside Down," *New York Review of Books* October 27, 1983, 78).

Thus, the reader's consideration of these first-order narratives inevitably involves the kind of rational critique—the power of reflective understanding which Jürgen Habermas argues for—a critique that the intertextuality of the essays demands. But it also inevitably involves an attending to each essay with a certain pragmatism, a pragmatism "where knowledge is conceived as the ongoing process of reflective adjustment between various cultural needs and interests" (Christopher Norris, *The Contest of Faculties* [London: Methuen, 1985], 148).

Deconstruction stands at the pinnacle of this collection, overshadowing and tempering a move toward both metanarrative and theory-as-firstorder narrative. Deconstruction, in the words of Christopher Norris, "is most importantly a textual activity that works to undermine the kinds of consoling self-image given back by a dominant cultural tradition" (165). It can operate, in short, against a pragmatic reading. But it is also undeniably a "handy ruse for dismantling the truth-claims of philosophers from Plato to Heidegger"—for dismantling, in short, metanarratives which privilege a "power of reflective understanding" (165).

Within the intertextual domain of these essays, deconstruction's voice modulates the reader's move toward metanarrative *and* toward theory-as-narrative. The Derridean sense of "trace" also modulates the traditional voice of historical survey, as there is in each of these essays a referring back to what is absent—a trace of what has come before in the chain of signification—as well as a referring forward to what is also absent— a trace of what ensues, of the future. There is a tendency to erase the present or, in an often-used word, to make it "indeterminate." The essays, then, are divided by past and future yet in themselves are not privileged constructions in the chain of signification that is literary theory. Thus by tracing literary theory we are not so much deconstructing that effort but placing it within the unprivileged ranks of rhetorical temporality. To some extent, this is commensurate with Terry Eagleton's view of rhetorical discourse and the structural implications involved. These essays attempt, similarly, to see how the interrelationship of different discourses has been structured and organized and, variously, to examine such effects.

However, the essential function here is dialogic—grounded in the openings of the theory body—and not structural—grounded in the regular surface of binary opposition. Language itself is the site of this dialogized heteroglossia. "The word, directed toward its object, enters a dialogically agitated and tension filled environment of alien words, value judgments and accents, weaves in and out of complex interrelationships, merges with some, recoils from others, intersects with yet a third group" (Bakhtin, *The Dialogic Imagination*, 276).

Our words make up a carnivalization of critical discourse, one which balances a continual dialogizing of one's own word and the alien word, a continual effort to reveal "ever new ways to mean" and discourse's "power to mean in real ideological life." Our words are always already laden with a pluralism of contending discourses, a heteroglossia, which seeks to reveal meaning "with dialogic vigor and a deeper penetration into discourse itself." Just as our own personal ideological development is "an intense struggle within us for hegemony among various available verbal and ideological points of view, approaches, directions and values," so too does each contributor in this collection seek to overcome heteroglossia, seek to achieve "a real although relative unity."

A reader's desire for ideological hegemony, for unity, parallels that of each contributor, but in the situation of each such closure is denied, is subverted by a carnivalesque interpenetration of voices. The awareness of a continual interplay of intertextuality ultimately exposes—traces—the lineaments of the theory body. Every text, according to Julia Kristeva, forms a mosaic of quotations, every text involves assimilation and alteration of another text. Because every "text echoes another text unto infinity, weaving the fabric of culture itself" (Jeanine Parisier Plottel, "Introduction" to *Intertextuality* [New York: New York Literary Forum, 1978], xv), a text of culture inevitably constrained by language, no one text has a "pure" being, in Bakhtin's terms, a voice that does not already partake, interact, emerge from other voices. In Derridean terms, each text—each essay, for instance, in this collection—holds a trace of another text, another essay. Derrida's notion of *différance*—of deferment (tying text to text, past and future texts) and difference (tying the existence of one text to its distinction from another text)—renders any text itself a trace of another text, a trace of a presence and absence only perceived within a never-ending chain of texts, of signifiers, of language.

Each essay here then serves as a context for every other essay, thus placing the 'meaning' one derives from any one essay within a dynamic back-and-forth reading of the whole, a reading in which similarities and identities may give way to differences, and differences may collapse into identities. What is present in any one essay is present in terms of its interpenetrations with what is absent in itself and in other essays; what is absent in any one essay emerges from a context of what is present in itself and in other essays. Presence and absence alter within the same essay as the force of intertextuality recreates both after the fact, so that the last essay here, on semiotics, may serve as the precursor to a reading of the first essay, on structuralism, and reveal what was always present but not perceived, what was always absent but not perceived. Just as the context of one essay serves as a frame for the reading of another essay, and vice-versa, so too does the reader, each reader of this collection, inevitably read through his or her own lens so that the reader's own history is a text which interpenetrates the texts of these essays. Within this wide-ranging, shifting universe of intertextuality, the reader attempts to shape interpretation, meaning, understanding, even against the force of a polyphony of voices interpenetrating the reader and the force of an inescapable *différance*. Therefore both presence and absence in any one essay are modulated, strung out in an intertextual fashion over the entire collection and begin to wiggle the reader toward a dilemma in reading, a dilemma with which the substance of the collection is engaged.

This intertextuality of voices is not grounded here in this prefactory point of origin, but the preface is itself somewhere in the interweaving, and intertextuality itself becomes subject to intertextuality.

....

The theory carnival then is loud with many voices, but each voice, each chapter, in this collection is tempted, if you will, by monologism. Each tracing promises the closure which all monologism promises, its own monologism ultimately subverted by the heteroglossia of the collection as a carnival whole. Tracing does not circumscribe but leaves openings; the past interpenetrates both the present and the future. Time itself—a continuity of past, present, and future, so necessary to the discursive tracing of each theory voice—is subverted by a carnivalesque interpenetration. Thus, both the Derridean sense of absence and the Bakhtinian sense of opening modulate through their own voices the traditional voice of historical survey. The smooth, polished plane of linear time becomes the irregularity of temporal hills and valleys, of the inside of the past and the outside of the future, fashioning the surface plane of the present. A tracing in the present is thus an interpenetration of the past, an exchange leading to a reorientation.

Preface to *Literary Theory's Future(s)*[2]

Theory as it exists now in the United States, within academe, awaits an uncertain future. It sits unobserved in a classroom within a context that is centered in a reality and that promotes a well-made experiencing of that reality, which Derrida in his Cornell address defines as a context of modern technoscience "built both on the principle of reason and what remains hidden in that principle" (Jacques Derrida, "The Principle of Reason: The University in the Eyes of Its Pupils," *Diacritics* 13 [Fall 1983]: 10).

Unless we can come within the sight of "humanistic education" *without being transformed into an agreement with it*, I doubt we'll get a hearing for any interrogation of "theoretical energies that promote the long-repressed analysis of *class struggle* as it approaches, and in extremely guarded or covert form circulates through, humanistic education" (Jim Merod, *The Political Responsibility of the Critic* [Ithaca: Cornell University Press, 1987], 14).

"There is a double gesture here," Derrida said at his Cornell lecture, "a double postulation: to ensure professional competence and the most serious tradition of the university even while going as far as possible, theoretically and practically, in the most directly underground thinking about the abyss beneath the university. Committed to the pursuit of a privileged experiencing of reality, academe cannot sponsor theory's difference, its transgression of academe's foundational identity. Committed to interrogating the reality of experiences, theory pursues an interrogation of our present academe's own special experiencing of reality. Derrida asserts that this sort of interrogation "appears unsuitable and thus unbearable to certain university professionals in every country who join ranks to foreclose or censure it by all available means" (Derrida, "The Principle of Reason," 17). Not only does a certain precariousness therefore result from the 'social analysis,' the brand of 'eying' that we bring to a consideration of the future of theory or cultural critique, but a certain precariousness in making such a social analysis involves the reality of the ways we have already realized our experiencing of what now comes under our eying. "If the police is always waiting in the wings," Derrida writes, "it is because conventions are by essence violable and precarious, *in themselves* and by the fictionality that constitutes them, even before there has been any overt transgression, in the 'first sense' of *to pretend*" (Jacques Derrida, "Limited Inc abc," *Glyph 2* [Baltimore: Johns Hopkins, 1977], 250).

Literary theory did not begin in the streets, nor is it likely ever to work up a public guise. Its move toward cultural critique goes on within academe. It is doubtless difficult for a cultural critique to retreat from the real world of hardball politics and entrepreneurial power, to back off and publish from a tenured spot for an academic coterie. The lack of worldliness threatens to enervate any self-respecting cultural critic. This sort of reaction buys into a scene without seeming to upset the hidden dualisms it contains: world versus academe, theory versus social practice—in short, the academic myth exploded by Lentricchia. What is seen as a retreat behind the walls of academe is a retreat underwritten by the realizing of such conflicts. It is an especially pernicious realizing, since it sets many of us off in pursuit of a real role within our culture and causes us to think of critique and life within academe as a retreat or a dead end.

Perhaps, for those who foresee that one day we all should be "registering for rooms in the motel of the state," this present dangling of academe is hard to live with. While the conservative Counter-Reformation yearns for *illo tempore* and despises those who are roadblocks to such a return, Marxist-socialists champ at the bit that keeps them powerless, incapable of realizing a future amalgam of power and people. I lean more toward accepting the world in its parts, with no template in hand for past or future unity.

Notes

1. *Tracing Literary Theory*, ed. Joseph Natoli (Urbana, Il: University of Illinois Press, 1987), 3–27 passim.

2. *Literary Theory's Future(s)*, ed. Joseph Natoli (Urbana: University of Illinois Press, 1989), 13–14.

Chapter Seven

Into the American Mass Psyche
of the Nineties

Hauntings: Popular Film and American Culture 1990–1992, Speeding to the Millennium: Film and Culture 1993–1995, Postmodern Journeys: Film and Culture 1996–1998, and *Memory's Orbit: Film and Culture 1999–2000* were published in the SUNY Press series "Postmodern Culture," which I edited from 1991 to 2009. We launched the series with Ray Federman's *Critifiction* and went on to publish forty-nine books that crossed disciplinary boundaries as well as sacred notions of popular and academic, fiction and non-fiction, narrative and argument, values and facts, stories and truth stories. We invited "submissions of short book manuscripts that present a postmodern cross-cutting of contemporary headlines and academic discourses from art and literature to politics and history, sociology and science to women's studies, from computer studies to cultural studies." We asked prospective contributors to "detour us off modernity's . . . Superhighway to Truth and onto postmodernism's 'forking paths' crisscrossing" and to develop a conversation "about a world that has overspilled its modernist framing" by linking "our present ungraspable 'balkanization' of all thoughts and events with the means to narrate and then re-narrate them." Style should "be readable across multiple narratives and culturally relative rather than foundational."

I offered *Hauntings* as an example of what we were seeking.

Hauntings: Popular Film and American Culture

Hauntings: Popular Film and American Culture demonstrated a kind of cultural critique driven first by postmodern theory's leveling of high and low culture, truth and truth stories, facts and values, eternal verities and everyday life, reasons and alibis. If we lived in stories that we, as a society and culture created over time, popular culture was doubtlessly a significant story-making enterprise.

A second postmodern assumption was that we lived within a cultural imaginary comprised of a hierarchy of our imaginative renderings of reality. If the world was filtered to us through what we said about it, we inevitably lived in a space, a zone between what the world was, independent of our consciousness and our narrations of this. That was a space wrought by the imagination. The 'things' themselves did not speak. We spoke for them, just as every religion speaks for deity, although claiming their words are divine. Whether our representations correspond directly to the world as it is divided from our consciousness and to what degree— could not be established to everyone's satisfaction.

The examples of universally accepted scientific accounts, or laws that science does not expect to change, are few. Chaos theory has set much of classical physics in a retractable position. We are enfolded within the fabrications of our own consciousness, always within the web of our own intentions, the personal ensnared within the social cultural. The periodic table of the elements and DNA, for example, establish indisputable evidence, but all enter the human life-world where they are narrated within human intentions. Johnny Cochran narrated hard DNA evidence toward O.J. Simpson's release, and, most memorably, Colin Powell presented hard evidence that Iraq had weapons of mass destruction. Undoubtedly, water is two parts hydrogen and one part oxygen, but whether or not human caused global warming is causing the oceans to rise is a hot debate.

Cyberspace not only is a visible screening of our imaginaries but increases the depth and breadth of this zone of human buffering of the world. Wandering in the images of social media is not a wandering in the world directly but in a designed space. Cell-phone and computer technology allow millions of opinions to bloom, fracturing the cultural imaginary with endless stories that take us further and further from things, as they are free of our consciousness. Cyberspace then is the greatest reality buffering or mediating zone the world has ever seen. Although humans can never be free of their mediating perspective of the world, it is clear that in our cyberspace age we erect an image of the world, more chaotic and conflicting than the vitriolic combat of a real-world congress, a phenomenal world that stands in place of the world. The hardware, so to speak, actualizes a realm of mediation that is as available as our cars and is at once a zone where "ignorant armies clash by night" and a zone also we can narrow to the breadth and depth of our own personal choices.

In this cyberspace realm, we are conscious and intend within a second configuration of our imaginaries. In Blakean terms, we have fallen into a construction of a fallen world, doubly fallen. Our imaginaries are dark because we are further from the light of true perception. Our imagination has collapsed into the dreams of a fallen world. Our reason, emotions, senses, and imagination have made dark affiliations here.

Hauntings was my expression of this state of affairs. I moved from postmodern theory to headline events and everyday life to popular culture in order to trace our fallen imaginary. I found these in the dark measurements of a Jeffrey Dahmer and a fictional Hannibal Lector, South Central L.A. Riots, the moral insensibility of the young shown in the film *The River's Edge*, the Rodney King beating and trials, the "greed is good" ethos of Gordon Gekko in *Wall Street*, the difficulties of doing the right thing, or the tragedy enacted by the unforgiving. We are both haunted by what Blake would say we have lost and haunted by all that we have done and continue to do to remain lost.

"What were you haunted by?" a no-nonsense, laconic Midwesterner asked me when the book first came out. By my own past. What was I taking into the 1990s with me? What baggage, what issues did the 1990s inherit? And since I held that the legacy of the previous decade was a darkening legacy, I felt that the 1990s would be haunted by the 1980s, just as the eighties were haunted by Vietnam, Watergate, and, for an emerging neoliberal movement, the counterculture. Growing up in the fifties in Brooklyn and spending my high-school years in Greenwich Village, I came to know how the "Howl" of Allen Ginsberg and the on-the-road escapes of Jack Kerouac were angry and desperate responses to a post-WWII world. That world had armored itself in a gray-flannel-suit business ethos that was absurdist in the light of what two world wars had revealed of both Western civilization and human nature. Just as the fifties came to a boil in the countercultural sixties, I foresaw a turbulent nineties because of the destructive dismantling of a middle-class democracy in the eighties by Reagan and Thatcher. And the failure to address this has led to plutarchy in the new millennium.

The 1980s were a psychic retreat from Vietnam, a retreat turned into an advance once the presidency, with the help of the Congress, put all the gathered fruits of our two-hundred-year-old democracy at the disposal of the Vietnam profiteers. The humiliation of that retreat as well as memories of profits made came to life after 9/11 and propelled the United States into a precipitous and wrongheaded response that triggered future catastrophe, similar to what followed the ill-conceived treatment of Germany after WWI. There was one lesson learned from Vietnam that was applied to the wars in Afghanistan and Iraq. And that lesson was to defuse protest at home by creating a volunteer army. Some of the young could continue on their career paths while others, without hope of a career, would be recruitable.

While one-third of my working-class Bensonhurst neighborhood buddies were destroyed one way or another by Vietnam—as were one-third of the working-class youth of every American neighborhood—the elite entrepreneurs with every variety of wartime contract were starting Swiss bank accounts until the investment climate of the United States improved.

And improve it, Reagan did—for the top 1 percent of the population. Trickle down went as far down as 1 percent paying fees, commissions, bonuses, retainers, stock options to brokers, lawyers, financial consultants, bankers, accountants, agents, managers, doctors, shrinks, architects, interior designers, and others in the professional classes.

I was haunted by that; we were all haunted by that. However, when the Soviet Union collapsed in 1989, most Americans were looking forward to the beginning of something new, something beyond the Cold War. It was a negative thing.

My attention was drawn to the murder of Yusef Hawkins in my old neighborhood in Brooklyn. I watched the Reverend Al Sharpton march through Bensonhurst, determined to show the whole world how racist this neighborhood was. My old neighborhood, the place I had been brought up. The past had a hold on me. And as we all sat and watched the Rodney King beating, our American racist past showed it still had a hold on us.

At the outset, I was haunted; the next three years only justified that feeling.

I went to the movies to see our cultural fears played out; everyone else was there for the entertainment. They could do the popcorn-and-Coke-we're-at-the-movies thing and then go home and get back to reality. My mind was crisscrossing headlines, digging up the past, running by a film's own defenses, finding the fear at the heart of everything. The surround of *Hauntings* was notable:

Eros and Thanatos were now brought closer together by AIDS so where there had been love, death's head now stood over everyone's right shoulder, just as Carlos Castaneda had affirmed.

Hannibal Lecter's real world counterpart, Jeffrey Dahmer, was a hell of a lot scarier than the urbane Lecter.

The moral insensibility of the young in *The River's Edge* was just a premonition of what was to come in this decade.

The Wall Street message that "greed is good" and its adoption right alongside the messages of the New Testament's beatitudes was a mind-boggling feat of multi-something or other.

The very fact that our national conscience and all the compassion Bush the Second would claim for Neoliberals had also dwindled to cold unconcern for losers—not fellow Americans or fellow human beings or fellow citizens, just losers—was like a solar eclipse.

Saddam's invasion of Kuwait in 1990, the Persian Gulf War in 1991 (a war that left a residue that would continue to haunt the 1990s), and the South Central Los Angeles riot and revolt in 1992 haunted the American cultural imaginary.

I ended *Hauntings* with Bill Clinton's election in 1992. For me his election meant that a man who understood we were in a postmodern world and who would therefore act within the new premises of that world was in the White House. While George Bush the First knew clearly that he was not to do anything as president that would hamper return on investment, Clinton was a mess of utopian intentions, a too-flexible conscience, an erratic hardball strategist, a truly divided man filled with his own childhood hauntings, hauntings that were eventually to lead to an impeachment trial. And yet he was a man of his times, a man who clearly represented the deep division in American culture. The United States was then and continues to be a country divided between an urgency to let the market rule and damn the losers, or let us try through governmental adjustments and interventions to correct the abuses of social and economic justice in the wake of market rule. It seemed clear that market rule was not keeping the United States from becoming a plutarchy where rule and power rested in the hands of the haves while the bulk of the population remained disenfranchised have-nots. Clinton went back and forth across this divide; so did every American not deaf to stories other than his own. Clinton attempted a Third Way that required Liberals and Neoliberals to do some leaning toward each other. How little Newt Gingrich's "Contract with America" was to lean toward Liberals, Clinton had not the opportunity to fully grasp in the last years of his administration, tied as he was with impeachment. But the futility of this Third Way came home to President Obama slowly as he began with the jejune optimism of the millennials.

Hunting the Haunted Heart[1]

In *Silence of the Lambs*, Crawford, Clarice Starling's FBI father figure, tells Clarice that she's to visit Hannibal Lecter because he, as a psychopath, may be able to shed some light on the workings of the mind of another psychopath, Buffalo Bill. But in order to keep Lecter from getting inside her mind, she is told to follow procedures and instructions to the letter. She doesn't want Hannibal Lecter inside her mind. That's all the inducement we need to look forward to meeting Lecter, that alien being who has the capacity to get into our heads and who is strangely different than anything we already have in our heads.

Clarice preserves the distance, unlike William Peterson who pursues Lecter in Hannibal's first film appearance, *Manhunter*. Peterson, the detective in that film, is able to enter Lecter's life-world and the visit leaves him haunted. It is not by objective methodology that otherness will be reached but through empathy with the narrative world or frame within which subjectivity is constituted and through which the real is configured. Subjectivity intersects subjectivity. Objectivity blocks off that intersection. But Clarice remains a good modernist detective, finally graduated into the world of investigation and, as such, a preserver of the distance between investigator and investigated.

At the same time, she has clearly not apprenticed under Crawford alone but also under Hannibal the Cannibal. It is his alien otherness that directs her and leads her to her climactic success—killing Buffalo Bill and saving the senator's daughter, the one lamb-victim she is finally able to save. Such a salvation salvages her own childhood self. All lambs, including her, are not necessarily victims to the slaughter, lost when their families are lost, lost when their father is killed. That lost inner child can be redeemed by a vigorous and sustained effort, by moving laterally into the perceptions and affections of otherness. In this way, Clarice brings disparate reality to sense.

But this is not the sense they want to preserve at Cambridge and in Springfield, Oregon. Clarice is guided by Hannibal's sense, the sense of the other, sense other than what we can sense or reach through the sense we already have. Intriguing. Lecter wants Clarice to know that he's out and that he won't harm her because he likes to think that she's also out there. He hasn't taken over her mind. They've intersected. Instead of maintaining the distance between them, instead of keeping him far below in the bowels of the sanitarium, she has gotten into a sort of play with him, a game of quid pro quo. In short, they cross paths.

Easily said "they cross paths." Doesn't knowledge ensue? If identity crosses difference, what new arrangement is made? What is rearranged? Is Lecter a sort of crabwise roamer away from conventional expectations? And how could Clarice roam laterally since she never gives up the path of an investigative, pursuing modernism? They play quid pro quo, a postmodernity truth or dare, through which Lecter leads Clarice away from the main highway of her investigation and onto side roads. And it is through the maze of these side roads that Clarice winds up eventually at Buffalo Bill's door. It takes her a while to realize that that is where she is. Lateral thinking isn't supposed to take you to modernism's destination but it is the postmodern encounter with the other, Lecter, that brings you to the right door. Modernist pursuit signified by Crawford and the FBI on a plane loaded with hi-tech pursuit equipment wind up at the wrong door. They wind up going places their technology can identify. Only tangential thinking takes you to the right door. Otherness, then, is the answer to waste and inefficiency, to entropy?

Lecter doesn't *lead* Clarice onto windward paths because he is himself not positioned either ahead or above her. His position is just tangential to the norm, a path away from the social order we invoke because we haven't the means to identify his precise location. We can't plug him into the equation until we know where he is and we know only where he isn't. Consider the fact that he is brilliant. He has a penetrating mind, gathers, sorts, and responds to lived experience at a phenomenal rate. Is he then an Enlightenment *lumière*? He conducts a course in logic for Clarice. Is he therefore sane? The jury ruled the serial killer Jeffrey Dahmer was sane because his crimes demonstrated all the joys of the scientific method. He could have made major contributions to the Foundationalist Project. Lecter already has contributed to society in a worthwhile way, as a practicing psychiatrist, as *Doctor* Lecter. Perhaps he has written or read scholarly papers in prestigious journals and at prestigious conferences.

Reason, Nietzsche tells us, is a pawn, a strumpet, an instrument in any hands. The desire for unity, coherence, and continuity is a cultural desire. You can summon reason and logic to fulfill it. You can also summon logic and method to fulfill madness, which then give to madness that coherence and so on that is *other* than what society says it desires. Jeffrey Dahmer's means are rigorous and methodical but the ends make our stomachs turn.

The modernist narrative latches on to reason and method. In its twentieth-century form, modernity increasingly distances itself from these as the historical record fills with atrocities and inanities performed within reason's frame. Crawford and the FBI are wary Enlightenment modernists and practicing twentieth-century modernists as they turn to Lecter to give them a perspective on their problem. Multiple perspectives, not only from the conscious, rational mind but from nightmare and the unconscious, are needed if the problem is to be solved. Method turns to madness for help, Clarice to Lecter.

Since Lecter does not share that which makes a modernist a modernist—-not the use of reason but a shared story about integration, solution, social bonds, and mutual alignments, stabilizing class and community structures, shared ideologies and ethics, and so on—he lies outside that story, however dynamic and efficient his mental powers. And since his mythos of reason is other than the mythos of our culture, it is not possible to use reason and method to track him down. For our reason to be seen as reasonable it must always operate within our mythos. The same goes for Lecter—he can't be reasonable the way we can be reasonable. Reason is denied that outside-our-mythos role that would enable it to roam free, scrutinize Lecter, and come back and give us a report. What it does is quite different: it stays home, scrutinizes Lecter from a distance, and gives us a home report.

In the game of quid pro quo both sides seem to be probing outward into the other. But the this and that reveal different probing devices and different results. Hannibal feasts on Clarice's mind within feasting rites that never change. If he were able to sidestep through a postmodern garden of forking paths everything that makes him godlike—his command and control, the very fixedness of his gaze outward, penetrating life like a laser beam fixed on one target—-all this would grow shaky as one way of seeing would trouble or parody another.

No, our Hannibal is a brilliant classic realist, his mode of being as stabilized and pinned to one frame of realizing as his physical being is locked deep down in the bowels of the asylum prison behind steel bars and thick glass. He fixes Clarice within a strangle hold of a gaze replenishing his own mythos of order and reason as he feasts through the eye and into the mind. While the biblical Jehovah moved to creation to strike an otherness to his own unity, Hannibal's unity pursues only itself. He is neither shaken nor troubled; he makes absolute, determinate connections with the world. He assumes his representations *are* reality. He feasts without variety; his own identity has a stranglehold on him. That he cannot move sideways, cannot get off the track he is on, is at the heart of his madness.

We see him at film's end pursuing his one way of feasting on what is out there.

....
We can't disassociate Hannibal's mastery from modernism: Lecter has all the gifts modernisms hold as its ideal. He fascinates because he is other than that cultural identity that is waffling. At the same time, he is bigger than life, a fantastic version of the dominance and supremacy over the real that modernity always promised. In the end, Hannibal is an otherness told within the modernist frame, a bright superhero whose lack of conscience and emotion is a sign of being value-free and ideology-neutral. His cinematic presence was haunted first by modernity before it haunted us.

Yet in admiring him at film's end, by rooting for him, by being glad he's still out there, we erode a bit further those firm moral categories, that clear sense of what's civilized and what isn't, what's sane and what isn't, which seem to be our only defense against Hannibal. And Jeffrey Dahmer. And all those who wander from the mythos of reason, sanity, and order we have made our norm. We wind up waffling. Hannibal's absolute, coherent otherness fractures, breaks up into tiny rivulets that wind every which way, crisscrossing endlessly like a flash flood in a dry arroyo, the American mass psyche. On the underside of that publicized smooth surface there are always cracks and fissures. You can see the seams of our real-izing, the stitches that make otherness a Frankenstein monster and expose us always as *Doctor* Frankenstein. Such deep and dark investigation and identification haunts us for sure.

Speeding to the Millennium: Film and Culture 1993–1995

The second book in my coverage of the nineties—"a sort of postmodern social history of this millennial decade"—required a full preface to the reader because it contained a mixture of gonzo-type reportage, a probing into the undecidables of the headlines, a focus on popular box-office movies, an interjection of theorizing, and finally an interjection of vignettes with reoccurring characters that alternates with the non-fiction.

The darkness of this collection is reflected in the chapter titles: "The Abyss of the Postmodern Film Noir," "Nightmares of Depravity," "Looking into the Abyss: Madmen and Fanatics," "American Maniacs: the Romance of Truly Natural Born Killers," "The Abyss as Reservoir: True Romance and Hard Love," "Stranger Murders in Strange Worlds," "The Last Seduction: Commitment Is Murder?," "Asking for and Getting Chaos: the Abyss of Human Sexuality," "Looking in the Abyss of Other's People's Lives," "Ghosts with Resumes/Vampires as Agents of Change."

The O.J. Simpson murder case offered two murders and a trial, both from the pitch blackness of the abyss, the trial appearing as a media circus within a culture mired in money, celebrity, and violence. "If it doesn't fit, you must acquit" was an apt mantra for a trial in which a commonly shared order of reason no longer fit. Jeff Dahmer, the Hannibal Lecter serial killer; Ted Kaczynski, the Unabomber; David Koresh and the Branch Davidians; Timothy McVeigh, the Oklahoma bomber could all be written off as lunatic outliers; but O.J. Simpson, an American sports icon, was on center stage in the American cultural imaginary. Through him, that whole imaginary began to trace its dark affiliations.

The essays were drawn repeatedly to a culture speeding to the abyss while the short stories drew upon the reader's power to sense and imagine that headlong journey. Speeding therefore performed a battle between an apocalyptic imagining and the darker imaginaries and affiliations of our nature. The purpose of the vignettes was to create a dialogic of many characters drawing us back into the richness of a world filled with paradoxes. Imagination remained the only way out of the abyss; but imagination itself could easily be narrowed to fit the dimensions of what Blake would call our own "fallen" perceptions.

Court and Culture: The Days of Our Life with O.J.[2]

One Hundred Days of the O.J. Trial

[T]he O.J. Simpson murder trial has been like a soap opera: it goes on like the flux of daily time itself; it insinuates itself into our daily lives. A great share of the American public has found speaking parts for themselves in this drama or, at very least, found seats in the courtroom and are listening interactively. Why this fascination, this absorption in a trial that has, at the moment I am writing this, gone on for one hundred days and shows no sign of losing its market share? For many, our culture shows no great enlightenment in such a fixation.

The American Survey column of the British journal *The Economist* calls this trial "Lance Ito's circus." Lewis Grossberger in *Mediaweek* reserves a room in Animal House for the trial. Frank Rich in the *New York Times* refers to it as "Judge Ito's all-star vaudeville." It is like a soap opera and not worth serious comment or attention, a serious intellectual tells me. Rupert Murdoch's *Star* and other tabloids will keep up the sensationalism for as long as it will sell papers, but for the serious minded, the enlightened, the sensational is the opium of the people. Geraldo has found a focus for his show. Talk-show hosts such as Geraldo can play into every nuance of the trial, milking it for higher ratings. From its very beginning, for the enlightened, this trial can mean nothing, except perhaps that too many darkened minds can be seduced by glitz.

Now, after one hundred days, the same enlightened observers note that there must be deep problems in our justice system. It has obviously failed to contain, in a lofty and expeditious fashion, a trial for double murder.

I am interested in this trial because we have culturally invested ourselves into it and it into us. And, like a soap opera we get addicted to, this trial could not have drawn us in if we were not in some mysterious ways accommodating. A real exchange is ensuing. Almost the whole country has found speaking parts. And this sort of symbiosis means that the trial will unfold in tune with the daily unfolding of our culture as a whole. What become facts in this trial and what facts become evidence, who testifies and who doesn't, whether the defense puts O.J. on the stand or not, what stories of prosecution and defense will be concocted for the jury, how Judge Ito will temper his rulings and his daily courtroom approach, what rationalities, realties, imaginings, emotions, and fears will be played upon will all be modulated by the daily changes in cultural disposition. But the trial goes on in this way because it is a way our culture enables it to go on. In short, we were a circus before the circus of this trial.

Our culture at this moment is constructing its daily reality in line with not only the Dow Jones, Newt and friends, Bill (Clinton) and friends, Bill (Gates) and friends, Rush and friends, headline contingencies, opinion polls, the weather, the soaps, blockbuster videos, the 1996 presidential campaign, the deaths of Jerry Garcia and Mickey Mantle, tabloid talk replacing Phil Donohue in New York City, Madonna on Letterman, who's on the cover of *Time*—and on and on—but also with this O.J. Simpson murder trial. We can sever ourselves from the web of interconnectedness here by merely choosing to be inattentive to this trial. We can say that we want no part of it. We can choose another channel, another column, another conversation. Then we imagine we are no longer interconnected. We have employed our interstellar Warp Drive and we are now somewhere else.

Good luck out there! Maybe you will run into Archimedes's fulcrum from which you can close the circus down here.

. . . .

The law should succumb to both deductive and inductive approaches—claptrap can be sorted out if one adheres to the rules of evidence, defense and prosecution. On the other side of this clash of arguments lies the truth. All it takes is disinterest on the jury's part, a disinterest that unfortunately must extend to their own lives and the culture they live within. And there must not be only a distance between the subjectivities of the jury and the evidence as presented but that same distance must exist between the trial and the culture. Nobody should have come from anywhere or have been any place or ever heard anything. We need every juror to wipe the slate clean, tabula rasa minds, if we are to avoid a circus.

If we cannot have that, if that cannot be created for us by some authoritarian order of things, if we cannot go back to a time when our culture was not permeated with the haunting belief that we construct the reality that constructs us, then our course seems clear enough. We are going to have to explore what all our cultural constructions mean and how they are valued. We are going to have to accept the fact that regardless of our attitudes and ideologies, our party affiliations and religious commitments, our lives come to meaning and value within our own cultural constructions.

As my intent here is to meditate in a postmodern fashion on what in the headlines, in film and on TV and radio, became staged for our culture as a scene from the abyss, I certainly cannot ignore the center-stage treatment we have given this trial. Every aspect of what many want to reduce to merely a simulated media event, a profiteering venture, connects with the fears and anxieties, haunting nightmares of our own culture.

....

Let's follow the money. If O.J. has enough money to buy a Dream Team defense, a top-of-the-line legal defense version of Bruno Magli dress casuals, then he's probably got a better chance of finding the kind of justice he wants than has a defendant with a court-appointed lawyer. Justice will have to be dispensed in an increasingly lopsided arrangement of privileges in this country. And it will have to do it as if were still blind to such inequities, which is, of course, a bedrock belief of our system of justice. This is a bedrock belief similar to our belief that the superrich can pour fortunes into elections without the outcome affected. A winner in our casino-logic system is entitled to use wealth to buy the best defense possible. Or, hire the right tax attorneys to hold off the IRA. Or, summon enough clout to get a minimum sentencing. Or, crush a parking ticket. Or, defy Anti-Trust, the Security Exchange Commission, the National Labor Relations Board, or the Constitutional Bill of Rights. Or, launder drug money through legitimate businesses. Or, grant favors to lobbyists. And so on. Money should be "free" and "no foul" declared.

The O.J. trial is part of the Monopoly game we never stop playing: its notoriety has become a profit-making business. Justice is all going on in front of the camera, on Court TV for the whole American audience to watch. If it becomes too clear that O.J. will buy his freedom, then our pretenses of objective, unbiased determinations of guilt or innocence will suffer yet another blow. "Money Buys Justice" will go prime time.

....

We are all equal under the law but because we now live within a corporate notion of social justice, some people are more equal than others. Now, because of the televised play-by-play of the O.J. trial, following on the heels of two other money trials—William Kennedy Smith and the Menendez brothers—we have right before our eyes a view of what happens to justice within a society that has abandoned any sense of social justice (concern for others is socialism which died with the Soviet Union) and yet presumes to still dispense justice to individuals.

....

Ultimately, because our coverage of the O.J. trial is simply that—a coverage and not a crisscrossing into the culture—what that event means and how it is to be valued blows with the same winds that sweep the country. Those enjoying a suburban reality frame, a perpetual summer whose only hardship comes in the shape of crab grass (and that is handled by one's lawn service), have little inclination to see the links between the O.J. trial and themselves or American society. In a summer frame, what our culture may be is not shaken for long by what this trial shows us. It remains wedded to an aggressive competitiveness that elevates a few to another level of justice. In other words, life is a garden party some have earned because they have demonstrated and relied upon winning values. The present system of social justice has bestowed their just desserts upon them, so it is obviously a system that works. If the Dream Team manages to get O.J. off, they will have reaffirmed our adversarial system of criminal law: justice goes to those who win in a competitive arena, just as success in life goes to those who win in the market arena.

The summer reality frame picks out the same irksome matters in the trial as they do in their own world. Our justice system is run too much like a liberal governmental agency of endless accommodation and not enough like a business. If every public official connected with the O.J. case had been held to corporate standards of competence and not governmental, bureaucratic ones, this trial would not be taking so long. It is not by accident that the Dream Team has focused on bureaucratic incompetence at the murder scene and in the gathering and testing of evidence. Theirs is an anti-government defense, which currently plays very well throughout the country. And it plays well because it suits the reality frame, the valuing and meaning disbursements of those few who are living their American Dream of having it all their way.

Some will argue that when our system of justice turns into a media event, a tabloid and talk-show carnival, then this becomes symptomatic of the wrong turn America took in the sixties. That counterculture demonized capitalism's winner while rewarding failure. Now this is a cultural connection of the kind that Newt Gingrich has been willing to make. It plays well even among those who were in one way or another enfranchised by a broad cultural revolution begun in the sixties and terminated in the eighties with the ascent of Ronald Reagan. Any act of murder and mayhem is linked to liberalism's soft posture on crime and criminals. Any outbreak of social unrest is attributed to liberalism's ready welfare program that brought up a generation of potential hard-working Americans as social parasites, as irresponsible threats to the rest of us.

Incapable of making any connections other than those that suit the best-off in this country, the salaried majority and the expanding underclass drift in and out of those hand-me-down views, inattentiveness, media disgust, and a nihilism born of frustration. Johnny Cochran relied on a widespread belief in governmental incompetency; and, in the case of the jury, eight of whom were black and two Hispanic, he relied on a readiness to believe that the police would falsify evidence in order to convict a black man. Cochran did not assume that reality was one and that all were rational in the same way. He adapted the rationality of his defense to what that particular jury would recognize as rational. The prosecution, on the other hand, proceeded as if the jury could jump out of the way they knew the world and accept, in a disinterested way, indisputable scientific evidence. The exposure of how the indisputable could be disputed, how evidence could be denied by a cockamamie conspiracy theory, generated not only anger and disbelief but frustration and confusion.

The Dream Team defense, the kind that most Americans, if on trial, couldn't afford meant indeed that money could buy justice. That realization should be incendiary. However, it failed to ignite because it was countered by the belief that those that have money should be free to spend it the way they wish; any restraint on this freedom means we are not a free democracy but a communist one. And yet, that drama of perverted justice added to an already-existing disgust and detachment from the public circus, from headline events to elections, which like jury trials darkened the private imaginary. A steady flow of mindboggling and disturbing happenings in the nineties foreshadowed a retreat from the public space to a private space, from politics in the world to a private politics, which could never be designed as a circus. That such a retreat would have disastrous effects on an already class-divided society seems inevitable.

Postmodern Journeys: Film and Culture 1996–1998

The series did end after the final book—titled, appropriately, *The Passing of Postmodernism*—was published in 2010; but the events of that year made it quite clear that a postmodern awareness of the narrated nature of our reality making had forever riddled the illusions and pretenses of modernity. Postmodernism as a movement comparable to early twentieth-century modernism moved on, as did modernism. But postmodernity as a way of knowing remains, just as Enlightenment modernity is still very much with us, but now its certainties and ambitions seem at best narratives and, at worst, pretenses. In effect, although the word "postmodern" in all its forms had been buried, the changes it effected endure and are now transparent in the American cultural mindscape.

First, everyone now has a narrative, is in need of one, or is advised to change the one he or she has because it is the wrong one, although no one's narrative, especially political ones can rise to the level of a universally acknowledged truth that dominates. Arguments prior to this state of affairs could be won with a reasoned representation of facts, but now we live in a world in which narratives can be countered only by other narratives. None could deliver the knockout punch. Also, a narrative was "like only your opinion, Dude" opinions you could share with others who had opinions endlessly and without closure in cyberspace. You can trace the ascendancy of enclaves of friends on social networks to a need to be part of a community in which a frustrating conflict of narratives filling the public sphere is eliminated.

Within the postmodern mindset, dialectic falls apart, synthesis is therefore unattainable, and politics, which merely mirrors this chaotic flux, moves closer and closer to irrationality and irresolution. A politics of postmodernity, one that could establish a regime of national order, a civil society, no less a government, seemed highly improbable, even if one could delve into this new alteration of truth to narrative or the attendant loss of any sure method to reach a consensus of what the truth might be. The retreat to private spheres of private freedom rather than the public sphere has been accompanied and underwritten by a libertarian spirit. And the emerging narcissism rests heavily on Max Stirner's "nothing is greater to me than myself" form of individual anarchism. What also fits this profile is the collapse of politics and economics as anything more than a "war of all against all." When the public social space means never-ending chaos, ideas of mutual aid and cooperation within that space vanish, which seems to be a good description of the millennial United States.

A sense that there is no authority trumping your own view and therefore societal and collective words and actions were worthless found a place in which to flourish—cyberspace. Here personal choice and design could rule, especially in domains occupied by those friends who shared or at least did not oppose your own views. One avoided negative attitudes and your critics were no more than haters. Ironically, the chaos that postmodernity's alleged anything-goes sponsorship has not been applied to the domination of personal choice. Let a million flowers bloom or, in other words, a million equally self-authorized truths flourish—and you wind up with the election of the present US Congress. Perhaps we do not associate unreachable opinions with political chaos because our personal arrangements in cyberspace can never create chaos but only what is personally appealing. In any case, a populace so self-deluded is an easy prey for those who have mastered strategies to spin narratives of influential logic.

Strategists and tacticians of both politics and the market found in postmodernity a manual of how to reach into a citizen/consumer's reality and brand their messages. If indeed reality was a cultural construction, and the most powerfully voiced narratives—volume and repetition—had the best chance of implanting their constructions, reason, logic, history, and even common sense went out the door. What was reasonable and what was logical was what a Humpty Dumpty-like power said it was. If you could attach your product or your candidate to the psyche of consumer/citizen, you could reach into their pocket as well as win their vote. Thusly, the 2012 presidential elections offered us an array of fools and clowns, idiots and addled in the Republican primary that could be matched in history but never so many on stage all at once. With these lessons learned and applied from the postmodern turn, politicians and profiteers buried their post-truth influences in the same way Dorian Gray kept the source of his eternal youth buried in an attic.

There are side-trip chapters throughout in *Postmodern Journeys* and a final cul-de-sac, which I see now as progenitors of online blogs. It seems that my entire gonzo social history in which an "I" is present, there are no footnotes, or argument brought to closure or question answered would now fit be a blogger's approach. And as blogging itself fades in the face of hashtag tweeting, I would now join a sally of back-and-forth anonymous tweets, open the issue in a fully democratic way. Social media, Facebook dominating, might have been a major venue for a discussion of Princess Di or Monica Lewinsky or the Dude or Ross Perot and any of the headline figures or events of this period but I doubt it. I doubt it because right now Facebook is an infinitude of isolated coteries of friends, like solitary asteroids each in his or her own orbit and the parlance more of the right-now-I'm-here-in-my-life sort than anything else. Headline events, all now potentially fractious, are therefore avoided among friends. This is a social media true to its title: an ongoing book of faces, a book though without pages but one that scrolls out endlessly, your interest only in what is at hand.

So now we have social media, hashtag tweets, rants, like my own here, blogs, online magazines plus all the old print matter. We have an encyclopedia resource, *Wikipedia,* which has expeditiously consigned authorities to the dustbin or made everyone an authority. "Bearcat" and "Woohookitty" have done over a half million edits on our millennial version of the *Britannica.* Democratizing every intellectual domain while defending wealth from such democratization seems to be an effective part of the defense. More choices mean, in the American cultural imaginary, "better." Unfortunately, however, one of the ways of vanishing something is to lose it in a crowd, multiply faces and words in a second-by-second outpouring until attention seeks escape. The young do not escape to lengthy tomes when easier stuff is available; the adults find their favored online bastions against noise, the sound and the fury of communiqués in a now unstoppable 24/7 cycle. Ironically, though, no one seems to be escaping the heated conflicts of the public sphere and finding a tranquil place to rest, a fortified psyche that is at peace in cyberspace. The astounding proliferation of attention-deficit and obsessive-compulsive disorders in the young no doubt has complex origin but as these disorders, like the expansion of autism, manifest now and not before, the surround of the present is key. And if we reduce this contemporary surround to a cultural dimension, we face two possibilities or narratives. Either the turmoil of the public space can't be kept out and thus overwhelms the psyche, or the private spaces we run to as escape do no more than jack up the quantity and speed of a virtual world that, unlike the real world, can never be brought to ground. We need either to go more completely into virtual worlds or reduce the time we spend there and increase real-world time. This is also a debate not resolved, as some have advocated an increase in the number of video-game hours as a way to expand an innovating intelligence and others connect poor reading comprehension scores of young Americans to the fact that they game and do not read.

I have selected a revised version of my chapter on the Coen brothers' film *The Big Lebowski,* "That Rug Really Tied the Room Together." In 1998, I reacted to reviews that declared, "*The Big Lebowski* is an empty frame" and "all the brothers' intelligence and skill can't make up for the sense of vacancy in their movies." Now the film stands as a classic, with a second generation of viewers quoting the Dude and Walter. The unrevised, original essay was reprinted in Oliver Benjamin's *Lebowski 101,* Abide University Press, 2014.

For me the Dude was happily affiliated with everyone he met, his imaginary resilient in the most instructive ways. He appeared at the height of the dot-com boom, a new Gilded Age that would soon collapse and yet another *époque d'or* appear, the inconceivable hero at a time when the Wall Street "Player" was America's hero.

That Rug Really Tied the Room Together[3]

All the brothers' intelligence and skill can't make up for the sense of vacancy in their movies. Until they find a way to let a little real life in (grownup reality, that is), Joel and Ethan Coen will somehow seem stunted—no more than the brightest kids in the class.

—Daphne Merkin, "Smart Alecks," *New Yorker,* March 1998

The Big Lebowski *is an empty frame.*

—Stuart Klawans, "Sex and Bowling," *The Nation,* March 30, 1998

Through this bewildering landscape . . . wanders our addled Philip Marlowe figure, toking herb, swilling White Russians and, truth to tell, looking increasingly heroic relative to the dysfunctional world around him.

—Andrew O'Hehir, "Everyman Must Get Stoned," *Salon*

One of the consequences of friends knowing that I may be writing about films that they've seen and don't quite know what to make of is their asking me what do I make of this or that film. Now they know whether they like or do not like a film but times are such—postmodern I mean—that just what they especially do not like about a film may yet be their hidden access to the whole film. What unsettles us and holds us off could possibly provide an epiphany, a transformative moment. Hold on another second and maybe the opaqueness here will attach itself to the dark holes of our postmodern age, move us into new figments of old figments such as cause and effect, linear time, non-contradiction, non-random order, external reference points, and grownup reality. I take it for granted that today everyone is holding on another second to see if their command of reality isn't going to be pulled right out of their hands, flung high in the air so that all the new movements, all the new revelations of an ever-changing us-and-reality relationship can be clearly seen.

That's not to say that everyone is ready to go along with the new swerve. Refer to our 'culture wars' here: On one side you have an army digging in and ready to hold on to grownup reality in the finest tradition of family values as displayed on Nickelodeon cable TV; and, on the other side, you have any number of radical, guerilla-like factions more than ready to admit that reality has moved on, say, from adultery or suicide or same-sex marriages or abortion or transexuality as destructive on all counts to the same as new constellations being brought to recognition for the first time in the firmament. We are never at play on a planet rotating on its axis and spinning in the heavens when we belong to the conservative cultural army but quite seriously grounded in truths, laws, imperatives, explanations, equations, and investment principles. Bend one knee, please. They are opposed by those who see themselves at play with reality, bending it, rather than a respectful knee, to fit the contours and dimensions of an infinitely flexible and varied human nature.

If you invest the spirit of one side with the spirit of the other, and vice versa, you get the sort of awareness each side needs of the other in order to have a good intense cultural war. You also get a cultural climate in which the two attitudes are to be found at all settings on a good blender. And, ironically, market imperialism—that on one hand demands an inert social order, which offers stability—makes its profits by pulping reality to push product. The market is at play with a pliable reality; return on investment is the only immoveable part.

When events—such as Princess Di's death or Clinton's sex drive—become like a movie we can't get control of, they now fall into this culture wars' miasma, a La Brea Tar Pit, which is our minds, in which white bones of all sizes swim about; and it's our job, as reconstructors, to put it all together. This is the sort of occasional acid-trip scene that Dude of *The Big Lebowski* might have. Which side is the Dude on? He is clearly at play with reality, skirting all the necessities that bind our present entrepreneurial society. Market players don't play the way the Dude does. They get into a competitive global arena, and they make sure they come out winners. The fact that in getting to be winners they are willing to obey no laws but those of profit, no principles but those of profit, and no tradition but only what profit requires at that moment does not turn them into Dude. His disrespect is for self-aggrandizement, his unconcern is for being rich, and his rebellion is against self-interest. And because he is so startlingly atavistic, so disturbingly non-entrepreneurial, after some twenty years of ascendant Dow, he activates a new clash of the culture wars but, at the same time, he and his crew of masterless men push the postmodern envelope a bit further. I mean to say that *The Big Lebowski* pushes us to wondering whether we can't command its subject because we're right and there is no subject, there is no rug that brings the whole room together, or that the fact that we can't command its subject and are wondering why, is precisely what the film's subject has led us to.

Dude and his friends are bowling outside our lanes and we've already rented shoes and are trying out bowling balls in preparing to join them. I'm not saying that we're all prepared to score this game according to rules we can't even begin to fathom. Nor that once we see the kind of game the Coen brothers are rolling here, we don't try to close it down at once. All I'm saying—and I sound like the Dude when we can't wrap things up or follow all the in and outs of the case—is that at this moment in America, market imperialized as we are, this is a postmodern flaunting of reality making and we're all bowling on those lanes, just scoring the results differently.

Let's explore the "sense of vacancy" that the *New Yorker* film critic mentions. Who possesses this "sense of vacancy"? And does it arise from a "sense of realism"? And, indeed, don't we reveal what sense of realism we hold when we begin to talk about "grownup reality," whose antipode surely must be infantile reality? Within this particular sense of realism, a certain "sense of vacancy" arises when not enough grownup reality is let in. But what if, say, we adopted the sense of realism of an eighteenth-century fruitcake like William Blake, who, because he was a fruitcake, confounded the realms of innocence and experience, childhood and adulthood. Because he was a fruitcake—sang on his deathbed, for instance—his sense of realism wanted to "let in" to "grownup reality" the joy, imagination, spontaneity, exuberance, emotions, playfulness, the dreaming and irrationalism of childhood.

None of this appears particularly appealing when viewed by those already in the realm of experience; it all appears frivolous, childish, disorderly, lunatic, and ludic; and where there should be grownup thought, there is only a failure to achieve cognitive grasp, a prepubescent assertion of the will, a bombardment of cognitive dissonance. In short, when time and space are not filled with the priorities of what now passes socially and culturally as grownup reality, then the observer notes a sense of vacancy.

This sense of vacancy is, however, a presence in this movie. It is not, therefore, the byproduct of *failure* to bring something into being but rather the result of the film *bringing* something into being. What does it bring into being? Well, from where I sit alongside you in our present grownup reality, I am not quite sure because it all first registers as unplotted, less than purposeful, fractured, disconnected, ludic, mazelike, discordant, surrealistic, incoherent jumble, a farrago. What does it appear like to the Coen brothers? I know from their film *Fargo* that they have a real grip on grownup reality as presently being manufactured in the Midwest. And they cannot see the whole of it without seeing the ludic, farrago dimensions of that reality. For them it appears that grownup reality is always already filled to the brim with unstoppable mania, is always tending to bring its own sobriety and control onto the snowy drifts of the cockamamie where the hard, cold edges of grownup reality finally melt away in the sun.

In *The Big Lebowski* all of the grownup reality the Dude becomes entangled in gives way to a musical number à la Busby Berkeley. And when the Dude is hit over the head and things grow dark as they do for Dick Powell in *Farewell My Lovely*, the Dude doesn't fall into a deep, dark pool and wind up running through a dark corridor of endless doors pursued by who knows what. Instead, he flies like Superman with arms spread wide over Los Angeles at night with all its lights fluttering below. He has a great, happy smile on his face; he surely dreams he can fly away. And then he's embracing a bowling ball, a look of surprise on his face, as he plummets downward, his flight canceled. He's weighted down and it's the weight of real-world gravity.

As in *Fargo,* all real-world gravity passes through human mediation, which gives it this role or that, assigning it wherever our sense of realism sees fit. Oddly enough, what the force of gravity is—often cited as an indisputable component of and proof of the real world—contributes to our sense of vacancy. It is a vacant force in a realm of vacancy. It is so real we bring to it nothing in our daily lives, living as if it meant nothing and did not exist. It is so powerful a force in the real world and at the same time lies unmediated in human life. We bring to it no meaning and no value, unless of course we are working for NASA.

I am merely trying to point out that a sense of vacancy inhabits all the hard stuff we connect to the real world. Observations of a sense of vacancy in a film which is—whether it is a film you like or not or the critics like or not—is a ludicrous claim, because all films film human mediations of reality. They film worldliness, the movements of people within the world in which they are already part. Electricity, nuclear fission, the synapse, photosynthesis, $E = mc^2$, LaPlace Transforms, and so on, are vacant lots in everyday human mediation of the world; we greet them with a sense of vacancy, even on exams where the only human transformation they have is in terms of grades, a symbolic enterprise whose meaning and value are socially and culturally manufactured.

So the Coen brothers greet grownup reality with a sense of vacancy and rather than put on gravitas they try to look at things as if they themselves were not obliged to obey the laws of grownup reality. And they literally film their attempt as a point-of-view shot from inside a bowling bowl. What sense of realism do we get from inside that moving bowling ball? If you are inside that bowling ball, do you project a sense of vacancy out there in the lanes, with the bowlers and their world? Or, do you take your gravity-bound sense of realism in there with you and hold on to the notion that vacancy is here inside the bowling ball and anything from this perspective results in a sense of vacancy? Who is going to mark the frame empty? From inside the bowling ball every frame is filled with action, every frame is a roll down one or another lane, and the sights along the way vary—pace, time, and speed locked into a new equation each and every time.

The flight of the bowling ball, like the Dude's flight over LA, is a metaphor of travel, Coen brothers-style; and it is a postmodern style. Every turn of the ball creates a new perspective. The world comes into our view from the position we are in; we are so framed and so accordingly frame the world, without a still point, an outside the frame observation point, a privileged place of neutral observation. It seems to me a profitless endeavor to object to the style of travel that the Coen brothers adopt and within which they plunge their hero, the Dude. Unless, of course, you are thoroughly convinced that grownups can and should travel only one way across a reality that allows for only that perspective of travel. Once you settle in for the ride on the Coen brothers' terms, you can see that every character in the film, not just the Dude and his bowling buddies, are coming at reality from separate lanes. And every dude on every lane has his or her bowling style and perspective.

Now I don't know about you but when I bowl, I am glancing at who is bowling on the right and left of me. I watch the lanes on either side. I distinguish mature bowling styles from amateur ones. I engage in bowling chatter and listen to that around me. I am on lane four and way over to my right someone is bowling on lane fifty; noise and movement blur where I am from where that bowler is. You might say that the reality of lane fifty lacks interest for me, but that is only an effect of where I am on lane four. I don't know how much I could say about life on lane fifty without filling you with a sense of vacancy.

Let's find a way to wander from lane to lane, although this sort of lateral movement doesn't take place in a bowling alley because we stand side by side, lane by lane, focused on the pins in front of us, moving toward them, releasing, and then returning. If reality is only ahead in our lane and if we are the only ones with the proper bowling form, we are the only ones bowling like grownups, then the plot and perspective on lane fifty should not mean a whole hell of a lot to us. On the other hand, if you take a postmodern view of things—and the Coen brothers do—then you're going to bowl laterally. Maybe your game will improve and your sense of realism expands; maybe your empty frame will get filled in and your sense of vacancy shifted back out to empty space.

Let's journey cross-alley in this film. Let's put the Dude in the center lane. The film opens with him strolling down the dairy aisle of Ralph's supermarket, stopping to sample from a carton of milk. The Dude is caught in a time warp: he experiences the occasional acid flashback, listens to whale song while soaking and toking in his bathtub, listens to the music of Creedence Clearwater Revival, and passes time at the bowling alley with his buddies, Walter and Donny. Reagan never happened for the Dude; he missed the film *Forrest Gump* so he does not know he has been declared extinct by Newt Gingrich, a wrong turn in American history.

The Dude's misadventures begin when he is mistaken for another Lebowski, the Big Lebowski, the Lebowski who has won, who apparently has all the toys. The goons that piss on the Dude's rug have been sent by Ben Gazzara playing Hollywood's creation of the porn-and-drug sleaze-kingpin behind the sleaze. But the Dude doesn't cross his path until later. Now he is set on getting restitution for his rug because this rug really tied the room together, a thought not his own but his friend Walter's. Walter has the gift of all true paranoiacs: he can tie together the most disparate things; and he certainly knows what the key piece is when trying to fit things together, trying to make sense of things. The counter presence here is Steve Buscemi's Donny, for whom the whole world is just a series of sentence fragments and conversations only partially heard. His constant interrogations elicit the same response from Walter: "Shut the fuck up, Donny." Donny is not privy to the real workings of things and in Walter's view cannot possibly be brought up to speed.

There is, however, a home base to Walter's thoughts: Vietnam. Everything, no matter how unrelated on the surface to that conflict, is inevitably linked to it. Nam is the rug spread out in Walter's mind that ties the room together. The discrepancy between that sense of order and what is in the world leads Walter and those who follow his 'logic' into strange conflicts and many casualties, a sort of microcosm of Nam itself. But no Tet Offensive daunts Walter, whose absolute certainty and determination never falter; no matter how distant the points may be on the map, Walter can connect them. He never experiences a sense of vacancy. Or, more precisely, he never experiences a sense of vacancy he cannot fill.

Seduced by Walter's logic that he needs to be compensated for that rug which really tied the room together, the Dude pays a visit to the Big Lebowski. Lest we ourselves forget that it's the nineties and Dude is all that's left over from the counterrevolution, the Lebowski of the nineties—the BIG Lebowski—a fat cat in a wheelchair, describes the Dude to the Dude's face early in the film. He tells the Dude how in spite of being crippled he has succeeded in becoming a winner, a success, and he did it because he was relentlessly, competitively entrepreneurial. In other words, he represents the shtick of the last twenty years to the Dude. He won't give the Dude a handout; did he personally piss on the Dude's carpet? No. Then he's not responsible. The Dude insists that he's suffered a great loss by being mistaken for the Big Lebowski. But the Big Lebowski does not share the Dude's sense of order and throws him out. The Dude nevertheless leaves with a Persian rug, which gets taken back later by the Big Lebowski's daughter, Maude, for whom it holds cherished memories of her mother. Maude will later mate with the Dude because she wants a child, but she does not want anyone connected to her life fathering that child. So, she picks the Dude; the lane he is bowling on is so far removed from the one she's on that even sex cannot really bring them together.

She fills the Dude in on the real success story of her father, the Big Lebowski: he has no money of his own; the money was her mother's and now it's in a foundation administered by Maude. She once let her father invest some of the foundation's money and he lost it all. He is an incompetent, lying, vain man who bought himself a trophy wife. He is, in short, a fraud; he did not earn millions; he cannot take the high ground with the Dude. In fact, the Dude is his moral superior: he is down, but he is not a hypocrite, nor is he vain and selfish. He does not make people trophies; a bowling trophy would suffice for the Dude.

On his way out of the Big Lebowski's, the Dude meets the trophy wife, Bunny, who later may or may not be kidnapped. As the Dude glances over at the pool, he asks, "Who's that?" "Oh, that's a nihilist," Bunny responds. "Oh, a nihilist," Dude says, nodding, as if a nihilist sleeping on a rubber float in a swimming pool was per usual. Bunny has been painting her toenails and now she holds up a foot and wants the Dude to blow on it. "Oh, you want me to blow on it?" the Dude says. But then he drifts off, following his rug being carried out. When he visits Maude in her studio, she isn't painting her nails; her own body is not her art as it is for Bunny the-porno-star-now-trophy wife. Maude swings naked over a canvas below and splatters paint on it as she flies by. Some of that paint gets on the Dude who is as unperturbed with the expression of 'high' art as he is with 'low' art. Art is not his passion, nor lust, nor money, nor ambition, nor the nothing of nihilism itself, which in fact makes as big a something of nothing as believers make of gods.

Neither is the Dude a committed artist of life or of profit or of nothing; the Dude carries on at his own pace. There is something stubbornly heroic about the way the Dude feels called upon not only to attend to all the ins and outs of the plot he has wandered into but also make some sense of it, come to some kind of conclusion. It's not a committed intent, a serious drive through the main street of this bewildering landscape. The Dude's command of the ins and outs of life's intricacies—and the bewildering landscape he has wandered into—never goes beyond his knowing the way to the In-N-Out Burger shop. You might say that while everyone else has an abstracted sort of connection with the world, the Dude's remains concrete and particular.

But he does take it as it comes; I mean he takes it as serious as life gets. He doesn't dismiss it as vacancy on his way to nobler ground. He hasn't adopted, for instance, a posture of scornful and amused aloofness as David Thewlis does in a brief cameo. The Dude has come to see Maude and finds only Thewlis sitting there, amused not only by the Dude's appearance but seemingly by his very existence. Later, when Maude shows up and answers a phone call, there is a three-way 'inside' joke that the phone caller, Maude, and Thewlis share. Theirs is a world in which avant-garde art and living life like art disdain the mundane, especially a figure such as the Dude, who represents all the messiness, disorder, and confusion that art seeks to transcend. Ironically, it's not aesthetic detachment that will impregnate Maude. For that, she has to turn to the Dude.

Quite interestingly, Thewlis is one of the only people in the film who provoke the Dude's wrath. "Who the hell are you anyway?" the Dude asks him after Thewlis has treated him to reeking condescension. Who indeed is Thewlis here but the aloof, scornful critic who will soon write about a sense of vacancy pervading the film?

Even though it is the Dude who has the occasional acid flashback, he lives without illusions. But he's surrounded by the deluded. Jesus, the Latino bowler, takes vanity to a new high; he is in his own mind the cock of the walk, all posture and braggadocio. He promises great harm but will never deliver; his delusion is harmless. But when the Dude winds up in the hands of a Malibu police chief, he winds up smack in the middle of a law-and-order, tough-on-crime worldly outlook. It is suddenly "Giuliani time," allegedly the words New York City police used when they were brutalizing a hapless victim. This sort of neo-Nazi barbarity and brutality is part of the nihilists' approach also; they throw an attack marmot into the Dude's bathtub as he is soaking, toking, and listening to whale song. Their violence finally runs up against Walter, the Vietnam vet, calmly telling the frightened Donny not to worry because these guys are amateurs. And Walter does go through them as if they were paper bags. A black-leather, German-skinhead-Sprocket look makes a good photo-op, but it's nothing but eighties and nineties hype compared to the violence Walter has seen. But the clash is too much for Donny whose weak heart gives out and he dies on the spot. Later, his ashes will be flung out of a two-pound coffee can into the wind and back into the Dude's face.

I can't help thinking: Who in this film are living as if they were mortal? As if they had one and not more lives to live? Do you counter mortality by committing yourself to something, such as art or sex or wealth or power or anger or service? The golden-age TV scriptwriter that the Dude and Walter visit, in the hope of getting back a million dollars from a fourteen-year-old thief, is in an iron lung set up like a casket at one end of the living room. Maybe every script that he's written is now being replayed in his mind to the rhythm of the iron-lung bellows. It is as if the reality of the present continues unscripted. There was always life going on outside the script; and the script was less enduring than the life. Was mortality held off by a script, no matter how golden age? Or does that inevitably lead you into thinking that you can't follow the ins and outs of life and world but that you are getting the most you can out of it?

The Dude is not entrepreneurial; he is no symbolic analyst; and he is certainly not shaping his own destiny. He is in fact being led through a maziness that confounds grasp. But maybe he is here in a way that no one else in the film is. Maybe the Dude is leaving his frame empty, and that is an accomplishment whose skillfulness we just can no longer recognize. But I see it as a reminder that while we may need to journey, the world does not journey. There is no journey but only movement; and that movement, foundationally, has no order, causality, time, speed, or space. I am not claiming that the Dude is enlightened in the way of the Dalai Lama or has reconciled in himself the paradoxes of consciousness immersed in what merely exists, what is outside of what we humans make of it. And yet the Dude is a pause on our journey here—perhaps a pause, received as vacancy, but a pause in our entrepreneurial rush to return on investment. There is something to humanity that abides beyond profit and loss. We can find that abiding in the Dude.

Memory's Orbit: Film and Culture 1999–2000

The theme or hook or MacGuffin for *Hauntings* was a walk on the dark side, a circle in the Inferno, prophetic, frightened. For *Speeding to the Millennium*, fiction interrupted the growing tragedies of headline events. For *Postmodern Journeys* it was a Céline-like journey to the edge of night but with detours and side trips and the possibility of a hero who was not out to eat the world whole but to roll in and through every life, picking up what was new and different. *Memory's Orbit* was a tale of a life running side by side with the American culture, caught up within it, trying to run apart, forever in an orbit of memory I seek "to cast off the rotten rags of memory by Inspiration." As such, *Memory's Orbit* is a forerunner of what I am about in *Dark Affinities, Dark Imaginaries,* an earlier look back when I was still "Nel mezzo del cammin di nostra vita."

Memoir was a form of writing Americans were born to, for it touches personal freedom and choice, individual autonomy and self-design, an Emersonian self-reliance, a Whitmanesque "Song of Myself." Memoir is an advertisement of self, an indulgence of the ego, endless selfies in endless locations, a plea to look at my life, now updated day by day in Facebook updates, posts to the world as to what I am doing. It does not fit the Scandinavian cultural psyche or the Asian one, but it reaches the very center of the American mass psyche. Reality TV is watching others in their display of *amour soi*, but it is also watching yourself, for every American is either a stone's throw from being that self-celebrating celebrity celebrated for that self-celebration or, the opposite, confident that he or she is not the hapless loser they are watching. This inclination has made it difficult for Americans to see the grievous wealth divide in the United States and the extravagances of the mega-wealthy as a real threat to democracy.

As the decade moved away from notions of society, the public good, the commonwealth, and toward winners and losers playing a zero-sum game where someone's loss was a requirement for someone else's win, toward a war of all against all, all things public were scorned and diminished. Society itself was destined for privatization. "There is no such thing as society," Thatcher had declared. Politics was public and, so, fated; history was analog and, so, fated.

I used the memoir as a frame to continue the story of the American cultural imaginary in the nineties. I used it to point out that everything personal was always and already interwoven with the social and cultural, that we forged our sense of private from what was public, that even though we sought to make the world our subject, its subject was not us nor did it share our subjectivity.

This is a hard view to broadcast in a society that "promotes individualism as a sacred concept," words Frank Barat used in asking Angela Davis about her focus on movements and not individuals. She points out that even though Nelson Mandela "insisted his accomplishments were collective . . . the media attempt to sanctify him as a heroic individual." (Frank Barat, "Q & A: Angela Davis," *The Nation*, September 15, 2014.) I yet maintain that Mandela was a heroic individual because from within the collective of both white and black culture at that time, he chose forgiveness rather than revenge though both sides were equal forces. Also, Mandela's sense of the collective referred to all those others who, like tributaries flowing into an ocean, melded their voices into his own. These were the like minded who brought his own voice forward. But every voice resonates within the chambers of its own time and place so that it is not a choir of voices, a collective of thought, a movement bringing together the like-minded, but a window into a time and place, a window into that collective, a window into what Heidegger called "the house of being."

My sense of memoir is not personal diary or spokesperson for this or that -ism back in the day but a glimpse through my own thoughts and experiences of a culture that made this person possible. My words bear the traces of a society at a certain time; and over time, my experiences, inclinations, and priorities made it clear through what windows I looked and what doors I opened or closed or never saw.

Some fifteen years after I wrote *Memory's Orbit*, the American cultural imaginary is awash in personal updates, second-by-second communiqués as to your state of mind, mayfly-like apparitions in cyberspace that spark and fade, YouTube videos of a multitude of undiscovered talent, of isolated souls in computer-screen cubicles posting the minutiae of their lives. We are awash in a truly vicious circle of comments on comments in a cyber country where no one has a real face or real identity but only the certainty of how the world appears to them, no apologies to how it may appear to anyone else.

My Blakean view is that we are now drowning in a cyberworld of single-vision:

> Now I a fourfold vision see
> And a fourfold vision is given to me
> Tis fourfold in my supreme delight
> And three fold in soft Beulahs night
> And twofold Always. May God us keep
> From Single vision & Newtons sleep. (William Blake,
>   "Letter to Thomas Butt," November 22, 1802. Quoted in
>   Geoffrey Keynes (ed.), *The Letters of William Blake,* 1956)

I used a memoir frame in *Memory's Orbit* to parallel a personal journey with that of the American culture within which I journeyed and was, in effect, shaped by it. But also, the story one tells of oneself reveals the life-world, that imaginative space which we fabricate and from which we deal with the world. So the memoir reveals the interface, the screening that filters all and, as such, it needs to be represented. To assume that there is no filtering or mediating of the world is to claim neutrality, objectivity, a confrontation with the world directly as if subjectivity could mesh with objectivity in a straight one-to-one fashion.

Although I positioned myself in all my books so that the reader would have some sense of my disposition, my angle of vision, and thereby consider my observations, my essaying from that perspective, I did not in my online writing pursue this line because the personal screed and rant, ego gone wild, had already saturated cyberspace. In the last essay for the 2014 season I wrote for *Truthout,* however, I united memoir with an essaying into poverty and gentrification.

As *Memory's Orbit* was the fourth and last volume in my portrait of the American cultural imaginary of the nineties, I summarized in my introduction what I had been up to in those works. Because the event that traumatized that American imaginary occurred just before the book went to press, I revised my introduction and titled it "After September 11, 2001."

After September 11, 2001[4]

It is ten days after the destruction of the World Trade Center towers and the attack on the Pentagon. I am writing a preface not only to this last installment of my history of the American cultural imaginary in the 1990s, *Memory's Orbit,* but also to the previous three volumes: *Hauntings, Speeding to the Millennium,* and *Postmodern Journeys.* They each had a preface but now that both the decade and this writing project are over and the cultural imaginaries we live in as Americans have so drastically and suddenly been interrupted, I need to bridge millennia. Our Y2K, that cataclysmic millennial event we anticipated, has happened. A belated millennial metamorphosis. We are in a post-September 11th world now; it is different. There has been a cultural sea change in America.

I think we all surmise that regardless of how well we come to know the causes of the September 11th destruction of the World Trade Center towers and part of the Pentagon, or how closely we can see ourselves as our attackers do, their crime remains unmitigated. We can say we don't care about the whys; we care only about bringing them to justice, bringing justice to them. And we care about how we will be able to charter a safe passage through the troubled waters in which we now find ourselves. We can say that it does not really matter what our peace of mind was before; what matters now is that it is gone and we must learn to live in a world where threatening dark shadows always follow our steps. It never made much of a difference to Americans that most of the rest of the world has always lived in such apprehension. This is new for this brave, new world. We do not know how brave we can be in a world where surgical strikes can strike everything but the cancer.

Whatever we imagined ourselves to be, whatever our 1990s psychic mind-set was, is now no longer. How to answer this question that has been raised again and again these past ten days.

Why this unspeakable, unthinkable, inconceivable act of terrorism against the United States, against a people who pride themselves on lending a hand all over the world, who provide more aid in every form than any other country in the world, against a people who welcome to their shores the downtrodden and oppressed, who impose no religious, racial, ethnic, gender, social, or political barriers on those who live in this country, who live in the most successful democracy of the modern world?

Are there reasons behind this attack or was it simply madness? What are the reasons? Who are our attackers? What do we look like through their eyes? What have we done to provoke this horrific response? How do we eradicate the evil of terrorism? Can our intelligence networks ever get to the root of this tragedy? Have we entered a new world of intermittent calm and madness, with a darkness never quite dispelled? How can our love of freedom vanquish this new devil, Osama bin Laden? Do we have the right team of problem solvers in Washington now? Do we have the best strategists at the Pentagon now? Or should we be looking to our corporate world and its brainstorming entrepreneurs to creatively destroy this recent threat to global capitalism?

The questions come out of different mind-sets, different reality-producing styles. The naïve realists deal in Cold War dualities, Boolean binaries of black and white, good and evil, true and false, right and wrong, just and unjust, win and lose, and so on. They don't ask the question that lurks behind this attack: Who are we? They already know. "We are the virtuous; reason, right, and God are on our side." The problem solvers whip out the durable Enlightenment Project, apply a rigorous system's analysis, isolate fact from fiction, and come up with a solution. But the optimism of that approach has already and most recently in the United States been riddled by Vietnam and Robert McNamara and General Westmoreland's unswerving application of the approach, while the North Vietnamese and the Vietcong remained steadfastly resistant to it. That Nam world overspilled the approach.

The darkness of twentieth-century modernism continues to seep into our country, leaving its impression in the 1990s on the Clarence Thomas-Anita Hill hearings, the O.J. Simpson trial, the events surrounding David Koresh at Waco, the Rodney King riots, the fight over Elian, Clinton's impeachment, the 2000 presidential election, the Seattle riot, and now this, what CNN calls "the Attack on America." The steady erosion of Enlightenment presumptions in the 1990s and our resulting sense of standing on shaky foundations run into that nationwide chatter of supreme confidence fabricated by Reagan's infectious nostalgia for an America that never existed. It did exist in Walt Disney's mind, and he gave it form in Disneyland; you might say Ronald Reagan's reality frame came out of his frequent visits to Disneyland—at least, from a postmodern perspective.

The angst-ridden vibe of twentieth-century modernism also runs into rationality and realism's new spawn: the Third Revolution, the computer revolution, the digitalizing of time and space. After our dramatic loss of confidence in technology both in Vietnam and NASA, we are, thanks to the likes of Bill Gates and Microsoft, back on the road to progress through technology. The road ahead is filled with computer screens; people are even supposed to be wearing them on their sleeves. The new e-world has us dazzled. But there have been other signs. There have been throughout the 1990s clear signs that America is having a hard time dispensing justice in the courts and social justice in the streets; becoming more and more class divided; becoming more and more cynical and cold in regard to the plight of the losers; scornful of the unionized working class; turning with the new Bush administration toward a global concern limited to return on investment; becoming more and more in the control of a limited and privileged discourse, and, tied to that, increasingly forgetful of powerful American narratives of value that had nothing to do with our "show me the money" attitude.

Our world has also been shifting from the uncertainty, nervousness, and always-looming darkness of twentieth-century modernism into the aimless playfulness of the postmodern. A good part of that playfulness extends to whatever we have inherited along the lines of traditional values and meanings, firm foundations, and reachable eternal verities. The market has found its port here, jacking into an attitude that buries the old and has us rushing for the new. New realities require new fashions, new homes, new cars, and new looks. In this new postmodern world, nothing has lasting, intrinsic value; value is in the newest line, the most recent innovation, and the new technological advance. If you are not always shopping, you are losing hold of this new digital world. You are doomed to be remaindered, discontinued, obsolete, dead in the water, your mind yesterday's product. But just as there are countercurrents dispelling dark modernism's darkness, there are postmodern countercurrents to what I have described here.

Revised Ending, September 2014[5]

September 11th was a tragic event, immeasurably tragic for Americans because unlike so many places in the world, the United States fought our wars elsewhere while the homeland remained safe. The homeland of the American mass psyche had only one time before been so traumatized, though that war, the War Between the States, had been a regional war— neighbor fought neighbor. There were not the dark affiliations of identity and an alien difference. It was all homeland, a rift in what had been united, what was vastly more familiar than alien, and for those reasons the trauma went deep and lasted long. But there is also a chilling dark affiliation here in a divided economics in both the ante-bellum United States and in the 2001 United States and an alien presence, African slaves and Islamic terrorists. Southern prosperity was built on the free labor of African slaves.

US prosperity owed much to its fossil-fuel diplomacy, a diplomacy that supported or turned a blind eye to oppressive regimes that continued and continue to enslave in every way their citizenry. Economies of greed then forged their own nemesis. The United States remains a society that will be continually at war with Islamic terrorists but also continually disrupted by African Americans who were gamed and tokenized, no psychic reparation possible, and who remain the first to suffer as wealth moves steadily upward for a very few, as in a long-running Monopoly game.

We could all measure a rising Dow Jones on September 11, 2001, coming out of the "Affluenza" nineties, a virus of affluence in which all seemed to share as the value of homes ballooned and the immeasurable opportunities of e-commerce seemed available to all. In short then, we were totally incapable of measuring the event for the euphoria of the nineties *fin de siècle* indulgence prepared Americans for nothing. Others, elsewhere, could measure the 9/11 tragedy because it showed up within their own imaginary. It was recognizable. Others elsewhere had memories by which this event could be compared, understood, and positioned. Others were already living within life-worlds in which sudden violence, lack of food and water, inadequate clothing and housing were as part of their lives as an American's car, fast food, and a protective law and order, which, though unequal in its actions yet exceeded what existed in so many countries.

Tragic, in every direction, was the unnecessary destruction and chaos that the United States visited upon the masses who were already living within a hardship that Americans, living within far different imaginary life-worlds, could not conceive. Everyone could live tragic lives day after day without hope of a vengeful retaliation—but not Americans. The United States did not have to accept in stoical fashion the deep violation to a long-entrenched sense of security within our own borders. A deeply rooted sense of our moral superiority of the rightness of all our causes, of never having to apologize because apology to anyone acknowledged our inferiority in the face of their superiority. The attack on the World Trade Center was more than a violation; it was a blasphemous act, not only against the image within which Americans lived, but also against capitalism itself. The response would have to be truly "shock and awe" in order to show the world that an American regime of order and the secure climate for business it provided could not be challenged.

What was threatened in Vietnam was a paranoiac's fear that a communist takeover in Vietnam would lead to the nationalization of American corporations from Southeast Asia all the way to Western Europe. We fought some fifteen years not as a matter of Homeland Security but the security of an economic system that was capable of making a very few very wealthy and a very many very poor. The price that was paid was high: "Estimates of the number of Vietnamese service members and civilians killed vary from 800,000 to 3.1 million. Some 200,000–300,000 Cambodians, 20,000–200,000 Laotians, and 58,220 US service members also died in the conflict" (*Wikipedia*).

The American cultural imaginary gravitated from obliviousness to annoyance with the daily news of Vietnam, until that war became entangled in a countercultural movement with a Left seeking a viable socialist tradition that it could really find only in Europe and flower-power pacifist beliefs. The counterculture's impact on the ending of the Vietnam War, still arguable, would have been scrunched at the outset if that whole countercultural zeitgeist existed after 9/11.

It did not; the US imaginary was not into "the greening of America" but into the opposite, "the greeding of America." Those who told us "the chickens have come home to roost," that 9/11 was a payback for the United States's own atrocities were pilloried. Those who blamed the counterculture for the loss of the Vietnam War were after 9/11 in no mood to tolerate any remnants of that dissidence.

So the injury was perceived as great to the American psyche and the threat to a Pax Americana within which an American style of free-wheeling capitalism could go on was perceived even greater. The price someone had to pay, anyone Islamic, had to be forever shocking and forever awe inspiring.

The depth and breadth of the repayment, of the retaliation remains haunting:

> The Iraq Body Count project (IBC) figure of 110,937–121,227 civilian deaths from violence up to December 2012 includes reported civilian deaths due to Coalition and insurgent military action, sectarian violence and increased criminal violence. The IBC site states: "It should be noted that many deaths will probably go unreported or unrecorded by officials and media." The IBC website currently states that, "Further analysis of the WikiLeaks' Iraq War Logs may add 12,000 civilian deaths." ("Casualties of the Iraq War," *Wikipedia*)

Add to these the casualties in Afghanistan:

The War in Afghanistan (2001–present) has resulted in between 18,000 and 20,000 Afghan civilians being killed. As of June 9, 2014, there have been 2,187 U.S. military deaths in the war in Afghanistan and additional 133 fatalities in the broader Operation Enduring Freedom outside Afghanistan. 1,808 of these deaths inside Afghanistan have been the result of hostile action. 19,964 American service members have been wounded in action during the war. In addition there are 1,173 U.S. civilian contractor fatalities. (http://military.wikia.com/wiki/ United_States _Forces_casualties_in_the_war_in_Afghanistan)

Hearing the Ping of Poverty—or Not[6]

McDowell County, the poorest in West Virginia, has been emblematic of entrenched American poverty for more than a half century. John F. Kennedy campaigned here in 1960 and was so appalled that he promised to send help if elected president. His first executive order created the modern food stamp program, whose first recipients were McDowell Country residents. When President Lyndon B. Johnson declared "unconditional war on poverty" in 1964, it was the squalor of Appalachia he had in mind.

—Trip Gariel, "50 Years Later, Hardship Hits Back"

You can't just come in the neighborhood and start bogarting and say, like you're motherfuckin' Columbus and kill off the Native Americans. Or what they do in Brazil, what they did to the indigenous people. You have to come with respect. There's a code. There's people. . . . So, why did it take this great influx of white people to get the schools better? Why's there more police protection in Bed Stuy and Harlem now? Why's the garbage getting picked up more regularly? We been here!

—Spike Lee speaking in Brooklyn, February 25, 2014

Are you sure you heard a ping from a black box, and if so, where did it come from?

In the seventies, when I lived in the original, 200-year-old Oxley Hollow homestead outside Athens, West Virginia, in a county neighboring McDowell, Mercer County, I noticed the ubiquitous presence of JFK's face on cabin walls, like the ubiquitous face of Jesus, often in velveteen brightness. I had New York plates on my 1972 VW camper and a noisy muffler, and I told folks I was from Brooklyn, describing a difference between that borough and the others that was lengthy, ferocious, and bewildering to all. I farmed land that had not been farmed in many years, answered the call to help 'folks out,' and though I announced myself a "Catlick," I was told that "we ain't gonna fall out over that." After all, JFK had been a Catlick. If not for him, Troy told me, with a twinkle in his eye, "some fellars might have burnt a cross on your lawn," not that any area where my wild chickens terrorized my dogs could have passed muster as lawn among the Michigan neighbors I would have some quarter of a century later.

So, a Bensonhurst/Borough Park/Dyker Heights, Brooklyn boy with a "Talley" (Italian) last name became "Joe Nat Lee" who lived "down there in Oxley Holl'er." We put a bell around our two-year-old daughter's neck so we could hear where she was, kept our two city dogs on a runner so they wouldn't spring a fox trap that were all over (fox pelts worth fifty dollars, a huge sum to all) and in a year or so rushed out of that holler so a second baby could be born, minutes after we arrived at Princeton hospital. She was born, today's *New York Times* tells me, amid the unconquerable poverty of southern Appalachia.

I know too that she was born surrounded by people who looked out for each other, who joined with me in the coldest winter to fell trees and cut wood when mine had run out. I had scant dollars to pay Coy and Tom for wiring my house, but for them even the little I had was too much. "We've had enough," Coy told me, shaking his head, refusing the twenty dollars I held out to him. In turn, I helped put up a barn, plant 'taters, burn winter grass, feed horses and cattle, and shovel a path to a cabin for an old woman who had left the hospital in mid-winter and wanted to die back "down there in the holl'er" where she was born. I owe my survival in Oxley Holl'er to my neighbors, to Mr. Parker, the retired high-school principal who ran a hardware store, sold his goods at Depression-era prices, and gave me without cost wisdom of Appalachia beyond wiki and Google. I worked alongside the Reverend Callier who sharecropped and picked cotton as a boy in Georgia and who showed me how to farm that Appalachian mountain soil.

As the Vietnam war dragged on toward a maddening always-deferred ending, I sought escape in Appalachia, not searching for the ping of poverty but only to be away from the ping of a mindless war, as deeply as I could go into a small world of spellbinding difference.

Time has provided a perspective so that one sees both a personal and cultural imaginary at work, a kind of buffering screen through which what is there and what is really going on is filtered, like a lens over your eyes. The imaginary trumps whatever any second order of observing reveals as fact and figures. That imaginary does not ignore facts from the outside but they nonetheless have no real impact, as if they were conceivable but out of place in that imagined space of self and world in which you live. Although we believe that sanity and reason avow that we live not within a mediating imaginary zone but within reality itself, we nonetheless live within narrations of the real, in what the phenomenologists call "Lebenswelt," or life-worlds, our being in the world of time, objects, other people, and self-image. The most powerful stories of what is what, of what anything is to mean and how it is to be valued, shape our personal thoughts, beliefs, and feelings.

Time also provides a perspective on how our cultural imaginaries have changed. After a long period of economic and social mobility from WWII to Ronald Reagan, a period in which working-class heroes joined and fought for working-class unions, in which a middle class did not conceive of an underclass as a danger to themselves or imagine it as a 'moocher' class, in which the poor weren't poor because they lacked the will not to be poor, the American cultural imaginary has descended into an imaginary painfully similar to medieval feudalism. Within that debased imaginary, we do not search for the ping of .poverty because the poor can help only themselves. In our millennial imaginary, we are what we choose and will ourselves to be.

The mutual interdependence and sustaining interrelationships that I experienced in Oxley Holl'er are now not comprehensible because they lie outside an imaginary that extends from narcissism to solipsism, that cannot respond to any societal ping because any idea of society, of others, has vanished, or remains the archaic platform of liberals or, worse yet, socialists. LBJ's "War on Poverty" fifty years later is like an alien undertaking we perceive as quixotic but also as pointless because the issue itself does not require a collective, national action, such as real war, but only a personal response. If you do not want to be poor, start a business. Or, say "NO!" to your poverty. Poverty is not a black box we are searching for because now we know that it is just something you personally own and can disown at will.

Before I left Oxley Holl'er, I saw a glimmer of what was to come in southern Appalachia when the first franchise fast-food emporium opened.

A "Long John Silver's—Think Fish" drew lines of curious people far and wide. To me, that journey from notched cabin to franchise fast-food was like an omen of what was to come, of what I had seen as desires were spun as needs and what was real was exchanged for simulacra. In the years I worked at the Bluefield State College library, in the beginning on night duty till closing, I got close yet again to battles for justice and protests for basic rights that no one ever escapes. I met coal miners seeking help for black-lung claims against the mine owners. One night, two young women who had been turned away from jobs at a coal mine sought my help in tracking down applicable West Virginia law to make a case of discrimination. They had come far for these jobs that paid fifty-five dollars a day and they were fighting mad that men were hired and they were not. These young ladies knew about Mary Harris "Mother" Jones, the fiery opponent of mine owners and politicians in their pockets; and they knew about the way the heroes of the Matewan Massacre, Sid Hatfield and Ed Chambers were murdered by Baldwin-Felts detectives. They knew that the appellation "redneck" applied to those brave miners who made a stand at Blair Mountain against the Coal Commission. In short, they knew the historical line of rebellion from which their own protest emerged. I had escaped nothing.

I left Oxley Holl'er before the practice of removing mountain tops in search of coal began. The MCHM leak of chemicals into the Elk River in January 2014 is the third major chemical accident in a state where both the legislature and regulatory agencies proceed, or not, at the behest of the coal and chemical industries, which dominate the state's economy. Chemical toxins are a by-product of an industry whose union, as unions elsewhere, no longer has power to protect or restrain mining operations. I never witnessed "family disintegration" but rather close bonds between family and neighbors. Family breakup in southern West Virginia did not become a calamity until the 1990's, after southern West Virginia lost its major mines in the downturn of the American steel industry. Prescription-drug abuse, which now devastates the region, stands like poverty itself as what closely bound families and church communities, what a perpetual stream of revival-tent gatherings, what a mutual sharing of each other's burdens had previously fought to a standstill. A communal life-world which so much of the United States had neither pursued nor had cast aside with a cold credo of "I've got mine, you get yours" was alive when I lived in Oxley Holl'er.

Poverty and hard times did not eventually bring a resilient way of life, an existential strength that stretched beyond the individual and into the community, to the sorry state today reported in the *New York Times*. An overpowering American cultural imaginary grounded in exactly the opposite of mutual aid, sharing, and communal concern displaced and conquered these virtues, tied them to values that made you a winner only if someone else was made a loser. What I had experienced in Oxley Holl'er was already scheduled for extinction by the rapid ascendancy of a market-driven politics. I guess there was something socialist in a society of closely woven interdependence. And as to this day, there is no gentrifying interest in Oxley Holl'er. I did not stay to see the tragic translation.

At the same time I am reading the *New York Times* front-page story "50 Years Later, Hardship Hits Back," describing poverty in southern Appalachia, citing towns that were part of the world I had been in, I read in *New Yorker* magazine, "Brooklyn's Ascension is Official." Brooklyn is a gentrifying frontier for young cybertech/Wall Street professionals working in Manhattan. Their medium is money, their gift, their refined tastes in everything from dining to nannies. For them, Brooklyn is a formless possibility awaiting a hi-end transformation. Wealth is the sole substance of gentrification; if you do not have it, you do not exist. The middle class is therefore like the underclass (i.e., simply not wealthy) and therefore excluded from the habits and lifestyle of gentrification. A gentrified manner of living supported by money alone has license to overrun what it witnesses as poor, a new norm of being poor that claims the truly poor as well as a struggling working and middle class. Gentrification hears the ping of poverty everywhere it has not yet colonized; rescue is not the intent but ingestion, like the hungry to the sound of a dinner bell.

I know neither an inchoate Brooklyn nor a hopeless West Virginia. I lived then neither in the Appalachian poverty that we revisit as we revisit our "War on Poverty" or in any vision of what my Fort Hamilton neighborhood in Brooklyn would become. I see both places now set up in our millennial view as polar opposites, framed, like the portraits of JFK and Jesus in a dovetailed notched cabin, within a way of being and seeing that was blind to how anything actually was or seen to be from an outside perspective. Each place was enveloped within a narration that disclosed a way of life that had a history, had heroes and villains, had hope, hard times, and happiness, noble acts, silly and sorry dreams, awesome revelations and dark suns. I knew no people in Oxley Holl'er who saw themselves as those who today read the *New York Times* article see them. I see only proud, tempered faces; I see bedrock faith and communal care giving, hear words weathered through like old boots, wise and never yielding no matter the hardship. And when I read of Brooklyn's

"ascension," I think only that my Brooklyn working-class neighborhood
had no need to rise beyond what it was, was never either high nor low,
gentrified or not. We could not know or care that 'the guy with the most
toys in the end, wins' and that what we already had, would not do, that if
you were not a winner you were a loser. We did not know "The Secret"
of a self chosen "will to power." The gentrifying way of measuring what
we were was unknown.

Sometime in the late nineties, I returned to Brooklyn and overheard
a conversation in which a friend had suffered a collapse and "no longer
wanted to be rich." He needed to go to a revival meeting, I suppose,
but not one to confess having fallen away from Jesus, but rather having
fallen away from wanting to be rich. A much older Brooklyn maxim had
been very different, closer to what Bernstein tells us in *Citizen Kane*: "It's
not hard to make a lot of money, if all you want to do is make a lot
of money." Jobs that paid a living wage, unions that fought for worker
rights, a tuition-free city university, dependable pensions, the absence of
credit cards as well as shop-therefore-I-am ethos and a respect for labor
created a world that had no need to send out a ping of poverty. There
was no existential distress.

More than all this was the fact that economic status and political
party were not as significant in our lives as the everyday customs, habits,
and affiliations that bound us and were kept alive by daily face-to-face
encounters. In my walk each day to the local stores with my mother, she
heard stories, told stories, became informed, laughed, cried, questioned, and
like a bee from flower to flower tended the spirit of our neighborhood.
We thrived on the persistent interaction with each other, exercised our
understanding of others' lives, extended imagination and empathy, saw in
the plight of others, ourselves. The nexus was not cash but the intangible
connections that you could not just bid for, move in, and own. The communal network was grounded. The vitriol and deception of anonymity
could not thrive.

I witnessed the descendancy of my neighborhood in Brooklyn commensurate with the denigration of the working class as an economy
turned from productivity to the Dark Arts of Wall Street financing, from
unions back to the noblesse oblige of owners who felt no obligation to
improve salaries or working conditions. I witnessed a collapse of a sense
of security and well-being that was content with what it had and did
not yearn for the ease and plenitude that seems now to signify what
the American Dream has meant all along. Those who did not yearn for
more, faster, and easier could not easily imagine what more was needed,

whether the speed of anything meant anything, and whether it was wise to make "easy" a cherished value.

What we see now in this first quarter of the new millennium is a kind of liminal life for the middle class, a confused sense of being as neighborhoods virtualize, neighbors become 'friends' on social networks in a radically different form of sociability, one that narrows society to your own 'likes.' The American middle class is transitioning to something I do not expect to see. It is being translated as Nick Bottom says in *Midsummer Night's Dream* into some new-yet-unrecognizable form. But perhaps what that may be is already observable in the bottom 40 percent of the population who are absent at the poll booths, who collect no shareholder dividends, who are invisible in quality-of-life assessments. They no longer send out any ping. And no one is searching. Existential distress follows economic distress "if all you want to do is make a lot of money." Life-worlds, personal and social, are not grown by the economy alone, or, as I discovered in Oxley Holl'er, dependent upon it.

I am not alone in failing to find American locales where the images of winners and losers, gentrified and moochers have not overwhelmed values and beliefs indifferent to such. The middle class in America is living on the fumes of former security and well-being, faint memories of not yearning for what we are each second now stimulated to yearn for. We have given up communal concerns and investments in each other. We have given up a variety of ways of being in the world in a variety of different places. We have given up a plentitude of close relationships with Nature and each other and have bought a gated, privatized isolation that defends us from each other, an anonymous virulence and cold-hearted mockery and disdain for those 'below' us. What has been erased is the humanity of the human life-world, a sad fate we subliminally recognize. Such recognition explains our drive toward a robotic technology that will extract the human. We are not in love with what we have become.

It's a terrible cultural imaginary we now live within; and both my West Virginia and my Brooklyn have been casualties, not simply because we are very far from taking any societal action to relieve poverty anywhere or because Brooklyn is now becoming a District 9 sort of place where the ungentrified are very rapidly being uprooted and enclosed, like public schools now colonized by charter schools financed by hedge-fund managers. What is most objectionable is the destruction of lifestyles that had greater merit, greater humanity, greater equality, neighborliness, social identity than the winner/loser/gentrified/ungentrified cultural imaginary that now filters all our perceptions. Call it the loss of existential habitat, the usurpation of a communal life-world built on values and meanings by a culture dominated by market values. What has been dissolved now leaves only poverty to be seen.

McDowell County, the *New York Times* reports, "was always poor." Economics creating asymmetrical power and a politics obliging that asymmetrical power erode the human life-world the way earthmovers, dragline excavators, and bucket-wheel excavators wear down a mountaintop. What is exposed clearly then is the various forms of debased and insulted life that poverty creates.

The close-knit community of concern I found in Oxley Holl'er slips away as poverty replaces that wood-burning stove we all gathered around, the inescapable and utterly controlling element in lives that previously were not weighed down by thoughts of their own poverty. Now we all ask: what could be more central and essential than having money or not having it? Now when the places I knew that I could point to and say, "There, there they seem not to care about who has money and who doesn't" are no longer there; I have only memories. Gentrifying my Brooklyn neighborhood will not bring it back because none of the values and interests of gentrification were ours. Gentrification is the everyday praxis of plutarchy. Waging another war on poverty in Appalachia would only be, yet again, a war to turn losers into winners and that is a battle no one I knew in Oxley Holl'er was fighting or even knew about. A war to turn the poor into winners apparently begins with a reduction of funding for the Supplemental Nutrition Assistance Program (SNAP) and a reduction of food stamps, which in the Tea Party view encourages dependence on government rather than on the casino roulette spin of Wall Street speculation.

Clearly, not all pings are equal. When you believe that someone else's poverty is someone else's problem, only a scam ping sounds. We are heading in the opposite direction from recognizing poverty as social. Our personal choice is to dream of wealth, not poverty. Poverty wears no clothes you would ever want to wear, has no line of credit, offers no relief in shopping, cannot afford to go online or buy that new hybrid to save the environment. The new gentrified class hears the ping of not being able to get their newborn into any of the 40K or so pre-K private schools in Manhattan. If Little Italy in San Diego reverts from its gentrified lifestyle back to the working-class neighborhood of yore, or if any now-gentrified Brooklyn neighborhood made the same return that would sound as an awesome ping, a real threat, and a collapse of future well-being. A ping sounds in our new high-priced enclaves when you cannot find your favorite artisanal cheese or the staff at Suzuki or Montessori schools for four-year-olds is not appreciative of your child's genius or when a homeless man accidentally wanders toward a baby-stroller pushed by a nanny ready to dial 911.

Imagine that the smartphone you hold in your hand and mourn the loss of so deeply that you insure it, that without it, life would end, is what poverty denies you. Impoverished, you cannot add the newest app or just use your GPS or upgrade to the Galaxy 5 or use Foursquare to see where your friends are. You cannot text or tweet. Your world grows dark. Poverty can't bid for that two-million-dollar condo in Park Slope, Brooklyn, fly to Rio for the weekend, or enjoy dining in the new haute Brooklyn style; and your child won't get that real American pre-K head start at Riverdale Country or Columbian Grammar for forty thousand dollars a year.

The idea of an egalitarian democracy shapes a cultural imaginary of societal concern; the establishment of a plutarchy shapes the opposite. Our brand of capitalism, a stochastic, Wild West play of increasingly opaque and questionable financial wheeling and dealing conducted by the super salaried has led to plutarchy, one in which, as Thomas Piketty points out in *Capital in the Twenty-First Century*, leads to a second Gilded Age of inherited wealth and family dynasties. The impoverished are no more than losers who can resurrect themselves as long as no one and no society intervene. The working class is slated for extinction and on the way, it must suffer a loss of reputation, a loss of privileged place in the American cultural imaginary. First, the unions are demonized and then the workers themselves, workers who refuse to become hi-tech skilled, refuse to be retrained, re-educated, reprogrammed, refuse to be the flexible pawns a globalized techno-capitalism demands. The middle class is in shards, their neighborhoods open season to invading hordes of gentrifiers, or left to rot, like the once vibrant neighborhoods of Detroit. Rich, fertile, and sustaining framings of everyday life, ways of imagining yourself and your neighbors, have been demolished like old buildings standing in the way of new multi-purpose real-estate developments—high-priced condos, high-end shopping, and new haute dining.

A scourging and burning, raping and pillaging of our former communal imaginaries, of what I lived within in both Borough Park and Oxley Hollow, stands as the most criminal, stands to be the most indictable. Appalachian life-worlds and ungentrified Brooklyn neighborhoods that signified much more than being impoverished, which did not bend to a measurement of have and have-not, are black boxes to an imaginary that has no imagination, that hears no pings from a ravaged Nature or a democratic egalitarianism now mocked.

And the ping of poverty? Steeped now as we are in a plutarchic imaginary, poverty is a ping that if you hear, you do not want to pursue. It is a ping coming from a black box you do not want to open because it contains not only what we have lost but what we have destroyed. If we search for it, we find a poverty that is the price the many pay for the triumph of a few in this plutarchic order we are busy gentrifying.

Notes

1. *Hauntings: Popular Film and American Culture 1990–1992* (Albany, NY: SUNY Press, 1994), 19–33 passim.

2. Revised and excerpted from *Speeding to the Millennium: Film and Culture 1993–1995* (Albany, NY: SUNY Press, 1998), 215–231 passim.

3. *Postmodern Journeys: Film and Culture 1996–1998* (Albany, NY: SUNY Press, 2001), 243–252. Revised.

4. *Memory's Orbit: Film and Culture 1999–2000* (Albany, NY: SUNY Press, 2003), 1–15.

5. I carried on this memoir style of *Memory's Orbit* in my admittedly gonzo online journalism, on display here in "Hearing the Ping of Poverty—or Not."

6. *Truthout*, May 23, 2014.

Chapter Eight

Railing through Europe

"Is This a Postmodern World?" 1995–2010[1]

By the time I wrote *This is a Picture and Not the World* (2007), I had been railing throughout Europe since 1995 with what I call my "Is This a Postmodern World?" road show (and which Andrew Mark Sivak will call "Rolling Thunder"), ostensibly a university study-abroad program welcomed by various universities throughout Europe. Indeed, I followed Foucault and so left it to the police and the bureaucrats to see whether our papers were in order. But as it turned out, with the continued encouragement, support, and energy of Professor Hans Bertens, who over the years ascended to what we in the United States call a "university provost," the program succeeded in blending classroom and experiential learning, everyday life and theory. I believe that in the fifteen-year duration of this program, it demonstrated that Europe was not the "open air museum" that Vice President Cheney mocked but a different and yet recognizable book of the world that young Americans needed to read—for all the reasons we assign to the enrichment of our being in the world.

I was intent on expanding the imaginative frame of my American 'heartland' students by bringing them into as many different cultural realities as possible in a month and a half.

You might say I gathered pictures of what a post-9/11 United States was doing and what it appeared to be from foreign perspectives.

A Senegalese cold-drink vendor on the Lido di Venezia told me I sounded "New York" like Robert DeNiro and then, smiling, called me a "capitalismo," which always needled my dissident heart.

A young Eastern European travelling salesman called me "New York" and told me he would get there someday and nothing would stop him. I asked "Why?" and he told me that it was the place where he could make a fortune without the government getting in his way. Besides, no one would ask him what family he came from. I took to calling him "New York," and his dream never diminished in the ensuing years I ran into him. A young Romanian woman trying to learn Dutch so she could become a Dutch citizen told me that "New York" would never get there. He had a wife and kids back in Slovakia.

I was invited into the office of the owner of a hostel in Paris who wanted to know why I brought Americans to Paris. I told him that they came from a provincial part of the United States but nonetheless thought they were exceptional compared to all foreigners. I told him then that I brought them to France to jolt them out of their illusions. Later that night we were told that we would get a free round of drinks, compliments of the owner. I had not told him that I believed one nation's pride and sometimes arrogance could only be jostled by running into another nation's similar self-admiration.

One late afternoon, as we sat on the small veranda at Eveline's bed and breakfast, Simone, who had been a chef in Milan and who spent days and nights playing *World of Warcraft* with one of the dozen or so Apple computers Eveline made available without charge, asked me for what reason my ancestors had left Sicily so long ago. "Per un lavoro, no?" he said, his eyes shaded by large tinted glasses, eyes with dark shadows beneath. *WOW* kept him up to all hours. I nodded. My father's father was hired to do stone work on the Ashokan Reservoir in upstate New York. I asked Simone why he had left Italy and he told me that he would not live in a country run by a pig like Berlusconi. He would become a Dutch citizen. He did everything but spit as he told me this and then minutes later: "Joe, farò spaghetti alla carbonara per noi, va bene? He was a masterful chef; we ate a kilo between the two of us.

In response to a Rom woman who pulled a sandwich out of a paper sack and, smiling, gestured to me if I would have it, I nodded and said, "Sure, I'm starving." A man seated by the window in the compartment, half asleep, told her what I had said. Her face darkened and she mumbled something. "She says you don't know what the word means." He paused and then said, "Like all Americans." I nodded. They were right. I was on my way from Trieste to Ljubljana, from a fantastic dinner the night before in a mixed northern-Italian-and-Slavic-cuisine restaurant and anxious now to experience Slovenian cuisine the coming night. I was "starving" between the two. Hilary Clinton, in defending the five million dollars she had made in speaking fees in fifteen months declared that she and Bill "were dead broke" when they had left the White House.

While tourism brings us into places and events designed for tourists, into an artificiality we escape to as we vacate the harsh realities of our own lives, enough travel in a purposeless, wandering style reveals to the comfortable what hardship is; to those who have never been hungry, what hunger is; to those who have no fear of the authorities, what such fear is; to those who luxuriate in their own freedom to choose, what tyranny is. And while it became clear after returning to the United States that there were an increasing number of Americans who had no need to travel the globe to find hardship they themselves faced, there was also an intensity in top-of-the-line living that remained indifferent to scaling back their own indulgence.

I recall offering to help a student from Saudi Arabia find what he seemed to be looking for under his bunk and only noticing the prayer mat when I too was on the floor in search. A thousand apologies and much embarrassment but he put all that aside with a wonderful smile and a hand on my shoulder.

Why did these Europe travels attract so many troubled students? As I look back now I believe I was looking for them; it was a subliminal criterion for selection. Fathers were the traumatizing hot spots for many of the males. A biological father known only just before his death, and then days before the trip begins, the foster father suddenly dead. This young man spends a good deal of time looking for stuff he has lost or says he has left behind. In a hostel or on a train. Lost. He spends so much time looking for a missing shoe that I am alerted and I go to see. And he is there in the room he shares with others, arms resting on his top bunk, journal open but not writing. "I lost my shoe," he tells me, his eyes wide as if he's told me something astounding and now he awaits for me to . . . I don't know what he expects from me and yet I do know, but knowing, even feeling, is not fitting.

Another young man tells me he wishes his father who works all the time and makes loads of money was more like me. I know he is not telling me that my one meditative, wandering reflection a day is not work and that I make a scant amount of money. He sees me as someone who does not care about such things. And when the Coen brothers' movie *The Big Lebowski* comes along and an essay of mine about the film becomes a highlight of the program and the recruitment. "Are you employed, Mr. Lebowski?" I was. Travelling around Europe with a pack of twentysomethings, all of us living in hostels and riding Eurail. It seems to all of them over all those years that like the Dude I just "roll" from one fascinating country to another, no worries. They all want to be that. Now when those who were in their twenties in 1995 are approaching forty, they might wonder if it was all a sleight of hand, or wonder how many hard knocks make it hard to abide. Or whether the flaw in the "flawed exiles" like the Dude is fatal to abiding in our millennial America. "Come on, Dude. Let's bowl" is either a waning exhortation or one that . . . abides.

The son who wanted to be a stand-up comedian? He is not going to be like his father. He is going to be a stand-up comedian. He will one day surprise us and do his act for us. But he never does. He is always sad and listens to the saddest music. And even if he went on to work 24/7 and make a load of money, I think the Dude could very well still abide in his life. At least I like to think so.

I was awakened in the middle of the night by a student going through what she called a panic attack; and then a student so ill from food poisoning, I took him to the Hôpital de l'Hotel-Dieu in the middle of the night, and we sat among a Balzac tableau vivant. The young man's father is a doctor; the young man has a satellite connection on his BlackBerry. I have not travelled with anyone who had this. He is a harbinger of what is to come. He speaks to his father who is a doctor and tells him he is in a hospital. The doctor-father speaks to me and I tell him his son will be released in the morning. He insists on speaking to the French doctor in charge though he speaks no French. He just wants the numbers. They speak and then I am given the phone and I am told the French doctor needs to do this and that and definitely not release his son. It seems the French doctor whom the American doctor cannot understand does not know as much as the American doctor who is thousands of miles away. I apologize to the French doctor who understands. "Il est un père inquiet pour son fils. Nous avons besoin des lits. Nous ne pouvons pas lui faire plaisir." The son is released and promises me he will not buy oysters from street vendors on hot summer days. He wants to be a doctor and probably is by now.

In Montpellier, Olivier Granier, the irrepressibly exuberant manager of the Hotel Nova, and I sat one whole night in hard plastic chairs as another of my travellers was brought to the ER. And in Budapest, another case of food poisoning, this time a hot midday, and a collapse of the student as Lash, my TA, and I bore him along between us, heading to a medical center that looked like Auschwitz, which we had just recently visited in Poland.

I am ill in Budapest; it does not stop raining. The bedclothes are damp; I am feverish. I go to the same doctor I brought a student to the day before in the same Auschwitz-like facility. A disease-control center. I

am berated for wanting antibiotics because all Americans want antibiotics but I say I do not want them. I just want him to listen to my lungs
so I can be reassured that I do not have pneumonia, which I have had
before without knowing. He does not use a stethoscope; he is dressed
in a three-piece dark suit, wears a bowtie and he's as old as I am. He
thumps my chest and puts his ear to it. Does the same with my back.
He asks me what my temperature is and I tell him I do not have a
thermometer. He tells me to get one, get some aspirin, and take aspirin
if my fever gets high. Otherwise, tough it out. I have some congestion
but not pneumonia. If I get worse, go to a doctor. You Americans take
antibiotics for needless things. We are soft. They are not soft in Hungary.
Or in Bulgaria. Or Romania. Or in the Ukraine and Georgia. Or in any
of the former Yugoslavia. I don't know mortality so I live in fear. He is
angry when he tells me that. All you Americans are alike. September 11th
brought death to your door. I cannot get a word in to say I am not one
of the indulged, that I am on the outside of that, that I am different. And
then I know it is not true. Otherwise, why am I there?

A former gendarme from Marseille living in the same boarding
house as myself and whom we called "Le Loup" because he was indeed
always on the prowl for the ladies told me he left Marseille because the
hoodlums had better weapons than the police did. "Do you know," he
asked me, "that more Arabic is spoken in Marseille than French? How
could that be?"

One afternoon in St. Jean de Luz my TA, Brian "Hosm" Hosmer,
now an illustrious winemaker in northern Michigan, and I wandered
around looking for a place to eat. We settled on a small place under
the trees, surrounded by mostly women, perhaps the French version of
the Tide Water Virginia Ladies Garden Club. Our waiter provided classic
French white-glove service, without the gloves and though he tried not
to show it, it looked like he shared our ribald appreciation of how out of
place we were. It was as if Céline had stumbled in. The waiter smiled, "Ah!
Ferdinand" and then told us of a place we might like. We went there that
evening and found our waiter, his tie at half-mast and his face red with
wine, among other serveurs unwinding after a long day of decorum among
the tourists. They filled every table but as luck would have it, a table was
free just as we entered. There was only one dinner choice, a lamb roasted
in a Piment d'Espelette, sheep yogurt, Dijon mustard marinade, and the
wine, a very drinkable red, was gratis as was crusty bread. Our newfound
friend, the Proper Waiter, took me back to the small galley kitchen where
one Falstaff-sized chef with a huge smile listened to me rave about the

glories of that lamb dish. There had been no sign on the door and when I looked for the place a few years later, it had been replaced by a hotel chain, and no one remembered that restaurant having been there. I began to learn that when one wanders and by chance finds what astounds, there is only sadness in a return, a disappointment that what once was, only a configuration at the very moment of chance, has vanished.

During a lecture by a visiting Utrecht professor, Maarten von Rossem, who was then what he called a "TV quizmaster," pulled some questions out of the latest *The Economist's The World in Statistics* and managed in so doing to turn the students against him. It happened this way: In response to the questions, which students believed the United States was at the top, he invariably had to correct them. Sweden, or The Netherlands, or Denmark, or Canada made the top list, and often the United States did not appear at all. For some fifteen years of guest lecturing in "Is This a Postmodern World?" Maarten troubled the minds of my students inciting them to recognize arguments contrary to their own and thus think dialectically, mediating between contradictory argument, as did all the fine guest lecturers in The Netherlands, Belgium, Italy, France, Spain, and Hungary. Very few nations and nationalities were not filled with their own self-esteem, their own exceptionalism that, like one's own ego, was not always pleasant to behold or to deal with. Neither of course was a demolished image that so many had to bear, from American slaves and Native Americans to every generation of immigrant.

The varied and contradictory pictures that travel provides lead you to think about the process of 'worlding,' of picturing everything in a certain way. Conflicting pictures puzzle the mind and bring you to ponder the how and why of differences, whether it be The Netherlands' portrait of individual and society or France's portrait of life and art or the Basque portrait of nation and identity, and so on. This sort of travel avoids the tourist agent's aim to give you a fun-packed trek, always entertaining, never provocative, rather like the way we like entertaining novels and movies that do not unsettle our realities. True travel is a wandering, an erring in the sense of going the wrong way because in truth the right way etches the path you're already on so that you may as well not have travelled at all and stayed home. We 'stay home' in our minds because it is a place we know and the dangers of difference are minimized. True travel away from home wanders into the ups and downs of everyday life elsewhere and inevitably leads you to compare and contrast your homeland's picture of the world with those you now experience.

Different cultures live in differed reality frames, live within different pictures of what the world is and was, though the forces of globalized marketing and financing are diminishing those differences, transforming the world as rapidly and relentlessly as global warming. And while the wealth and power resulting from such globalization had in actuality created a situation whereby it was easier than ever before in history for such wealth and power to exploit and victimize the many to the benefit of the few, Chance could play all against their own interests. The attacks on the US homeland on September 11, 2001, would very quickly lead to a reaction that brought dividends to investors and injury and death to the many, both Americans and Afghans and Iraqi. The tragedy of 9/11 privatized warfare beyond what Eisenhower had predicted, but it also created a mass paranoia that could be triggered henceforth against all opposition to that picture of what the United States should be that the few had painted on the American cultural imaginary.

The American cultural imaginary has not strayed far, in spite of the Great Recession and continuing unemployment, from the words of *Wall Street*'s Gordon Gekko: "Fifty, a hundred million dollars, buddy. A player. Or nothing." The wealthy measure the world in a far different way than those who work for wages, don't have stock options, six-figure bonuses, elite travel accommodation, and inherit nothing but unpaid medical bills and unpaid mortgages. Inherited wealth is what Thomas Pikkety in *Capital in the Twenty-First Century* sees as the coming knockout punch to an already-fading democracy. Wage earners in the United States have fallen off all statistical charts and polls, are mesmerized by the seductions of cyberspace, or identify with the wealthy in some strange psychodrama tragic to their own interests. How the world appears to them and how the impact of anything is measured remain hidden and inconsequential, a "whatever" matter to those who don't really know what starving or being dead broke might be. Every American, not just those in inner cities where violence is ritual, didn't know what violence was until 9/11. They did not know what a plutarchy the United States had become until Occupy Wall Street began to paint that portrait. They did not know what catastrophe could be wrought by a runaway Wall Street financial sector until the 2007 Great Recession, and how unequally dispersed the painful consequences of that looting and the 'austerity' strategies following have been. These are all pictures in the making.

Along with the entire country, I was propelled into a different way of looking at the world after the 9/11 attacks; we had in moments journeyed into a new and very dark world. I tried to follow that new imaginary in *This is a Picture and Not the World*, which was finally published in 2007. At that moment of attack, our democracy had already replaced any sense of egalitarianism with a winner/loser ethos, and the country was prepared within its cultural imaginary to respond to a no-discussion "us against them" battle cry. Why wouldn't economic warfare fought on a zero-sum basis automatically translate into bloody warfare? And why wouldn't it, like economic warfare, go on and on? Inequities of all sorts, and all rooted in a growing wealth inequity, were put out of sight and replaced by only one divide, a divide between us and Islamic terrorists. The terrorist fever has not ever been allowed to abate, fueled firstly by a politics that needs to keep propped in our cultural imagination a fear of "them" and not a fear of what is being homegrown by a wildly reckless financialized capitalism. We have created by our blind world economic hegemony monsters, including the monster of ISIS, a distorted aberration of its own avowed religion, a religion which, unlike Christianity, does not render to Caesar a worldly rule. September 11th vacated from the mindscape of the American cultural imaginary a rising battle between our capitalist Caesar and some 80 percent of the American population. Skirmishes have arisen now and then since that time but terrorist, deficit, illegal immigration, and the always-present 'rising socialist' fears have kept the calamities of climate and plutarchic devastations repressed.

This Is a Picture and Not the World

From "Behind the Scenes: A Preproduction Q & A"

Kevin Nicholoff: People died. That was real. Those towers are gone. That's real.

Joseph Natoli: Sure. It's an historical fact. Place, date, and all. Like Pearl Harbor. Vietnam. Wait. Aren't those historical events, like all historical events, now imagined within the dimensions of a present cultural imaginary? Their existence is at once a matter of representation, which is a matter of cultural mediation. The 9/11 attack was unique in that it happened on our TV screens at the same time it happened in the world. From the very first TV images of a plane and a building, the event went through the kind of mediating filtering TV gives to reality and we give to TV. At once, what we saw on TV was like a movie, and we could digest it in no other way. Bush's responses were also from a movie, the only way to reach a culture already residing in the hyperreal. He became John Wayne. He had a Texas walk, a tobacco-chewing smirk, a twang as needed, and he cut brush a lot "out at the ranch." It was pure PR genius to give Bush a part in that movie, pure genius to see it all so quickly as a movie.

From "Outtake: Postmodern Screwball"

Key Grip: *"The Big Lebowski* is multiplex realities? . . . What does the Dude do? Soaking, toking herb, the occasional acid flashback, listening to CCR, a penchant for White Russians, and bowling. He's a flashback dripped like acid over the entrepreneurial American 1990s. He's what's now called a "loser," and the Coen brothers fascination with him proves they're not in grown-up reality. That view was made by a film reviewer in the *New Yorker* (March 1998). Everyone is now bowling alone in our fiercely all-against-all society, except the Dude. He has buddies. The spirit of egalitarianism abides in the Dude."

From "Futurescape"

Outtake: Note the multiplexing here: The writer takes up a discussion of sci-fi movies through sci-fi characters who take up a discussion of whether or not a discussion of sci-fi movies can be objective and whether or not such premised objectivity leads to realism, and the nonhuman—the android who is programmed without subjectivity—concludes logically that only a human who had never seen a sci-fi movie could render an objective account of sci-fi movies, to which another character facetiously remarks that at the very least someone should be chosen to write about sci-fi who doesn't use voices putting the reader on the trail of the origin or grounding voice, the "Natoli-author" signifier, which links to us through characters considering the complexities of communicating outside the frame of one's own observations, one's own always-already-present cultural scripting.

From "Noirscape"

Outtake (voice-over sounding amazingly like Michael Moore): America after 9/11 is paranoid and terrorized, but the landscape is not darkened, the mood is not set for film noir. "Get out to the mall, to Disneyland, to NASCAR. Nothing indelible has been written on your soul." Yet the war in Iraq has gone badly with a thousand soldiers dead and almost seven thousand wounded; twelve thousand Iraqis—civilians, soldiers, 'insurgents'—killed. More Americans were glued to *American Idol* than listening to the Democratic presidential candidate John Kerry make his acceptance speech. And Americans watch *Survivor* on TV where 'real world' reality TV 'real people' compete in an exotic setting to be the "last man [*sic*] standing," the recipient of a million dollars. This is a picture, and not the world.

Voice-over: A picture of Americans after 9/11 shows us that human nature is neither haunted by a primordial sin nor caught in an existential battle between authentic being and bad faith, nor, as in classic film noir, buffeted by the play of Chance, driven by desires exceeding rational control, and caught in a web of misfortune, corrupted by power, past sins, and violence that foundationally crack the veneer of a moral, rational social order. In the years 1941–1958, the time when classic film noir flourished, Americans were heading for prosperity but were shadowed by the horrors of war and haunted by not only revelations of the dark side of humanity but their powerlessness in the face of it.

From "Sneak Preview: Magic Town: America's Heartland"

Script Doctor: "Bringing in *Twin Peaks* right away is good. Why? David Lynch jumps on this American psyche small-town mythos vibe and blows it apart. Okay, here's how: It's part of the American Dream; ergo, it's part nightmare. Why? Small-town America is magic town because it's harmony town; it's where the neighbors greet neighbors in the town square, at the soda fountain, at the church on the hill, at Baldwin's grocery, at the Sunset movie theatre on Main Street. It's a picture-perfect unified reality. It's a one-peak town, because everybody shares the same reality, which means they can communicate with each other. They share the same basic values; they're on the same page because they live on the same block, in the same small town; they live in the same reality frame. But if you double the peaks, you double the realities. And if reality can divide like that, why can't you have four realities? Why can't you have multiple realities living in one small town? All of a sudden, with Lynch, you have a postmodern small town. It's always been multiple realities, but part of the mythic allure of small-town America has been the fact that it isn't multiple, that it's the one place you can go to and find not clashing, crossfire pictures of things, but simple, true, honest, wholesome, authentic being-in-the-world. If you fracture the mythos of the American Disney small town, you're on your way to forming international coalitions before you jump to preemptive attacks. The indivisible isolation and completeness and the self-contained harmony that we invest in our vision of small-town America is no more than an illusion, a delusion. As long as we hold on to this illusion that unity beyond all diversity lies at our beginnings—a simplistic, Hollywood created harmony—we will never move within our imagination toward any globalism except what global capitalism defines" (14).

From "Documentary: The Short-Term Memory Detective"

Voice-Over: The "United States of Amnesia" is what Gore Vidal calls the United States of America. We are in a market-induced or market-spun cultural amnesia. The ideal in this market-driven technoworld is the homo sapien of fifteen-minute memory. A short-term memory, a memory that locks onto the present, consumes it, and then loses it, and stands ready to lock on to a totally new present.

Imagine the marketing delirium over this state of affairs. We fall in love with the newest new, purchase it, and then in fifteen minutes can't recognize it, or our desire for it. Obsolescence on a fifteen-minute cycle! We're out shopping again. Endgame consumer capitalism. Imagine such a brave new world, such a society, where continuity in thought, word, and action is rendered meaningless. Coherence would vanish, as nothing from the past would need to be tied to the present and everything said would need to meet—or not—the requirements of a fifteen-minute intelligibility. Identity would also need only meet the requirements of a fifteen-minute present and would, therefore, be free to remake itself continually. No one would need a psychiatrist because no one would be trying to find a true self—a unified, coherent, continuous self. Authenticity of self is a fifteen-minute achievement. Welcome to the United States of Alzheimer.

Have we come close to describing the present generation of primary-school students? Perhaps the latest computer-software programs will dissolve fragmented and fractured attentiveness, and the market will, thereby, resolve the problem it creates by the very means it created the problem. Only a fifteen-minute memory span would, of course, believe this.

From "Shortscape: Never Far from Melodrama"

Voice-over: We no longer value an emotional or an imaginative life, and our senses have degraded into a purely passive, receptive mode. Everything is reduced to exchange value. What profit is there in our emotions? In our imagination? Our intellects are not sharp, surgical instruments but blunted gatekeepers of Boolean bytes, of the endless deferment of email [text] messages and replies. Just as the peptic billionaire John D. Rockefeller envied the digestive system of a humble worker on his estate, we now envy the power of classic Hollywood melodrama to exercise the emotions, imaginations, and senses of its audience.

From "Fearscape/Thrillscape/Nightscape"

Voice-over: "What in me is dark" may find its way to the screen and scare the bejeezus out of me. Maybe we fear falling back into alcoholism, or cheating on our wives or husbands once again, or not having enough of a retirement pension to get by, or that mole on our back becoming a melanoma and eventually killing us, or having someone run a red light and crashing into us, or someone finding out we pursue some weird sexual fantasy in secret, or a stranger who raped us and was never caught coming back for us, or the phone ringing and that one person we love with all our hearts has been killed, or Anthrax sent to you in the mail, or a dirty bomb going off not too far away, or the airplane you're on suddenly bursting into flames and spiraling toward the dark, cold waters of the Atlantic . . . whatever your mind now touches and you feel fear.

Can we call these personal fears? Surely, whatever the origin, they occupy the private spaces in our minds. We bring it inside and become haunted by private fear. This is fear privatized, and the genre begins here.

. . . .

Harry Favorite: "Fear is universal, Doc. What you're saying is that only a few whackos know what fear is. Fear is universal. Which means you need a universal cause. The Devil. The Dark Side. Where the dead go who ain't happy. You close your eyes, Doc, for the last time and you go someplace. Maybe it's a happy place; maybe it's a dark place. But it ain't no place. Why? Because if dead people were going no place for all these centuries the story that we go some place would have dried up a long time ago. In point of fact, Doc, that story would never have been told. Do you see any other creature on the planet trembling in the dark? What separates us from them? I'll tell you. We're jumpy. And we've got a right to be" (17).

From "American Cool"

Script Doctor: "Hollywood linked coolness with rebellion. Who's cooler than Rick in *Casablanca* (1942)? Or, John Garfield in *Body and Soul* (1947)? Who's cooler than James Dean in *Rebel Without a Cause* (1955)? Who's cooler than Peter Fonda's Captain America in *Easy Rider* (1969)? Who's cooler than Donald Sutherland and Elliot Gould in *MASH* (1970), John Travolta as Vincent in *Pulp Fiction* (1994)? Who's cooler than The Dude in *The Big Lebowski* (1998)? Who's cooler than Jack Nicholson in *Five Easy Pieces* (1970), or Linda Fiorentino in *The Last Seduction* (1994) when she walks into that redneck bar? Rebels all. Totally American. And why not? Who's a bigger rebel anywhere than Tom Paine? We didn't have a revolution; we had a rebellion. Rebellion is in our blood, in our roots. What are Americans rebelling against? "Whatya got?" Brando responds in *The Wild One* (1953). Young blood, young guns. Every guy willing to fight the law when the law always wins, from Billy the Kid, Clyde Barrow, John Dillinger to Jesse James, Jack Kerouac to Bob Dylan, Elvis to Tupac. Who's cooler than Paul Newman as *Cool Hand Luke*? Ask them that."

....

"You start with a search for the coolness code and wind up with a bunch of views tearing each other down. You get no place, which is where postmodernists take us, but we've got no time left for going no place. Here's the code for coolness—*betrayal*. Coolness after 9/11 means being cool about the future, about being secure, about the social compact, about the American Dream. A deeply submerged sense of betrayal by country, history, reason, reality, words, and pictures puts Americans in places where they can't be betrayed again: virtual realities and realities emptied of real thought and feeling. These are realities in which you become one of the survivors in exotic locales far from the real America, or realities that are so flagrantly unconnected with the real world that they are sadistically referred to as "Reality TV." Coolness is now no more than being cold about the world you live in."

After writing *This is a Picture and Not the World*, I turned to online writing because I was beginning to feel "time's winged chariot" at my back, to feel an urgency to broadcast my approach to reading the American mass psyche to headline events and crossing disciplinary boundaries. The first piece I wrote for *Truthout*—"When the World is Turned Upside Down"—pulled in more readers than all my books combined. And there was not something like two years between finishing a piece and seeing it published. I believe that if the doors of cyberspace had been open to William Blake, his magnificent letters would have become a daily blog, his art imaged everywhere, his poetry recited on YouTube. On the other hand, he may just have disappeared in a snowstorm of hashtags and viral YouTube videos with the longevity of a Mayfly. Blake, just another unpaid "content provider" lost in cyberspace. That haunts me too.

Note

1. Excerpts from *This is a Picture and Not the World: Movies and a Post-9/11 America* (Albany, NY: State University of New York Press, 2007).

Chapter Nine

A Long Journey to
Find an Online Political Home

Upon retirement both from teaching here and in Europe, I took up pro bono publica online writing. I had long been a fan of *Bad Subjects: Political Education for Everyday Life* and became a member of the editorial collective. I follow Aristotle's lead in believing that through politics we secure a civic morality that functions not merely for private interest and gain but for the public good. Our politics, both as practiced by our politicians and pursued by the electorate, has collapsed as we have embedded ourselves in the illusions offered to us by private domains of personal autonomy and freedom. Our chosen economic beliefs sponsor such illusions in order to keep us from "doing" politics as an expression of and nurturing of the public good, a "doing" that creates the moral life of a society.

I had an interesting, and, of course, turbulent journey, in my political online writing, which I trace in this chapter, starting with *Truthout*.

Truthout's Public Intellectual Project

The Public Intellectual Project on *Truthout* was launched with the following announcement by Henry Giroux:

> Within the last few decades, the emergence of public intellectuals
> as important cultural and social critics has raised fundamental
> questions not only about the social function of academics,
> but also about the connection between higher education and

public life, between academic work and the major issues shaping the broader society. *Truthout's* Public Intellectual Project will provide progressive academics with an opportunity to address a number of important social issues in a language that is both rigorous and accessible. All too often, academics produce work that is either too abstract for a generally informed public, or they separate their scholarship from the myriad of issues and contemporary problems that shape everyday life in the United States and abroad.

The Public Intellectual Project will solicit and publish work from both younger academics who have not yet ventured into the public realm to address major social concerns, and from those scholars who are already actively involved in speaking to multiple audiences about serious social issues. The project is designed to provide a platform for the public to think carefully about a range of social problems that affect their lives. It will also allow a generation of scholars to reflect on their own intellectual practices, discourses and understanding of what it might mean to embrace their role as public intellectuals.

The website *Truthout* had not descended into the fury to draw eyeballs to the 'page' that even a ten-second attention span could capture. The idea was to combine journalistic attention to the present moment with an unapologetic erudition. Opinions and personal takes could be left at the doorstep; this was to be background that drew upon history, connections to cutting-edge theory, argument in a dialogic with counterargument, interpretation that measured what forces led anything to mean what we held it to mean. I saw it as a return of Frankfurt School dialectic, no diatribes or paid endorsements but a maneuvering between contrary arguments.

Drawn to the format and a readership that dwarfed the few eyeballs *Bad Subjects* was attracting, I saw no sign of a future contretemps. My postmodern slant put out versions of a sentence like this: "The view that the truth is out here and not there, that our words seal in a determinate way 'the truth of things" and The Other's words don't, is a view that preempts any possibility of engaging in the necessary struggle to imaginatively infuse the world with a liberating vision." My critique also of what I saw as the dark side of our cybertech enthusiasm and its already deleterious effect on the minds and imaginations of millennials troubled *Truthout's* mission to attract more millennials to the website. My notion that the millennials weren't 'post' anything but in fact were disinterested in everything that was outside personal interest and everything resistant to personal opinion profiled me as a back-in-the-day Ned Ludd. Nevertheless, I continue to see our unquestioned welcoming of all that hi-tech develops as an accommodation that the need for new profit derived from new technology has engineered.

In my writing for the far more Leftist journal *Bad Subjects*, I had repeatedly suggested that the Liberal view was cowed by a market-driven neoliberal politics and at the same time embarrassed and reluctant to strike against that politics with a well-developed arsenal of Leftist critique. Libertarians, who had no problem with market rule, had assumed the radical, dissenting spots. The Libertarian appeal to all those who wanted no government, no rule but personal rule, to all the young to whom anarchism is exciting, persists because the sine qua non of anarchism, as in all socialist views, remains concealed. Libertarians will not mention economic equality because it is government and not market rule they protest. Some Liberals want to trim the sails of an out-of-control globalized techno-capitalism but they will not reroute toward economic equality with a populace that does not understand the connection but does understand "economic equality" as communist.

No brand of socialist, from social democrat and democratic socialist to communist to anarchist, can reach beyond a cabbalistic fringe to mainstream America. Liberals step back from the idea that you have as much political equality as you have economic equality and that when the two are seriously awry, you have a plutarchic rule.

The liberal view has grown dark in my mind because it had become servile to market rule, admitting what should have been opposed in that rule as a 'reality' not to be resisted. I stood with Blake and imagined that such a rule was like Urizen's, only real because we acquiesced in recognizing it as such. It has always seemed to me that if Liberals would get out of the way and stop providing Neoliberals with the compassionate gestures that come after blood has been spilled, we wouldn't be in the one side only fighting the war we are in. The result of a too accommodating liberalism is to create the impression that the public good is indefensible or only laughably defensible. The "public" in Romney's view cannot be reached because they are degenerate bloodsuckers, losers who need to be dealt with, like an infestation of rats. Why keep Liberals around to bring up the humanitarian blather or chatter about a social conscience or the need to treat your neighbors biblically? As long as such feel-good words are mouthed, the American conscience is salved while the well-being of the many is ransacked by Neoliberals. But a winner's indifference to the public good is permeating the society, top to bottom. Bukowski captured the winners' view here: "The Bible also says leave your neighbor alone. Let every soul look out for itself and let your neighbor do the same" (*Factotum* [Black Sparrow Books, 1975]). When there are enough Americans who imagine a world like this is right and reasonable, just to the way things "really are," there is no need for Neoliberals to keep Liberals around. They are redundant, obsolete, and soon to be as extinct as is required.

This is a dark imaginary; I did not make it up. I observed it.

Besides my dark affiliations with liberalism, my postmodern bent recognized that myriad realities announced that the truth was what each reality said it was. And each had statistics and facts to offer evidence in support of their truth, which I called a "truth story" that played variously as the truth, depending upon time, place, and audience. Reason did not work both sides of the street, as Nietzsche saw, but only on the side you were on. This did not play well with *Truthout* editors and neither did my harping on what seemed to me as clear as the emperor without clothes. Those suckled in cyberspace, learning to walk with a smartphone in hand, and carrying on a 24/7 *World of Warcraft* addiction in a real world that was turning very harsh for very many, did not need to be told that they were the most informed generation. They didn't need to be told they could multitask, connect, reconnect, post, update, tweet, and text that they were on and off the bus and all that really meant something. Einstein's words pointed to a single, long and steady focus of mind: "It's not that I'm so smart; it's just that I stay with problems."

What I saw was that those born into a cyberspace world became bored because the off-line world moved too slowly, and that history was analog and analog was dead. Attentions flagged in the real world because that world was analog. Nature itself is analog. It no longer matters, which may be a reason why the destructive consequences of global warming do not register. What I saw was that the young were enchanted and seduced by their own circling choices, choices that could never break the vicious circle a know-nothing choosing self inevitably created. What the alternative reality of cyberspace had done was provide a home for illusions and delusions that could never be challenged as long as one's own consciousness was the 'final arbiter of truth' and as long as one remained imprisoned within the prison house of one's own choices.

One was free to Google and wiki till the cows came home but one would always be choosing the same cows. And if by chance anyone fell upon what was outside their own locked box, they would unfriend. No one who loves his or her own choices and never asks, as does Montaigne

"What do I know?" ever takes to what challenges and opposes them. No one who is secure in the knowledge that their personal design of the world is all that matters is ever a fan of what dismantles that design.

Although I persisted in saying that this unfortunate state of affairs couldn't be laid at the personal doorstep of the young who were subjected and not controlling subjects, my observations didn't go down well. *Truthout,* like the countless online broadcasts of the truth, was trying to draw the young into a particular view of the world. This was a difficult enough row to hoe in a climate when neither politics nor reading beyond 140 characters was in vogue. And the fact that polls indicated that millennials had great confidence in their own power to overcome all odds only meant that any criticism was an attack by a superseded mentality.

And so I took a long sabbatical but returned as a "Public Intellectual" with a piece titled "Dark Affinities: Liberal and Neoliberal." I attempted to show that these rivals were joined at the subliminal dark hip in regard to issues in which real opposition was needed and that neither represented the interests of about 80 percent of the American population.

Political Affairs: "From each according to his ability, to each according to their work"

For a brief time, I wrote for *Political Affairs,* partially because I had developed as much of a critique of Liberals as Neoliberals, discovering in both underlying affinities of wealth and a mutual rallying around the same flag of market rule. It seemed to me—and this is an ancient position—that Liberals were no more than shills for that rule. They seemed like corporate, established workers' associations that corporations could point to as proper worker representation. In reality, such mockeries only succeed in keeping real, challenging unions from forming.

I did not want to assist in any way in keeping this proper front man viable, this field arbitrage that kept victims of the winners from bleeding to death, just barely. My preference was to clear the field of apologists for looters and looting and make a full-scale assault on that gang, mostly the ones who had carried out the Great Recession and continued to do so afterward. It seemed clear that after the biggest collapse of the economy since the Depression, it was time to retrieve a critique that was not a sham. It was time to unpack what Alex Ross in a *New Yorker* article called "naysayers," the Frankfurt School "thorny theorists."

I was therefore understandably impressed with Elizabeth Warren's appearance on the political scene and the ensuing divide that has developed

in the Democratic Party between those who accept market rule as a starting point and those who wish to challenge it at every point. The divide
is growing between, in short, The Third Way developed by Bill Clinton
and Tony Blair in the nineties and may continue under a Hillary Clinton
presidency, and a politics that recognizes that profit making does not bend
on its own, for any reason. Therefore, all compromise has to be made on
one side, the side where 80 percent of the American population struggles.

Because I saw the absence of any challenge by Liberals at the time
to market rule, I took up writing for *Political Affairs,* self-described on
their website:

> *Political Affairs* is an online magazine of the theories, ideas,
> politics and culture of the socialist and democratic traditions
> and visions of the United States from a working-class point of
> view. We are partisan to the rise of working people's wealth
> and culture as the foundation for the rise of the whole people
> toward a more just, prosperous, and peaceful nation.
>
> Over 150 years ago near the dawn of industrial capitalism,
> Karl Marx, the father of modern socialism, gave the most suc-
> cinct and essential expression to this ideal in the slogan: "From
> each according to his ability to each according to their work."
>
> In the labor movement; in the associations of every trade
> and profession; in the struggles of communities of color and
> diverse nationalities against racial injustice and inequality; in
> the movements of women, youth, seniors, the disabled, and of
> gay, lesbian, bi-sexual and transgender communities for equality
> and dignity; in the strivings, achievements and aspirations of
> the many people's that comprise the American people, and in
> the genius that arises from their wisdom, works, science and
> art—we seek enlightenment, truth and the fullest realization
> of the abilities of humankind.
>
> We seek the paths to global peace, prosperity and the
> end of oppressions in the fraternity and cooperation of all
> who do the work of the world and in the highest aspirations
> of all peoples.
>
> *Political Affairs* is part of the People Before Profits network.

I wrote for them until someone detected my postmodern tail and
I suddenly was 'Siberia-ed.' Besides "Why the Rich Get Richer, and
Other Truth Stories," I wrote "The Most Dangerous Game," "Our Market

Regime and Republican Ethics," "Unions Serve the Tea: the Rage against the Employed and the Unionized," and "Where Are 'The People'?" before my own trustworthy political affiliations apparently came to light. I have selected this piece on the rich not because they are a particular target of a rabid leftism but because the American cultural imaginary is so full of very seductive stories about the rich. And one of those stories—that we are all a stone's throw away from joining that elite group—has made any critique of the economic system that created them difficult. Likewise, attempts to recuperate some semblance of egalitarian democracy are prevented by entrenched oligarchs working to defend and preserve their elite status. The most efficient way to defend and preserve is for the oligarch to become the plutarch, to use wealth to gain power. There is more of the axiomatic than diabolical choices and conspiracies against 'the people.'

An economic system that is stochastic and not rational is a true casino system, although the winners here do not admit that the Goddess Fortuna has turned the wheel in their direction, but rather argue that innovative genius, indomitable will, hard work, a savvy sense of human nature, vision, and smart choices, and so on, create their good fortune. Bad luck only lays low those who fail to turn such into a winning opportunity. And so on. What percentage the minions of Chance—genetics, inheritance, time, and place—play in good or bad fortune is not something the fortunate care to discuss nor is it ever more, in their view, than an excuse made by the unfortunate. We hold onto the belief that Chance is always preempted by reason, even in the case of an economic system that can only be rational after Chance has made its play. We could not, for instance, foresee the 2008 Great Recession, still ongoing, although after the event, we discern a great deal of empirical evidence and clear indicators, a sort of traceable logic, leading to the event.

Our present form of cowboy capitalism could be tamed with a good deal more rational, political legislation and regulation, and could perhaps, be aimed at a less utopian and mystifying goal than 'trickle down' prosperity. We could place greater obligations on our entrepreneurship, innovation, investment, and profit distribution, obligations to workers, the planet and its species, and egalitarian and not plutarchic politics. This is hardly a campaign that a resident plutarchy will endorse. What seems more achievable is some retraction in the view that winners are 100 percent responsible for their winnings and the losers are 100 percent responsible for their losses. If we could recognize that Chance, sometimes landing a sequence of blows and then a knockout punch, lays people out through little or no fault of their own, we could take compensating societal action.

The American cultural imaginary needs to free itself from a mis-diagnosis of 'moral hazard.' Assistance to those who did not choose their misfortune does not imperil their moral constitution, does not make leeching 'moochers' of them. However, wealth and power and the strategies to protect the same test the individual moral fiber as well as imperil the moral fiber of society by establishing a perverted moral sense. It is difficult to follow a Kantian moral view that holds you to acting only as you would wish others to act toward you if others are already in your view despicable moochers. Others may be only those who have lost in the zero-sum game we play in order for you to win.

In short, the rich one's moral sense has little to do with the way he or she treats those who have failed to achieve on the rich one's level. Shades of *The Big Lebowski*: "Since you have failed to achieve, even in the modest task that was your charge," the corrupt rich man tells the Dude.

Why the Rich Get Richer and Other Truth Stories[1]

Here are some stories I've heard:

The truth is that the rich get richer because they're smarter and bolder than the rest of us.

But do you want to know the truth? It's luck not smarts because if it were smarts, every smart guy would be rich and every stupid guy would be poor or just getting by. The real truth is that the rich get rich because they're in the right place at the right time. From then on, compound interest does it all.

Truthfully speaking, every means of redistributing the wealth available that would prevent a democracy becoming a plutocracy has been eroded, except thievery, and the wealthy run the game there.

If truth be told, the rich will themselves to be rich—like Oprah—and they keep on getting richer because they never doubt themselves. They have a will to be rich.

But here's the truth of it; the rich get in there and compete with great savvy and strategy, like on the reality TV show *Survivor*, and they come out the winner because they out-strategize everyone else. Think of a general in a war: the rich are skilled Napoleon tacticians while the rest of us take orders.

People that aren't rich can't handle the truth but it's this: rich people see business opportunities where the rest of us are content just to earn a salary.

Whatever anyone may say, the truth is that rich people pass their wealth and property on from one generation to another so every generation starts off privileged and gets a head start on the working and middle classes.

Let's go to the foundation of things where the truth is. What do you find? It's in the genes. Rich people have the sort of alpha/Über genes that make them rich.

This is truth and not truthiness or truism: we're in a zero-sum Monopoly game here in the United States, and it's going to happen that pretty soon all the cash and all the property will be in one guy's hands. We don't play Socialist Monopoly; it doesn't exist.

The bottom line truth of it is that we all like the rich to get richer because some day when we're rich—and that's just a lottery ticket away—we want to keep getting richer.

It's a hard truth to accept but the rich get richer because they shine in the light of God's favor as chosen for salvation while the poor and struggling bear the dark marks of their eventual perdition and damnation.

But here is a truth that cannot be denied: the rich may get richer in this mortal vale but it will be as hard for them to bear their riches into paradise as for a camel to pass through the eye of a needle. Meanwhile, the poor and meek of this world will earn the riches of paradise.

When you step back and look you see not one truth but a gaggle of truth stories, some on totally different tracks, some conflicting with each other. Of course, if one of the stories happens to be your story of what truth is, it isn't a story, but 'the truth.' You go to www.truthout. com for the truth only if you are already in a truth story that says this is where the truth is. The truth is out here and not there. You tune into to Cenk and not O'Reilly or vice versa. You go to where your truth story says the truth can be found, a truth that fits into the truth story you are already in, a truth story which is never a story but 'the truth.' Knowing what the truth is and knowing how to find it is something you've probably never thought it was: a vicious circle.

Americans prefer to reason their way to personal truths, which can have social or even universal applicability but they need not. It doesn't matter. Truths made to hold in society matter a great deal less than personally discovered truths. Reason does the discovering. It sorts and sifts through until it finds the truth. Not only are our reasoning faculties free to do this but we are free to choose what reason reveals as truth. No outside force lobbies us away from our personal choice nor infects our reliable reasoning.

If you're in this sort of mind-set—and who isn't in our design-your-own-reality millennial clime?—you can easily winnow through the responses as to why the rich get richer and you can find the truth. You're in—if you don't mind my saying so—a truth story regarding reason and choice that enables you to do that. We won't quibble if you want to call your truth story "the truth" because none of us are prepared to descend into a chaos of truth stories we can't climb out of so as to reach some Archimedean point where we can leverage truth from falsehood. Nevertheless, I am not deeply embedded in a truth story that contains chapter and verse on reliable reasoning and unconstrained free choice. But I am deeply embedded in a truth story that is in pursuit of truth stories that keep the many embedded in a reality in which the few get richer and the many are retrogressing to feudal serf conditions.

What are the stories we tell ourselves not only in regard to why the rich get richer and the poor get poorer but why Wisconsin protests won't rise to Egypt-like revolt? Why we won't give up nuclear energy even while the nuclear catastrophe in Japan reaches apocalyptic levels? Why increasing global warming has less and less impact on us? Why our wars in which 'volunteers' continue to die have less and less impact on us? Why an economic collapse manufactured by wealth speculators needs to be salvaged by savaging the working and middle classes? Why we can disassociate the amazing story of former American class mobility from the struggles of unions and unionization, from the hard-won victories of collective bargaining? Why beneficiaries now and in the future of Medicare and Social Security must be steadily badgered into accepting the inevitability of failure and collapse of these programs? Why the word "public" produces as much disdain in 90 percent of the population, who benefit greatly from all public programs, as it does in the wealthy 10 percent, who have no need of such programs? Why we continue to accept the truth story of the wealthy that no class warfare exists even though that warfare, unilaterally conducted, has, since Reagan, brought the middle class to its knees alongside an underclass already flat on its back?

The truth stories we are in concoct our answers. Some of these are in motion and some persist and hold on leading us to think that such longevity is proof of their truthfulness. Political campaign strategies and marketing strategies are engaged in tracking these stories and do so without being impeded by what's empirically verifiable or ideologically faithful or logically anticipated. Such tracking, however, has progressively taken a back seat to the actual fabrication of truth stories. Stories now reach us online as well as off-line so you might say the capacity of political lobbyists and Madison Avenue marketers to reach us has gone from uni-verse to multi-verse, from single dwelling to duplex to multi-plex. Why track what truth stories people are in if you can produce them and thereby, like a celestial entity, know the minds you yourself have created? It's the simplest access, and it is now done with astounding success.

If I believed reason was more than what Nietzsche called it—that is, a strumpet who works both sides of the street, works for power, bends to power—I would have the means to reject in a flash the possible existence of a great many truth stories, which are in fact now in existence. But how do you get out of a truth story you yourself are already in as a character, a truth story you yourself tell, a truth story through which you pursue your understanding of the world? How do you stop the lobbyists from lobbying for space in your brain? The marketers from selling you what you then call "your thoughts"? I think you have to get to know the field you are playing on, or more truthfully, the field upon which you are being played. Once we begin to search for the stories that have attached us to what we hold true as well as attaching us to our ways of knowing what is true, we have a chance of taking back our own minds and with that done, taking back our share of our democracy.

We have the numbers; those economically wounded and hurting plus those already in the ER vastly outnumber those who have benefited from a trickle-down economics and politics, from the deregulation of everything that would have kept the wealth gap in the post-WWII to Reagan-era level, from the collapse of an effective progressive income tax, and from the high-speed expansion of corporate "reachability" power to nothing short of the brain washing of individuals and the corruption of egalitarian democratic processes. Unfortunately, the truth stories of the wealthy few have inundated the minds and hearts of the many, tsunami-like. But the truth story the Tokyo Electric Power Corporation tried to tell gave way before the overwhelming reality of increasing radioactivity. We all have to believe that eventually a story of the truth gets out that does justice to the reality we have framed for ourselves, that eventually what we believe and say corresponds to a state of affairs that exists, to conditions here on the ground that are actually going on. Unfortunately, too many are deep within truth stories that have little or no connection to a present state of affairs that is oppressing them mightily.

Bad Subjects: Politics in Everyday Life

After someone at the *Communist Party USA,* who published *Political Affairs,* realized there was an enemy in the camp—namely, me, the editor of

SUNY Press's "Postmodern Culture" series—my submissions entered a dark hole of no response. I would have liked the chance to reconcile my postmodern and leftist positions in *Political Affairs*, but it was not to be. I subsequently joined the editorial collective at *Bad Subjects*, the oldest political online magazine and continued to write further to the left of Liberals who had in my view moved to about where Eisenhower and Nixon, two Republicans, had been, although Neoliberals placed Liberals, including President Obama, about where Norman Thomas and Eugene Debbs had been. A nation that had long ago given up on politics and retreated to private freedom in private spaces, and had abandoned teaching civics or any economics critical to globalized techno-capitalism, made political identifications the way hard-shell Baptists identify good and evil.

Among the essays I wrote and continue to write for *Bad Subjects* was a series that eventually was tagged "National Psychoanalysis." I put Liberals through the ringers in three different psyches. I devoted only one to the Neoliberal psyche, "The Neoliberal/Right-wing Psyche" because the axiomatic consequences of a very simple mantra did not need to be belabored. In "The Leftist Psyche," parts of which I include here, I attempted, among other things, to clarify the class, order, genus, species of Leftist so that at least Barack Obama could be rightly identified, or, less presumptuously, at least not identified as any kind of Leftist.

The essay is my shrink session with the American mass psyche, the ground or subterranean level in which we find 'reasons' for our political persuasions, fixations, and mystiques. It was written before the advent of both Elizabeth Warren and Bernie Sanders, the former implored to run in the 2016 presidential election and the latter running for that office with surprising success. Now in 2016, one third of millennials look favorably on socialism. I went on to write a Kindle book, *Occupying Here & Now: The New Class Warfare*, with the intent of providing Occupy Wall Street (OWS) protestors both a profile of the politics they had adopted and some history, in neither of which did it turn out they were much interested.

The Leftist Psyche[2]

Tout est possible!

—The Popular Front, 1936

The Leftist is the DB (dead body) in our proliferating TV autopsy dramas, proliferating gruesomely and oddly because Americans recognize on the level of *psychomachia,* the cultural psychic battlefield, that their avenging and resurrecting self is psychically comatose.

Because Liberals thus have already made absent the Left's presence, the Left remains in a dark abyss of *"That Which Cannot Be Named."* The Left has been enfolded within all the deadly bedeviling mumbo jumbo that surrounds the Harry Potter nemesis. That psychic happening allows the right wing to tarnish Liberals by associating them with this darkness, by tagging them as Leftists and socialists. Nothing can be brought to presence and the psychic terrain remains empty of real critical force.

The Left wants to take on the right-wing Neoliberals but they are denied a language. In our psychic drama, Liberals have faint recollection of a reality behind their words while Leftists retain a clear reality of their critique but have no space to represent it, a space owned by Liberals but vacated by them. The Left's language has already been repressed by Liberal apologetics and a Liberal collusion with the Right to go along with the erasure of the Left's representational power in political discourse. What remains is a situation in which an authentic populism on the Left cannot appear in American politics because the Left is packaged in and by the Liberal 'absence/lack' pathology.

Socialism, in all its various forms, has no future in the present American mass psyche. It is always already a venture, a mapping that has led to nothing, to failure, to darkness. The Left is where Milton's Satan finds himself: "no light but rather darkness visible." The devilish Left is already devoured by the collapse of the Soviet Union. The Left is what has already happened in the American mass psyche. And here it always happened disastrously.

"You might well ask," Michael Burowoy writes,

> why the critical intellect might draw on such a supposedly moribund doctrine as Marxism? Did not the death of Soviet communism drive the final nail into the Marxist coffin as it was being lowered into its grave? Did not the burial have both concrete and metaphoric meaning, lying [*sic*] to rest not only a social, political, and economic order but also a whole way of seeing?

Buroway answers his own question:

> The magic of Marxism lies in somehow holding together these three contradictory elements: that is to say, first, its objectivity, diagnosing capitalism as a totality riddled with contradictions,

limits, and insurgent social forces; second, its engagement, challenging capitalism on its own terrain, and thereby also generating an intimate knowledge of its weaknesses and its resiliencies; and third, its imagination, daring to postulate a freer world beyond capitalism, knowing full well capitalism's ability to deny, obliterate, and ridicule the very idea of an alternative to itself. The vitality of Marxism lies in the tension among its objectivity, its engagement, and its imagination. The revival of Marxism depends on the reconfiguration of these three moments but without abandoning any of them. (*Theory and Society* 29 (2000): 151–174)

And yet in our psychomachia, a battle within the psyche, the reasons for discarding Marxism after the fall of the Soviet Union as well as the reasons for reviving it quoted above are not empowering. What are empowering within the cultural psyche are affinities absorbed on a prereflective level so that one has an immediate tacit attachment or repulsion to, say, 'socialism,' or 'free markets' or 'competition' or 'mutual aid.' One's cultural imaginary becomes filled with narrative and spectacle dramatically and repeatedly offered. You could say the most forceful representations perform in our place, on our behalf, the mediations of everything.

In *Society of the Spectacle*, Guy Debord writes, "In societies where modern conditions of production prevail, all of life presents itself as an immense accumulation of spectacles. Everything that was directly lived has moved away into a representation." Ironically, the strength of telecommunications to interface reality for the individual has increased at the same time that a belief in the personal design of reality has increased. The more one feels in control of a personally chosen reality either through a proliferation of apps on a smartphone, or through an accumulation of thousands of friends on Facebook, or through a personal determination of politics on a blogging site, the more one is experiencing within a virtual world. Instead of consciousness mediating world, it is now mediating within cyberspace. One therefore spins further from 'great outdoors' than ever before in history within a space where one can avoid the mediations of others. What results is a reduction of worldly interplay to the vicious circle of one's own choices grounded in one's own preferences. Your vulnerability to a world already branded for profit is great because you believe you are by your own choices both the creative force and the beneficiary.

Reasoning and its reasons, then, derive from narratives and spectacles that have a compelling power to shape what is 'reasonable' and what is 'unreasonable.' The expansion of the media from print to cyberspace is applauded as an expansion of information, of instantaneous communication from text to tweet, an expansion of awareness and literacy, of knowledge itself. We deceive ourselves because greater access means no more than an expansion of illusion.

"The media" Chris Hedges writes in *The Death of the Liberal Class,* assists

> the commercial culture in "need creation," prompting consumers to want things they don't need or have never really considered wanting. And catering to these needs, largely implanted by advertisers and the corporate culture, is a very profitable business. A major part of the commercial media revolves around selling consumers images and techniques to "actualize" themselves, or offering seductive forms of escape through entertainment and spectacle. News is filtered into the mix, but actual news is not the predominant concern of the commercial media. (New York: Nation Books, 2010)

We are presently living at a time when the world is being branded in ways that benefit globalized techno-capitalism but not at a time when the job has, as in Huxley's *Brave New World*, been completed. Globalized techno-capitalism owns the future when it totally owns the spin-making machinery; but cyberspace has shown that while it can make a solipsist out of everyone, it can spin in opposing directions. Nevertheless, much of cyberspace's countering force remains to be seen or is lost in the chaos of cyber communication that one assumes is somehow guided by Google. A world in which the voice of the Dow Jones speaks the loudest is both online and off-line.

Every manifestation of a vestige of socialism whether in Scandinavia or Cuba or South America, or in American university faculties, or in workers' unions, or in co-operatives of any stripe, has been greeted with amused disdain, with the patience of a parent confronted with a slow-learning child, with the pity the sighted have for those who cannot see. But this response lacks real subliminal potency, the kind that fear, in all its forms, can provide. In order to demonize on the psychic level, in our cultural imaginations, the target must be presented as a threat and a fear of that threat kept on the boil. It is very difficult to deal with those who are frightened; reason cannot get them out of a place into which they have not reasoned themselves

Fear of terrorists, no longer bin Laden but now ISIS, now resides alongside a fear of engaging in another losing war, fear not shared by those who stand to profit from yet another war. But the Great Recession of 2008 has not led to fear of a repeat. Wall Street and the excesses of a vulture capitalism that have brought an obscene amount of wealth to a few and great woe to a great many remains in a safe zone within the cultural imaginary. Other fears are transfixing: fear of a deficit inherited by our children, fear of illegal aliens overrunning the country, fear of gay marriages undermining our biblical faith, fear of Obama taking away our guns, fear of a Leftist media and a Leftist academy, fear of Iran with a nuclear bomb, fear of Islamic terrorists, fear of the underclass and their ungentrified neighborhoods. Many fears. But no fear of a plutocratic wealth divide or a planet collapsing as a byproduct of a reckless capitalism.

Every blow to the vestiges of our egalitarian democracy and to the future well-being of the planet are converted by Neoliberals, in what Naomi Klein calls *The Shock Doctrine*, as opportunities to dismantle social safety nets, target unions as obstructionist in a time of crisis, and impose austerity measures designed to reduce the size and therefore power of government. "Austerity" has deep psychic roots extending to a religious sense of restraint and denial, of abstinence as purgative after an orgy of excess. Both the sense of sin and penance are, unfortunately, not deeply rooted in Wall Street, its traders seeing the financial crisis as an opportunity to make a lot of money. Only the injured are shadowed in our psychomachia with guilt and a need to repent.

On the stage of our cultural psychomachia, we have great power, Jung called it "mana" power, extended against taxes, government control and regulation, and against 'victims' who have chosen to victimize themselves. Here we have only thin shreds of empathy, compassion, imaginative understanding of 'losers,' of those living on welfare, on those 'underwater' in every way, on those who can't retool themselves to meet the new demands of the information age, on those who haven't the will to will themselves into success. The Occupiers occupying street space, living on the street, and not assuming personal responsibility for their own improvement cannot earn the respect, regardless of the case they make, of those already seeing through a lens designed not to see or hear or understand them.

How to break free is a question repeated repeatedly, but not directed to the Left. As long as Liberals occupy the space of critique but lack critique or offer only a critique of "lack," Leftist can only be identified as superfluous, as redundant, and worse, as defunct, extinct, back in the day, as millennials say when something is too removed from their reality to remain conceivable. The Leftist psychic space is leased by Liberals at the direction of Neoliberals.

The Left is also removed from any time continuum that has a psychic hold. The historical time line is not in the Left's favor, not simply because the illusion of being post-history is strong in the mass psyche but because the Marxist promise of a golden age in the future dead-ended in 1989 with the collapse of the Soviet Union. Once again, the irrationality of discarding a needed critique of capitalism because Stalin, a tyrant, corrupted the Russian Revolution has no hold in our psychomachia. The Left is now belated at best and belated means done in high-speed hyper-reality in which what is past may be prologue to something back in the day; but tweets, without end and only endless middle, need no prologue.

In a market-driven mass psyche, where the past is yesterday's Dow, yesterday's horserace, the future always makes investment returns in a present and not in the future. The future is no more, within the movement of time in this psychomachia, than a bit of vocabulary that hides a desire filled NOW, the instantaneous gratification that must be NOW. War or child poverty or racism are always not problems that will haunt our future but problems already solved, already in the past and not a concern of the present. Scenarios of global warming's future effects or the emerging semi-literacy and defective critical intelligence and moral indifference of millennials are not problems represented in the present and therefore there is no future to them. The future has no impact in our psychomachia when contrasted with a need to devour the present as an ontological necessity. And that is a need the right wing has established, like an American flag on the moon's surface. The present moment devours any thought of the future. Liberals go along with Neoliberals in this faith.

The American cultural imaginary's paradigm shift toward a hyped and hyper-consciousness—that is, a consciousness fantasized, fantasizing, and over-stimulated—has totally upstaged the Left's relentless focus on historical, material, and objective conditions. Turbo-charged capitalism has branded the mass psyche to define itself in ways compatible with market values and to refuse and dismiss any critique of such. The Left's mission lies outside this branded ontology.

The Left's own psychic drama, which had a life of its own back in the day, now does no more than shadow the Liberal drama which is not a force in itself but only in terms of its defensive and alleviative relationships with the right wing. Liberals are defending psychic ground that they have allowed to sink beneath them before the battering rams of the right wing. Only their words act as a salve, a skin-deep only palliative that permits the illusions of an American moral high ground. The Left, on the other hand, has no defensive tactic but only offensive, which involves dramatic action that frustratingly cannot take place on our stage, in our present psychomachia. Neither is the Left useful in mouthing noble aspirations to conceal the zero-sum game to which our democracy has been reduced. Liberals escape the history that would give them meaning, deny the radical critique that Neoliberals fear. And like a censorious schoolmarm they 'regulate and constrain' the golden age promised the millennial hyper/d-consciousness by the right wing. They stand like a superego before the flooding liberalities of the id, liberalities that capitalism's minion—cybertech—can easily provide.

The 'decathecting' gesture here is for Liberals to not only fight to bring the world to meaning with their own word/world connections but to face its connection to a socialist critique—thus creating a Left created by the Left and not by the Right—that would make the success of such a fight against the right wing possible. For that possibility to occur, the Left would first have to become conceivable within the present American psychomachia. To overcome our psychic arrangement is a matter of psychic politics that expands on the worldly stage of everyday politics to nothing less than a 'soul struggle,' of no less import than the allegorical pyschomachia of Prudentius or Bunyan. Knowing the arrangements of that territory, that established disorder, is a first step toward a new mapping.

It is upon this psychic stage Occupy Wall Street emerged and then vanished from the cultural imaginary, replaced now by the fiery Elizabeth Warren and the presidential bid of the socialist, Bernie Sanders. But turning left on the street demands that we first turn left within our American cultural imaginary.

The "Free Exchange of Ideas": Our New Normal[3]

I set out to grasp the mechanisms of the effective exercise of power; and I do this because those who are inserted in these relations of power, who are implicated therein, may, through their actions, their resistance, and their rebellion, escape them, transform them—in short, no longer submit to them.

—Michel Foucault, *Dits et Ecrits*

I have been rattled by a video sent to me wherein, according to the *Detroit Free Press* "a noted professor at a large Midwestern university" was videoed as he railed against "Republicans and closet racists in class last week." The video found its way to YouTube and will, I suppose, as all viruses do, run its course and then fade from memory. The words, however, of a university spokesman in regard to 'a free exchange of ideas' going on in a classroom brought back to me some words by Foucault, quoted above, regarding power's reach, words I extended to the classroom. In *Discipline and Punish,* Foucault himself had made a frightening comparison when he asked, "Is it surprising that prisons resemble factories, schools, barracks, hospitals, which all resemble prisons?" ([Pantheon, 1977], 228).

On the most obvious level, one that angry responses to this professor's rant point out in referring to his abuse of power, students are a captured audience, wary of angering those who wield the power of the grade, now more than ever a linchpin in our zero-sum game of winners and losers. But I am also mindful that another sort of power, one not wielded by the professor but already instilled in the societal surround is at play here, unrecognized and therefore unindicted.

This sort of power invades the classroom under the disguise of phrases such as "free exchange of ideas," a phrase which is now as faddish a credo as "free to choose" but like that phrase conceals dark complexities which can be disturbingly linked to our present asymmetrical arrangement of power. That arrangement, most certainly the product of our zero-sum competitive Monopoly-like game of winners and losers, infects places, such as neighborhoods and classrooms, and practices, such as politics. But minds also, minds which are already subject, not simply to the wielder of the grade, but to the exercise of unequal power that aligns students with the goals and objectives, ejections and destructions that support the preservation of that power.

No manner of free exchange of ideas can go on given this situation because already-existing priorities rearrange all critique into what is palatable to those already-existing priorities. If that initial defense is overcome somehow, one is yet in a classroom in which a clash of ideas and arguments has become no more than a clash of opinions, a clash without resolution as each disputant retreats to the sanctity of "my own opinion." The task of reaching young minds already 'friending' and 'unfriending' words in line with powerful overriding societal priorities is a formidable task but one not deterred by disingenuous notions of the free exchange of ideas. Such a task should not be deterred also by the frustration of discovering that all attempts at unpackaging those priorities lead to the dead end of a student's personal opinion.

Pre-existing conditions of asymmetrical power make a farce of free exchange as does a belief in the inviolability of personal opinion. Both conditions preempt any attempt in a classroom to dismantle asymmetrical power. A society in which power is asymmetrically arranged cannot be exposed or dismantled by the pretenses of an objective, disinterested, and balanced approach. Such an approach confirms the illegitimacy of a corrupted status quo. Unfortunately, it is an approach that lingers on and comes tied to the equally problematic pretense of a free exchange of ideas.

Why would we not expect that what we now mean by the free exchange of ideas is a free exchange of opinions, no one's opinion overruling another? We are in a post-truth era, which means that the age of absolute and universal judgments, judgments made from outside the furor of clashing subjectivities, is over. None on either side of an issue holds their truths to be merely stories or that their judgments should not be universal. No one, in fact, who knows in his or her heart what was true, or knows by rigorous rational or empirical methods what is true, believes we live in a post-truth age. Nonetheless, a mere survey of the last half century would show us that no universally accepted universal rule of truth judgment has been at play in the world, humankind's or any celestial entity's. To say we are in a post-truth age is merely to affirm that truth is a transactional arrangement of varying longevity. And like all transactional arrangements, it is arranged by the effective exercise of power.

The troublesome aspect of opinions is that although they seem personally inspired with each person creating for him or herself a response to conditions she or he observes, our opinions are more certainly shaped by the surrounding conditions than our own original genius. Surrounding conditions, the social and cultural milieu, the economic and political arrangements are the waters within which our minds swim. And in asymmetrical power distributions, you can expect that our opinions are not being shaped to disturb those distributions.

How do we reorient such an arrangement? It seems that when our opinions are serving a foundational inequality, we should not be trumpeting them but rather investigating them. We need to question the unquestioned mantras of the day, especially the illusion that we personally design the world the way we personally design a Facebook page or a website, that all things personal exceed and are opposed to all things societal.

The media is loathe to point out in the dramatic way it deserves that our democracy has turned into a plutocracy, and I suppose the reason for this has much to do with the media's ties to the top 20 percent. Americans remain unconcerned with this slow but progressing alteration of democracy to plutocracy because the story gets lost amid other stories, a tweet amid a never-ending downpour of tweets. It does seem as if Pandora's box has been opened when it comes to story making, what some call a "democratization" of journalism, a freer, in short, exchange of ideas because everyone is now involved, free to comment, to like, to blog, to opine. Surely, it is as possible to impede ideas and the ability to interpret them by chaotic downpour as by Gestapo-like censorship. Ironically, asymmetric power now oversees this confusion of public discourse while privatizing everything else with the word "public" attached to it.

In the absence of any Solomon of judgment or oracle of truth, or what scientists call "an external point of reference" to which all claims can be adjudicated, what we have now is a cacophony of voices. We have a whirlwind of opinions that either blow heatedly and often viciously but always emptily in cyberspace, or they take the shape that an asymmetrical power gives them by virtue of owning the mechanisms of influence (i.e., volume, spectacle, and repetition).

Again, how to challenge such an arrangement? One of the ways that this is done is in the classroom, which is a societal space but not in the sense that its mission is to inculcate the priorities of any particular society. Whether a society is enjoying good or bad economic times, the classroom mission is to impart the highest level of societal awareness which itself depends upon an understanding of the achievements of the past and the development of a critical awareness grounded in skepticism.

Our classrooms have travelled far from this view because our US society has travelled far from this view. In a society in which power is asymmetrically arranged, any level of education must serve the priorities that transfer all social and public enterprise to the personal and private level that is itself governed by market principles. There is no freedom in this because there is no equality in the powers of representation, although a sense of personal and individual freedom as well as a sense of self-empowerment prevails. If we could see through such illusions, we could see the dominance of a free-market economic rule leading to a severe asymmetry in wealth and power. Such rule has self-protectively fabricated illusions of a personal freedom although such freedom, upon any examination, has been curtailed severely. This rule makes only one demand of the classroom: that it lead the young to accept that rule and detour them from any opposition.

The way you lead students in this fashion is ensuring that balanced neutrality oversees any discussion. Students are, in this scenario, like jurors listening to a case as presented. The professor is a judge who makes sure that the rules of the court, in this case, objective balancing of all views, are upheld. But teaching is not anything like this; the role is not passive nor is there any pretense to a balanced treatment when every aspect of the enterprise, including the already-existing dispositions of the students as well as the societal forces that dominate their thinking, are far from balanced.

The easy course is not to trouble those already-existing preferences and prejudices. The easy course is to stay clear of the credos, illusions, and presumptions that block any development of thought. The easy course is to stay clear of taking on the already-existing distortions of thought ensuing from an outside-the-classroom surround imbalanced and distorted. The easy course is to avoid any disruption of resident student values because your dissidence antagonizes students and creates a hostile audience. The easy course is to make sure that if a hidden camera is on you that you say nothing that will lead to the public humiliation of a YouTube video. The easy course is not to unravel opinions and expose the subtle machinations of power seeking to maintain its position as the status quo or, philosophically, a true expression of 'things as they are' when things as they are are only what a plutocracy wants them to be.

There is now a great deal more pressure to take this easy course when every student has some hand-held device to broadcast your dissidence globally.

In an already dangerously deluded and divided society, no one can go on as if an enormous power disparity can be amended by going on as if such a disparity did not exist. Nevertheless, an enlightened, objective disinterestedness is rolled out to protect such a disparity from the rigorous critique needed. Any attempt to correct such an imbalance is greeted as extreme, as radical. However, the nature of inquiry is not to presuppose or impose a balance that does not exist but to expose the deceit, illusions, and blindness of what does exist.

The university classroom has been, whether frequently or not, a place where young minds can be challenged. It is difficult now to find any place where such challenges are made. You would have to range beyond the power of money and the political power it achieves and is able to hold on to in a plutocracy. Print newspapers go extinct and head online where they join a faceless horde of 'citizen journalists' and thereby, in the chaotic, unsearchable mix, all distinction is lost, all solidarity dissolves into personal tweets and photos on Facebook. Popular culture takes its shots, but market values quickly commercialize such threats. Art, however, high and serious or low and popular, has historically found a way to fly by all nets. But it is the classroom in which the challenge to a resident order, especially one so askew as our own, is launched. There is some hope in the classroom that minds exploited by an exploiting culture can be redirected. There's a chance that the baggage piled on students by a society that already has them bending to the mantra of "let markets rule!" can be exposed, like the Wizard of Oz behind a curtain, as impostures and fabrications serving the very narrow ends of a very few.

Just as Dietrich Bonhoeffer in a classroom at the University of Berlin was seen as an enemy of the state, a state ruled by the Third Reich, we now have teachers in classrooms whose words oppose the injustices of our own plutocracy. I hesitate to mention Bonhoeffer and the treatment of his dissidence by the Third Reich because the victims of our market rule cannot be so imagined, if imagined at all. But the supremacy of our market rule prime directive has made not only our egalitarian democracy a victim but also the health and sustainability of planet and people, except a wealth minority. One wonders as to what sort of free exchange of ideas can go on when progress and growth are reported by and experienced by a top 20 percent who also steadily work on 80 percent of the population to assume responsibility for their own misery. This is perhaps the most mind-boggling of all our new 'new normals.'

There is a very hard course to take in the classroom now, especially so because what goes on in the classroom is a battle for young minds already driven to commit, for reasons of economic survival, to values that do not go beyond profit to shareholders. What is now required in the classroom is almost a 'shock and awe' campaign, a sudden shock of recognition that gross inequities in a society cannot and will not foster an open and free exchange of ideas.

Because the free and open range of a cyberspace twittering is replaced in the classroom by the simple privileging of the instructor's 'bully pulpit,' plutocratic power cannot drown out classroom challenges with a hailstorm of personal opinion. What plutocracy does is target all classroom challenges as a danger to itself in the same axiomatic way that globalized techno-capitalism axiomatically responds to governmental regulations and entitlements that it sees as a danger to itself. We are now witnessing a powerful lobbyist effort to privatize public education not only for reasons of profit but also to place teacher and classroom in a competitive customer/business relationship, thus explicitly confining free exchange of ideas to the dimensions of market rule. Unfortunately then, parents, now customers, already committed to the values that asymmetric power has arranged will shop for the classrooms that support those values. Possibilities of expressing challenges of such values to the young thereby decrease.

As Bonhoeffer discovered, it is difficult and dangerous to expose the ills of a society from within the institutions of that society, but some take that hard course and do it and in doing so re-acquaint us with what a free exchange of ideas could mean.

Counterpunching

In the fall of 2015, I decided that the late Alexander Cockburn and Jeffrey St. Clair's *CounterPunch* was a better fit for me than *Truthout*. I had long been an admirer of Cockburn's *Beat the Devil* column in *The Nation,* tracking further to the left than traditional Liberals, mocking the Third Way. *CounterPunch* went online in 1998, and by 2007 it had as *Wikipedia* reports "become one of the biggest websites on the English-speaking Left with "around 3 million unique hits a month."

While I admire and enjoy the benefits of online writing and publishing, now 'posting,' easy access and a sandstorm of choices buries the good with the bad, inflates egos beyond any mission of empowerment, and puts fools at their own rudder of vicious circling. Stuff indeed gets posted faster, but I reserve "fast" to fire trucks, ambulances, and police cars. The 'short of the long' or the tweet of the essay is, I think, exposed in Jenny Holzer's "Truisms," no one wise saw standing unchallenged by its polar opposite. As a writer, I worry not only about a future Shakespeare not going viral and thus lost in the sandstorm but also writing itself devolving into an harangue of tweets that a severely limited capacity to follow argument or plot produces. Of course, who will be there to point out any of this?

To write in the footsteps of Montaigne, one would need his public or, in truth, the reading public anytime since then. But Montaigne would now be lost among a horde of bloggers, his approach swallowed as creed or rant. And the bloggers of yesteryear, meaning a time before the smartphone, would stand just above the printed-book and magazine writers on a tier where texts and tweets now represent writing that is actually read. In lieu of joining Montaigne as he wandered toward a discovery he had not made in advance, we now all wander in the virtual corridors of cyberspace itself. And what we find serendipitously must not wander but get to the point: "Who exactly is on the bus?" "Are you here or there?" "Do you like or don't like?" Writing, like the algorithm itself, is Boolean: presence/absence. Profit or loss? Win or lose? Young or old? Conservative or Liberal? Pro-choice or pro-life? Go beyond 140 characters and you go into negative territory and nothing will be communicated until you discipline your words. If a thought cannot be expressed in 140 characters, it is not a message and messaging is all that writing is. Thoughts are left to the individual free to choose to think of in any way he wishes. We get into fights over thoughts but not over messages. Unfortunately, a great deal of vitriol can be let loose in 140 characters. After all, "Fuck you" is a message.

I had spent a few years as a pro-bono online writer responding to the mounting tragedy staged in the American cultural imaginary. Some of what I wrote produced rancorous, pungent "comments" from the abyss of anonymity. But mostly my own writing acted like blood in the water attracting sharks that tear each other apart. Debates in the online Comment sections go on energetically, often ferociously, with dramatis personae and plot threads from Gogol or Chekov, always Russian, often like group-therapy sessions beginning with something and then wandering into a maze of psychosis. I seldom recognized where I came into it all and generally felt apologetic for having stirred up so much ill will. To those who wrote and said I had done something of a clarifying nature, I am grateful. To those who found me obfuscating but went on to clarify my obfuscations, I am also grateful. However, I am not sure whether the Comment portal is damaging to the quality of our intellectual and imaginative life or beneficial. A plutarch friend of mine believes that it allows people to vent harmlessly without otherwise occupying Wall Street or his own treasures. There is that.

All—online essays and comments—however were within days archived, forever buried and awaiting resurrection on Google. Google resurrects or "searches" based on what is being searched the most, what is hot at that moment. The topic may be a perennial classic but nonetheless, it is the most recent and most-searched online sites that Google records. So, the future of such retrieval is tragic if you consider that in a very short period of time we are severed from the past. The writers who fill the first page are writers whose erudition is built on prior Google first pages. You will not find Jonathan Edwards on the first two pages of a freedom-of-choice search but rather Rhonda Byrne, not Aristotle on the notion of politics but breaking TV news. You will find *Wikipedia*'s "group think" entries on these topics; the idea is that a consensus over time will shape an entry into something reliable. Only Jonathan Swift could do justice to these hopes. There is nothing stopping the scholar who might have been hired to write an entry from adding his or her expertise to a *Wikipedia* article. That scholar can join the ranks of the unpaid 'content providers' and await his amendments amended by an anonymous, uncredentialed wiki enthusiast. You can also anticipate that polemical issues, such as those that divide Liberals from Neoliberals, will convey just enough gridlock to turn an emerging intellectual back to video games.

We are all one among equals, especially now when it comes to intellectual background but certainly not when it comes to income and wealth. A leveling of intellectual work so that it cannot ever rise to a telling and concerted critique on the usurpations of capitalism has always been a longtime goal of capitalism. While capitalism remains tightly focused in its own profit-making mission, brooking no detours or deviations, all outside attacks are fractured into billions of noise bytes echoing in cyberspace.

I remained committed to the public sphere not because I relished the way it was abused by what Spinoza called the "ordinary human sentiments"—fear, greed, tribal hatreds, jealousy, love of power. Neither was I a fan of the way market rule had diminished the public good through a relentless privatizing for profit, or the way the public space had been inundated with the mounting piles of digital information that corrupted our social-learning space. I remained committed because I believe in what Goethe showed us in *Wilhelm Meister's Apprenticeship and Travels*—that human self-development compels us to move from the private life and travel into the world of others. And I believe he imagined that to be a journey beyond Facebook. And the Internet is a vehicle of travel, and cyberspace a testing ground whose potential remains unfulfilled. In practical terms, I remained committed because the administrator and designer of my website, Einar Nordgaard (NOWE) as well as my Kindle book, *Occupying Here & Now: The New Class Warfare,* who has also brought me into Facebook, LinkedIn, Skype, and Twitter, has been my cyberspace guide and mentor. *Skyping with Einar: Conversations Beyond Imagining* is a book, a Kindle book, we someday may do.

My *CounterPunch* essay "Gun Control, Illegal Aliens, Moochers, Planned Parenthood, Gay Marriages, 'Big Brother' Government, and Obama" did not bring any of these hot topics to nationwide agreement. My interest was in moving from rock-hard cemented positions to undecidability, a state in which obdurate views give way to a numbing doubt as to what might be the best path to take. And in that position, one begins to examine and interrogate beyond the cloistered confines of one's own sacred personal opinion.

On all the issues of my title, and many more also, we are presently like boxers in a ring, each in a corner, each fortified in his or her own website niche, punching and counterpunching opponents as we imagine them to be. There is then no actual counterpunching because all our punches land, all are knockout punches. The real counterpunch is like a fast left we don't see coming because it comes out of a reality so other than our own, we cannot conceive its existence. Advancing to undecid-ability is the first step in conceiving the existence of the other and the beginning of a real face-to-face engagement that may end as a draw until the surrounding culture arranges changes we cannot now foresee. The gridlock that we see in the US congressional arena is disengaged, each shadow boxing in his or her own corner anti-politics.

Gun Control, Illegal Aliens, Moochers, Planned Parenthood, Gay Marriages, "Big Brother" Government, and Obama[4]

The reason Sanders is unlikely to win the nomination for president is because only 31% of Americans "react positively" to the word socialism. However, among 18–29-year-olds, about half view socialism favorable and only 47% see capitalism as a good thing.

—R.Muse, "According To Polls Most Americans
Are Socialists Like Bernie Sanders," *Politics USA,* June 3, 2015

It is not easy to write about any of these hot issues without taking one side or another and so join an all-shouting-and-no-listening match. We are not even close to listening to each other about these issues. That I can write about.

I do not believe that "telling the public what's really going on," as Paul Krugman puts it, is an easy matter. Affective, prereflective responses make us human and come out of our own experiences, so that even though we may dismiss anecdotal evidence or our gut feelings, they remain at the root of our convictions. Appeals to the affective/emotional/sensu-ous way of being in the world have more power, a magnetic charisma that emotion generates, than do sequential arguments, historical references, comparative framing, and close readings of position papers, platforms, and encyclicals.

When a level of public discourse falls more deeply into 140 character tweets of sharp, determinate assertions, seeking to rouse a following in a daily cyberspace Bastille Day, you wind up with a Donald Trump who trumpets loudly or a Doctor Ben Carson whose soft-spoken, beyond-argument delivery tells us that we all instinctively know what's what, that no long harangues will replace what we know is true in our gut. On that gut level, George W. Bush knew Putin was a man he could deal

with, that weapons of mass destruction were in Saddam's Iraq, and when
it was time to declare victory in Iraq.

When you get to a level of response emerging from the mind and
not the gut, from reason supplemented with a sympathetic imagination,
what the poet Shelley referred to as a "capacity to imagine intensely and
comprehensively" the life-worlds of others so as to legislate an appropriate
just politics, you task listeners and readers beyond their personal interest
level ("A Defense of Poetry"). For "everyday Americans," as Hillary refers
to people not in the salaried political class or those who profit by lobbying that class, there are no wages paid or degrees granted for studying
and researching issues, even those that may directly affect them. I am
thinking first of human-caused global warming, and second of a wayward
financialized capitalism twisting democracy into plutocracy. When a fiery
emotional response has already settled the issue, why dig deeper, and question the soundness of our own personal opinion? When personal opinion
rules there is little need to re-examine or heed contesting opinions. No
voice sounds better than our own.

There's all of that and also the fact that any proper examination
requires an understanding of an historical and comparative framing of an
issue—steady trips to *Wikipedia*—and a kind of deconstructive adeptness
that unravels and exposes hype and façade, and a self-reflexive scrutiny of
one's own experiential and emotional positioning. As sexy and exciting as
this sounds, a title not out to incite already-packaged emotional responses
would not only not be pithy and sharp but rather more like an endless
prolegomena to all future politics. In other words, the long of what we
can get short elsewhere. The tweet of endless characters.

So here are the issues of that sort of catchy title list:

> Top 0.1% of US households own as much wealth as the bot-
> tom 90%, adjusting for inflation; Today's average hourly wage
> has just about the same purchasing power as it did in 1979;
> Fifty-nine percent of self-identified conservative Republicans
> said they don't believe that climate change is happening now,
> and 70 percent said they don't believe humans are responsible
> for it; The only people for whom war was a success are the
> super-rich CEOs of war industry corporations who made a
> killing during the wars we launched since 2001; Finance has
> penetrated every aspect of economic and social life, and turned
> towards extracting profit from individual income; Government
> is not willing to touch the financial system at present.

These phrases at once become problem issues that may not register as problems or may be immediately rejected or demolished, but each certainly, if pursued, requires study. Those we don't pursue dwell in a domain of undecidability. With many issues, the American culture is not ready to come to any clear decision. And it is hard to say that events can push such a decision. We remain racist regardless of our proclamations and legislation. What is distorted in our imagination, emotions, and reasoning may not dissolve when confronted with the *Black Lives Matter* movement. Neither the destructive force of the Great Recession nor the Occupy Wall Street protest has led us to any clear, concerted effort to remodel our economic system.

Sometimes the unreadiness of a culture itself nixes our proclamations and legislation, as with the Equal Rights Amendment (ERA), and most recently, immigration, taxes, and a strategy in Syria. What becomes decidable extends beyond the purviews of reason, which not only comes afterward but also arms all sides. What leads us out of undecidability is as hard to foresee as the movement and eruption of tectonic plates. What seems to be suddenly conceivable to us becomes representational, not as we would have it but in its full otherness. Undecidability sounds bad but it is an advance when compared to the immoveable imperviousness of where we are on so many issues.

We are approaching but have not yet reached an undecidable state in regard to our present corrupted form of capitalism. It has not sufficiently darkened in our minds to bring us even to that point where doing something corrective is counterbalanced by continued laissez-faire. We live in an unquestioned idea of free market, innovative, liberating capitalism, an ideal that may have Platonic worth but has not been seen in the United States since before Reagan's presidency. Whether we have a progressive/liberal sense that the damages of capitalism need to be field dressed—a triage approach—or a conservative/neoliberal idea of a "true, ideal" capitalism—the model David Brooks evokes—or a democratic socialist view that Bernie Sanders advocates that deep structural changes to capitalism need to be made, the fact remains that with the Great Recession the scaffolding upon which our capitalism was resting collapsed. Something was rotten in the financial practices of Wall Street. And something was rotten in a capitalist economic system that has led to the dark and deep, untraceable legerdemain of those financial practices. A financialized capitalism is not what we signed on for. Both liberal and neoliberal politics, each in its turn, are complicit in this gradual but steady fabrication of the monster that now rules what is very far from an egalitarian democracy. No form of socialism has been an accomplice in this crime.

Unfortunately, the word "socialism" is not undecidable in the American cultural imaginary. We are not even ambivalent. Its catechism: "Socialism is loss of both economic and individual freedom, a relinquishing to a totalitarian State our own personal freedom to choose." What Bernie Sanders may succeed in doing is bringing the word "socialism" to a questioning stage, to a point where it may provide us with a critical rod with which to tame our miscreant capitalism. Hillary Clinton goes so far as to admit that our capitalist system is out of whack, an admission that signals she has placed the Third Way politics of her husband under investigation. Why lean into a system and seek to rob some of its fire if doing so taints you? Why touch the Tar Baby of a corrupted capitalism? Why be conciliatory when what stands before you deserves no such conciliation?

It seems clear that Hillary Clinton has a long way to go to reach the position Bernie Sanders is already in—that is, knowing that triage does not work but that the battlefield itself must change. The grounding drive of socialism is a hunger for economic equality emerging from the belief that without such intention, political equality erodes. Democracy gives way to plutocracy when wealth and the leverage that wealth provides to tilt all decisions in its favor is not countered by thriving working and middle classes who can leverage their own power in their own interests. Such power to lobby on behalf of have-nots and have-less-each-day, on behalf of an environment being "creatively destroyed" in the name of profit, and on behalf of democracy itself has been diminished, eroded by an economic system in need of major surgery.

A pundit has remarked that Sanders would be served better by not using the term "socialist" because it sets him up for immediate destruction if not by Liberals but certainly by Neoliberals. Would you ask a Christian to hide the New Testament? Or a Jew to hide the Old Testament? We may, unjustly and blindly, be hoping that every Muslim will hide the Koran but we do not expect our Western sacred texts to be denied. Socialism is Sanders's critical rod; it provides him with his principles, arguments, and understanding. It is the fount of his tutorial of societal regeneration that guides such regeneration. Sanders's democratic socialism does not seek a dictatorial imposition of economic equality but rather in democratic fashion urges recognition of the relationship between wealth and power in a democracy and the need to legislate toward an equitable distribution of both, a distribution that turns us away from plutocracy and toward our long-lost goal of egalitarian democracy.

In practice that means limiting the reach of profit making while at the same time strengthening the economic muscle of what our high-flying winners call "the losers." Neither directive is in an undecidable state but rather both summon instant and sharp rebuttal. Profit making must be denied the frontiers to which it has no right. What the democratic socialist stance does is take profit making out of war, prisons, and education and allow a reasonable return on investment in health care, pharmaceuticals, and energy. It also continues to support and expand public media as a counter to the media's dive to the bottom to attract the most eyeballs and computer clicks.

To what degree a loser is in dire straits because of personal choices or for reasons beyond personal control remains unknowable to a society deliberating whether to aid and to what extent, or not aid at all. Liberals may take the high ground and assume some people are losers because they are overwhelmed by circumstances—illness, job loss, home loss, mental and physical impairment. Neoliberals may take the tough-love ground and assume handouts destroy the will to win. Democratic socialists want to change the economic conditions within which so many are losing and at the same time exchange the capitalist bred notion of winners and losers for an egalitarian notion of one among equals.

We are far from bringing issues such as abortion and gun control to a state of undecidability. A cemented determinacy preempts a probing questioning of other views as well as our own. Gay marriage moved from determinate refusal to undecidability where, for most, once under such review moved on to a "why not?" And while some few argue that the science is not yet in regarding human-activated global warming, a growing number are convinced something must be done. Our need now to deconstruct the mythos of a capitalism that is far from what it is hyped to be requires that we move from dismissal to consideration, to a point we are undecided what path to take. And then a probing interrogation will be a beginning. And that is an advance.

Notes

1. *Political Affairs,* April 22, 2011.
2. *Bad Subjects,* August, 2013; revised.
3. *Bad Subjects,* editorials, 2013.
4. *Counterpunch,* October 16, 2015.

Chapter Ten

Popular Culture

What I Did at the Movies

The approach that I had used in my books regarding popular culture was what I transported to my online essays. I was fortunate with Rolando Caputo, editor of *Senses of Cinema*, as well as Gary Morris of *Bright Lights Film Journal* because both went along with my use of film to roam widely into extra-filmic domains. *Americana: The Journal of American Popular Culture* had published an interview with me (http://www.americanpopularculture.com/journal/articles/spring _2007/natoli.htm) as to why I thought popular culture had to be plugged into the latest fluctuations in the American mass psyche. They asked me why I thought it was key in any cultural-studies approach, an approach that traced the interweaving of, for instance, film and American culture.

Popular film performed the very important task of disclosing what was disturbing and threatening, the troubled mass American psyche, of putting us into play with such. It did not matter if there was no resolution, no answers, and no relief beyond a Hollywood closure, which too might be withheld. All that, including attempts to transcend the messiness exposed and so on, was of no importance compared to the simple display of our dark imaginaries and dark affiliations. If we could see them performed on the screen, we would move a step closer to recognizing what we feared to recognize and so was destined to grow worse.

The approach was phenomenological psychopathology. We needed to be brought into play with our own darkness, bring it all to a level of representation. Popular film attempted to do this because it needed to sell tickets and it could only do that by tapping into what was magnetic, what touched the wellsprings of subliminal fear, desire, anger, frustration.

Doing the American Hustle[1]

People believe what they want to believe because the guy who made this was so good that it's real to everybody. Now who's the master, the painter or the forger?

"American" and "Hustle"—the words are redundant. *American Hustle*, the movie; American hustle, the reality.

First, the movie and its characters "doing the hustle," like a dissonant disco party. Money, sex, greed, and ambition are at the party and the DJ is a con man spinning the discs and keeping everyone moving. Wise guys stand at the bar, the guys you fear and do not want to go near. There is a poor boy at the party, stupefied, immobile, doing the dull federal-bureaucracy hustle.

This movie has a history, shades of the carnival family life of P.T. Anderson's *Boogie Nights* (1997) as well as Scorsese's *Goodfellas'* (1990) ubiquitous larceny, lust, and laughs. An even earlier film version of the hustle of sex, politics, and a con man on the loose is Hal Ashby's *Shampoo* (1975). But the film actually stretches back to screwball comedies. Jennifer Lawrence like a crazed Carole Lombard in *My Man Godfrey* (1936) or in a film filled with the hustle of the con, *To Be Or Not To Be* (1942). Lawrence's scenes as Rosalyn Rosenfeld with Christian Bale's Irving Rosenfeld are reminiscent of a zany Judy Holiday with Broderick Crawford in George Cukor's 1950 *Born Yesterday*.

Whacko hustle but now this new hustle is not sparked by a Depression-era anxiety heading toward the Dada of the Marx brothers whose hectic mania permeates a whole society, as in *Duck Soup* (1933), when the brothers become the ruling government. Licentious, larcenous, anarchic, the Marx brothers turn the whole world upside down at a time when speech is cut loose from sense but money was not yet the speech that ruled.

There is a difference but there is also continuity, a continuity of hustling toward a madcap world in which all moorings are breaking loose and all that is solid melts into air. In the early screwball hustle films, we have the very beginnings of a post-truth world where bullshit has no boundaries. The difference between our new millennial hustle and these earlier screwball versions is that now the hustlers and the hustle can never successfully be brought to trial and the most flagrant machinations are never prosecuted. Reality and truth are no longer waiting in the wings or secure in the minds of the audience. In the post-truth world, all is perpetually in motion, intercrossing and intercommunicating with no solid external, Archimedean point in sight. You could once step out of the world of *Duck Soup* in leaving the theatre and return to an order of things commonly shared; there is in a post-truth, new millennial world no such return possible.

American hustle, the practice and not the movie, the type of hustle that will lead to the 2008 Great Recession as it had led to the Great Depression some eighty years before, begins a rehearsal period with the Abscam scandal of the late seventies, a scandal, which the con man of *American Hustle* tells us, never caught the big guys but just some legislators trying to bring relief to their constituents. But it's this small con game now brought to the screen in 2013, a small-potatoes con game when compared to the dark and deep intricate hustling of Wall Street in 2008, a hustle that points a finger at Big Brother and not Wall Street as the evil gamesters. Whatever untoward behavior that seems to be coming from Wall Street "whales," deep-pocket financiers claiming to be doing 'God's work,' and Ponzi-scheme tricksters, all such behavior and such villainy seem to be actually initiated by a regulating, interfering governmental bureaucracy. This is, at very least, a mind-blowing deduction, itself a bit of Rufus T. Firefly rationality. By passing the political mine field of confounding conclusions regarding the 2008 Great Recession, *American Hustle* avoids the mystifications of that hustle, which still looms as an unsolved case with no one found guilty. However, the movie extends wider and plunges deeper into a hustle drive that infects both the American cultural psyche and the psyche of every American. This is a drive that the Puritans failed to repress and what Melville soberly glimpsed in *The Confidence Man*, Twain made hilarious with the Duke and the Dauphin in *Huckleberry Finn*, and P.T. Barnum carnivalized across America.

The victory of appearance over reality is sealed in the twentieth century and extended into the infinitude of a virtualized cyberspace in the twenty-first century as brick and mortar, paper and ink, the physical presence of friends and enemies, work and wages, warfare and spying have all been translated to an entirely different plane of existence. Call it forgery. Irving Rosenfeld, the con artist, gives Bradley Cooper's Richie Di Maso, the FBI agent, a lesson as both look at a painting the agent thinks is real but Irving tells him that thinking something is real doesn't mean it's not a forgery. The con artist's artistry lies in this making what is not true or real appear to be so in the eyes of the mark.

Di Maso is ambitious as is his FBI superior, Amado; but ambition itself is expanded in the new millennium beyond egoism, beyond narcissism and on to solipsism as virtual communities composed of virtual friends exist within the design priorities of individual choice. So the hustle will expand beyond the hustle of this film where the question of reality and forgery re-emerges at the very beginning of our post-truth era, an era in which narratives of truth and reality can no longer be clearly seen as distinct from truth and reality. The forgery of the hyperreal that has no link to the real but stands, as Baudrillard predicted, in place of it, opens the door to the world that the audience of *American Hustle* is in.

We are clued to the supremacy of appearance over reality in the first scene of the movie as Irving slowly and carefully arranges tangles of his hair into a comb-over supplemented by tufts of faux hair, all of which is glued, patted down, and sprayed into position. "What you think you are seeing," this scene informs us right off, "may not be as real as you think." Every movie photoshops reality, but not every movie makes this its subject. And unlike films, such as Antonioni's *Blow-Up* (1966) or *Cinema Paradiso* (1988) or *Pan's Labyrinth* (2006), *American Hustle* hustles us into a world not studying the dilemma but transitioning us into the instabilities and zaniness of a forged world. The film is part wide-eyed and perplexed realism (Louie C.K.'s Stoddard Thorsen), but it is not a naïveté that a hyper/hyped audience can share. Being outside the hustle is not anything the new millennium offers.

Every viewer in 2013 knows that Irving's one-man game will expand to the hustle of the Great Communicator, Ronald Reagan, and beyond that expand in the cyber age to mindboggling proportions. The movie chooses not to show what we know but we already know this because we have lived it. Every viewer knows that the whole world indeed may be photoshopped online and seem true to everyone's eyes. Replacing the real with simulacra is the marketer's stock-in-trade. And the simulations of the market itself are the stockbroker's stock-in-trade. The real now far exceeds Irving's hustle, extending to insurance, real estate, cars, breakfast cereals, sleeping pills, fashion, politics, and of course, film where spectacle is its true métier. And so while *American Hustle*, the film seems to evade all the dark consequences of our cyberspace/post-truth world of perpetual hustle, none of this can possibly be avoided.

The film is indeed a masterful deflection of all the partisan uproar that would occur had the film pitched its tent not in Irving's backyard but in Wall Street, like an Occupier. And that partisan uproar would not be limited to the political scene but pitch cyberspace enthusiasts against those not so enthused and, most dramatically, winners against losers. In place of this entire furor, the film pulls us all into the hilarity of the con and the players while never contradicting the fact that hustle is the quintessential ingredient of American success, the very heart of Americana.

Hustle here is bullshit as the philosopher Harry G. Frankfurt (*On Bullshit*, 2005) describes it. The bullshitter

> is neither on the side of the true nor on the side of the false. His eye is not on the facts at all, as the eyes of the honest man and of the liar are, except insofar as they may be pertinent to his interest in getting away with what he says. He does not care whether the things he says describe reality correctly. He just picks them out, or makes them up to suit his purpose.

Creating faux realities is easier in our new cyberspace millennial world because reality itself has been virtualized. Determining what is true and what is false has been made easier because that determination has been personalized. Empirical evidence and validation have been removed from any disinterested investigation to a personal view, indeed a personal 'like' or a personal 'whatever.' With the gatekeepers of a real or forged world dismissed from their posts, the world can go full-tilt boogie in all directions as in a three-ring circus, a hyperreal of hype and hustle.

The American economy grows on the hustle of its innovators, entrepreneurs, advertisers and marketers, celebrities and financial 'players'; its hustlers, who open new marketing frontiers or lobby legislators, hustle voters who will not in any way prosper by being so hustled. After Abscam times, the American hustle will head toward a market-rule apocalypse, which will leave the hustlers at the top and the hustled wondering what game they were in and how it was played. The focus of this movie is on the hustle dance, the rhythms, and the movements as it plays on in as many places as the film can reach. What the film seems to say is that taking a good look at this dance as the very soul of the American *comédie humaine* tells us more about ourselves than the events and scandals that are its symptoms. The characters are caught up in the dance; they actualize it, but it's the hustle dance itself that draws us.

Amy Adams's Sydney Prosser wants to concoct a bullshit identity for herself and finds Christian Bale's Irving Rosenfeld who makes a living concocting bullshit stories that result in five-thousand-dollar checks from greedy marks. Bradley Cooper's Richie Di Maso wants to bring the hustler to justice by hustling them, allowing us to think that the dispensation of justice is a hustle, something perhaps O.J. Simpson's Dream Team had already embedded in the American mass psyche. His FBI associates include a mid-level bureaucrat Amado, whose ambition is pushing him to hustle up the bureaucratic ladder, and Louis C.K.'s Stoddard Thorsen, who remains temperamentally outside the hustle.

The most kinetic hustler is Irving's wife, Rosalyn, who works a marriage hustle, in which Irving is also a player. It is as if they cannot work themselves out of their own bullshit. The marriage hustle works like this: Irving the hustler needs a reality that's hustle-free and for him that is being a father to his son. His son, young Irv, is like a solid that will not melt into the nothingness of bullshit. The marriage is a packaging of this true zone of the real but it proves no respite from hustle because Rosalyn is all the movements of hustle in one body but propelled by a mind that is fractured, but not to multitask. She thusly represents a foreshadowing of the hyperkinetic, ADD, OCD, addictive, narcissistic reality to come.

Sex, which all the women in this film exude, in the world of hustle is a constant energy feed. You cannot seem to have a con without it as if when reality is hyped, sex is the lubricant of the hype. Sex is never off-screen, always in our face, whether we're looking at cleavage cut to the navel, or long shapely legs stretched out for Di Maso to hold, or trim ankles getting into a car, or lips inches away from other lips. This American hustle literally takes to the disco dance floor where heated exchanges there lead to a rush to a bathroom stall for a tryst that never happens. Everything involved in the hustle is deferred until the payoff, tempting and alluring and just out of reach until then. We stay hungry, primed for the con. Sex and the hustle in American life are kept ever on the boil, never evaporating. It permeates the culture because the hustle permeates the culture. It is what an economics of "greed is good; greed works" requires. Greed thrives on the juices of sex and the hustle, the juices of the American Dream. The good con man, like the skilled sales-man of all stripes, from politics to marketing to investing, is always at play and sex is the medium of transaction, the capstone, the climax of all play.

Two notable collisions with this hustling reality barely stop the flow and dance by more than a caesura in the beat. Louie C.K.'s Stoddard Thorsen is all that his name suggests, a stolid bureaucrat without rhythm, which means he not only cannot do the hustle, he cannot hear it or see it. In his scenes with Di Maso, Thorsen is positioned squarely behind his desk, the true man behind the desk, the man defined by his job and its procedures. Procedures reveal the real. But in this film, he is really at the Mad Hatter's Tea Party. While Thorsen remains fixed in place, Di Maso plunges deeper and deeper into the madness of the hustle, so deep that he can no longer see what is real and what is not. The hustle here now in 1978 is still analog, do-able on the off-line movie screen, but Thorsen, the bureaucrat, cannot quite keep up with it all. We sit there in the audience as he sits behind his desk, somewhat dazed and confused, seeking control by telling his back-in-the-day story. Thorsen's Michigan fishing story is an old-fashioned, before-the-hustle story, what in a few years will be called mockingly "an analog story" in a digital world. The hyped-up Di Maso cannot wait for the story's closure; he has lost all patience for the world moving in an unhustled way. Each time he interrupts with his own story ending, a moral that clearly seems to be the one Thorsen was heading toward, Thorsen says no. He will not let his flow of procedural, linear, continuous reality be pre-empted by the erratic intrusions of Di Maso. He will not learn. He will not move. He will not dance.

There is no need to nail down truth or reality in the world of hustle, or bring the hustle, which is multiple and not one, to closure. The economic system that rules requires an endless game of hustle, an endless replacement of the real with simulacra and a continued campaign to have the profitable appear as the only real. Such a system does not wait for the need for rational connectivity, purposeful continuity, and meaningful closure. Hustle cannot wait for Louie C.K's Stoddard Thorsen to catch up.

Not surprisingly in this P.T. Barnum world, Thorsen departs the scene of hustle victory abused and ridiculed. But as Irving, the master hustler, hustles victory away from Di Maso and the FBI, the ridiculed are now reinstated in a way that reality reinstates itself periodically in the hustle dance. Irving knows this; he has, here in the late seventies, a respect for the limits of bullshit and of trespassing too far from reality. That reticence will all but vanish as cyberspace joins global market rule and kicks the hustle of façade, spectacle, the virtual, the hype, the bullshit into high speed.

The second notable collision between the real and a forged reality comes when Robert De Niro as Victor Tallegio, feared mob boss, sits opposite Irving, Di Maso, and the pawn of both, Jeremy Renner as Mayor Polito, and delivers the words that hard reality uses when confronted with any whiff of bullshit. Hard-faced and scary, De Niro's Tallegio leans forward and tells the hustler that there's no mystery when they deal with him, that what happens if anyone is trying to pull something on him will be very real, no bullshit. On the other hand, all he has from them are words and there could be nothing real behind them. When hype collides with hard reality, the result, in this case, will be deadly. Irving, the experienced hustler, knows that his hustle has to avoid possible retaliation by those he hustles. He bottom feeds on the helpless but greedy, those who become embarrassed by being hustled. Trying to hustle Tallegio or congressmen is way outside Irving's game. Di Maso forces this game, telling Irving flat out that he's now Irving's boss.

We also have a brief caesura in the hustle, a fleeing image of Mayor Polito's family lined up on the staircase, distressed as their father is taken into custody. The hustle pauses again here. This is where the con cannot go but it does not mean that Irving has not used his Bronx background and family life as a means to bond and lure Polito into the hustle. Nothing sacred in the hustle but this yet remains something that Irving regrets, a regret that will lead him to help Polito out of the worst of his indictment, by yet another hustle of course.

It's a crazy carnival of a hustle here in the late seventies, one not yet accelerated by smartphones and second-by-second tweets, Facebook postings, and so much personalized hi-speed online communication that has resulted in no one knowing anything in common, a blow to the notion of communication as 'social.' We, the audience in 2013, know this hi-speed world; we know the entire exciting tech that awaits these seventies characters. They amuse us in their analog, back-in-the-day lives. Rosalyn places metal in the new "science oven" and the whole audience laughs more than at any other scene. And what credibility do we extend someone in 2013 who is without a cell phone? Here all characters are cell phone-less, not even a flip phone. The world is not yet online. Our amusement distances us from other, darker thoughts.

All the signs of what will be are here in *American Hustle*. The federal prosecutor will remain many steps behind the 'wolves of Wall Street' they pursue, clueless as to how the Magister Ludi hedge-fund managers ply their intricate financial cons. Compared to these wizards and their wizardry, the federal government remains a dumb show. Stolid beef-witted bureaucrats, unteachable in the sly ways of the hustle.

What camera do you think will capture the hustle of both the off-line world and the online world? The world we think is not a forgery and the world cyberspace runs alongside? We need the equivalent of an electron microscope to capture the hustle that a post-truth market-rule world moving globally at cyber hi-speed produces. The difficulty of getting this to the screen is on the level of getting the Higgs-Boson particle into view. No matter. We are no longer making an attempt at capturing the Big Picture but rather have opted for personally designed views of reality, indifferent to whether our realities are forged or not, whether we've been hustled, whether we've been conned into believing that we're somehow outside the hustle in a separate world of our own that's true and real.

I approached politics, history, racism and violence in "*The Hateful Eight*: History's Dark Bounty." Just as war, blood, violence, and guns are fixed in American roots, racism has remained so fixed." It was not surprising that The Academy of Motion Picture Arts and Sciences chose to ignore the film following the whole culture's failure to follow racism and violence to their roots.

The Hateful Eight: History's Dark Bounty[2]

"We are not enemies, but friends. We must not be enemies. Though passion may have strained, it must not break our bonds of affection. The mystic chords of memory will swell when again touched, as surely they will be, by the better angels of our nature" (Abraham Lincoln).

Nothing remains sacred in Tarantino's eighth feature film, *The Hateful Eight*, certainly not the sacred character upon which American exceptionalism is rooted. This is a film deeply embedded in the unresolved turmoil within the contemporary American cultural imaginary. The thriving mythos of a people forever at war with evil, bringing evildoers to the justice of a hangman's rope, is brought into a disturbing killing field, back to a fallen world of bloodlust, greed, misogyny, and racism.

Revelations summon questions yet unanswered: "Why can't Americans give up their guns?"; "How deep are the roots of racism and misogyny in America that they cannot be reached and destroyed?"; "What is the true bounty of blood and violence?"; "Where can we find a sign of a moral imperative being fulfilled in war?"

I see the film on the day President Barack Obama is to present his final State of the Union address and that evening, fresh from viewing Tarantino's version of the state of the Union just after the War Between the States, I ponder the two stages, past and present. Rather than preface his speech with his assessment of the state of the Union, President Obama waits until the very end to tell us, "The state of the Union is strong." My immediate responses are, "Maybe" and "in regard to what?"

I am, however, more certain about the roots of this union. Bloody. Very bloody. And maybe bloody because the Union is "strong" where it should be as the Taoist suggest, "bendable," or as expressed in the Beatitudes, "meek." What I realize more certainly is that Tarantino takes us on a shocking, imaginative, and dark journey into the American past, into the *Id* that every State of the Union address works hard to conceal although all the nightmare effects of that past remain alive in the present.

It is the changing nightmare, yet somehow always the same, that must be addressed. What *The Hateful Eight* seeks to do is to enter the abyss, uncover the damages wrought in the past, traumatic damage that infects the present and eludes the platform of any politics.

The journey Tarantino takes us on in this film is like a Dantean excursion into the progressively darker reaches of America's mass psyche. The stagecoach rattling through a snow-filled landscape with a blizzard on the horizon and heading for Minnie's Haberdashery is a journey from light to darkness, from the purest whiteness of newly falling snow to the black pitch of unwinding circles of violation, abuse, rage, mayhem, mutilation . . . blood, and violence. Bullets eventually speak more than words, but words are themselves like angry projectiles that explode all conversations, taking us by surprise though we uneasily anticipate that every occasion, no matter how seemingly everyday and banal, will so explode. And the language, before any gun is fired, is the weapon.

But the whiteness, what is that? The snow is the cover, the façade of purity, of evangelical innocence, of noble exceptionalism; it is the snow of what Lincoln called "the better angels of our nature," ironically summoning at Gettysburg a side of the American psyche not on display. Neither is it on display in this film. We are on a stagecoach rattling through the persistent snow job that fills American history, the cover-up spin that, like fallen snow, must continue to fall, or otherwise it will melt away.

These hateful eight, who will taunt, mock, poison, dismember, and shoot each other, have escaped the blizzard and sought refuge in this way station. They were never part of the whiteness; not of it, never the better angels but always like pitch, which as Falstaff reminds Hal "doth defile" as "doth the company thou keepest." We are in such company, not apart, but of it. We are already defiled and that defilement, though covered, is easily observable in the present, in the very present that President Obama's address surveys. We would rather associate ourselves with *"The Magnificent Seven,"* the Samurai of equitable justice, of selfless humanity, of, in short, noble whiteness. We are not allowed that escape that sham in this film.

Amazingly, in such a long film, there are no places to rest, no moments in which we can settle into comforting scenarios already in our minds, no words that do not provoke and conjure, no action that does not unnerve us. All is here to jolt, unsettle, disturb, overwhelm defenses, do violence to pretenses, and dismantle the equilibrium that never existed in our past but is evoked in the present for its own purposes.

"America will be great again," Republican presidential candidate Donald Trump trumpets, burying a bloody past while at the same time making a campaign promise to spill more blood. If greatness then lies in blood, in the military supremacy that President Obama boasts in his address, then Tarantino's film takes us to the heart of that greatness. And he takes us further and deeper into the darkness at the root of such a pull toward violence.

Violence, profit, and a societal order of things are quickly connected.

The stagecoach stops for Major Marquis Warren, a bounty hunter with three dead bodies, redeemable for eight thousand dollars. He joins John "the Hangman" Ruth, also a bounty hunter, who has Daisy Domergue as prisoner, redeemable at ten thousand dollars. Marquis says it's safer to shoot the bounty, but Ruth insists on bringing the mean ones to the hangman. It's a capital punishment that later in the film the hangman, Oswaldo Mowbray, who is really outlaw English Pete with a bounty of fifteen thousand dollars on his head, will tell us upholds a society's notion of justice. And because it is this man, English Pete, who violates as an outlaw society's laws, who connects violence with justice, it seems clear that any claims of justice being related to violence and profit are concealing artifice, false illusions that violence and partnership of profit preserve a social order.

At film's end, in their last act, Marquis and Sheriff Chris Mannix hang Domergue because, as the major puts it, they have no say in their dying but they do have a say in the way Domergue will die. The film has feasted visually on her bruised face, on the blackened eye she sports the first time we see her. She is, throughout the film, smashed, punched, and elbowed to the face a number of times, once so hard it knocks her out of the stagecoach. After being shot in the leg, she is finally, slowly hanged from a ceiling beam. We never know what the Domergue gang has done or what the three dead men Marquis has killed have done, but it does not seem that reasons matter when it comes to violence. The violence here is a free-floating performance, sometimes tied to profit but not needful of it. The little we know of Daisy is that she has a brother who has come to rescue her. The only exchange they have reveals their closeness: "How ya' doing dummy?" he asked. "Better now I see your ugly face." Whether we like it or not, this is one of the few signs in the film of "the better angels of our nature." He's shot and killed, and she's hanged. It seems that back in the day, the social order was preserved not only by a bloodlust but by misogyny as well.

The bonds that dominate in this film, the bonds that are taken up by subsequent generations are not the bonds of solidarity, of any kind. "Fraternity" is a foreign concept; what is rooted in the American past is distrust and fear of what others may take from what is yours, including your life. John 'Hangman" Ruth's fear of losing his property—his captive, Daisy Domergue, and the ten thousand dollar bounty—structures his entire relationship with others. And that reduction of the social is a bequest to the present that fills the contemporary American landscape as wealth compounds in few places while hard times pursue the many. The person who has ten thousand dollars looks warily at the person who has nothing. The trust and aid, sympathy and empathy, compassion and "love thy neighbor as thyself" descend, in time, to the vitriolic of cyberspace comments and tweets. Minnie Mink, Six-Horse Judy, Sweet Dave, Charley and Gemma—who are the welcoming characters at Minnie's Haberdashery—are trusting of the strangers who arrive and are murdered by them. John Ruth and Marquis, however, trust no one and engage others with fists and bullets. Suspicion does not wait long for proof with either man. This is the dog-eats-dog and war-of-all-against-all brand of humanity that is the present's inheritance.

Tarantino does not draw back from giving us a display of humanity bereft of all humanity, a watchful circling of wolves ready to dispatch each other at the slightest provocation. The tension of the film is here but also in the way the film provokes the audience into a recognition that they too are bereft of concern and compassion for others, that empathy for others has been replaced by negligence, that others are threatening and therefore to be feared. "I don't give a damn about them, or you, or your sister, or any son of a bitch in Wyoming for that matter," General Smithers tells Jody Domergue. That testament captures the feeling of fellowship the film lays down. That it resonates in an audience as the operative brand of humanity in the world they are in does not tie that audience warmly to the film. This amounts to an antagonism between film and audience that shows up in film reviews of all of Tarantino's work, which sets no boundaries in its laying open the dark bounties of the American mass psyche.

When they are all at Minnie's Haberdashery, John Ruth and Marquis Warren form a partnership to protect their redeemable bounties from what Ruth sees as possible threats. We have thus an eye on the spot killing or a future hanging as a profit-making business venture pursued consequentially, either because killing has become a profitable trade or because war has made violence a natural way of life. All of this has clearly been genetically transmitted to twenty-first century US as bloody violence continues on American streets as well as in wars in the Middle East that linger like radioactive fallout. There is not much distance between that war which serves as the close horizon for all the action in this film, a War Between the States that was the deadliest war in US history, a war in which 750,000 died, and present day wars—fought differently but fed by the same wellsprings of bloodlust in the American mass psyche.

There is a deconstruction of war in this film as well as a rising cascade of blood, like the Mississippi overflowing, that we cannot escape as easily as we can the blood spilled in city streets and on foreign soil. The war deconstruction begins with Major Marquis Warren describing Sheriff Chris Mannix as one of the Mannix Marauders, "the scourge of South Carolina," who, according to John Hangman Ruth, was a "bunch of losers . . . wrapping themselves in the Confederate flag as an excuse to kill and steal . . . in particular emancipated blacks." Mannix is our Satan, until we hear Mannix give an account of how Major Marquis Warren escaped a Confederate prison by burning to a crisp forty-seven Confederates and thirty-seven Yankees. To this, Marquis replies, "That's the thing about war, Mannix. People die." The contretemps does not end here. Marquis avoids Union justice by killing "his share of redskins" and so endearing himself to the reunited United States of America. And when Mannix argues that the Marauders fought for Southern dignity in defeat, Marquis asks him, "How many nigger towns you sack in your fight for dignity in defeat?"

The muddy and indeed non-existent moral nature of any side's view of war is extended further in Marquis's baiting of the old General Smithers, who has come to Wyoming to bury his son. Marquis lays a pistol down alongside the general and proceeds to tell a story of how he got the general's son to strip naked and "stuck that big black johnson right down his goddamn throat." The general is finally provoked to go for the pistol, and Marquis shoots him dead. Marquis is seeking revenge on the general's shooting dead a whole colored command. The general responds that they had neither the time nor inclination to care for Northern horses or Northern niggers. What is designed to be unsettling here is the link between the lack of clear-cut good and evil in that war between the North and the South and the possibility that all wars, whatever is avowed, devolve into a confused nightmare in which there is no winning to be declared that is not equally fraught with loss. We cannot find our Satan in that one place because he shows up everywhere.

Because the American audience for this film remains haunted by the unnecessary war in Iraq, and further back, haunted by a conflict in Vietnam, whose purpose few could identify, once again, defensiveness sets in. The film indicts an American identity built on sins and congenital faults never absolved, though repressed and built on an image of exceptionalism that economic hegemony requires. And so, Tarantino must be accused of playing for sensationalistic effect, stretching action and character to comic-book entertainment-only proportions, and ignoring both the facts of history and, once again, as in *Inglourious Basterds,* lacking the moral dimension with which all serious art wrestles. Anthony Lane in *The New Yorker* represents the view. Tarantino cannot "resist the blandishments of extreme bloodshed. Such is the climax that all his movies seek, and trusting fans will relish the eagerness with which the new work accelerates into carnage. That was true of Jacobean tragedies, too, but in those we sensed the intolerable burden of moral risk, whereas the characters here are dispatched with snickering glee, and little seems to hang on their demise" (1/14/16).

But what if "extreme bloodshed" lies at the roots of the American character, so awash in blood that the moral sense is either comatose or a mockery, something like the moral sense of a Wall Street "player" doing "God's work" or a politics that defines "moral hazard" as the government acing as the Good Samaritan did in the New Testament? The "extreme bloodshed" in *The Hateful Eight* is like the fires in Dante's Inferno, the milieu of the hateful; and these hateful portray what continues into the present. This milieu of blood is no more than the wellsprings of what continues to flow into the present.

Tarantino is called upon to obey a moral imperative and control the flow of blood, control the violence portrayed on the screen, even though that moral imperative remains difficult to see operative in our past. Just as no claims of righteousness any of these characters make regarding their behavior in war are allowed to stand without being impugned, all claims that violence here exceeds what either historical or artistic imperatives require cannot stand. A society that protests control of everything but guns, blood, violence, and rapaciousness here defends, in its criticism of Tarantino's film, his failure to control guns, blood, violence, and rapaciousness.

It should seem clear now that Tarantino's film has us swimming in blood and carnage because our past is soaked in both. Just as Rabelais expands our human nature to gargantuan proportions and Swift expands and contracts the sizes of his characters to display the proportions of their nature, Tarantino employs excess to drive his vision home. A film that begins in a covering blanket of whiteness is soon foregrounded with a gruesome pile of three dead bodies. From that moment on, we are never allowed to cover ourselves in a concealing blanket of whiteness.

Just as war, blood, violence, and guns are fixed in American roots, racism has remained so fixed. A brief period of what was called "post-racism" seemed to exist; but after a burst of reported racist incidents, it has become clear that the country never was post-racist. Personally choosing not to be interested in a matter does not make that matter go away. A society immersed in the illusions of personal determination has a difficult time in dealing with the persisting presence of matters that extend beyond personal choice. And just as the Occupy Wall Street protesters woke up a good part of America regarding the wealth divide, Black Lives Matter protesters point to a racism that is very much alive in America. But is it true that "the film's (*Hateful Eight*) treatment of the subject doesn't *go* anywhere"? (Camilo Hannibal Smith, "Tarantino and the n-word: Why I Hated *The Hateful Eight*," *Houston Chronicle*, January 5, 2016).

The n-word appeared 110 times in *Django Unchained* and some sixty times in *The Hateful Eight*. That's excessive use in a post-racist society, the bogus kind of post-racist society that doesn't use the word because it's connected to the now totally inconsequentiality of back-in-the-day. In other words, it is an "analog" age word and has no digital presence, no *emoji* life. And in a severely wealth-divided society, color becomes segregated in ways reminiscent of the Antebellum South. Headline reports of police violence to blacks, however, tell us that suppression of the n-word has not cleansed the American psyche of its racism. Tarantino's expressed view is that the only way to de-taboo a word, deflate its potency, is by overuse. Use it so often that the psychotic attachment in the American psyche is decathected. This is the exact opposite of the political correctness view which calls for a suppression of "hate words" and thus cut words from reality. That an unrepresented reality soon withers and dies is the hope here. Whether no use or overuse is the plan, American society does not seem to be going anywhere in regard to cleansing itself of racism, especially now when people of color are caught on that side of the economic scale where the winners say the moochers live.

But does *The Hateful Eight* go anywhere in regard to race?

The film is set at a time when the sight of emancipated blacks is offensive to defeated Southerners. As in the case of our rooted affinity to blood and violence, we are transported to that moment in US history in which hatred for blacks was not concealed but expressed openly. An antebellum relationship between black and white marked by abuse and infantilizing is in the emancipated setting marked only by hate. The subsequent life and expression of that hate is what *The Hateful Eight* incites us to review.

Daisy Domergue does not want the nigger Marquis to sit in the stagecoach not because the stagecoach is like a private, gated compound that keeps the moochers out but simply because he's a nigger. The general once again nails the attitude here when asked whether he has met Major Warren: "No, I don't know him but I know he's a nigger and that's all I need to know." Present-day profiling is grounded in this never-expressed but fervent belief that it remains sufficient to see the color of a person's skin to "know" him or her. What General Smithers knows and cannot tolerate is that slaves, once property, are now free and told they are as human as whites are. But if that cause for racism no longer exists, what impulse to racism has taken its place because we are deluged with proof that black lives don't matter, or they matter less than white lives? If viewers of this film distance themselves from General Smithers and all the other racists Tarantino puts before us, are they not put on a search for why racism continues to exist?

The entire South votes Democrat only to disassociate itself from the party of Lincoln, the Republican Party. It is only until President Johnson's Civil Rights Act upsets the rule of Jim Crow in the South that Johnson's Democratic Party is shunned and the South votes Republican and Republicans henceforth can win Southern votes by playing the racist card. And a sign that racism has grown can be seen in the 2008 and 2012 elections where President Obama won two states in the South in 2008 but lost the whole South in 2012. Racism, like a parasite looking for a new host, is not now lit by the sight of emancipated blacks but by the sight of "loser" blacks in need of "Big Government" assistance. This loser class, both black and white, is now offensive in the eyes of a totally segregated gentrified class. That situation lights the fire of present-day racism in the United States. We don't use the word because the reality of blacks is further now from the private, gated compound life of the wealthy than ever before. There is no need to use the word or extend any kind of representation to those who do not really exist for us. Perhaps this is a more pernicious form of racism than that expressed openly by General Smithers in *The Hateful Eight*. So Tarantino indeed goes somewhere with racism, goes deep into the dark roots of the American psyche.

Lincoln did not see the better angels of our nature at work on the Gettysburg battlefield. He was urging those in the North and the South to go in search of what they had lost. Or, discover what remained hidden. Tarantino presents us with a film in which he too cannot find the best in Americans at work. His fellow citizens are what they are in the present, war wearied and creating carnage as the stochastic play of the stock market goes on; because he sees them rooted in darkness, the claim to be "the greatest nation in the world" cannot excavate. And the falseness that results from such disingenuousness in turn makes everything false, or, as Americans are experiencing it now, makes it impossible to distinguish true from counterfeit.

Lincoln's bogus letter to Marquis is on one hand, as Marquis tell us, a ploy which the black man needs as an edge, as just something extra, to get what he wants. "It got me on that stagecoach," he tells John Ruth. But when Mannix, dying alongside the dying Marquis, reads the letter and they both laugh and the letter is crumbled and thrown away, we witness that act which reminds us that humanity itself has not yet heeded Lincoln's urge to go in search of "our better angels."

Notes

1. *Bright Lights Film Journal,* January 30, 2014.
2. *Bright Lights Film Journal,* January 19, 2016.

Chapter Eleven

I Roam into TV

Rebel Sons, Foodies, DBs, TV Pharmacy, and Sports

I was drawn to the psychopaths, sociopaths, and timeless rebels repre-
sented in pop culture, what Shakespeare called "masterless men," Malcolm
Gladwell called "outliers"; and in "TV's Rebel Sons: The Anger of Deep
Revolt" I work my approach into the young rebels of *Breaking Bad*,
Dexter, and *Sons of Anarchy*, TV's exploration of our dark imaginaries and
dark affiliations.

TV's Rebel Sons: The Anger of Deep Revolt[1]

*There is a subterranean river of untapped, ferocious, lonely and romantic
desires, that concentration of ecstasy and violence which is the dream life of
the nation.*

—Norman Mailer

*Today's constipated politics, the eroding civility of our public life, and the
virtual disappearance of generosity from our political debates are the predictable
pathologies that emerge whenever most of the population loses its sense of
getting ahead, and loses as well any optimism that renewed gains are on the
horizon. But the manifestations visible today are likely just the beginning.*

—Benjamin M. Friedman, "'Brave New Capitalists' Paradise':
The Jobs?" *New York Review of Books*, November 7, 2013

TV's *Sons of Anarchy* are, for many, America's favorite sons. They are the
sons of the dark side of the American cultural imaginary. If there is now

a bright side, I do not know where it is in either pop culture or political culture or economic culture. Exception: there is a bright side for those who shop at Prada, Tiffany, and Cartier, not the many. Exception: there is always a bright side in religion but it is on the other side of life, apocalyptic Rapture a current favorite.

Meanwhile, like the *Sons of Anarchy*, we are urged in this mortal coil and vale of tears "to look this life in the eye." In numbers probably exceeding those who have adopted TV's *Sons of Anarchy* as their own, there are those looking at life through the eyes of the *Duck Dynasty*, the Robertson Family, who cling to "guns and religion."

If the Robertsons believed politics went beyond the family and its business, they would join the Tea Party. But the Tea Party's political activism is contrary to the disdain for politics that is far more popular than any activism. The *Duck Dynasty* is very close to where the American cultural imaginary wants to be right now, which is very strange because few look and live like the Robertsons in West Monroe, LA. It is perhaps where that imaginary escapes to, where headlines do not exist, anger never seethes into revolt. Yet this dynasty remains puzzling.

I'm much closer to understanding where the *Sons of Anarchy* are in that imaginary and what they represent and mean, what they tell us about an archetypal anger of son against father, of rebellion against the dynasties and regimes of authority and power. True, these regimes are mostly divided into senseless gridlock. True, these dynasties are divided into the rich who grow richer and richer and those who lose, following zero-sum game rules where winners need losers.

My interest lies in places where a son named Dexter works day-by-day to create a moral and social way of being that he has to find with the help of his dead father. My interest lies in Mr. White, who "breaks bad" and takes a surrogate son along with him. The anger of deep revolt in my title is to be found in *Sons of Anarchy, Breaking Bad*, and *Dexter*, expelled in different ways but all emerging from a dark side of the American cultural imaginary. This is a convergence that tells us something of protest and revolt that OWS only reveals in the way any sudden eruptive action signals what is subliminal, what I call an imaginary not personal but cultural that runs like dream footage, dream footage that is dark and telling.

I.

I liked it. I was good at it. And I was really—I was alive.

—Walter White, *Breaking Bad*

You break into this darkness, this "badness," what Mailer called "a subterranean river of untapped, ferocious, lonely, and romantic desires," appropriately with *Breaking Bad*, but it is the young Jesse Pinkman and not Walter White who represents us and where we are positioned in the cultural imaginary. Pinkman is our deputy here, the one with whom we break into badness.

Breaking Bad premiered on AMC January 20, 2008, the year of the Great Recession. The youth unemployment rate in 2007 was 13 percent and it jumped to 21 percent in 2010 as the Great Recession took its toll. According to the *Huffington Post*, "In 2000, the United States had the lowest non-employment rate for 25- to 34-year-olds among countries with large, wealthy economies. By 2011, America had one of the highest youth non-employment rates compared to its peers" (May 9, 2013).

Notorious B.I.G. sums up what new millennium social mobility in the United States means for youth: "Either you're slingin' crack-rock, or you've got a wicked jump-shot" ("Things Done Changed"). Under the auspices of market rule and its zero-sum game, the path to a middle-class life has eroded as union salaries and industrial and manufacturing jobs have eroded and been replaced with McJobs. With the rungs on the ladder of economic and social mobility now missing, it remains difficult to get from nothing to a beginning. A serious jump is now needed. The business of how money is made in the United States has become as arcane and opaque as Wall Street's investing 'instruments.'

The surround out of which a Jesse Pinkman emerges then is one in which slingin' crack-rock is a more practical path than owning a wicked jump shot, which itself is a more practical path than the neoliberal advice: "Start a business." So you can think, from a rational point of view, that Jesse Pinkman, not employed by any business is a long way from starting a business. What he needs to do is the impossible: He needs to innovate, literally bypass experience and invent something new, something out of nothing because nothing represents his skill sets. This sort of irrationality is all that is offered by his society. And the absorbing drama of *Breaking Bad* emerges partly from this: that Jesse does start a business, alongside Mr. White, and makes oodles of cash, bricks of stacked bills that fill storage units and fifty-five gallon drums and suitcases and car trunks and safes and. . . . The sight of piles of cash not counted but measured in length, width and height, so much cash it has to be weighed, plays on and on in the cultural imaginary. It is the shape of a mass-cultural desire.

Our first sight of Jesse, a former high-school chemistry student of the authority figure he calls "Mr. White," is when he is fleeing a raid on a meth lab. Our last sight of Jesse, when the series ends after a five-year run, is of him ecstatic, finally free, in a car crashing through a gate, getting as far away from a dying Mr. White as he can. What happens in between when his life cannot break free of Mr. White, when the two run in diametrically different moral dimensions, fascinates within a society whose moral sense is calibrated by profit. In this dynamic duo, we have widely different confrontations with what I will call "occasions for a moral review."

What propels Jesse into a new life with Mr. White is what propels air into a vacuum. Jesse, however, is not empty in himself but only in a deflated state, without anything to nurture his development, without anything or anyone to push him forward until Mr. White. What there is about Jesse that saddens Mr. White is Jesse's turn to drugs to escape a world with which he cannot come to terms. As the horrors mount—the death of his heroin-addict girlfriend, Jane, his killing of the lab assistant, Gale, the murder of his friend, Combo, the killing of Andrea's son, Brock, and of her brother—Jesse assumes a crushing amount of guilt, although he slowly begins to see Mr. White's role in his tragedy. Jesse has no defense mechanisms to protect him from the guilt that floods through as if a dam had broken, although there has been no chance for any fortifying installation to be erected. The huge piles of cash and all that it can buy, a new life luxuriously funded, a sure hold on the American Dream to have it all, has no hold on Jesse. He literally throws money out of the window of his car. He collapses under the burden of his sins, not ever a tragic hero of any stature and yet is heroic for revolting in his own fashion from the self-deceit and illusions of his father-figure, Mr. White.

Perhaps it is systematic method and analysis, the control of variables as well as chance that Mr. White projects onto his meth-cooking enterprise that organizes all his deflections from a moral review of his actions. He has at hand, defenses against putting himself in the place Jesse so easily and naturally falls into: a burden of guilt. Nothing can become a tragedy in Mr. White's life because he refuses to allow it through force of his own will. His choices are almost axiomatic, as if when one is given a cancer death sentence, everything is taken off the table, no rules apply, no obstacles recognized. It is all then a push forward toward having what he feared to take before. Death opens the doors of ambition in a way that the daily routine of unthreatened life has not. And what he sees suddenly and clearly are piles of cash, a happy family life filled with family values, an awesome presence as "Heisenberg," and the triumphant role of a clear winner.

Mr. White has become, in other words, the personification and emblem of the society that has left Jesse no more than his victim. He thrives as an entrepreneur with a highly prized product—his blue meth—and cleverly outplays all threats and challengers. "I did it for me," he tells his wife, Skyler. "I liked it. I was good at it. And I was really—I was alive." That feeling of being alive is the result of being 'on the inside,' being where the action is, where the game is played and winners can dominate.

"If you're not inside," *Wall Street's* Gordon Gekko tells us, "you're outside." But now both inside and outside are only one place: a primeval, barbaric, blind, and lightless place. What the popularity of the *Duck Dynasty* confirms for us is that many Americans imagine economic nightmares in religious terms. "I think our problem is a spiritual one," Phil of *Duck Dynasty* tells this 90 percent. "Where there is no Jesus, evil always reigns." But it remains clear that the winners of a game that has no moral dimensions also have invoked Jesus's name. What remains clear is a dissociation of moral priorities from the priorities of market rule. There is then no moral valuation made in precisely that domain where it must be made, the domain of market rule where the 'players' dismiss moral concerns as delusions of a Nietzschean slave mentality, the distractions and weaknesses that make losers.

There is no room in Mr. White's moral imaginary for him as bad; in his own mind he breaks beyond good and evil—pious being good, worldly being bad—and regains what Nietzsche described as an ancient warrior aristocracy's good and bad, the good being bricks of cash, the bad being no bricks of cash.

Jesse Pinkman feels guilty because he has accepted the notion of one morality-for-all while Mr. White has detached himself from the herd morality and accepted his own unique determination of the moral. As he evolves in the five series, he accepts at every stage what he has become, placing that expansion of self beyond the shackles of any morality, relishing at every stage what he is becoming. And so he expands as Jesse contracts, as when in a culture the few expand at the expense of the many.

II.

I'm the helpful handyman, how evil could I be?

—*Dexter*

I am imagining that Jesse Pinkman's feverish excitement as he crashes through the gates, racing away from Mr. White, will, at some point, disappear; and he will begin to fashion some moral code within himself that defends him against all charges of criminality, of peccancy, of culpability and reprehensibility, of guilt. And when he arrives there, he will begin to live without reproach.

In truth, I cannot imagine any of this. There is nothing in *Breaking Bad* that tells us or shows anything about *Breaking Good*. We remain fascinated in our cultural imaginary with those stacks of bills in barrels and storage facilities, in the trunk of YOUR car. There was eighty million dollars in those barrels! Selling a product for those who choose to buy it, use it, and assume personal responsibility for the consequences—what part of 'the market is always right' is violated here?

The question now becomes, "How do you create a moral code for yourself in a society that gives you no instruction, in a society that mimics a moral sense but your eyes can't find anywhere, not in Detroit, not on Wall Street, not in the Hamptons, not in Washington, DC, not anywhere enacted, though diplomatically mouthed globally?

From a Homeland Security point of view, a need to create your own moral code in the perceived absence of the lack of a societal one puts you on a potential terrorist list. It registers a deep dissatisfaction with the resident order. It registers a challenge to a society's values, achievements, and struggles. It means that you will not go along with a society's struggle on behalf of what is good and right because you have adopted alien and alienating notions. And yet, when the moral sense offered by that society has brought that society to a state described in the prefatory quotation of this essay, is it moral to acquiesce?

Dexter Morgan in the TV show *Dexter* can provide what Jesse Pinkman cannot: a way to establish a moral code in your life when the one society offers you is rejected. Whereas Jesse Pinkman is carried along Mr. White's headlong rush to egomaniacal power, mo' money and mo' money, like benumbed baggage brought to pained awareness, Dexter Morgan steers his own course as a renegade, outpacing and outthinking all around him. Whereas Jesse Pinkman's sad course shows us that revolt from all that the American Dream has been reduced to—ego, greed, duplicity, and moral apathy on display in Mr. White—is what is now required, Dexter Morgan shows us a bit of how that requirement is fulfilled.

The same dilemma regarding the individual and society holds true, however, with Dexter as with Jesse. Is society culpable here or has Jesse, a loser surrounded by losers, failed to make the right choices and suffers accordingly? Mr. White can also be seen not as a logical exemplum of the market principle of 'winning is the only thing' but as a mind traumatized by terminal illness. Is society culpable for Dexter's psychopathology, one arising from childhood trauma? Dexter then in this view, is not a rebel against society, a rebel without a cause but rather an injured mind forging a functional compact with the world. He develops a moral code that allows him to satisfy his pathological urges to kill without the pangs of conscience that torment poor Jesse. The messages seem clear: Jesse has no one but himself to blame; Mr. White is an unstable, dying man who loses himself in greed, power, and ego; Dexter Morgan is a psychopath intelligent enough to kill and avoid capture.

Things, however, play out quite differently on the terrain of the cultural imaginary.

The root attractiveness of Dexter Morgan is his rebel, anti-heroic status that outshines all other responses. Admiration on this level is at best intermittently shadowed by our recognition that we are admiring a serial killer and that this is an insane man incapable of freely choosing, and he is, therefore, totally unlike ourselves. Because market rule rests on the notion that we all choose freely on a level playing field, our fascination with a man who demonstrates that his experiences have distorted that freedom bears a truth market rule suppresses. Our freedom to choose can be impaired, to disastrous degrees, by our experiences and by our surround that leave us choosing 'freely'—a false freedom—within that impaired state. Neither Dexter's transgression of our moral sense or our sacred market rule, however, gets in the way of our magnetic attraction to Dexter.

What I think we are attracted to is his overriding our societal regime of order, on all levels. Merely doing that is a relief for us; he provides us an example of how to slip by, time and again, the blindness of our bureaucratic methods, power struggles on all levels, unequal dispensing of justice, the interminable gridlock of our courts, and the hype and hypocrisy of what passes as civility. In a society so divided into factions—those that indict the winners for being the cause of the hardships they suffer, and those who feel they unfairly bear the burden of supporting those who won't work—there is, on both sides, a receptivity to a heroic outsider, to one who pays no heed to that fractured society but pursues his own life, liberty, and happiness. Only a society that has worked itself into the cultural imaginary as a nightmare could put forth a psychopath as a liberator, as the one they have been waiting for.

Dexter's is a cold, surgical ruthlessness, the kind that legendary revolutionaries have found necessary; nothing sweeps cleaner than a bloody coup. There is an equal moral dimension also as the revolutionary takes the lives of tyrants whose own tyrannical order will not bring them to justice. Dexter takes the lives of monsters whose own societal order cannot bring to justice. In the liberal/leftist view, he is an avenger who refuses to abide by legislation corporate lobbyists have written or by the greed version of the American Dream that market rule brands into every soul but the avenger's.

Somehow, Dexter has escaped the influence of those regimes. It does not matter here if childhood trauma is offered as a reason. Such reasons do not matter. What matters is that he is fully aware of the branding manipulations that others are blind to, that he flies by the nets set out to arrest him, that he launches his own counterterrorism and succeeds. This one man undermines a false order by showing us, first, that it is no order at all but a maze of ineffectual confusion, and second, that we can all launch our own revolt, be our own government of our own lives, and outsmart all our pursuers.

The conservative/neoliberal attraction to Dexter's quick dispensing of justice can be explained, on one level, if at all, by studying the state of Texas and its rationale for capital punishment. But on the level of a cultural psyche, the conservative need for a speedier and more definitive criminal processing is rooted in fear, fear of an increasing number of citizens, have-nots and having-less-each-day, who threaten the sense of security that winners require to enjoy their winnings. Here on this unsayable, irrational but potent level of response, Dexter is indeed the handyman who gets the job done, the one man, like a superhero, who could efficiently bring offenders to justice and justice to offenders. Here is an individual, not a government, who by his own choices does what governments fail to do. This deflation of government to personal choice makes Dexter a Libertarian hero, an honored member of the Tea Party.

Dexter's sociopathic lack of affect is indicated in the efficient, emotionless preparation and execution of his kills. In the course of the series, Dexter struggles to confine that coldness to his kills while extending the growing embers of feeling to those he sees as innocent, most demonstrably to his sister, Deb, who is a living thread to his own beginnings and to the whole course of his struggles. Her death in the last episode destroys all the human compassion and feeling he has built; the cold killing has tainted that side of his life where he was not cold and did not kill. It is a moral impossibility to kill the monsters without remorse and yet hold on to a ruthful life, a life of compassion. In the end, Dexter gives up the struggle rather than accept the hypocrisy of believing he can succeed. The hypocrisy of a so-called compassionate conservatism does not follow the path of a fictional Dexter but rather pushes its compassion harder as the force of market rule coldly and axiomatically pushes many toward desperation and thus belies the presence of any compassion at all.

If we want to see the anger of deep revolt extended beyond the individual, we need to become a member of The Sons of Anarchy Motorcycle Club, Redwood Original Charter (SAMCRO/"Sam Crow" or SOA for short).

III.

That a new society be founded in the heart of the old society.

—Pierre-Joseph Proudhon

Got to look this life in the eye.

—"This Life," Curtis Stigers, Dave Kushner, and Bob Thiele, Jr.

The *Hamlet* theme of *Sons of Anarchy*: Clay kills "JT," John Teller, Jax's father, and then marries Jax's mother, Gemma; Jax discovers the murder, is in anguish, and begins his slow plotting of revenge. That personal psychic drama, that psychomachia, is a good fit for the millennial turn to the maxim, "Everything is personal." But what precedes JT's murder turns the screw toward "Everything is political." Shakespeare's eye is on the broader maladies out of which this drama emerges: "Something is rotten in the state of Denmark." The civil society is not so civil, nor does it appear that a livable, balanced spread of prosperity arises from the zero-sum economic game being played.

SAMCRO (Sons of Anarchy Motorcycle Club, Redwood Original) begins as all separatist endeavors begin: struggling to remain apart from a culture they cannot accept. The Shakespearean analogue that more closely reaches the cultural imaginary is *The Tempest's* Prospero and his island kingdom, one he shapes after his exile from the debauched society his brother, Antonio, has created. Prospero's goal, however, is to redeem that debauched society, which is not the goal of JT, who seeks a separate peace, as if there is no hope of redeeming the United States, to which he has returned. He has limited redemption to a tiny separate island: Teller-Morrow Automobile Repair shop, the home of the Sons of Anarchy. A sense of tragedy is present at the club's very beginning, for this is an experimental, alternate society that can fulfill its charter only outside society.

The club is formed by JT and fellow Vietnam vets in an attempt to retain the close comradeship, the brotherhood that had sustained them in that senseless war. They attempt to create a society within an overshadowing society that plunges into depression after Vietnam and is then 'reborn' by Reagan's attempt to convert a middle-class democracy to an oligarchy of winners. The problem that JT faces and cannot resolve is namely this: What form of economics will sustain their club without falling "under the weight of greedy men who believe in nothing"?

These are words spoken by Jax to Clay, his stepfather, in the sixth season of the show, as Jax assumes the mantle of his dead father's mission to free the club from the greed surrounding them. Jax has read the typescript his father has left him—*The Life and Death of Sam Crow: How the Sons of Anarchy Lost Their Way*—and is determined to find ways of earning that do not involve dealing in guns or drugs, although, like for the Dutch, porn and prostitution remain legitimate. The search is for an economics that sustains and does not transgress the charter of the club, a charter that privileges communal interrelationship and interdependence, a charter grounded in the sort of brotherhood Ursula Le Guin speaks of in *The Dispossessed*: "We are brothers in what we share. In pain, which each of us must suffer alone, in hunger, in poverty, in hope, we know our brotherhood."

There is an order here and a hierarchy of leadership and authority that is democratic, not anarchistic, but this democracy is struggling to free itself from the market rule that has turned the American society they are enmeshed within into a predatory oligarchy. Thus far, they have protested against that form of capitalism by earning illegal profits. In doing so, they have entered a world of violent chaos, a world Jax, as the club's new president, attempts to manage. He will get through, he repeats each time the club faces a new threat, the shit they are facing now and bring a club that has lost its way, in the words of his dead father, back to what, in truth, he cannot clearly see.

If SAMCRO can reconcile democratic government and leadership with 'ways of earning' that do not turn the brotherhood into the "greedy men who believe in nothing," the men Jax is set against, then this revolt and the patch *Men of Mayhem* will disappear. Success in this will be a model for the society at large enabling the United States to rediscover so much that it has lost, including its downsized moral sense.

You could say that our cultural imaginary of "untapped, ferocious, lonely and romantic desires," will dissolve, that the chaos that casino capitalism has created will turn into the "voluntary order" that Alan Moore speaks of in *V for Vendetta*. But the difficulties the Sons face, which extend from their hometown-charming problems to problems with international drug cartels, IRA gun dealers, the CIA and "Pope," a man of extended Koch brothers pontifical power, reveal all ways of earning have already been appropriated by institutions, legal and illegal, 'too big to fail.' The monsters that do not know brotherhood own all ways of earning. And it remains quite clear that the Sons want these monsters to fail.

We wind back to Dexter who is a one-man assault on the monsters.

It is a very successful assault, but Dexter, in *Sons of Anarchy* terms, is a man outside the brotherhood, a man without a patch of belonging, a man whose fate is like any son who loses his patch and is sent into an uncivil world where "greedy men believe in nothing." And there in the end, as in the beginning, we find in Dexter a pathology that cannot serve as a model for societal revolt, regardless of how much his outlawry touches the deep-and-dark reservoir of our own anger. He is doomed to an exile from any familial or societal connection; there is no hope of any brotherhood for Dexter.

The Sons fear that fate of being voted out of the brotherhood, of losing their patch of belonging somewhere, but they cannot find their way to preserving the bonds they cherish. They cannot revolt from the society around them and at the same time find a necessary economic relationship with it that does not violate their moral charter. This dilemma closely parallels that of a US society that cannot reconcile a deeply divided politics regarding the culpability of its economic losers and the culpability of its market rule. Further, the opaqueness of a future in which such rule does not totally extinguish democratic civility, to say nothing of the fraternity the Sons cherish, is shared by both societies, Sam Crow's and that of the United States.

With both paths of revolt blocked and dysfunctional—Dexter's and the Sons'—we remain pliant and branded, adrift like Jesse Pinkman, seething but pathless and unprotected in the chaos greedy men who believe in nothing create.

....

"The fear of death follows from the fear of life," Mark Twain wrote, which is a version of what I observe in what I call "autopsy TV," or TV returning our gaze to dead bodies (DBs), either at the murder scene or on the autopsy table, the camera in close on damage and mutilation as well as rip sawing, slicing, and dicing performed by indifferent or sharp-tongued medical examiners (ME's). Intermittently, we are presented with commercials revealing to us a wide variety of illness and disease, of pain and suffering, alleviated by this or that purgative or curative. The dark imaginary of death shadows life, generating fascinations and fears that the market exploits like a never-exhausted fossil-fuel frontier. And in many ways, it's an American fear-and-fascination syndrome, or, more exactly, the dark repression of modernity's secular materialism, more a familiar companion in hardscrabble or war-torn countries, or in countries where death is a welcoming to paradise. Oddly enough, both Christians and Muslims believe in a paradisiacal afterlife but in Protestant America, it is clear that material possessions trump an unknown afterlife. What I observed in US TV was the shock of the DB followed by an urgent message to hold off this or that mental or bodily complaint with this or that prophylactic. That dynamic linkage is endlessly profitable.

Autopsy TV[2]

Everything to be imagined is an image of truth.

—William Blake

The aughts began with the fearful Y2K and ended on Christmas Day 2009 with a terrorist attack, thankfully failed, on board a plane from Amsterdam to Detroit.

Call these "macro-fears" and include everything that is going on in Iraq, Iran, Afghanistan, Pakistan, Israel, Palestine, Lebanon, North Korea, Yemen, Somalia, and the newest exotic locale that a primarily xenophobic American cultural consciousness has no "ap" for. Undoubtedly personal fears—fears closer to home—trump global fears, at least for all the victims of "outplacement" (job loss), home foreclosure, all manner of bankruptcy, loss of health care, and cracked nest eggs. Call these the "micro-fears." Perhaps it's a class thing: the haves and have-mores have the macro-fears and the rest of us have the micro-fears.

However, what I observe in what I call my canaries in the coal mine—the "entertainments" of popular culture—lead me to believe that we are all in this new hype(r)(d)modern world fearful on a deeper ontological level, a primordial genetic level, perhaps a shared archetypal level, that no amount of Twitter and Prozac, friending and unfriending, outplacement and outsourcing, bailouts and stimulus, surges and drones, Mii and Wii, nunchusk and netois can displace or subdue.

I can offer neither justification nor defense of my treating the American hype(r)(d)modern psyche as a deranged patient and pop culture as an outpouring, a free-association of that cultural psyche. But I can offer this: at this moment we live wholeheartedly in the story of individually designed reality and a self-chosen, self-willed autonomous psyche. The illusions of individualism and personal choice have reached the extraordinary level wherein we now believe we can simply choose what we want and the whole universe will support that choice. Such illusions are pathological certainly but they are also widespread. The pervading presence of this hype(r)(d)modern attitude is a mass-psyche phenomenon: all of us are in some stage of infection.

At this hype(r)(d)modern moment the notion of an "American cultural imaginary," a "mass cultural psyche," seems "so five seconds ago." I am also aware that the expression "so five seconds ago" is belated. It is difficult in our NOW obsession not to be belated, and belatedness is as shunned a malady as leprosy once was "back in the day." Unfortunately, Nowness has a built-in elusiveness while belatedness cannot be evaded. Nowness is only implicitly and defensively revealed as in the phrase, "That was back in the day, right?" "Back in the day" here covers everything that happened before you opened your Facebook account. This disassociation from the past along with a fear of revealing one's belatedness by any recognition of the past—as well as a turn to a totally personal design of destiny—are for me, as a starter here, glaring symptoms of a psychopathology. Our illusions do not announce themselves as illusion but always as fascinations, desires, fears, obsessions, hatreds. Every illusion comes packaged with reasons. Every illusion becomes a need. Enlightening secrets, charismatic presences, the tattooed brands of individuality, virtual warfare and pornified lives, the prosthetics of technology, private argot and *Brave New World* mantras, pharmacological living and dying—the imagination creates but also reaches to find these expressions of the cultural psyche.

Here is some back-in-the-day talk, which drowns in its own belatedness: A culture both fearful of its own end, terrorized by its own fall from grace (its own "exceptionalism"), engaged since Vietnam in a defensive death-dealing in order to preserve its own way of life has death on its mind continuously. A way of life must oddly and perversely become a 'way of death.' Death is the cultural métier. It pervades the dominating economics wherein the most savvy work freely and competitively toward a 'creative destruction' which creates profits for few and destroys the habitats and lives of many. The illusion that by killing others—surgically and without injury to ourselves—we secure our own safety has its beginnings in the primordial mud, of creativity in the service of survival.

But the American Dream whittled down to the nightmare of money, of filthy lucre, the coin of death and the devil, of a "theatre of war" as a new market to be opened, new profits to shareholders to be grown, now more surely drives the illusion than our instincts to survive. The creativity of Eros has given way to the destructiveness of Thanatos. The creation of profit has nurtured a death wish that turns back on us, even as it surges outward and away from the safe zone, the Green Zone, of our own hearts and minds.

This is, as I say, more back-in-the-day talk than *CSI* autopsy talk, but, its belatedness aside, it is nonetheless talk inspired by our TV death shows. That the American repression of its own mortality has reached crises levels is evidenced, perversely and ironically, by our obscene fascination with dead bodies lying on autopsy tables, Y-stitched chests à la Frankenstein, or cut open with surgical SawzAlls, blood splattering on the goggles of the mad scientist—here a medical examiner—gloved hands pulling out organs, sliced and diced, churned in blenders, human bodies processed like butcher meat. One show has not been enough. Like the *Alien* mother whose prodigious fertility spawns egg after egg, the *CSI* shows breed. Unlike the *Alien* movies, which seem to have terminated, these TV shows will be syndicated till the end of time. Surgery upon the dead. Surgical strikes and smart bombs and man-less drones, stealth fighters with a Darth Vader look. An ivy-league grad sits at a computer in Arlington, Virginia, and programs death from long distance and then goes home to watch a *CSI* TV show. Or take his daughter to a soccer game as Russell Crowe does in the film *Body of Lies*. Long distance, regentrified death dealing.

Each *CSI* show seems intent on showing more gruesome stuff than its rivals as if the ghoulish addiction to seeing the human body on a slab, mutilated in the quest for the "physical evidence which speaks for itself" must be steadily fed a richer diet. Counterpointing this fascination with death is the erotic inclusions in the *CSI* shows as if near-porn and dead bodies were fit companions, like salt and tequila. This is a belated observation: death and sex (it was one of Norman Mailer's fixations back in the day) but consider that these are network TV shows of immense popularity. Somehow it is encouraging to think in the end you wind up a piece of meat, soulless, on a slab, evidence. Evidence of what? Carpe diem. Seize the pleasures of the day, of the body while it lives and breathes. Mud lies on the table with no sign of God's breath. This evidence will destroy all illusion that there is something good and wholesome, something miraculous and everlasting to which death will bring us. What I feel when I gaze at the autopsy table in autopsy and hospital TV is that I am alive now and have escaped the obscenity of death. That feeling is culturally shared.

Perhaps popular culture has staked this ground only because every culture that binds itself to the credo 'the guy with the most toys in the end wins' cannot look away from the end but must turn to it and mock or dissolve it. This is the electrifying spot, the toxic location. When you show it, they will come. And there is longevity here as the matter will not easily or ever dissolve, the gaze upon the dead body never leaving us certain, no matter how intense the desecration, that this body will not be held accountable for its own desecrations of other beings, of its own nature, of Nature itself. Regardless of how long we gaze upon this dead body we cannot be reassured that what we see is no more than a confirmation of our desire to fulfill our own desires, to take all and want more, to make use of all the world offers before we end on the autopsy table. The dynamics of this uncertainty, of this struggle of deep ontological dimensions that results in a psychic angst is a marketing target, a cultural disposition as vulnerable to the assaults of branding as any audience of weak minds before a charismatic demagogue, a fiery preacher. It is a struggle that has proven accessible and profitable in American culture, one that has replaced or supplemented religion's use of the very same contentious haunting.

For two-thirds of the time you are watching a *CSI* TV show you will experience *schadenfreude*, fully enjoying the relief of not being dead, that you have not suffered the humiliations that fascinate and revitalize you simply because *you are not this dead body*. Everyone has to die, but right now someone is dead and it's not you. You are alive now and that DB is proof. You are so vulnerable at that moment to any and every cure-all pitch that Madison Avenue can make. Thusly, one third of the time you will be watching commercials ingeniously tied to the profile of you that marketers have. The proliferation of dead body programming attends the proliferation of pharmaceutical advertisement. The pharmaceutical industry with millennial-level research and development offers you all you need to hold off your own autopsy. There is little sense within this drama for you to 'help save the planet' or 'wipe out poverty' or, in short, do anything for others beyond a social networking that allows you to friend and unfriend at a safe, virtualized distance. You will be a dead body before Nature is salvaged or poverty is no more, a dead body regardless of what you've done for others who will be, in spite of your humanity, no more than meat for autopsies.

All your attention then goes to your restless leg, your limp penis, your weak stream, your need for Beano, your cholesterol number, your memory loss, your overactive bladder, your facial lines and wrinkles, your fungus toenails, your sleep problems, your depression, your migraine, your joint pain. After such continuous programming of the dead body, of the autopsy, you seek every defense against death, every suggestion that this melodiously named drug will delay the autopsy moment. Millions whose legs have not been restless, whose sleep has not been disturbed, whose penises have not failed, whose stream is not weak, whose flatulence is only laughable, whose problems have not led to depression, whose everyday neurosis is tame, whose hearts give no pain, whose attentiveness is not hyperactive, whose thoughts are not suicidal, whose joint pain is bearable—and so on and on—suddenly question their sleep, their own minds, their sex lives, their quirks and jerks, whether they are steps away from a heart attack or a cerebral hemorrhage, whether fat blockage clogs the coronary arteries, whether a pissy mood is deep depression, whether a memory lapse is a sign of early dementia. . . . Everything becomes a sign of the death that awaits you, of the autopsy. Unless you take these pills or those pills or all pills each and every day.

Every TV show dealing in death and dying now provides for our pathography a description of the cultural psyche. But the most inventive and pressing and revealing aspect of popular culture—marketing and advertising—provides the verification of the picture here drawn. In describing a pathography, as in criminal investigation, you follow the money. And where money stops functioning and fails to make sense of what we fear—9/11, Katrina, oil spills and global warming, incomprehensible wars, the Great Recession of Now—there is only dread ahead. We are hype(r)(d)modern now, perhaps the last presentation of a long illness that a switch to *Activia* will not cure.

....

I found the proliferation of food shows on TV puzzling. In a country whose palate was attuned to fat, sugar, salt, and chemical food additives, who mostly has dinner at a fast-food drive-in (30 percent of Americans eat in their cars all the time), who 'nuke' and barbeque, either abjure bread because it's fattening or because gluten is the new enemy, who eat fish and vegetables raw because they can't cook them in any tasteful way, who think 'American' cheese is exceptional because it's American even though no cheesemonger would identify it as cheese, and who couldn't judge a 'scratch' cake from a box one, and who want wine to come as close to tasting like Mountain Dew as possible, who like 'mild' fish and mild olives and olive oil, who think tomatoes are slimy, and who think small tidbits of food, tweezer arranged, described by a waiter, and costing a week's salary are somehow admirable.

Why so much interest in watching others on TV make what they themselves can neither identify nor make, and will probably never eat? I detect a cultural pathology here that I have never been able to reduce to anything comparable to our fascination with dead bodies on TV and the attendant relief of pharmaceutical commercials, to fear, fascination, and salvation. The best I can come up with is that America's descent to the lower depths in regard to cooking and eating—not by the top 20 percent who have gentrified and artisanaled both—and its addiction to TV's wallowing in both is either a penance for transgressions made against food, or a kind of susceptibility or impressionability. It could be a kind of awe similar to what goes on when the down-and-out watch the British TV drama *Downton Abbey*, where life is different from their own. At any rate, whatever dark affinities and dark imaginaries exist here, all aspects of food are a marketing frontier beyond buying milk, eggs, and butter, also items it's now faddish to avoid.

I admit I like Bourdain and Jaime Oliver, and I think Jacques Pepin skips the 'haute' in haute cuisine, and I understand that the competitive Reality-TV food shows fit the American winner/loser profile. I also see that a turn to Reality TV accommodates an audience that has lost a sustained focus as well as the patience to work through the works of the imagination. If you think that texting and tweeting do not represent a dumbing down of language, then you will not agree that our passion for Reality TV is a passion for "Tony has a pony" language, the everyday language that a society that tweets and texts finds most comfortable. Besides, in our 'my opinion rules' mindset, why struggle to understand what you wouldn't say yourself?

I took the persona of "The New Gulliver" in writing my food, cooking, and farming pieces for *Dandelion Salad*, a marvelous online site not at all about dandelion salad or, indeed. food. The metaphorical salad here is mixed, like the culture.

Food TV [3]

[O]ur culture's food madness tips into food psychosis, at least among those with keen appetites and the means to indulge them.

—Frank Bruni, "Dinner and Derangement,"
New York Times, October 18, 2011

One night, a waitress revealed that the fish-tempura taco with cabbage, and lime mayonnaise was made with "baby shark," prompting one diner to wonder aloud, "Should I feel bad about this?" She should not; the term is a colloquialism for cazon, a small school shark common in Mexican cooking, and not the veal of the sea.

—Silvia Killingsworth, "Table for Two,"
New Yorker, September 19, 2011

[T]his decade's best food programming has plied our species' basic need for sustenance with our culture's love of competition and thirst for voyeurism into shows that are suspenseful, hilarious, challenging, maddening, and stomach-rumble-inducing—often all at once . . . we find ourselves passionately invested in food we can't even taste.

—*Paste Magazine*

Kind of neat to see what makes these chefs tick and their take on areas other than food.

—Comment on "Serious Eats" website regarding
the possibility of an HBO food show

In one way at least I am like a shark, maybe a small school shark: I am as attracted to American cultural psychosis as a shark is to blood or smelly bait and chum in the water.

Once riveted on what I called "Autopsy TV," I am now speechless before "Food TV," quite honestly transfixed by the mélange of odd elements that comprise our fascination. By "Food TV" I am not referring just to the Food Network presenting 116 food shows from *Ace of Cakes* to *Worst Cooks in America* but also *Man v. Food, Bizarre Foods, No Reservations* on the *Travel Channel*, *Top Chef* on *Bravo*, and the many local and regional food shows on PBS.

American culinary genius recognizes no boundaries of ethnicity or tradition. In our strange Food-TV world we have zany extrapolations of the basic food groups, over-the-top fusions of what should never be fused, rather like the fusion of Jeff Goldblum and a fly in a remake of the classic *The Fly*. We also have a stupefying mission to 'contemporize' classic dishes and denationalize and deregionalize cuisines in deference to the new drive to personalize and self-design every little bit of everything in the world. We fuse and brand in the name of inventive change, as if you could take any number of Renaissance painters, blend all their canvases, flourish with a squeeze-bottle squirt of mystery compote and voilà—pure American genius! The squeeze bottle has a potent, mysterious allure; its contents can equally glorify the Donner kabob and West Virginia barbeque. It can colorfully lace the perimeter of a white plate in which a tweezer-arranged creation rests distinctively in the middle.

In the heartland of the United States, "European" just means *foreign*. Of course, special attention is paid to the French because they are foreign *and* irksome. It is clear that Old World caviling ignores America's inventive spirit, its refusal to bow to any tradition, political or culinary. Here we invent what suits us and recognize no foreign claim to a superior quality of life, including food. Here we add our own ingenuity to the old and outworn. For instance, the addition of Philadelphia brand cream cheese to an oil-based processed cheese produces—voilà!—the cheese ball, that ubiquitous delight of the American heartland. Put aside Umbrian olive oil and Spanish Shiraz 8 percent wine vinegar—and the whole magnificent tradition of creating great vinegar—and grab a bottle of Ranch, comparable only to Coke in its pricey nothingness but far superior in its chemical properties. Demand a meatball with your risotto, fry a whole turkey in an oil drum, stick gratuitous chocolate bits in any recipe, turn the chocolate itself into a chemical concoction, allow a machine to make your bread, throw away your pots and pans and 'nuke' your food, and enjoy your choice of a boutique coffee in plastic covered individual servings which emit no aroma, no trace of that bygone scent of bygone early mornings in America.

Why after an endless proliferation of food TV can't Americans break away from dried grain dregs coated in sugar called "breakfast cereals"? The drug-free meat and chicken of yesteryear now is rediscovered in gourmet food stores and sold at prices only the plutocrats can afford. 'Designer' food supplies, which are free of preserving chemicals, high-fructose corn syrup, and spray baths of fungicides and pesticides are now sold on websites for a discerning top 20 percent, whose lifespan increases while those who may reach Social Security age are destined by diet to need Medicare. The increasing need for both these government programs is running neck and neck with a need by plutocrats to undermine both programs.

There is a definite oddness, a certain derangement of logic, about a fast-food culture lusting for grease, salt, and sugar, and doesn't mind more chemical additives than in a lab report. There is a definite oddness to a culture whose cooking skills begin and end with a microwave, a culture that no longer has time or skills to cook yet manic about watching others cook on TV. Why are Americans, who think cooking is a leftover enterprise of an extinct analog generation, who flock to fast-food emporiums, who have less time to cook and eat than to text and tweet, who have been largely unconcerned with nutrition and healthy eating, who are not obese because they cook like Paul Bocuse but because they gnosh at will, all the time popping some ready-to-hand comestible in their mouths . . . why are they so fascinated by all these food TV shows? Why fascinated by competing cooks who are preparing dishes no viewer will ever make, with ingredients no viewer has ever seen, or ever have the time to eat? What gives here?

The psychology behind all this is deranged but not impossible to follow. But we need to take an even closer look at the derangement itself.

Here is a culture where the few whom the Goddess Fortuna has blessed seek 'an elegant hideaway whose conceits include the pairing of each dish in an eleven-course meal with a lukewarm, flavored water in a lidded grappa glass' while the many whom the goddess has tied to wages seek . . . well, they seek grease, salt, sugar, food additives, a Happy Meal in an eatery with colorful plastic conceits. Food identifies you; it is a clue as to who you really are. Michelin-starred restaurants are like gated communities keeping out those moochers who eat low on the food scale. Food is a defense the wealthy use, the way the English language is used in Shaw's *Pygmalion,* to tag the masses. Once you've enormous wealth, you don't try to culturally catch up to your wealth by reading the Harvard Classics. Instead, you learn to deal with a *sommelier,* to order from a French menu, to knot your scarf à la mode, to ply your knife and fork like Lord Grantham in *Downton Abbey,* to have your name recognized at fashionable restaurants, to know where to dine in the Hamptons, in Cobble Hill, or the East Village.

The need for food to survive is not incidental among the wealthy alone. Most Americans do not eat to survive but eat for pleasure, eat to forget, eat for the orgasm, eat to confirm an illusionary elite status, or eat addictively. Eating is another palliative, like shopping: the more you do it, the better you feel. Or, oppositely, it can be seen as a threat: the more you eat, the more you risk your need to be thin, like a celebrity; the more you eat, the more you risk becoming fat, like a loser. And in these ways, food plagues the wage earner in insidious ways.

Food must be fast for Americans because everything must be fast for Americans because fast gives us our competitive edge. If the winners are lingering decadently at table, mainstream eaters do not know that because they have no opportunity to see that. A very plausible reason as to why some 80 percent of the American population is not upset by the fact that 0.01 percent owns 40 percent of the country's wealth is that mega wealth lives privately outside the 'street view.' Their excesses are not experienced. And, indeed, excess is always represented in the media as something to be envied. Mainstream Middle America has a much closer view of their own backyards and those of non-competitive, dole dependent loser cultures. Loser cultures degenerate over long five-course meals in midday, followed by long siestas. Time slows down in southern Europe for food; food itself becomes a respite from the mantra 'time is money,' which is a mantra in the Northern Hemisphere but not the South. You could say that the American Dream of fame and fortune is braided into the American cultural imaginary's relationship with food. And it is a crazy relationship. A psychotic one.

Our food psychosis is like this—the more we tie food to chat as on *The Chew*, the more we see that the way we talk about food is like the way Tony Soprano talks to his shrink—words are distant from the reality we know. What I can do is describe the way food fits our American materialism. Let us face it, the fact that gluttons are on ring five, the Ring of Gluttony, in Dante's *Inferno* in no way affects a culture driven by its economic mandate requiring us to 'eat up the world!'

Regardless of how much a force the Christian Right is in conservative politics and how 'evangelical' we have become (for "evangelical" read "personally designed relationship with a personally designed celestial entity"—what is more American?) the fact remains that Americans are gross materialists, either wannabes or in actuality. Right now, the wannabes far outnumber those who live at the very top of the food chain. That food and everything associated with it from cooking to eating has become a means to stimulate, seduce, and distract the many from their increasingly bad straits is there to be seen on Food TV. Food is a distraction; cooks of every level of ineptitude and hubris take to YouTube and countless more watch them. Why? Because TV is too restricted a venue to satisfy the need to jump onto this mania. Your special and personal relationship with food becomes yet another expression of your own individual freedom, your own uniqueness. No one can tell you what to eat; yet, paradoxically, you cannot stop watching and listening to other people tell you what to eat and how to cook it. And you tolerate them because you know you can jump in with your own video as to how to prepare a five-bean casserole out of five cans of beans with marshmallows and chocolate topping.

Food, like all 'stuff,' is a soma that Romney's moocher class ingests and that can bring you some relief from your economic woes. The tougher the times, the more relief you seek, the more cheap burgers you buy. Relief is in the eating; and the more you eat, the more relief you get. You might say our prevailing economic system has a profit interest in keeping fast-food cheap, which means nutrition-free.

Recall that soma tablets in Huxley's *Brave New World* were free handouts. The reason fast-food emporiums regularly, dramatically advertise mouth-watering specials on TV is to boost the addiction. No effort is made to make dark, leafy greens mouth watering because neither Food TV nor the food industry know how to un-bewitch the taste preferences for grease, salt, sugar, and chemical substitutes they have created. A child's palate rules. The difficulties of acquiring tastes for what is healthy and nutritious are the same difficulties we face with adults as we face with children. There is no maturing process, no development from ignorant to wise but rather your childish tastes segue without alarm into adulthood. You keep eating burgers and asking for the Ranch dressing.

The resulting health calamities are only calamities profit-wise if those who profit from illness are forced to pay for its remediation. On the other hand, if an obese, diabetic, and hypertensive population has to pay for pharmaceuticals, doctors and hospitals via HMOs in the free market, profit is made on both ends—food and health care. If the health insurance business was turned over to the federal government or some amalgam authority representing profit AND the public good who would set payment levels for drugs, doctors, and hospitals, the profit loss would be heavy. And because taxes would be paying for all this gratis health care, taxpayers themselves would be seeking the elimination of toxic food additives and processing, which has led to bad health, more health care, and higher taxes.

Fast food is an instrument of appeasement, distraction, seduction, like cyberporn, cyber-shopping, endless sports talk, the chat and photos of social media, addictive video games such as *World of Warcraft*, like the feast of apps on a smartphone. All these are release valves that we can turn to after our house is taken away by a bank, or our job is 'outsourced,' or our credit cards are maxed, or our college financial aid is still unpaid ten years after graduation, or our 401K dipped below the poverty line, or we need a ninety-thousand dollars a year cancer chemo treatment, or we sold our pension and bought into Bernie Madoff's Ponzi scheme.

Bewildering fads rocket across the culture like shooting stars and are announced as ancient cure-alls or fountain-of-youth elixirs.

Deep in our food syndrome lie eerie fascinations with inventive and innovative fare and the ludicrous fussiness of presentation, a great laboring that puts forth a mouse, or less dramatically, a whole lot more Limoges plate than food. We are offered 'medallions' which I see as signifiers of beef or duck or veal or scallops as if the reality of food was the first victim heading toward total virtualization. After we all become cyborgs, what Boolean software will we eat, when quantum processing takes us to The Singularity, will merely *thinking* we have dined magnificently replace the reality that we have not dined at all?

Pierre Bourdieu has pointed out that if one is to achieve a cultural distinctiveness, some sign of a civilized discipline, rather than a barbaric appetite, must be presented. Thus, French *cuisine minceur* shows more distinction that an overflowing plate of spaghetti. Why? Because control of the appetite implies a discipline out of which order emerges whereas no control means chaos is on the horizon. Italian food breeds chaos; French, civilization. The more minute the portion, the more elaborate the presentation, the more knowledgeable you are of both the wine and the cork, the more this dining experience reminds you of a time in Paris, the more everything is *comme il faut*, the more distinguished you and your life become. Although, once again, this is distinctiveness that only a top 20 percent of the population seek and can afford.

Call this a "gentrification" of food. This is not a reversal from low to high, say, from peasant/ethnic to haute cuisine or from fast and fatty food to 'slow' and organic food. No, what I believe we see now is a virtualization of food, its removal from any reality, high or low, to a cyber world of endless personal design, which mishmashes all off-line boundaries, from history, region, language, customs, and agricultural domains. Food follows money, labor, and products as free-floating, transnational entities. While perhaps 80 percent of the world's population cannot exercise this new freedom but remain in enclosed regional and ethnic domains of eating or queue up in their cars for fast-food service, 20 percent of the world's population are developing a language of foodie expertise that endorses gentry status as surely as Oxbridge inflections.

I remain drawn to such food derangement that no logic can wrap itself around, although this may all be as inevitable as a descent to the bottom in regard to the quality of everything that de Tocqueville tactfully implied would be the American fate. Americans have already reached that in regard to food and cuisine. What is new is what I call the virtualization/gentrification of food by the new 'foodies,' who know the details of new microbrews, how quinoa has replaced arugula as fashionable, the lineage and provenance of artisanal fare, and much more. But there is a political dimension to being a foodie, just as gentrification of neighborhoods is a natural foodie affiliate. Foodie erudition is a way of separating the gentrified from the ungentrified, the connoisseurs from the louts, and the bottom 80 percent of the population from the top 20 percent.

What defenses do the non-foodie and ungentrified have? Is there an offense?

Big Government to the rescue. Or, maybe just a mythical government that competently responds to, say, the pollution of air, earth, water, and food. Unfortunately, food safety is like drug safety—it is so bureaucratically fractured or it is in the hands of those miscreants we need to arrest. We are a society without some sort of French Academy-like authority to say "Impossible!" That is the sort of Big Government authority against which Americans are exceptionally opposed. Market rule has left us with the McDonalds' Golden Arches, diabetes, hypertension, obesity, allergies, and "Thirteen Serious Toxins Lurking in Your Food," more toxic bodily oxidation going on than antioxidants can defeat. It has left us powerless to keep junk food out of our schools, powerless to challenge in the name of public health the 'personal taste' already instilled in the young before they come to school, and powerless to resist the removal of region, history, and farming to a virtualized concocting that is detached from any of this.

What Americans do to food is not just growing, cooking, and eating it but what I call "weaponizing" it. This is done not in the service of feeding an increasing multitude but in the service of an array of reasons I list as if they had sprung from Pandora's box:

1. We seek to provide the consumer endless choices to satisfy the American ontological need to exercise "free choice" and therefore confirm individual uniqueness. "I express my individuality by rejecting the ordinary purple eggplant and seek out a striped eggplant";

2. We look to the laboratory to create endless hybridized Frankensteins (tomatoes crossed with watermelon and a rubber plant, or is that a strawberry?) in accordance with the rule of designed obsolescence: eating an 'old school' Cortland apple is like using a flip-top phone;

3. We package our food not to oblige what may be its needs (you cannot wrap real cheese in plastic and put it the frig) but to oblige our own need to control (dominate) and technologize (advance) beyond the organicism of Nature which we have also removed ourselves from. Technology knows best; Nature is analog;

4. We 'technologize' cuisine by reducing time consuming/labor intensive primitive food preparation to instantaneous nuking, and we do this as a sign of millennial hi-tech advance;

5. We dissociate ourselves from a moral review of our treatment of the 'lower orders' that serve as our food supply by disassociating meat from 'bodies,' by plastic wrapping what can never be identified as carcass, by cutting filets and putting out-of-sight heads, necks, eyes, snouts, beaks, feet, and even bones. Surely if we do not face our own mortality, why should we face the mortality of the lower orders?

6. We have been subjecting food and cuisine to the changing politics of an equal sharing of kitchen duties, from shopping to cooking to serving, and cleaning up so that both men and women, in a battle-seeking equity, seek to escape these enterprises altogether. Everything dealing with household chores, including cooking, is used by women working out of the home as long and as hard as men are as a weapon to achieve their freedom from a historically unequal share of domestic duties. Whether men seek the easiest way out or contribute their equal share, there yet remains a mutual desire by both men and women to escape the kitchen in every way possible. The home-cooked meal and the family dinner become special-occasion events: birthdays, Thanksgiving, the Seven Feasts of Israel, and Christmas. Everyday family dinners become restaurant or fast-food trips or pizza delivery as well as a 24/7 individual food foraging for snacks by each family member. There is a whiff of socialist solidarity in family meals whereas 'let each eat what and when he or she wants' conforms to a creed of individual freedom and personal choice. Having to eat what Mom has made, or Dad, is a fascism, a bloody form of oppression;

7. We have found it easy to weaponize food through adopting the branding philosophy that ties personality type to product. Regardless of the taste, nutritional quality, or overall healthfulness of any product, it can be marketed successfully (launched like a missile) to its target audience because an indelible psychic connection has been made. Let food fit the profile, and when the profile is not marketable, create the conditions that create the profile. What we get after a generation or so of such weaponizing of food is what a

weapon barrage normally gives us: toxic ground, destroyed homes, ruined lives. I mean we wind up with an unhealthy and mostly toxic way of growing, cooking, and eating, destroyed palates so that memories of what anything in a natural state tasted like is lost. We like what we have grown used to and so we can easily like a tomato that tastes like a potato because that is all it is ever tasted like to us. If you make butter out of sawdust and start a whole generation on that butter, the reality of butter is that and nothing else. In the end, profits are made but the quality in food, cuisine, and taste lie in ruins.

'Weaponizing' implies risks but just as in war, we are apparently ready to accept such risks. For example, in a search for a plant's genetic resistance to pests and diseases, we are willing to ignore what the future consequences of such may be. Profit takes many risks and food, like illness and ignorance, is a frontier to be exploited for profit. After all, this is a reality in which we choose what we want, so we can choose not to worry.

....

I played baseball in the PAL (Police Athletic League) in Brooklyn in the 1950's. The movie, *Blackboard Jungle* (1955) captured the 'terrorist' fear of the time; namely, juvenile delinquents. So the PAL was a strategy to keep the juveniles off the streets and out of trouble. Of course, when members of one gang played a baseball game against members of another gang . . .

When the Dodgers left Brooklyn for the allure of Los Angeles in 1957, it seemed like a final, crushing blow to the Brooklyn ego, long diminished in film, novel, theatre, and song as a cultural Siberia. Its present gentrified status is not so much an accomplishment of native Brooklynites but of an invading army of the young and well-heeled, mostly from the heartland that we summarily referred to as "Oshkosh" in my neighborhood; that is, a place as uncool as it sounded. But I did see some of the legendary greats play and the memories linger so much so that the contamination of the game with doping brought me to this sentence: "Can I say that the heart of resistance to technology's impact on sports is America's love of baseball?"

Baseball does not move at nano-second video-game speed; it is not an interactive game; you do not sit in the bleachers with a joystick. You sit, sometimes for many hours, and watch others play. It is a slow game. It's low-tech. Bat, ball, and glove. It is an off-line game; it is analog and perhaps the only way it will survive in fifty years is online, a virtual game in which you become a player. We are becoming aware that everything analog, like everything public, is scheduled for extinction. We are also in a 'whatever' mood in regard to the past. Perhaps this is so because what is important remains what we personally choose, and we were not around in the past. We did not choose it so it is meaningless. Soccer somehow has appealed to the gentrified class; perhaps it is because it is not baseball, which has the taint of working-class Americana to it. Lacrosse has an even more gentrified ring to it, perhaps because it sounds French; and while the hoi polloi may despise the French, the American gentry join with the French in admiring the French. Lacrosse originated with Iroquois, however, which muddles the whole distinction link because while it's impressive to say that one is one-eighth Native American in the South, the remark has less clout out West.

Baseball, however, reeks of history. Its legendary players shadow those who play now. We are not in a mood for the past because technology has made only the future, in eighteen-month installments, important. And one of the ways technology can undermine the rich heritage of baseball is to make today's players superior models, rather like the way the auto industry seeks every year to offer a car that "outperforms" last year's model. If you can bury the legend of baseball and its legendary players in the same cemetery where you've interred everything and everyone that has been surpassed, from cowboys on horses to sailing before the mast, you can establish a reign of greater-than-human sports. Baseball will not be permitted to say no to the march of technology toward The Singularity and, along the way, increased profits.

This sort of sleight-of-hand game is what I sought to expose in "The Emergence of Greater-than-Human Sports . . . and Baseball," which I wrote for *Magazine Americana*, one of three sports essays I wrote for that magazine, the other two being "The Wellsprings of Football and Blizzard," and "The President and the Tiger: Just War, Pacifism, and Enlightened Self-Interest."

The Emergence of
Greater-than-Human Sports . . . and Baseball[4]

Baseball is a spirited race of man against man, reflex against reflex. A game of inches. Every skill is measured. Every heroic, every failing is seen and cheered, or booed. And then becomes a statistic. In baseball, democracy shines its clearest. The only race that matters is the race to the bag. The creed is the rulebook.

—Ernie Harwell, *Baseball Almanac*

Regardless of what narrative spin rules the day, we face certain inevitabilities, none of course universally acknowledged as inevitable besides death. Some inevitability seems to be a much surer bet than others. For instance, what technology, especially cybertech, offers will not one day vanish. Unless of course it loses itself in its own complexity, or, quite the opposite, its own complexity falls before some quite simple invasion, rather like the way box cutters brought down the Twin Towers. The probability is, however, that it's pretty much a sure thing that the future, near or far, will not go off-line, at least not by choice. Older generations of smart-phones, Xboxes, iPads and so on will vanish but only to be replaced by even more fascinating technology.

Probability also leads us to believe that chemical enhancement of sports performance is such a technology that will not go away. Once 'innovated,' it will not succumb to any resistance but rather will shape the "new normal," as politicians now refer to our continuing recession blues.

I think this is so, first of all, because we are very much attached to growth through technology; we prefer continuous-growth economics rather than steady state/sustainable. To grow ever larger you need to expand profits; and this is done by offering new products, which are the creation of new technology. So our economic system, which everything else queues behind, including politics, is more liable to view sports' performance enhancement via technology as part of inevitable growth goals.

Second, and connected to our competitive rather than cooperative notion of economics, we are very much attached to getting into the competitive arena and winning. Why wouldn't the newest technological innovations apply to winning in sports as they do in our most important domain, that of economics? Entrepreneurs play a hard-ball game just short of criminal arrest, most of the time but not always. The entrepreneurial idea here is to push the envelope, to go to the very edge of risk, to push a self-empowerment to the max, for the bold to leave the timid behind, in the dust.

Doping is the sports' world's version of insider trading: it's illegal but the very nature of the enterprise encourages its existence.

Third, we have pushed ourselves toward a need for accelerated response and an attendant impatience with 'slow, dial-up speed' and certainly for the speed of the off-line world. We have pushed ourselves online to virtual realities that make our off-line world seem boring and slow.

Wikipedia describes a virtual game world, which more and more people inhabit: "Massively multiplayer online role-playing game (MMORPG) is a genre of role-playing video games in which a very large number of players interact with one another within a virtual game world." Ten million people inhabit the *World of Warcraft* domain, for example. These cyber-space, substitute, fantasy worlds are knocking at our off-line real world, urging it to keep pace. Real-world sports now has a competitor no one foresaw, a competitor that offers not only the enhanced performance of virtual characters but the opportunity to interact within the worlds those characters inhabit. You are no longer sitting in the bleachers watching the game; you are in the game. You don't go out to the ballgame because it's no longer 'out there.' Everything that was once out there is now in cyberspace. The world has collapsed into just you, virtual faces of friends, 140-character tweets, apps for all cyber connections.

What off-line reality can rival this? How much doping must be done to real bodies to compete with virtual powers?

And last, I would say that whatever resistance we muster against the invasion of biotech into sports, it cannot withstand every form of technology's march toward a future in which all manner of constraints and limitations are surpassed. We can stimulate the brains of infants and increase IQ; we can replace worn-out or diseased organs with new ones; we aim to put a world of information behind our eyelids; we aim to mesh our nervous system's synapse with a microchip and move from bionic being to cyborg. It seems inevitable to us that we will reach this prophesied "technological singularity."

So what is the especial resistance sports can make to all this?

Take me out to the ball game,
Take me out with the crowd.
Buy me some peanuts and Cracker Jack,
I don't care if I never get back,
Let me root, root, root for the home team,
If they don't win it's a shame.
For it's one, two, three strikes, you're out,
At the old ball game.

—Jack Norworth and Albert von Tilzer

Bryant Gumbel once said that the other sports are just sports, but baseball is a love. Can I say that the heart of resistance to technology's impact on sports is America's love of baseball?

The tradition here is built on Olympian gods, from the legendary "Bambino" like a true force of unbridled Nature to Jolting Joe DiMaggio's disciplined mastery, to the heartfelt tragedy of Lou Gehrig's story, the victory of talent over racism in Jackie Robinson, the perfection of Ted Williams's swing, the all-around perfection of Willie Mays hitting, fielding, running the bases, the long-time heroics of 'Hammerin' Hank Aaron, the miracle of Sandy Koufax's fast ball. There's a theogony here that exceeds that of classical Greece.

In the American mass psyche, baseball is more sacred than is politics, so the intrusion of the profit calculus into sports incites real anger in the streets. The cancellation of the 1994 World Series seemed an outrageous extension of capitalism into the sacrosanct world of sports. But the obscene intrusion of doping into baseball is a trespass against Olympia and its gods.

When you love baseball you love the game now but you love it within this great tradition in which baseball runs alongside the 'birth of our nation,' baseball beats with the heart of Americana. And you do not want that sullied, tampered with, violated. You don't want the triumphs of baseball's legends to be overwritten by the quick fixes of biotechnology, the deck, if you will, of natural performance stacked so that winning and losing lose meaning.

Technology threatens to hollow out what has been so magnificently created. And because baseball is at the heart of the American cultural imaginary, all violations to the honesty of the game weigh heavy on the American soul. Mark McGwire, Sammy Sosa, and Barry Bonds tarnish the soul of sports in a way that Lance Armstrong cannot do because cycling is more closely linked to the French and the Italians and the Dutch and Europe itself than to the United States. The French connection alone should be fatal in the American cultural imaginary.

The resistance to the inevitability of doping in every sport fades as baseball itself disconnects from the heart of Americana. And this disconnect has occurred in the new millennial-cybertech generation. Red Smith accused dull minds of finding baseball dull; but today it is more apt to say that all back-in-the-day analog reality is dull in the view of those such as Jane McGonigal of the Institute for the Future who in her TED talk called for at least twenty-one billion hours a week of game play in order for us to solve the world's problems and insure the survival of the planet. The virtual game here is one in which the players are not on an off-line field but on a virtual field, and winning is something they can achieve by gaming in cyberspace. The 'epic win' is the reward for deft play and smart choices. It is an individual not a team win; it is personal and not social; private and not public. All this meshes nicely with a broader American cultural mind-set.

Baseball cannot move as fast, cannot jump cut, sidebar, and enable the interaction that cybertech can. The winning cannot be as personal; it can never be interactive as long as we are playing in the real world. It cannot make everyone in the bleachers a Derek Jeter. If cybertech has both overstimulated and abridged attention span at the present three billion hours a week of online gaming, you can imagine that at a recommended twenty-one billion hours a week, a virtualized online reality will be jacked up to levels of interaction and affiliation against which off-line reality, for all the vagaries Mother Nature as well as human nature throw at us, cannot compete.

And yet it tries because our off-line sports are still multibillion dollar businesses. Therefore we now face, and perhaps only for a brief transitional period, the urgency of enhancing all aspects of off-line sports to keep pace with the acceleration of fragmented stimulation. Doping is both a response to this state of affairs and part of the technological advance that has created it.

The superheroes of pop culture, including all the heroes of online gaming, of TV and film, are struggling to inhabit the sports fields, accomplishing the superhuman feats that performance-enhancing doping allows. A new notion of what skill and strength are, of what endurance and agility are, of what a championship level of toughness is becomes inevitable as every sport succumbs to the ubiquitous presence of doping, as every sport revs itself up to meet the accelerated awareness that our cybertech new world has created.

A good part of our baseball mythos in America is to believe that its legendary heroes of the past would be too proud of their own God-given natural gifts, their own natural and trained prowess, to accept an 'enhancement' from the tech lab, an enhancement available to all and therefore ultimately destructive of one's own natural and trained prowess. But we live now within a technological mythos that grants to technology the power and beneficence of the Greek gods. Only a foolish, archaic Luddite would deny technology its superiority over the unenhanced functioning of brain and muscle.

What is 'natural' has come to be seen as only that which an off-line world has, because of its analogue roots, defined as "natural." Digital reality is in the early stages of extending the notion of natural to levels that remain inconceivable to us now. We are more focused on that as yet-inconceivable future than we are on what anything might have been achieved in the past. We envision a technologically enhanced world of baseball as well as all sports. This is a human advance; and in this scenario, Babe Ruth, for example, would be an early form of human, like Homo naledi. The playing field, if you will, is different, alternative, and preferred.

Right now only historical memory resists this.

What we could do with our chemically *unenhanced* bodies, what kind of toughness, strength, and endurance we could summon without technological prosthesis, what we could do when Nature rocked us hard throughout our history—all this is not an insignificant record, though our online realities accelerate the obsolescence and extinction of all historical recollection.

I think of sports as a grueling challenge, in some ways more than others, as making demands of body and mind, of deftness of hand and foot, as summoning a force of intent to go a step further, to give more when the body says it has no more to give. I think of it as a physical and mental toughness directly opposed to any biotech trespass, as opposed to any artificially enhancing intrusion. To own your performance is to own your body, to reject its purchase by the newest, under-the-radar doping. To reject a chemical accommodation to your own fitness is a rejection of all technological attempts to make you 'transhuman'; to perfect you based on a machine model, instrumentation without consciousness.

This now appears to be a nostalgic, romanticized view, one that faces not only the relentless progression of biotech and cybertech but the bedrock creed of zero-sum, winner-take-all competitiveness that drives our prevailing cultural narrative and, finally, the total collapse of a pre-cybertech historical memory. If, however, a mythos deeply implanted in the American cultural imaginary exists on a totally different dimension that any advance in technology, the legends of how the game is played cannot fade.

Notes

1. Revised version of "Sons of Anarchy: Rebels and Bad Subjects with a Cause," *popmatters*, April 8, 2010; "Dexter at the Tea Party," *Bad Subjects*, 2010.

2. *popmatters*, March 4, 2010.

3. This is a revised and composite version of food articles I wrote for *Dandelion Salad*: "Gulliver's Tale of Three Food Stores: Part I" (August 28, 2013); "Weaponized Food—Do We Really Need a Striped Eggplant?" (April 14, 2013); "Our Strange TV Food World" (February 24, 2013).

4. *Magazine Americana: the American Popular Culture Magazine*, May, 2013.

Chapter Twelve

Dark Affinities

In "Dark Affinities: Liberal and Neoliberal," *Joseph Natoli opened up a line of thinking about our political quandaries that is profoundly important but little understood. His piece is grounded in a rich understanding of the deep cultural dimensions of our political dynamics.*

—Michael Johnson, "Transforming Our
Dark Affinities," *Truthout*, February 1, 2014

I begin with an article published on *Truthout* that prompted an immediate response by Michael Johnson, "Transforming Our Dark Affinities," and an interview invitation from Washington, DC, radio host Garland Nixon. What I attempted was a phenomenological psychiatrist's analysis of the political scene, focusing on the points at which Liberals and Neoliberals were joined. If you can discover the narrative framing of the world someone is in, the ways an individual life-world is narrated into being, you are observing a processing of the world that precedes views and opinions, reflections and arguments. Those reflective narratives sometimes expose a preflective narrating, a seminal life-world; and sometimes the psyche's deep affiliations are obscured and hidden not only from the world but from the consciousness of the individual. In this latter case, a resident order of moral acceptability, political correctness, inspiring traditions, the pretensions of exceptionalism, and entrenched norms of social behavior compel a masking of dark affiliations that comprise a life-world.

There may be no divide between one's deep narrating of the world and what one says and does. Sometimes other people are openly described with racial, ethnic, religious, homophobic, or misogynistic epithets. However, a political solidarity that can win elections is more easily formed if it is not transparently running on a platform of such epithets. Of course, the more beleaguered by wealth inequities and the more confused by politics a society becomes, the more liable it is to respond to a candid expression of dark affinities. What's more prevalent than such transparency, however, is a masking of deep underlying feelings, both from others and from oneself, so that it's difficult to trace, say, a political position or a personal philosophy or even random responses to headline events to their wellsprings.

Neither Liberal nor Neoliberal will announce a preference for indifference as opposed to compassion, or, that the ambition to "Show ME the money!" outweighs family and country. No one claims to wage war for profit, or admits that illness is more profitable than health. No one claims to be more suspicious and annoyed by neighbors than anxious to love them. No one tells us that their conscience goes no further than where our dominating mercantilism takes them: you need to feel bad when you don't pay your debts. That's not a pure moral imperative but a mercantile-driven one. Beyond that, the moral sense and the conscience directing it are just fronts that a society pretending to be about something other than business requires of us. Guilt has a mercantile beginning and it really goes no further, *pace* every religion's testaments. Liberals and Neoliberals are equally attached to the notion of a personal will-to-power, to the notion of 'moral hazard,' and to the belief that competition is preferable to mutual aid. It follows then that both have an equal absence of guilt for those who suffer in any way.

The wealthy may mouth liberal causes but at bottom they want to preserve their wealth, employ it to give their children all the advantages they can, and not be drawn into a codependent relationship with the less fortunate. Enough of those not in the top 20 percent of the wealth distribution vote Neoliberal because they share the life-worlds of the Neoliberals regardless of the fact that Neoliberals see them as moochers. They share life-worlds, not real-life conditions. Compared to the number of wealthy in the United States, those just getting by or failing to get by are overwhelming, and yet US politics does not represent this because a life-world sharing favors Neoliberals. The righteousness of Liberals is no more than blather to Neoliberals, but it is useful blather because it provides the whole country with a sanctimonious front behind which drones can fly, poor people can be bulldozed aside by gentrification, and a third of the world's species can be 'creatively destroyed' while profits are 'grown.'

We have gridlock in Congress because no one political side is able to overwhelm the other. Those who are losing or have already lost are repelled and angered but are as likely to rise up against those losing and those who have already lost as those who have exploited them. The have-less-each-day seek to protect private hoarding of wealth and property as readily as the wealthy. There is never an obscene amount of material possessions because both haves and have-nots share an antagonism to any limits, especially those set by the government. No one, poor or rich, Liberal or Neoliberal, wants to give the government any of his or her money, even if the government will use that tax money to give health care or retirement benefits to those who have neither. The wage earner's conscience is not superior to the mercantile conscience of the wealthy. Money is to be made wherever it can be made. No one unfortunate wants to be suckered into a codependent relationship with the unfortunate, which means, of course, that we have deep in our dark psyche a masochism that cannot come to the surface.

Dark Affinities: Liberal and Neoliberal[1]

Each society determines which thoughts and feelings shall be permitted to arrive at the level of awareness and which have to remain unconscious. Just as there is a social character, there is also a "social unconscious."

—Erich Fromm

Newly elected Mayor Bill de Blasio's "tale of two cities," referring to the wealth divide in New York City, sounds nicely Dickensian, but the 'boots on the ground' reality is not divided so clearly. Roughly speaking the bottom 40 percent of Americans are what Dickens's Noddy Boffin called "scrunched" while a top 20 percent, if we follow the counsel here of 'scrunch or be scrunched,' are doing the scrunching. A middle 40 percent are, as Gradgrind facts show, decidedly more of the scrunched class than the scrunching class although their confusions, misrecognitions, and dreams of former well-being render them as liable to identify with the scrunchers as with their fellow scrunched.

So we have some 80 percent of the American population in need of legislative action that 20 percent of the population either does not require or requires precisely the opposite. The numbers are on the side of have-less-each-day and have-nothing-at-all and not on the side of the have-mores. However, the top 20 percent are already holding positions of power while 80 percent are fractured, disillusioned, disinterested, confused, and pliable; and so our expectations of victory by overwhelming numbers fade.

The situation is yet darker and more complex as to why we cannot right an upside-down ship of state. I want to introduce what I call a "melding" on the level of the American social unconscious of Left and Right that also must be considered when we wonder why our democracy has turned to plutocracy, why that fact is not recognized, and why the many cannot put a stop to an aggrandizement of the few at the expense of the many. Only when we delve into affinities between Liberal and Neoliberal on this level of social unconscious can we comprehend the puzzling inexplicability of American politics since Reagan.

Legislatively, we are close to a flat tax or a 'fair tax,' the former a tax where $50,000 is taxed at the same rate as $400,000, and the latter a sales tax replacing any income tax. We are closer to undermining entitlements than bolstering them. We are closer to eliminating unemployment compensation, the Earned Income Tax credit, and the Federal Reserve than holding on to them. Obviously rational attempts to constrain the Wild West free play of the American financial sector such as the Dodd–Frank Wall Street Reform and Consumer Protection Act including the Volcker Rule section of that act somehow get entwined in American paranoia regarding governmental forces taking away personal freedom. Clear scientific evidence that humans are disastrously mucking up the environment does not produce real anxieties and thus defensive action; but rather these actions are waylaid by dark anxieties regarding the effect the national debt will have on future generations. Although the Affordable Care Act aids some of those on the majority side, the majority of the country takes the stand of the minority.

Most obviously and outrageously of all is that fact that it seems as if the 80 percent who live humbly, poorly, confusedly, increasingly anxious ridden, in the shadow of 20 percent are not plaintiffs at all but are 'the accused.' If this was a criminal trial and the courts proceeded to rule the plaintiff as the accused and the accused as the plaintiff, that legal system would be overthrown. In the 2012 presidential primary, Mitt Romney voiced a case against 47 percent of the American population, demonstrating this Mad Hatter convulsion of sanity and order.

It seems crystal clear that the overwhelming majority of the American population needs a reliable representation in Congress, one they do not presently have. If they did, they would not be in a state of continuing collapse, the rush of democracy toward plutocracy would have stopped just after the S&L crisis when deregulation proved disastrous, and we would not now be living in a country in which the top one-hundredth of 1 percent make an average of $27 million per household while the average income for the bottom 90 percent is about $30,000.

It is not surprising that a plutocracy in sway in a country that was at one time a middle-class democracy has the money and power to convince all that a plutocracy does not exist. What is surprising is that an irrational notion that wealth in a few hands is not a problem to the aspirations of an egalitarian democracy continues to hold sway. Nonsense and absurdity appear now as sweetness and light.

If we delve into a social unconscious in which such a topsy-turvy event can occur, we find whole scenarios invisible to rational discourse. Dark affinities appear where we discover that 'the accused' lean heavily into the accusations made by the 20 percent. They share a great deal within deep recesses of the American culturally imaginary or the American mass social psyche. On this level, there are no opposing ideologies or parties but rather a conjoining of subliminal responses that create an almost identical imaginary of the world and who lives in it and how they live in it. We need to explore these deep-rooted connections, sever them, and seek legislative representation that is not bound already on this level of unconscious affinities to the policies we need to contest.

Ironically while Americans seek to change the "minds and hearts" of Islamists, the hearts and minds of Americans victimized by the chance-like dispensations of casino capitalism remain attached to what is victimizing them. The rest of the world more readily apprehends this state of affairs than do Americans, thus explaining why we do not shine elsewhere as we do in our own eyes. Foreign judgment, however, does not make it easier for Americans to self-scrutinize not simply because 'American exceptionalism' preempts listening to foreigners but because the sort of pathography I am conducting here finds the winners and the losers sharing the same values. They share the same mass-psyche desires, fears, antipathies, repressions, traumas, blindness, compulsions, dreams, and nightmares, the same American Dream, if you will. If the losers did not connect here with the winners, we would face the clarity of a moral dualism, of innocence and guilt, of oppressor and oppressed, of hero and monster, of, most aptly, the dangers to democracy of a severe wealth divide and the nurturing of democracies that aspire to egalitarianism.

There is no such clear opposition within the cultural unconscious.

If the complex incestuous state of affairs on the American mass-psyche level could be reduced to the good guy/bad guy polarities of the wars we fight—Nazis, Communists, Terrorists—the American disastrous wealth divide would surely become a class war with a dangerous outcome. But because every American, whether employed or bankrupt, solvent or insolvent, luxuriating or underwater, wants it all, admires and envies those who have it all, hates those who interfere in any way with the chance to get it all, believes that rich and poor alike are free, independent, proud, and playing always on a level field, that those down on their luck today can be kings of the hill with the right turn of the wheel, and that carping criticism comes from whining anti-Americans who want nothing more than have us all equally poor and queuing up for government handouts, there is no moral divide but only a moral monism.

When minds and hearts are bound together in deep subliminal recesses, quarrels are a sham, a cover behavior meant to defend a civilized, rational, high ground from a low, untamed place that is neither civilized nor rational. We fear going into such recesses because we find there what darkens our American exceptionalism. We find there hostilities and avaricious hungers that mock our Jesus evangelism.

That there is no real fight on this mass cultural unconscious level is paralleled by the so-called fight between the political parties. There is no two-party system on the level of the American social unconscious; no one is across the aisle but actually seated where you are. Partisan conflict and polarization that we witness in Congress would belie my claim of subliminal affinities if the divide were somehow equal. It is not; there is no reason why 80 percent of the population whose well-being has decreased since Reagan has not legislatively overpowered a dividend-fed 20 percent. There is no reason on a conscious, rational level explaining gridlock. What has been going on in American politics can be compared to a rewriting of the War Between the States in which Union forces lost—although they were three times the size of the Confederate forces.

Wealthy Conservatives are like wealthy Liberals in that they relish the wealthy life-worlds within which they live; poor Conservatives are like poor Liberals in that they both believe it is up to them to build a wealthy life-world for themselves. The common core here is buried very deep and traverses matters over which legislative action is gridlocked, matters such as education, immigration, moral hazard, class warfare, gentrification, tax warfare, entitlements, global warming, stimulus and austerity, national debt, regulation, indictment and prosecution of the financial sector, Eternal War on Terror, Gitmo, and torture.

The new Common Core education proposal is one that Liberals and Conservatives commonly share because they both accept that capitalist growth requires what David Brooks calls a "mechanistic intelligence" and that the young should be schooled in that sort of intelligence. Neither party sees education as giving the young an opportunity for liberating themselves from this mission to "grow the economy" under the direction of market rule. Both parties agree that this Common Core best serves the needs of corporate human resources, ignoring how obsolete hi-tech training becomes in our hi-tech world.

Both parties disbelieve the Blake quote, "What is now proved was once only imagined," and if they do, the Common Core proposal does not reveal that belief. At the level of mass cultural imaginary both parties find it reasonable to pursue the math and science that will produce the technology that will in turn produce the patents that will lead to profit for those already positioned to receive those profits. Here the powerful code that captures the psyche of both Liberal and Neoliberal is dominating size and power, at root the mantra that profits always need to be bigger. Exercising the imagination is not only profitless but always, for any hegemonic state, a possible threat. Imagination is reduced to "innovation," which is bounded by apps, robotics, and everything cybertech.

Illegal aliens are a cheap labor supply for home and business, the liberal wealthy as needful of nannies, cooks, and gardeners as the conservative wealthy. Here both factions adhere on the psychic grassroots level to an image of hardworking help who have a Third World sense of class privilege and the respect that it is owed, something that American workers fail to display at this level. This desire to dominate is in need of the dominated, a truly dark need to be hidden from the grounding text of American democracy.

Very few of the top 20 percent, regardless of whether they are blue or red, find a progressive income tax fair. The idea that some people, especially those who have done well, should pay a higher tax than others, those who have not done well, is counter-intuitive to the American sense of equality and fair play. On this level, any sort of unequal treatment is patently un-American, and Americans are slowly working toward equality in all domains. However, on the social unconscious level we are observing, inequality seems to be the force at work, call it the subliminal disposition. It explains why it took so long for a love of equality and fair play to show up in regard to black African slavery or the treatment of the native population or women's rights. Much below all historical analysis lies the magnetic psychic attractiveness of white, male, Anglo-Saxon, and protestant. Darker and deeper lies an imaginary mapping of duality that Liberal and Neoliberal share, of the firmer and more certain presence of good when opposed with a clearly defined evil, of the superiority of white shown in the degradation of color. A perverse paradox results when a nation conceived in equality is yet on an unsayable level searching for its exceptional superiority, for a standing above equality.

In regard to moral hazard, Liberals are at best undecided whether "giving a man a fish" will destroy his incentive to start fishing and selling fish for profit, or whether moral hazard is what Wall Street and hedge-fund managers face in their everyday pursuit of high returns. This liberal irresoluteness, however, is itself a sham. There is no energy forthcoming to point out the absurdity of tying moral degradation to welfare and entitlements. It seems that Liberals will allow the notion that the poor are corrupted and corruptive in society while power, especially plutocratic power, is beneficial. Consider that key beliefs regarding freedom of choice, personal responsibility, and the play of Chance are not critically scrutinized by Liberals, though public instruction here would do much to deconstruct the conservative bible on these matters.

The hotspot that connects Liberal and Neoliberal in the American mass social unconscious is the magnetic attractiveness of individual free-dom and will that has abided since frontier days. A fierce independence crosses party lines and unites all in a suspicion of and antipathy to col-lective action and aid. We observe then that the party of a bare minimum of governmental intervention, the Liberals, is as magnetically attached to non-intervention of market rules as are the Neoliberals. And both fac-tions are proud that Chance is no more than what American have a gift for overcoming, and so it enters a mythos of powerful national memory.

A huge wealth divide in the United States in which the top 10 percent of US earners claimed about half of all before-tax income in 2012, including capital gains, is not an issue either party will campaign on for obvious reasons: the wealthy 20 percent of Americans are not themselves positioned to perceive any problem with income and wealth inequality. They literally do not see it in the same way a man living in Grosse Pointe does not see the poverty of Detroit. They do not swim in the same waters. Personal economic well-being gives no one an incentive to see wealth divide as a problem nor imagine that a class war is really going on, one that Ralph Nader called a tug of war in which only one side is pulling.

Once again, however, this disinterest in class divide is shared by the bottom 80 percent whose own well-being might be best served by a political party that saw this as a devastating problem, one that legislation could do much to amend. Unfortunately, the legislators of our two-party system are of the wealth party and share deep down affinities. But the many remain magnetized by the prospect of 'having it all' and are thus unable to recognize or enter a class war that may turn against them when they too 'have it all.'

An extended period of middle-class prosperity, increasingly eroded since Reagan, still nurtures a sense of an American equality unlike the entrenched class divides, economic and social, of Europe, though statistics show that only Chile, Mexico, and Turkey have greater inequality than the United States. This feeling that 'we are not like them' is buried deep in the American cultural imaginary; only socialists and envious losers talk of "class warfare." Aristocracy and peasantry are always elsewhere in the US psyche; Horatio Alger is the unconquerable American who always climbs the ladder; and hardship is always ended by social and economic mobility, which is also not factually verifiable. Thus, class divide, no matter how *ancien régime* it becomes, is a topic willingly repressed by both parties.

Gentrification—the taking over of poor neighborhoods by the wealth class and highending all real estate, products, and services to meet the expanse of the gentry class's pocketbooks—occurs when a native but poor population is in possession of what a minority but wealthy population desires. Where do the poor go when pushed out of their neighborhoods? No one knows, and neither party seems to care. Gentrification is not an issue that troubles the gentry, or it troubles them only as to how to move out a rent-controlled class. And the gentry are to be found on both sides of the so-called political divide.

Tax reform strikes a welcome note at any time in the American mass cultural psyche because it signifies an enforced compulsory sense of society, of mutual interdependence, that is contrary to what reigns supreme on this level (i.e., the independent free-spiritedness of the individual). 'Reform' thus is a reform of a progressive tax system that benefits the 80 percent. Lying close by is the repugnance with which this independent spirit holds the government that imposes socialist social concern through taxation. Americans see themselves as altruistic, charitable, compassionate, generous, and so on; but all of that is by personal choice and not societal compact. The tax reform that is sought on this fantasy level is one in which each individual decides what taxes he or she is to pay and where that money is to go. Because you can have neither a government nor a society that can function in this manner, 'tax reform' has the mesmerizing power that "Rosebud" has in *Citizen Kane*.

Quick work of the remaining:

Global warming is like ill fortune that is no more than an opportunity to show your mettle, a challenge to be met. But deeper is the cross-party affinity, once again, of domination, this time of Nature. Technology does not adapt to the vagaries of Nature but rather overwrites them and thus strengthens humankind's hold on the planet and the superiority of the species.

Stimulus is an extended government handout that goes far beyond the extent of welfare handout and thus violates the cross-boundary attachment to unaided independence.

Austerity in order to dissolve the national debt obliges the ingrained Puritan spirit of the American soul. Paradoxically—and paradox is no problem in the social unconscious—stoic and epicurean 'elective affinities' flourish in the American social unconscious. Ironically, however, Puritan austerity and discipline is required of the many while the few oversee the penitence.

Regulation, indictment, and prosecution of the financial sector are understandably not pursuits of those who are deeply invested; but, to repeat, the wage earner tags along here because the red cape of Big Brother tyranny is waved.

Eternal War on Terror, Gitmo, and torture are like the Ego's defense mechanisms: they are there to protect a resident order of things. And here the wealthy on both sides of the aisle represent that asymmetrical order while the imprisoned in impoverished lives absorb this fear and anxiety because it's what they do—fear and anxiety being for them a way of life.

The Clintonian Third Way in politics that President Obama has moved toward after abandoning his 'post-ideology' naïveté brings subliminal connections between liberal and neoliberal views into the light of day and does so boldly as if some adequate representation of the plight of 80 percent of Americans was here offered. Leaning into a market rule that has colonized areas in which it does not belong is an incomprehensible tactic unless one acknowledges already-existing dark affinities between liberal and neoliberal views. In its present overextended and overweening form, market rule is like the unruly child who is not corrected by adopting his behavior.

What signifies in all these strange perversions of rational expectations is the enormous potency of subliminal desires, fears, and anxieties shared by all Americans to camouflage the strangeness and the perversity while at the same time detouring any rational remedies. If we could free ourselves, in a sort of mass therapy of the American social unconscious, from our cross-party, mutual fixations, desires, antipathies, and fears, we would see clearly that a Monopoly game sort of economic system has knocked eight of the ten players out of the game and has left two with all the money and all the property.

Because Liberals are linked in more ways than I have indicated to the neoliberal social unconscious, Liberals can do no more than make a poor, stumbling defense of the majority of Americans, can make no decisive indictment of crimes and criminals but allow the modicum of any purpose to dwindle and meander into mindboggling confusion. Too many Americans are infected and are thus so confounded on this conscious level while disastrously tied on a yet unreachable level, and yet barely enunciated level, to the perpetrators and causes of their immiseration.

The Economics of Immiseration/The Politics of Seduction[2]

The domain of seduction is the sacred horizon of appearances.

—Jean Baudrillard, "On Seduction"

"[I]mmiseration" concerns not just the wages workers receive, but how long and how hard they have to work in order to get them.

—Frances Wheen, *Marx's Das Kapital: A Biography*

The genius of the internal combustion engine engineered by Etienne Lenoir in 1860 was to release the pressure of such combustion to pistons, rotation, and movement. Explosion was controlled and detoured; ignition could be repeated and catastrophe avoided each time. Rising pressure and calibrated release equals relief. Psychology responds to this analogy as do politics. Increased pressure on low-wage workers makes headlines: "The Walls Close in: Low Wage Workers Finding It's Easier to Fall into Poverty, and Harder to Get Out" (*New York Times,* March 17, 2014). But all wage earners, underclass or middle class, are feeling the pressure. Thom Hartmann reports that "wages have gone down almost seven percent since the recession. And, that decline followed more than three decades of stagnant wages thanks to Reaganomics" (*Truthout,* October 3, 2013).

Neoliberals, moderate or immoderate, pragmatic or crazed, attribute this sorry state of affairs to a number of variables that Liberals agree with, mostly referring to a transition from a lo-tech society to a hi-tech society, from a manufacturing base to a financial base, from a hunting, farming, and manufacturing economy to an information economy. None of this has any drawing power. But the neoliberal steady refrain, from Reagan's Welfare Queen to Romney's 47 percent, has seductive power with that pivotal, crucial, voting middle class. The seductive spin is well known: "The slow degeneration of working-class family life and the creation of a 'moocher' class too lazy and indulged to get a job results from 'big government' nurturing and coddling. There is a seductiveness also to other neoliberal reasons as to why immiseration is like the wolf now at every door but those of an elite few. Each 'reason' touches a hot spot already fully charged within us. The collapse of a nuclear family is the collapse of a patriarchal order that is itself an order preserving male desire. The bureaucracy of public education is no more than the resistance of what is public, governmental, and socialist to personal choice and individual freedom. The power of unions resides in a communist-like solidarity that obstructs the free and competitive play of business.

All of these briefs are seductive spins within the American cultural imaginary not because they rest on uncontested fact and evidence but because they rest on seductions and repressions already deeply embedded in that imaginary. In other words, the way we think now is so heavily layered in fantasies and illusions that the argument that wins the day does not appeal to rationality but rests on those fantasies and illusions. As I have suggested before ("Dark Affinities: Liberal and Neoliberal," *Truthout,* January 20, 2014), this imaginary and its accompanying fantasies and illusions are not partisan, there being no politics ruling imagination. But there is a political use of the imaginary, what I call the "politics of seduction," and that arises from an economics of immiseration. There would be little need for the former if such an economics had not led, as it has, to immiseration for an increasing number and the anxieties that emerge from a fear of inevitable immiseration for many more.

There are numerous varieties of seduction from Eve's in the garden to Baudrillard's sense that we seduce by enacting a weakness that we see in ourselves as well as others. We all harbor a never-fulfilled appetite to eat the world whole; and we choose an individual freedom, a supremacy of self-interests and desires, that urges us, like Milton's Satan, to rule in hell rather than serve in heaven. The fantasies of desire are Janus faced as are the illusions of power. They have their weaker side—an impotency of desire, a feckless command, and a captured will. Romney's 47 percent of the population would eat up the world if they could but are totally impotent and cannot do so. The totalizing power that the elite seek can never be blocked by the feckless command of unions. Big government is no more than a ridiculed domain of power, not our own, that presumes to rule us. The fantasy links to male desire and personal choice are too transparent to require exegesis.

Seductions work because the appeal is to what is in us, both the desires and the fears, and therefore connections are made and recognition ensures response. And while both appeal and recognition are felt, they are unthought and prediscursive. We do not think what is unthinkable. We do not express what we fear to think. Nevertheless, power remains here. Eden's garden is no more than a confinement we need to go beyond, explore what's outside; God's one law, call it regulation, blocks our libertine and liberty-seeking nature. We do not need to be tempted to bite the apple; as unthinkable as this may sound, we were made to bite it. And much more. We have an appetite to possess and not to share. All that we have never quells a desire to have yet more. Mutual sharing and aid has no seductive power in our elemental level of being, but domination does. All other species, according to Genesis, awaited Adam's naming, their identity and place in the world forever held within the province of human need and desire. Global warming can be conquered just as we have conquered Nature all along the way. Global-ecology movements thus have little seductive attraction and rational arguments, especially in regard to human-caused climate change, have not been able to deactivate the seductiveness of what is irrational.

While we can recite all this as a reprehensible darkness relegated to Freud's Id, it all yet remains the fire that drives us to compete, own, and dominate. What most compels us is not what we legislate for a social good, or what disciplines and bounds our own will, but what gives these free reign, a 'road of excess' that leads not to Blake's "palace of wisdom" but to an oligarch's domain. The power of seduction lies in appearing at barriers that we ourselves have built to restrain our own dark side. The 1956 film *Forbidden Planet* envisions an extinct race destroyed by their own great and final hi-tech breakthrough: they can materialize their own will, including what the film calls "Monsters from the Id." Because our defenses against our own uncivilizing drives are never as real as our own desires, seductions have no difficulty in passing through. Every rule and restraint made on society's behalf is never as real as our instinctual appetites and our personal will to power. This is the hidden truth of Thatcher's assertion, "There is no such thing as society." Such an assertion means that an economics of immiseration and a politics of seduction now exists openly ridiculing all civilizing attempts to restrain us from playing out at will our own dark imaginaries.

Capitalism gives us an economics of the Id, an economics that liberates every hidden energy, striving against any confinement, offering a gratification that grows because it is unfettered, releasing instinctual forces that drive competitiveness beyond what commands can organize. The failures of socialist economies lie in their reliance on what is disciplinary in the service of all, command economies that restrain and regulate the full licensing of the Id. In globalized competitive economics, such self-disciplining cannot stand against the full force of a capitalism of the Id. Socialist economics champion the Superego, to enlist another character from Freud, allied with a common and public good, with 'one for all' and not 'all for one' mentality, and thus has no seductive power. You have to work hard at distancing yourself from your basic instincts, your own will-to-power, in order to feel the attraction in an economics of the Superego. Immiseration finds no release in restraint. The failure of "Just Say No" rests in this morality of discipline, which the gentrified are pleased to impose upon the immiserated, though not on themselves.

The capitalism of the Id inevitably shapes, as it has done, an economics of immiseration for all those ravaged by an economics of the ravenous, driven over and plowed under by the winners. We are on what is a democratic 'level playing field' only in the eyes of those destined to be driven over and plowed under. A politics of seduction emerges as naturally from an economics of immiseration as a steam engine is equipped with a pressure release valve. Some have engaged our open-throttle economics with an equal amount of open-throttle energy, or, to put it another way, have extended successfully their own uncontrolled instincts for power and ownership into an economic arena built on those instincts. What are not seductions from outside but only already energies and appetites inside, now are externalized on the national and international stage. What was inside, as Goethe remarked, is outside.

Because the politics of seduction arise from our economics of immiseration, the two join forces to easily and instinctively create a climate of seduction that diverts critique and spins the immiserated into distracting fantasies and illusions. This is a much more sophisticated version of Roman bread and circuses but just as directly targeting what any moral review would call the weaker side of our natures. Had Louis XVI been a mere figurehead, or a president democratically elected, in a capitalism of the Id and a politics of seduction, the pressure release of revolution and the vengeance of the Reign of Terror would have been tampered down daily by seductions and the fantasies and illusions they inspire.

Only a seductiveness that plays into such fantasies and illusions can make the neoliberal case against the poor, against wage earners, against a so-called underclass magnetically compelling. Liberals join with Neoliberals in pretending that the emperor is not naked, that an economic system that is nakedly exploitative, rapacious, and stochastic is fully clothed in efficient rationality. What we have is an economic system that makes the possession of wealth itself the medium of achieving wealth while at the same time making work and workers irrelevant to the country's needs and aspirations. This is an economic system that puts wealth at the disposal of a few, compounds that wealth like a snowball rolling downhill, and solidifies a class divide in which the possession of wealth is the price of membership. The sidling of Liberals toward Neoliberals in regard to the inviolability and venerability of market rule is simply a result of the sharing of good fortune and the subsequent sharing of lifestyles. Neither wealthy Liberals nor wealthy Neoliberals are positioned to undermine their good fortune by targeting for demolition—or even prosecution after the Great Recession—an economic system run by a financial sector brokering the rising returns of their stock portfolios.

Regardless of how winners of both political persuasions maintain and protect market rule, the pressure is building in the lives of about 80 percent of the US population. A number left astray on this stage in the United States are gathering in protests from the 1999 Seattle WTO protests to Occupy Wall Street. They threaten the order of inequality and an economics of immiseration. The coordinates of attack on unions are recognized in the 2011 Wisconsin Protests while the Google bus protests in San Francisco put gentrification, a plutocratic and not egalitarian creation, in the sights of the 'ungentrified.' These scattered but continuing outbreaks are signals to an order established by market rule that there is limited release of such opposition in a politics either imposed or self-restraining. Hypocrisy is transparent in asking many to expect nothing and live with less when surrounded by those profiting from an economics that knows no restraint. The jobless are each day less likely to assume personal responsibility for being jobless. Those always on the edge of hunger or on the edge of sickness or already over that edge, are each day less likely to assume personal responsibility for their hunger and their sickness.

The functional and successful release valve brought into play is a steady campaign of seductions distracting the immiserated from their misery, a steady campaign to repress former solvency, on the part of the middle class, and continuing hardship on the part of the underclass. According to Thomas Piketty's *Capital in the Twenty-First Century*, market rule has set up a relentless disparity in wealth in which the owners of capital will expand their wealth while wages stagnate. The case made here is solid but not seductive. It implies that release could be organized democratically but what hope is there of that if we are already entrapped within fantasies and illusions that arrive already packaged to turn reality, even the most visible and defined, into even greater diverting seductions. What hope is there of that if we are already allied with such seductions, already self-seduced?

US Higher Education:
The New "Treasure Island" for Investors[3]

I

This government's [England] whole strategy for higher education is, in the cliché it so loves to use, to create a level playing field that will enable providers to compete on equal terms with public universities.

—Stefan Collini, "Sold Out,"
London Review of Books, October 24, 2013

Stefan Collin's review essay of two recent books on higher education in England (Roger Brown and Helen Carasso's *Everything for Sale* and Andrew McGettigan's *The Great University Gamble*) begins with some unnerving facts regarding the "explosive growth of the for-profit sector" in US universities. It is the sort of preface that provides some relief to his compatriots as he proceeds to describe how higher education in England has become "a treasure island" for investment banks and private equity. At least, an English reader will think, the situation is not half as bad as in the United States.

So how far are we in the United States in turning higher education into a good return on investment?

Something called "Bridgepoint Education" boasted in 2008 of having seventy-seven thousand online students but also had "dropout rates of 63 percent for Bachelor's degrees and 84 percent for Associate degrees." University of Phoenix, owned by the Apollo Group, reported six hundred thousand students and annual revenue over $4 billion with a dropout rate of 60 percent. The most appalling revelation was that after the Educational Management Corporation was taken over by Goldman Sachs, recruiters were directed to target applicants' problems and offer college as a solution.

Public school 'reform,' one concentrating on K–12 is what is exercising the American imaginary right now, 'reform' here being closely tied to 'family values,' state and federal control, teachers' unions, taxes, the compulsory nature of K–12 in the United States, and parents' fears that their children might be hampered in their race 'to the top' by an unreformed public-school system. Parental concern is a ubiquitous nerve that politicians can appeal to with the word "reform" and not worry about a furor that tax reform or health reform or entitlement reform or regulatory reform would occasion.

The word "reform" wouldn't be magnetic if something indeed wasn't rotten in the state of education in the United States; but what's rotten may have more to do with issues other than a lack of market-driven competitiveness. Consider a staggering wealth divide and shrinkage of federal funds to education resulting from a federal budget sequestration capping spending. But the cultural temper has long been in line with a neoliberal drive to shrink the federal government by shrinking taxes. The American temper has also, in a very puzzling way, not been aroused by the wealth gap, *pace* the Occupy Wall Street movement. Both shrinking tax support and an almost feudal-age division of needs and resources have, one could reasonably suggest, an eroding, putrefying effect on education.

If public institutions cannot rely on government funding because less tax revenues force less funding, then public institutions need to turn, as they have been, to student tuition and fees. The one who pays, now or later, is the student who immediately becomes a comparison shopper amid an array of public and for-profit products and services. Such a market arrangement favors market-driven, for-profit enterprises because here they are in competitive buy-and-sell waters they know. The trick is to move the American cultural imaginary away from a sacrosanct John Henry Newman's "idea of the university" to a Walmart world where nothing matters but price.

In regard to public K–12 education, this sort of transformative path has found a hospitable terrain. Americans are already convinced that reform is needed and that the Superman they are waiting comes clothed as new 'alternative providers.' Some of these providers come clothed as nonprofit charters fighting for the right to feed at the public tax trough. But while public schools do not attract lavish philanthropy, the charters do. The Promise Academy of the Harlem Children's Zone and the Knowledge is Power Program, for example, receive tax money as well as support from the Gates and Walton foundations. The Koch brothers are lobbying for charters through their lobbying group the American Legislative Exchange Council (ALEC). "In a December, 2011 opinion piece critical of ALEC which appeared in *The Nation* magazine, John Nichols described ALEC as a "collaboration between multinational corporations and conservative state legislators" (*Wikipedia*).

The road upon which public school "reform" has become an imperative is confounded by an underlying reality; namely, that it is difficult to see how the poor will not be left behind in a country that fails to point to the stochastic chaos of its economic system as the root cause of such poverty.

No doubt, the poorer you are in the United States, the more the schools in your neighborhood will also be poor and thus educate you poorly. If you are child of poverty in the United States, there is a far greater chance you will be left behind than you will fulfill one of the rags-to-riches stories pulled out whenever the matter of poverty and success is aired. And there is great probability that you are destined to be left behind, regardless of how charismatic your third-grade teacher may be.

No doubt, a race to the top will leave many at the bottom and few at the top, enacting in the adult world that childhood game of King of the Mountain. The game that produces such results should clearly be ended or at least amended, but this is not what we learn. Tests that show so many are failing have become a clear sign that the same Chance-ruled game that has produced so many losers should now be applied to the means by which we hope to escape such a destiny (i.e., education). Enter now the "new, alternative providers," the Supermen we have been waiting for.

No doubt, any summary of what every American needs to know in order to succeed in our zero-sum game of winners and losers will not be included in our Common Core State Standards. Beyond eliminating standards of critical thinking, our Common Core is skeptical of or, at best, indifferent to the idea that ideas matter simply because there are no ideas relevant to money making and there are no standards that have anything to do with making money beyond the standard that money making is a good, a summum bonum. That underlying reality of market rule—that success is detached from any rationality or methodology leading to it— places all value to results, to ends not means. It is not how you play the game, fairly or rationally or morally, but whether you get a high score and win. We are here very far from Socrates's words: "All men's souls are immortal, but the souls of the righteous are immortal and divine." This foundational unenlightenment is a necessary state of affairs because market rule is itself stochastic, casino-like, and therefore it is what fundamentally stands outside any educational mission that ideally directs young minds into discursive and nondiscursive ways of knowing the world.

A market-driven approach to education therefore is not concerned with core knowledge or standards that deliver that core knowledge, but is only results oriented. But such testing becomes a convenient means to expose public education as in need of reform. This very approach is already reforming anyone's sense of anything signifying beyond a competitive winning.

II.

[T]he only questions being asked about knowledge production, the purpose of education, the nature of politics, and our understanding of the future are determined largely by market forces.

—Henry Giroux, "Public Intellectuals Against
the Neoliberal University," *Truthout*

Think now of public college and universities standing in the wings—as all this K–12 reform theatre is going on—and thinking, in some magical way, that they will escape the humiliation of it all. Public colleges and universities long dependent upon the government dole naïvely assume that the luster of tradition and honors they are clothed in will see them through, if such a wholescale reform campaign is directed at them. We cannot, however, blindly accept higher education's sterling image of itself. We cannot assume that the unenlightened standards of market rule are contesting enlightened standards or a universal core of knowledge and knowing, already in hand. What the value of higher education may be, beyond its usefulness in supplying market needs and preprofessional programs, seems to be increasingly difficult to define in a way that seems able to answer, without scorn, the question, "How does it help us grow the economy?" These difficulties of defining 'value' in higher education in our market-driven culture dissolve the Delphic oracle mythos that higher education relies upon as a protective shield. But what seems nebulous though grandiosely defined cannot withstand the enveloping ambience in the United States, where all value is measured in terms of cost and profit.

President Obama, in response to the 'start up' for-profit corporate rush to dig into the 150 billion dollars in federal financial aid to students, proposes a rating based on value received, a rating of which institutions give the student/consumer 'more bang for the buck.' You can expect that a for-profit institution such as the University of Phoenix will convert its high dropout rate to a high graduation rate, leaving the question of 'value of goods received' to an interminable debate: what the value of higher education is in a society that values results and not the getting there, where 'winning isn't everything; it's the only thing'?

American universities have been ducking these unsettling conditions threatening their own self-image. Professors have long resisted unionization because they stand on the inviolability of their intellectual freedom, their own venerable charter to conduct a free exchange of ideas in the classroom. Students are here in these hallowed halls not as customers, clients, or consumers but as inquiring and open young minds. Politicians, lobbyists, agitators, and filmmakers cannot presume to lead a reform charge against these deep and venerable traditions and presumptions.

Nevertheless, in our millennial clime in which history's accolades seem nothing more than analog and therefore passé and irrelevant in a new digital world, it seems probable that courses, as apps on smartphones, are more attractive than Mr. Chips at the blackboard.

Students are now consumers shopping for the best buy, in most cases for the best place to spend their government financial-aid money, money that the "new alternative providers" will pass on to investors and shareholders in labyrinthine, opaque ways as needed. The biggest players in the United States in for-profit higher education are Bridgeport Education, Inc. and the Apollo Group; but in higher education as in K–12, those who declare themselves "non-profit" bear closer examination. "McGettigan's analysis," Stefan Collini writes in his review of McGettigan's *The Great University Gamble*, "demonstrates why it is important to analyze the corporate group structure, rather than simply accepting that, if the teaching institution itself is described as not-for-profit charity, there can be no question of profits for private investors further along the line" ("Sold Out," *London Review of Books*, [October 24, 2013], 3–12).

What public universities put their faith in and stand upon—namely, the habits of time and mind that feel the weight of history and can trace its present-day role—the millennial imaginary has overwritten, not in conscious rebuttal but simply as a result of wandering in new and disassociated habits of time and mind. Whether old notions of higher learning can add to themselves an aura that respects its traditions and yet accommodates those who have no interest or understanding in such is itself an academic question. I say this because academic committees are not determining change, but rather the tide of change is propelling higher education.

We see such change both in the role of student as well as in the cybertech innovation within which communication and learning go on. Public universities have no experience with consumers in contrast to the new alternative providers who have all the experience that our US Wild West financial sector has given them. The transference from book to website, from reading lengthy discursive writing to texting and tweeting, from sustained critical focus to a multitasking attentiveness are not unexpected or unwelcome events for the new alternative providers. The goal of consumer marketing higher education as e-commerce is a familiar market goal. Market rule brought to higher education arrives without the baggage of traditions and expectations that millennials are also without. It is not difficult to see that the competitive advantage here is with new alternative providers.

"Reform" is not yet a word ubiquitously and daily applied to US higher education. And yet the same compelling rush of hi-tech transformations, the same hi-speed cyber forces that are rushing so many vestiges of an analog Dark Ages into the dustbin of history are morphing higher education, at warp drive, into something new and not yet totally recognizable. So much of what universities have been in the United States—books and libraries, brick-and-mortar campuses and classrooms, professors and lectures—are destined for cyberspace relocation, like the last furnishings in a condemned building.

An ever-accelerating and expanding rush of computer networking and social media held in hand and accessed at will have broken through the sacred chambers of higher education. Every lecturer in every classroom now faces a student whose attentiveness is in need of constant 'refreshing.' This student welcomes the advance and improvement of the new online and for-profit higher education in the same way we have learned to accept the old as retrogression and the new as progress, in the same way we bond to the new when we have no recollection or interest in what was before.

A subject revealed through the length of a course under the control of a professorial voice and direction in a classroom on a campus seems now more than ever to be not at the heart of learning itself but impedimenta, accessories, delivery systems of a particular time and place. The market viability of universities has depended upon delivering what students cannot possess on their own, on locating the delivering of that service to a resident faculty adept in time-honored methods of teaching and on attaching graduation to the fulfillment of a curriculum delivered in a university setting. All that now stands as a diminished marketing enterprise as the market itself ranges into the new profit-making frontiers that cybertech offers. There are shades of Luther's Reformation here as Christianity suddenly finds that the heart of a New Testament message did not require the impedimenta of pope or Catholic canon.

Cybertech privatizes and personalizes all that has been public and social. We are experiencing individually and culturally a drawing inward to the self as online access replaces worldly experience, as we shape a self-designed analog of the world on cell phones and cyberspace. Older notions of what "social" means give way, including the social enterprise of education, which fades as we are liberated into a new world of knowing, where we are knowledgeable, savvy interpreters, and adept critical thinkers.

Higher education in the United States has already conceded to the sense and logic, the justice and humanity of market rule and thus has failed to critique that rule which is now uploading it and dealing with it as one of many online choices. Some appraisal of conditions surrounding education in the United States was, and is, prerequisite to any critique. What are the difficulties of educating the young to fit into a society where the minimum wage, adjusted for inflation, was two dollars higher in 1968 than now, where the income of the top 1 percent has gone up 20 percent whereas income of 99 percent has gone up 1 percent, where 400 individuals have as much wealth as the bottom 180 million? What sort of education can proceed when a crippling level of ignorance is not addressed? For instance, only 42 percent of Americans believe that inequality has increased in the past ten years although this inequality has undermined public education's claim to defend democracy from oligarchic rule. The fact that American democracy has been devolving into oligarchy seems not to have been a matter serious enough to address in the classroom.

The mission of US higher education has been a mission that a collaborationist would follow. Why public universities have not taken on the many serious challenges to the well-being of democracy as well as their students elicits more than one response. The same question can be put to liberal politicians. The most obvious answer is that since Reagan, the inclination of the American cultural imaginary has been toward letting markets rule. That game has made a minority very wealthy, and that wealth has greatly influenced our politics. But higher education was affected somewhat earlier by a conservative reaction to the sixties. That conservative reaction engaged in a purging of 'radical' and experimental movements in higher education, initiated in the American countercultural period. The view that 'everything was political' was, in essence, a view that challenged the idea of a neutral presentation of any topic. What were the conditions within which any discussion took place? Up until then it was not difficult for academe to use the pretense of a neutral, objective, and disinterested approach to all issues as a screen to hide behind, to, in short, ignore the effects market rule had on which subjects and courses of study were valuable, and what was to be valued in a free democracy. Once the radicalism of countercultural influences on higher education was eliminated, mostly by eliminating the classroom practitioners as well as the like-minded administrators, the political and economic surround could once again be ignored in the name of a disinterested and unbiased pursuit of truth.

Instead of enabling students to develop a corrective rod to a devastating and corrupting market rule, higher education has set itself up for a takeover by those market values. What higher education in the United States faces now is its reward for failing to lead its students away from what Carlyle called "the cash nexus" of human relationships. The rewards of higher education in the United States are to be reaped by investors who see it as the new Treasure Island as well as by those students who observe and learn the message in that.

I could not describe this relentless passage to the rule of a market mentality, which is not a mentality at all but a resurrection of Fortuna, the goddess of Chance, if it were not already on public display. There is also a defense blocking that rule underway in various guises, from the "We've Had Enough!" worldwide protests of OWS to the 2010 student protests in the United Kingdom, and the Free Cooper Union Movement. Jeff Bryant's "Education Spring: A Growing Revolt Against 'Reform' Mandates" (*Truthout*, May 2013) points out where in the United States the word "reform" is viewed with distrust. I am not alone in realizing as Solzhenitsyn remarked that the "name of 'reform' simply covers what is latently a process of the theft of the national heritage" (interview with Joseph Pearce, February 2003). And surely awareness and defense will lead to a renewed effort toward a university's active stand against market loyalty to the perverse logic of 'creative destruction,' extended most dangerously to critical and creative thinking outside the box of profit. "Universities," Henry Giroux writes, "should be subversive in a healthy society, they should push against the grain and give voice to the voiceless, the unmentionable and the whispers of truth that haunt the apostles of unchecked power and wealth."

Plutocracy, Gentrification, and Racial Violence[4]

You know Southie's gotten gentrified. I guess you can't stop progress.

—Ray Donovan, *Showtime*, 2015

It was a real wake-up call the other day to realize that evictions and gentrification don't just mean losing your home but really losing your life as well.

—KQED News, San Francisco, March 31, 2014

My God, is no place safe? Bensonhurst, perhaps?

—*Brooklynian*, March, 2013

For consideration: if you are poor in a plutarchy, where wealth has the power, you are in trouble. Let us also say that you are in a country that has not experienced feudalism. No aristocrats, no peasants, no French Revolution, just a colonial real estate and tax revolt back in the day. This self-professed classless country picks up on a competitive economic system that is lauded as being self-regulating, elegant in its eventual efficiency, and capable of 'raising all boats,' economically speaking. What turns out however is that this system plays out like a Monopoly game where Chance and a cold-hearted eating up of your neighbors ensues, a zero-sum game where for you to win, someone has to lose.

Right now in the United States, we have more than the 1 percent possessing the power that wealth buys. If you want to understand how gentrification is a byproduct of a Grand Canyon size wealth gap, is indeed the praxis of plutarchy, you need to accept that roughly 20 percent of the United States population now enjoys a surplus capital snowballing on the stock market, business investments, and inheritance. The top 20 per-cent have an average $100,000 income; 8 percent make over a $150,000 income. With a population of about 2.5 million, Brooklyn, one of the most talked about faces of gentrification in the United States, has about one million people and at least two hundred thousand with enough funds to turn a former working-class/lower-middle-class borough to a borough with an average monthly rent of $3,139.

Because a former working-class/middle-class well-being has slid downward into the anxiety, frustration, insecurity, and discontent that has been the lot of the bottom 80 percent of the population, neighborhoods have become vulnerable to a gentrifying takeover. Once affordable places are no longer so, landlords work hard to push out longtime renters so flush gentrifiers can step in, and housing offers are made that exceed a wage earner's lifetime savings. The gentrifiers are not villains, nor are the improvements their money and influence effect insignificant. However, if we had maintained a solvent, secure middle class as well as a blue-collar working class confident in a work/progress democratic, egalitarian social contract, neighborhoods would be more resistant to gentrification, and gentrifiers would not be an invading army but unremarkable within a society in which all were moving 'on up.'

The sharp divisions of plutocracy has erased a secure middle class and plunged them downward where blue-collar workers have no sense of what advance might be. All the tactics of takeover have been accelerated and supersized by a mindboggling wealth gap, one that has left very little ground upon which a middle class can stand.

Here are some facts, now more clearly brought to our attention with Bernie Sanders's run for the presidency.

> In the United States, wealth is highly concentrated in a relatively few hands. As of 2010, the top 1% of households (the upper class) owned 35.4% of all privately held wealth, and the next 19% (the managerial, professional, and small business stratum) had 53.5%, which means that just 20% of the people owned a remarkable 89%, leaving only 11% of the wealth for the bottom 80% (wage and salary workers). (William Domhoff, "Wealth, Income and Power" *Who Rules America,* www2.ucsc.edu)

While productivity has increased by 80 percent since 1979, the income of those who live on wages and not interest and dividends has not risen at all.

Wealth is not innocent of leveraging that wealth to exert power in our democracy in which people, like products and services, can be branded—a clever marketing process of manufacturing ways of seeing and thinking. Of voting. And it is clearly money that fuels that capturing of a democracy voter already led into thinking he or she is impervious to any influence outside his or her own personal choices. Believing that money is spent equally in support of opposing ideologies is like believing that PBS has as much influence on us as FOX, and that the financial clout of vanishing unions equals that of corporations. Why would the pursuit of the maximization of power support a leftist, or even liberal politics intent on either displacing that pursuit or regulating it?

The zeitgeist, mass psyche, or what I call the American "cultural imaginary" has changed from a proud sense of an American working-class hero, perhaps rooted in the image of G.I. Joe, the soldier made of galvanized iron and to whom Eisenhower referred "as the truly heroic figure of this war." That image of respect stood behind both private sector and governmental bolstering of a strong middle class, arising out of worker initiative and industry. Mobility from blue-collar, working class to middle class was insured by union efforts, overtime pay, job security, pensions, job health benefits, and effective unemployment and workman's compensation safety nets. And egalitarian spirit stood where now an 'I've got mine, you get yours' attitude reigns. Real economic and social mobility began to erode in Reagan's first term. While the middle class descended into the hapless confusion of the present, the blue-collar 'Everyman' was targeted to become 'Joe Sixpack,' a loser, a moocher, a miscreant; while those reaping the chance dispersals of a financialized capitalism become heroic icons celebrated for their fame and fortune. Simply put, wage earners never making enough to buy that home in the suburbs but remaining in the neighborhood became the bad guys, and the entrepreneurial wealthy became the good guys. The middle class was destined to exist as middle class only in their own minds.

A zeitgeist of gentrifying wealth fueled by a desire to privatize the public space to fulfill personal design arrangements now pushes both working class and middle class to the curb. Neighborhoods are now customized to meet the requirements of high-end shopping and costly leisure activities. Americans have gone from imaginatively identifying with Chaplin's tramp persona, the beleaguered poor man who not only endures but also wins our hearts and our admiration, to becoming admiring 'followers' of those Chaplin had parodied as "moneybags." Donald Trump is no more than a moneybags whose absurdity we are no longer able to parody Chaplin-style. We went from laughing at the arrogance and pretensions of the wealthy to idolizing them, from promoting a social and economic advance from underclass to working class to middle class to the rigid class boundaries of Europe before the French Revolution.

We now have a winner discourse, practices that degrade the working class and heel to the wealthy, and institutions that enforce this new regime. For the wealthy to have everything the way they want, they need to dismantle entrenched neighborhood arrangements that fall below their own lifestyle standards, which amount to no more than consumption and leisure regardless of how much one is devoted to yoga, veganism, and meditation. Gentrification is thus class warfare waged with both political sides pulling in the same direction. Both Liberals and Neoliberals are either openly applauding or giving a rapacious capitalism's creative destruction the benefit of the doubt. This is done in the same fashion that the charter school invasion of public schools as a campaign of profit making somehow seems to be a creative process. What is staring us in the face, however, in regard to gentrification is that it is an assault on and invasion of the losers by the winners. This has feudal and not democratic egalitarian dimensions.

The resistance point that has now hit the headlines has emerged from the racist treatment of blacks escalating to police violence. Many Brooklyn neighborhoods, and I use my own home borough Brooklyn as an example, are traditionally black neighborhoods, though some such as Red Hook and Williamsburg are no longer. Neighborhoods surrounding Bedford-Stuyvesant remain majority African American such as Brownsville,

Canarsie, East Flatbush, Crown Heights, Prospect Lefferts Gardens, East New York, Coney Island, and Fort Greene. The most offensive neighborhoods in terms of a gentrified perception are the ghettoized neighborhoods, the sanctuary neighborhoods of those who have not found their way into the mainstream of American life, either economically or culturally, Top of the list are African Americans, the heirs of American black slavery.

Gentrification in "Southie" Boston has gone on at great speed, but the Irish and not African Americans are the ones being displaced. The Latino population in The Mission district of San Francisco has been steadily evicted but clashes with the police do not take hold as do clashes with African Americans elsewhere. In these places and elsewhere across the United States a struggling blue-collar and lower-middle class, which have been scheduled for extinction since outsourcing and robotics, since the collapse of manufacturing and sustaining salaries, are now being uprooted from their neighborhoods. Only the explosive, deeply troubling issue of racism has brought attention to an incursion that we are otherwise wired to call "progress."

The congenital memory of black African slavery haunts the American mass psyche in incomparable ways. It draws the headlines. A gentrifying force initiated by a plutarchic wealth gap ignites an always-latent American racism, and the point of explosion is police enforcement. The poor have proven to be easy to ignore or degrade; but when the poor are also black, racism, the haunting nightmare of the American mass psyche, comes into play.

The answer to the question as to why this new millennial American society, which has declared itself "post-racial," now brings us each day a new report of police clash's with blacks has all to do with a black presence in those neighborhoods scheduled for gentrification. Police uphold the laws but they also uphold the values of a culture that demonizes the moochers and the losers. The poor are not others who "but for the grace of God" would be us; but rather they are those who, in the words of the Big Lebowski "have failed to succeed," are too lazy to get a job and too canny at working a welfare system (almost non-existent in the United States) to their advantage to start a business or buy stocks.

The advance of gentrification has run into the perennial racist issue in the United States but neither Liberals nor Neoliberals find it useful to make the connection. Poor whites could be easily displaced without arousing too much attention. But violence to blacks is a hot point; to repeat, it goes deep into the American mass psyche. The young millennials think of themselves neither as homophobic nor racist. These are back-in-the-day, analog hang-ups to which their own attachment to online life shows no interest. And yet, the topic has legs, almost as newsworthy as Donald Trump. Blacks have gotten caught being poor in the neighborhoods that the gentrifiers want. Law enforcement is now in a place where the gentrifying invasion must be carried out. If you are poor in a neighborhood that the wealthy want, your days are numbered. If you are black and poor and in those neighborhoods, police brutality precedes racism charges made against the police, a Praetorian Guard protecting a resident order established by and for the winners.

Police chiefs, mayors, and governors will take all manner of antiracism measures, face all manner of abuse, or make all manner of defense. The focus, in other words, will be on the site of clash and the actors involved; but this is like condemning the knight in a game of chess for eliminating the pawn or, you can take a wider view and scrutinize the game strategy of your opponent.

When the game being played is a zero-sum game, a scrunch-or-be-scrunched doctrine, and the results represent progress, the march of gentrification cannot be questioned because doing so would question the underlying premises of capitalist competitiveness. Only a socialist preference for mutual aid would launch such a critique, one neither Liberals nor Neoliberals will make. Capitalism is a forbidden "c" word in the American mass psyche, like cancer and class. It is a word even Bernie Sanders on the campaign trail refrains from using. But to amend the victimizing, exploiting, and dehumanizing of the poor—the designated losers and moochers—the wealth gap that the Monopoly game of capitalism will inevitably produce, and has produced, must be addressed head on.

A serious blow is struck against structural racism when the wealth status of African Americans, who remain a preponderant presence among the poor, gives them resistance power. This amounts to what leverage a secure prosperity provides, and beyond that, as much ownership of law enforcement, the justice system, and as much lobbying power and media power as the gentrifiers now possess. Neither brutality nor invasion occurs easily when one is so fortified.

Notes

1. *Truthout*, January 20, 2014.
2. *Truthout,* March 31, 2014.
3. *Truthout,* November 12, 2013.
4. *CounterPunch,* August 31, 2015.

Chapter Thirteen

Dark Imaginaries

The ways in which we as humans are affiliated, regardless of our religious, racial, political, and wealth divisions, in this enduring struggle between doing the right thing and doing whatever it takes—doesn't go too far beyond the ways in which we imagine.

The lines of battle, of bitter feud, and rival allegiances play out like subplots within the overshadowing power of our imaginaries. And because no politics or belief can stand solely on one side of our divided imaginaries and not the other, we are affiliated. Darkness crosses over into the hero just as light crosses over into the villain. The poor white man can hate a man of color as easily as a rich white man can. A Catholic can cheat his neighbor as easily as a Jew; married gays can commit adultery as easily as married heterosexuals. Men can be selfish and so can women. Liberals fear a 'street' tainting of their children's classroom by the poor as fervently as do Neoliberals. Both look anxiously toward their stock portfolios and both are equally obedient to the mantra 'I shop therefore I am.' Neither wants his or her child to fight in a war and both rally around the flag and sing the praises of American exceptionalism. Both acknowledge the evils of unions and extend the same freedom to market enterprise as to their own free choice.

We imagine in our great epics variants on this play of hubris and greed contesting with a romantic Cyrano claim to an unadulterated white plume of noble virtue. *The Epic of Gilgamesh, Beowulf, The Iliad* and *The Odyssey, El Cid* and *The Aeneid* supply templates here that have not faded simply because the struggle of dark and hopeful imaginaries has not faded. The great religious sagas from the Torah and the New Testament to the Koran, the Vedas, the Analects, to the Book of Mormon all witness an overpowering of our dark imaginaries by some variety of obedience and belief in either an immanent or transcendent divinity. There is farce and absurdity accompanying all attempts to isolate a dark imaginary as the 'other's' and ours as untainted, affiliated somehow more closely with a prelapsarian world than a fallen one. Cervantes mocks a romantic idealism that ignores the real conditions of the world and quests in an imaginary space destined to fail. Rabelais mocks the hypocrisy of the faithful and the obscenities of the powerful; Diderot sends his Jacques into the world as does Voltaire his Candide, and Swift offers the Yahoo as a portrait of humanity.

In Blake's *Marriage of Heaven and Hell* one finds that the imagination of four-fold perception is not divided into dark and enlightened. The energies in that expanded state of perception of what we call "evil" and the realm we call "hell" are necessary contraries to what we call "good" and the realm we call "heaven." However, in the fallen world, a collapse of the imagination has occurred, leading to dark affiliations and dark imaginaries that are corrupted, distorted, and equally shared by all. There is not sufficient imagination on any side to perceive the sameness we share, nor sufficient emotions and senses to break from the confines of the logic of a fallen world. All adversaries claim reason and assert a logic that has no more validity than that of the blind man holding the tail of an elephant and affirming that an elephant is shaped like a snake.

What Climate Scenarios Do We Imagine?

Even with a deal to stop the current rate of greenhouse gas emissions, scientists warn, the world will become increasingly unpleasant. Without a deal, they say, the world could eventually become uninhabitable for humans.

—Coral Davenport, "Optimism Faces Grave Realities at Climate Talks," *New York Times*, December 1, 2014

In a *New York Review of Books* article on climate change, William D. Nordhaus runs through the usual suspects in answering the question, "Why has progress in climate change policy been slow?" He concludes that "the fundamental reason for the lack of progress is the strong incentives for 'free-riding' in current international climate agreements." In short, you pay for the costs of a public good, and everyone else free rides. He finds to be less significant the following reasons: a poorly informed public, a difficult and not determinate science, industry opposition via strong lobbies, climate deniers' control of the Republican Party, expense of any solution, present hardships, and remote benefits. I believe, however, that these reasons are not less significant and very much in play. They fabricate very persuasive narratives, very dramatic scenarios scripted in the American cultural imaginary.

The US government would not be deterred from taking action for fear of others free-riding if some 90 percent of the population were imaginatively attached to the scenario that unless we act we face "the end of the human adventure on this planet, as we now know it" (Gernot Wagner and Martin L. Weitzman, *Climate Shock*). In fact, no reason for not taking action would survive if as many people who now affectively and prereflectively attach smoking to cancer attached in the same way fossil fuels to planet collapse. Re-imagining smoking as not a cool, rebel act, or a sophisticated social action, but as a slow contamination of the lungs and a painful death was, in effect, a translation of one imaginative state to another.

One could argue that compelling reasons effected this transformation. This would mean that the young choose not to smoke because they are informed as to the dangers and have dutifully gone through the reasoning. But the reasoning here goes on within a cultural imaginary that already has staged the smoking/cancer connection. And this is an imaginary into which the young are born.

Such is not the case with climate change. We are yet caught within ways of imagining that are promoted by far more industry widespread provocateurs than the antismoking campaigners faced with the tobacco industry. All the reasons that seem not as important as free-riding are actually in play and forceful simply because we have not consolidated an imaginative awareness with climate change as we have with smoking. We are, it seems, closer to reimagining sugar and the Baconator as real dangers than we are to reimagining driving fossil-fuel cars as a deathblow to the planet. There are reasons why we attend or do not attend to climate change but they emerge, once again, from the ways we imagine climate change. And these ways are many and have not yet coalesced.

First, there is very little interest in the United States in a politics in which it is not quite clear to the majority what is going on and where truth may lie. It may be that the American public is so angry and frustrated with a pitched battle between political ideologies that it turns away from public issues—issues that require legislative action and cannot be personally resolved. Climate change is a public issue, a planetary issue requiring global government coordination, and it comes at a time when all things public are eschewed, all things private and personal deified.

Our millennial politics has become a privatized one. On this private level, self-interests do not extend to imposing as much discipline on our own gratifications as this global warming problem requires. It's a problem that exceeds the faux societal representations of Facebook. This is a whole human race issue. This is an unfolding tragedy that we have relegated to a matter of personal interest and preference, to personal choice. In a culture, that has replaced any notion of a common good with a personal well-being of the moment, climate change denial is moral because it's a personal choice. Such denial preempts a realization that something monumental is going on in the world, which is not ruled by our personal choices. An economics of consumption and leisure fits nicely with our personal self-interest, though such affiliations work against public and global concerns and the development of a social moral sense. Our social and communitarian selves, our public and political selves have collapsed into discord and inertia, manic and depressive, subsistence and survival. Out public interest is weak; our private interests consume us.

Basic interests of survival are also at play. A great percentage of the populace are already too beat up by economic realities to worry about something so removed as the planet heating up to a possibly dangerous point at some not yet known time in the future. The scenario of global-warming prevention measures making life even more miserable has force. In the grip of this imaginary, any legislative action that slows down economic growth in order to slow down the pace of global warming is no more than a plot to dismantle the free-enterprise system. It is a plot to cripple our economy while other countries too savvy to slow their own economies in the name of some possible future event, become powerful enough to impose a Chinese- and North Korean-type tyranny upon us. In this scenario, government is not only useless but also potentially dangerous if it intrudes on the free flow of the market to regulate on behalf of the environment. Tragedy is imagined as an impeded market fails to grow properly and develop market solutions to global warming.

Once you are drawn into the imaginings of these neoliberal productions, it is difficult to develop a counterimaginary. It's possible, however, that the millennials who are likely to be alive when the bad stuff happens may feel a greater need to imagine differently than the *après moi, le déluge* crowd. What motivates the *après moi* group, the prominent adults in charge of government and business, against human-affected climate change is their own age, the likelihood that they won't be around to experience catastrophic devastation of the planet. Unless The Singularity happens in their lifetime and they become immortal cyborgs, they will not be around to suffer the consequences of their offensive against climate-change legislative action. Those now enjoying the power that wealth has given them have no incentive to change a world that has so gifted them. In a culture where self-interest rules and the most selfish blather about "true compassion," sacrifice is not the rule. Self-interest points to no diminishment of profits now.

The so-called winners in both business and government might also welcome a planet-threatening dystopic event because winners welcome crises. In the midst of the complexities of climate change, the collapse of a sustainable environment, there will be, it is imagined, winners like "the fabulous Fab" who crowed like a rooster as the Great Recession rolled in. The psychology of this scenario sounds too perverse, too fantastical; but it is in play for the players who have played recklessly and have, thus far, remained cultural heroes and icons.

For the winners who fear climate doomsday will happen in their lifetime and are not sure they can make a profit on the event, there is emergency evacuation insurance in case the rise in temperature is suddenly lethal. There is escape to that part of the world not flooded, with a protective amount of the ozone layer, and less heat than elsewhere. There may also be a flight to a space station and luxury accommodation toward which privatized space tourism seems to be heading. Technology is imagined as the hero here; though it may have caused our problems, it will get us out of them. For entrepreneurs and venture capitalists new beach real estate may open up as well as oil exploration in the previously frozen parts of the planet. A global warming dystopia may propel us to reach out to other planets, to explore, as in the *Star Trek* mantra, new frontiers. As fantastical as these narratives may seem, they yet link tightly to our overriding economic metanarrative. We dominate and prevail against Mother Nature; we don't bend our will to it.

There may be a vast number of new marketing frontiers as well as a creative destruction that a bold, adventurous form of capitalism, our US form, welcomes. So while half the audience of the doomsday production is cringing in fear, the other half is boldly looking forward to capitalizing on a crisis or escaping to a safe space station. When you have an escape plan or you think like those who boldly and recklessly continue to sail through the Grand Guignol of Wall Street's arcane bait-and-switch tactics, you do not pay much attention to the issue at all.

There remain scenarios of our intellect and imagination far less perverse and depressing. It may be that our planetary environment is too complex to computer model, a view that emerges from Heisenberg Uncertainty Principle; namely, that experimental conditions alter reality and that observation itself intrudes on what one seeks to observe. What may actually be going on in the world may be different from what the results of our human experiments and computer modeling may indicate is going on. Hope rises here when one considers that our classical physics has not been validated by what we have observed on the quantum level. And while we have mathematics, we have no understanding of what remains opaque and can only be termed "chaos."

As far as the Earth is concerned, we operate on a few islands of predictability on a vast ocean of unpredictability. The Earth, according to quantum theory, may be always in a state of superposition, in which elemental particles in different states can lead to different possible outcomes. Observation from an experimental position closes down this superpositioning so we see not possible outcomes but only one. A consensus of all studies done by scientists throughout the world that reach the same conclusion regardless of the divergence of their experimental circumstances cannot then exclude the possibility of this superpositioning. Nevertheless, the consequences that an accelerated global warming is happening and is caused by humans may be a macro-level judgment, but scientists have made many of those that have been realized.

A more hopeful imaginary, at least for the planet itself, poses a planetary self-organization triggered by the 'noise' of global warming. That reorganization may entail the end of the human race however. The Earth itself becomes the struggling hero, beset on all side by persistent efforts to dominate, alter, uproot, creatively destroy, exhaust, poison, and deplete its astounding and still-mysterious symmetry, a fearful symmetry that, as William Blake questions, who dares to dominate?

The last act here is an imaginative portrayal of the Earth's reorganizing itself to accommodate greenhouse gases while making their further production impossible. A self-organization ensuring Earth's survival and not our own cannot exhilarate a humanity driven to dominate and exhaust the resources of the planet. We do not see ourselves as easy to extinguish as the dinosaurs. The dinosaurs, however, never had a choice in their extinction, as do we collectively, not as individuals deluded by a personal will-to-power but in solidarity with societal efforts made throughout the entire planet.

. . . .

Once the whole point-counterpoint is in ruins, a proper satire can operate and thus, perhaps, expose/disclose what it seems reason no longer can in our post-truth world. My first humble offering in Dean Swift's path was the following essay, "A Modest Proposal, 2014," which whet my appetite for both satire and Swift; so in the years following, I wrote *Travels of a New Gulliver* and entered the publishing domain of Jeff Bezos, literary agents being as repelled by irony and satire as Little Miss Muffet was by spiders who sat down beside her.

A Modest Proposal, 2014[1]

For preventing the poor, wage workers, the un-gentrified, and Mother Nature from being a burden on the Alpha class of the country, and for making them beneficial to the publick. . . .
I have been assured by a very knowing American of my acquaintance in London, that a young healthy child well nursed, is, at a year old, a most delicious nourishing and wholesome food.

—Jonathan Swift, *A Modest Proposal*, 1729

It is a melancholy object to those who travel through these American towns or travel in the country, when they see the streets, the roads, and public places crowded with beggars, welfare recipients, the perennially unemployed, the wastrel gadabouts, the gangbangers, malcontents, and whiners, the losers of scant ambition but to feed on the winners, importuning at every turn the federal government for all manner of 'freebies.'

This lot, instead of being willing to work for their honest livelihood, spend all their energies scheming for food stamps, unemployment compensation, rent control, legal aid, earned income-tax credit, welfare without work, Medicaid benefits, and all that can be gotten when a politics of endless aid to the parasites of our society is at the wheel of government. I propose a zero-tolerance for such devilment and the federal government from which it originates.

I think it is agreed by all parties that both the winners and the losers would be best served if the losers were cut free of government handouts and, thus, like children ready to walk and free of their mothers' hands, step out and develop those skills necessary to earn a living in the world. Thereby whoever was thus liberated would soon be filled with a personal ambition to succeed, a will to compete, and, most wonderfully, a keen desire to assume personal responsibility for either success or failure on the most consistently level playing field that our society offers and the world has ever seen. The real glory, as Mr. Lombardi reminded us, is being knocked to our knees and then coming back. Without a good knocking, no glory can ensue. The miscreant class is already on their knees, and it is best, for their own sake, to keep them there if they fail to rise on their own.

Those who contribute nothing to society but sponge off the success of others thanks to the largesse of Liberal taxation are in no way ennobled by such a practice. If such liberality is ended, there is a possibility that such liberation will cause a people to stand on their own two feet, get into the arena and compete, perhaps start a business. Those habituated to handouts will not rise and walk, whether they are on the dole or not.

The liberation must be as sudden, penetrating, and extensive as to rouse the lethargic and insensate in the same manner that electrical shock treatment of the addled jacks them up to a new state of being. Any attenuation of the dramatic change sought will give time for not only a scam defense but a condemning outcry from coddling Liberals.

My intention is very far from being confined to the lazy beggars but extends to the wage class, to those who live precariously on the fumes of lost middle-class well-being and fading memories of vibrant workers' unions who could bargain with the proprietary class for wages and conditions of employment, who lived in neighborhood communities neither gated nor underwater. May I remind the reader that living on the fumes of yesterday preempts the rewards of today?

I can think of no one objection to driving the dependent to their knees where they may find the strength to compete and succeed, perhaps to start a business.

Such success can be properly recognized and admired by those who have themselves competed freely, encouraging all toward a conversion of a loss to a win, a debit to a credit. Those who suckle on the government teat can never know what winning is. They fail to applaud the winning in others but rather endlessly moan and groan and vote for the Liberal who promises them succor from cradle to grave. They can neither comprehend their own responsibility in their failures nor recognize what a sad dehumanized state to which their dependency has brought them.

Let none talk to me of the virtues of denying fellow men and women the chance to test their mettle, the opportunity to be free to choose their own course in life. To those who accuse me of a lack of compassion, I observe that those who lack all self-respect and the necessary will to win that survival demands cannot be saved by Liberal largesse from the deserving fate that awaits such feckless lives. The highest note of humanity is played by enabling shorter life spans to those failures whose misery would be prolonged by misguided benevolence.

A perennial scene of misfortune and tragedy result from all blockades to self-initiative. These continue because a misguided notion of compassion is at work as when the sapless watch a wounded creature suffer and fail to put a bullet in its head.

The mothering that will not end rears the child who is never free to discover his or her own worth, perhaps start a business.

I am not so violently bent upon my own opinion as to reject the play of Chance in the lives of both winners and losers. But before Chance can be allowed to reconnect the miscreants to the government teat, I need point out that the accidents that lay some low are no more than opportunities for others to rise higher. Climbing out of a trash can and into fame and fortune is the essence of the American Dream. Deprive people of the trash can and you deprive them of the American Dream. No one should be denied that privilege.

Further, the ones who are self-empowered and project their will into the world are less liable to be detoured by Chance and more prepared to face the consequences than those whose lives will fall apart if a monthly hardship allowance is not received. The aged do not find themselves suddenly aged but have had a lifetime to prepare for the event. Similarly, poverty, whether lifelong or sudden, upends the lives of only the dependent and un-self-reliant. Those who make the future for themselves are not waylaid by Chance as are those who put their lives in the hands of others and, like Dickens's Micawber, expect something "to turn up."

As to my own part, having turned my thoughts for many years upon this important subject of Chance, and maturely weighed the several schemes erected to keep the weak from blaming the Goddess Fortuna for what should clearly be laid at their own doorsteps, I have concluded that straight talk is required.

None can doubt that a series of misfortunes, one upon the other, can come upon people so hard and so swift that no act of legerdemain can change their lamentations to hallelujahs. And there is no concealing the fact that Chance plays a part in the winner's life as well as in the loser's. It is, however, not in the interests of the winners to admit this, neither in their lives nor in the lives of the losers. The losers' fate may be partially of their own making or not at all; but such shirking is no more than what we expect from losers. Winners, on the other hand, accept losers as a natural result of their own winning. A zero-sum game in which for one to win another must lose replaces Chance with an inviolable creed.

There is then, in short, no way for the losers to free themselves from the winners' arrangement of Chance; and the sooner such appeals are terminated, the sooner losers will face up to the winners' arrangement of all. All efforts to plead conditions and circumstances—from slow-witted genetics, parental abuse and slum-level poverty, to wallet-draining cancer, loss of limb, sight, and job, and so on—should impact the losers in the same way they impact the winners: as the excuses of those who fail to assume personal responsibility. I propose that we drive hard, pedal to the metal, in reorienting society from excuses to responsibility and declare a zero tolerance for excuses.

If we push the envelope toward a totally cold-turkey treatment in all those places in which some liberal and socialist tempering of the efficiency of market rule is at work, we will very quickly be able to separate those few who are unfortunate through no fault of their own and those upon whom personal connivery is at play. And the discrimination required must be local for it is well-known that every neighbor has a tale to tell of whose plight is legitimate and whose plight is a scam. We then rely on the disposition of informed, targeted private scrutiny in the same fashion as we rely on private philanthropy rather than the blind bureaucratic dispensing of welfare that taxation enables.

I have been assured by a very knowing Mauritanian slave owner of my acquaintance in New York that if the wages of the American salaried class were to be uniformly and immediately dropped to the 2,000 *taka* a month paid to Bangladeshi workers, a very wholesome upswing in top 20 percent prosperity would result, thus benefitting that class. At the same time the bottom 80 percent would experience relief from the anxieties of modern life by being thrown, like a Finn out of the sauna and into frigid waters, into feudal circumstances.

The virtues of medieval peasantry are many, from a reassuring faith in the hereafter to a secure sense of place and purpose in feudal society. This seems clearly preferable to the apprehensions and insecurities of 80 percent of the American population, half of them without any sense of place and purpose and the other half moaning over a defunct well-being.

There should be no liberal pretense and delay in rushing the losers into a feudal way of life. The certainty of that state will incite a will to power aborted at birth by liberal nanny-ism.

I do therefore humbly offer it to public consideration that sixty-three million will rest easily in gentrified fashion, with all the perks accrued, while 252 million have a shot at reaping the undeniable benefits that a life that is solitary, poor, nasty, brutish, and short can deliver as cleanly as a bullet to the brain. The struggle begins or has a chance to begin, and the competitive spirit is awakened when the cost of living itself is pumped to the max. This agrees with the perennial wisdom of 'what doesn't kill you, makes your stronger.'

Thus the gentrified squire will learn to expand his life's longevity by the intake of organic, non-toxic food at gourmet emporiums, the assistance of personal fitness trainers, nutritionists, 'talking cure' analysts, illegal nannies, gardeners, cooks, personal assistants, house cleaners, and body guards, as well as platinum-level health care, including access to the organs of young peasants.

Those who are most thrifty among the lost and losing classes may live long enough to receive Social Security benefits had that age not been raised to accord with the gentrified class's increased longevity and not their own, which, unfortunately and in no way owing to the stochastic nature of market rule efficiency, has decreased.

I propose the matter to be inconsequential if socialized security is replaced by a privatized pay-as-you-go arrangement thus giving some 252 million of the population an opportunity to assume personal responsibility for their last years of solitary, poor, nasty, brutish, and short existence. The carrot of trophy wives, extensive real-estate holdings, obedient servants, gold bars, luxury yachts and ready-to-hand organ transplants push everyone forward except those whose indolence has been nurtured and whose will-to-power unmanned.

As things now stand, matters of illness and health, crime and law, defense and war, education and schooling are managed in ways that maximize illness, crime, war, and ignorance. This travesty is achieved by putting forth the public good rather than private concern, public expenditure rather than personal profit.

If hospitals and emergency rooms were not forced to provide 'charity care,' not only would profits to shareholders increase but the poor would take better care of their health, and, possibly, work toward being able to pay for their health care. I think it is agreed by all parties that if people cannot muster sufficient power of will to lead healthful lives then it matters not at all if the federal government provides them with affordable health insurance or not.

The sooner people face their own mortality—and illness is the great conveyor here of that message—the greater the chance that they will opt for health and long life if, of course, the illness, without medical help, does not kill them. However, any interference with this tough love accommodates liberal compassion but brings no one closer to assuming responsibility for his or her own life. Unnecessary cost is added to inevitable tragedy.

If the law were privatized, crimes and criminals would be pursued on a pay-as-you-go basis, thus affording another level of protection for the gentry class who has the wherewithal to define what they see as a crime, pursue perpetrators in private courts, and confine them in private prisons. Those who cannot avoid the misfortunes of thievery, murder, and mayhem in their own neighborhoods will come immediately face-to-face with the brutish aspect of their lives and thus, once again, be incentivized to get a job and possibly start a business.

I desire those politicians who declare wars and pursue them to step aside and leave all war-making decisions to private enterprise, which is best able to conduct war for profit. What does it gain a country if it wins a war but shareholders suffer a loss? Privatized warfare steps back from all engagements in which a quick return on investment is not forthcoming, except in those cases where a slow and long-term profit-making campaign is being waged.

I am studious of brevity so I will state that without public tax support there will be no public education but only pay-as-you-go education, thus, once again, incentivizing parents on government handouts to get off their arses and pay for their children's education. Parents who care not whether their children are educated will hardly be amended in this uncouthness whether the federal government picks up the tab or does not. The virtues of for-profit, privatized education are many, not the least being a curriculum that prepares students to start a business.

Many disadvantages can be enumerated when regulatory agencies intrude amorphous and contentious social concerns into the efficient workings of market rule. First, as things now stand, federal government sanctuary and bailouts for the casualties of creative destruction are putting a drag on not only global competitiveness but also an inevitable rush to the bottom that the useless must face. Character-building epiphanies are forestalled by governmental interjections. And second, interrupting market efficiency in order to protect and preserve an environment that we control and adapt to suit human needs is preposterous. Human civilization has been built on bringing Nature to heel and not the reverse. Here again we need to push the envelope, in this case, by not de-accelerating growth through technology but pushing it further, heedless of climate change, toxic air, water, food, plastics, and so on.

Any retreat from pushing the envelope of technology, as with hampering market rule, will only succeed in diminishing the innovative drive as well as the intensity of competition that results when the game of survival of the fittest is not corrupted by French notions of fraternity and cryptic, lunatic Gaia bonds with the planet.

The faster we muck up air, water, and earth, the faster will our responding technology grow, the faster will that tech take those who have the price of a ticket off the planet and onto a whole new world, which we will subject, as we have on this planet, to the wondrous efficiency of market rule. Those who doubt this need only observe how Iraq has benefited from the sudden, unchallenged implementation of market rule under the leadership of special Presidential Envoy Paul Bremer. Those who unpatriotically believe that the poisoning of the planet will stump human technology can expect that the gated compounds of the gentry will be domed and that the purest oxygen will be pumped in.

Market rule efficiency will push technology to its profit-making limits and should be allowed to do so without concessions to the whims and tantrums of Mother Nature. To repeat: we should push Mother Nature to the limits and thus incite those technological innovations that human-kind produces in response, thus augmenting profits to those positioned to reap them.

Ice and meteors were planetary catastrophes in name only but, in truth, opportunities Nature provided for the very beginning of human civilization. We are now able to push Nature toward new cataclysmic events without fear because we have reached a level of technological inventiveness that is more than able to respond to the benefit of those positioned to benefit.

The planet Earth will be left behind the way Detroit was left behind by the wealthy after the 1967 riots—the fate of the planet, like that of Detroit, bankruptcy.

A flight propelled by fear of angry indigents will in the future be a well-planned departure and not a fearful escape. When we creatively destroy the planet, we do so consistent with a mission of unstoppable growth in full expectation that technological innovation and human inventiveness will take us to a higher plane. Private space-travel entrepre-neurship and Google-sponsored robotic technology are not products of a retrogressive, nostalgic imagination but an aggressive, forward-looking imagination. Virgin Galactic now offers a $250,000 seat to space for six hundred wishing to join the most exclusive club in the world, and so the seeds of leaving behind an exhausted and poisoned planet have already been planted. While cowardly and fatigued imaginations envision humans as victims of technology, those who imagine outside the box of apprehen-siveness foresee a cyborg amalgam of human and computer impervious to sickness, to cancer, and death itself.

In a manner similar to pushing all non-human fauna on the planet to their own end as speedily as possible, sparing them the slow, painful dissolve and extinction that a creative destruction of their environment foretells, or pitiable confinement in cages, we must more ambitiously push the feckless from their roosts and engage in a gentrification of the planet. This has already begun in the cities. The universe is there to be gentrified, a fact that a gentry class, swollen with stock-market gains, realizes as it invades the last of the smart and faddish locations on the planet.

I can think of no one objection to releasing to the freedom of homeless tent camps and the joys of communal, shanty-town *favela* life those who now stubbornly and tastelessly occupy real estate greedily eyed by the new gentry.

The lesson to be learned here is simple and elegant: the faster the losers face the conditions of their own plight, the faster will they be motivated to change those conditions. Meanwhile, the new gentry must swallow whole that choice real estate which ill suits the pedigree of its current squatters. This is being done in Los Angeles, Tampa, Portland, Chicago, Atlanta, Washington, D.C., San Francisco, Seattle, Boston, and New York City with the same speed and relish as an earlier gentry used to push the Lenape tribes out of Manhattan in the eighteenth century.

Such a project has been underway quite successfully in New York City, true to its legacy of commandeering real estate at wampum prices, under the lordly guidance of Mr. Bloomberg. Developers, spurred on by cash-in-hand new gentry, are evicting and thus liberating the non-gentrified of Red Hook in Brooklyn, who for their part will ride that horse of freedom across a frontier never before envisioned in American egalitarian democracy, a frontier that as Rod Serling intoned "not of time nor space but of mind."

My ancestor, Dean Swift, was metaphorical only in advising that the Irish eat their babies and thus improve the quality of their lives. We need to eat up the world and all its resources and turn a deaf ear to the Liberals of retrogression who would have us check our own energies, shackle our own creativity. We need to eat up the losers, swallow them in the voracious maw of globalized techno-capitalism and thus allow them, as Mother Nature allows the wretched caterpillar to turn into a monarch, the chance, now denied them, to metamorphose beyond servitude.

We need to swallow this planet and everything in it in order to fulfill our human destiny. Our destiny is to utilize our consciousness of our own destiny, which no other creature on the planet shares, and the will-to-power that develops from that consciousness to truly own this world.

I modestly propose that we not back away from such ownership merely because there are many who are not fit for the struggle and who seek the leadership of the weak. As Sarah Palin reminds us, "Only dead fish go with the flow." I propose that we not join hands in a brotherhood of the enfeebled and impotent, grinding out our days in one step forward and two back, setting ourselves up for a tragic apocalypse, a hopeless defeat in the way that cowards always defeat themselves before the battle begins.

I profess, in the same words as Dean Swift, in the sincerity of my heart, that I have not the least personal interest in endeavoring to promote this necessary work, having no other motive than the public good of my country. We face a moral imperative to allow an efficient market to raise all boats, to liberate losers from the apron strings of the federal government and permit them the opportunity to know what Aristotle so wisely said, "Happiness depends on ourselves," and to resist the call to put the unconscious force of Nature before the technological growth of civilization.

The Coming Transformation of Work to Leisure

Whether or not technology liberates us all into leisure in the future, as Google's Larry Page envisions, the problems of NOW, which include profits, dividends, and leisure for a minority wealth class and a collapse in income for the many, are pushing our democracy toward a breaking point, one which threatens angry, violent eruptions scattered like the eruptions of our warming environment itself. We can make work and workers matter now, a first step in pulling the reins from the "invisible hand of the market" and enabling the many rather than an elite few to deal with both technology and the plight of the environment from the perspective of the well-being of the many and not the profit of a few.

> *Smart machines may make higher GDP possible, but they will also reduce the demand for people—including smart people. So we could be looking at a society that grows ever richer, but in which all the gains in wealth accrue to whoever owns the robots.*
>
> —Paul Krugman, *New York Times*, December 26, 2012

> *Capital isn't just winning against labor: there's no contest. If it were a boxing match, the referee would stop the fight.*
>
> —John Lanchester, "The Robots Are Coming," *London Review of Books*, March 5, 2015

If capital goes to the owners of the robots and not to the workers, then it's clear that the severe economic equality existing in the United States today will only grow more severe in the future. This is not an uncontested view. Dean Baker, for instance, asserts, "There is no real evidence that robots are displacing workers on any substantial scale" ("Don't Worry About the Robots: the Fed Might Take Your Job," *Truthout,* March 30, 2015). The real threat to workers in Baker's view is the actions of the Federal Reserve. I do not see that, but I do see that while we can challenge the Federal Reserve we cannot challenge the inevitability of robots and AI. Ironically, this same AI will one day replace the engineers who created AI. The replacement/retirement here will be indiscriminate and universal.

I also see that Larry Page's vision of a future in which hi-tech liberates workers into a world of leisure is a future already being enjoyed by those who are making a living in our new 'share economy' as 'independent contractors.' We are redefining the unemployed as free agents and all manner of back-in-the-day anxieties and insecurities as either bad personal choices or incentives to start an online business. 'Leisure' has already for some become an amalgam of work and leisure, if you define both as doing what you will. The old adage that work is fun if you are doing what you choose to do is now strangled within the twisted illusion that in a plutarchy in which middle class well-being has collapsed into the same dark rut as the bottom 40 percent of the population one remains 'free to choose.' Whatever miserable fate plutarchic rule allows you, you remain exhilarated by your freedom to choose. Your life can never be solitary, poor, nasty, brutish, and short because you always remain free to choose a magnificent life of leisure and consumption. In the order of things in which we now live, we were made for consumption and leisure, and we have the power to personally choose to have both. Work is now not only peripheral but also vestigial, something like a tail that vanishes when we evolve. It is a stage in an evolutionary process that we will soon, thanks to robotics and AI, leave behind.

Meanwhile, back on a warming planet, there yet remains those, maybe 80 percent of the population, the same percentage who remain ungentrified, who are not already in that glorious, evolved future. And like the FedEx workers who have been given the title "independent contractors" so that they can be denied employee benefits, or the Uber drivers free to insure themselves, or the fast-food workers who can choose between a living wage or having a job many still live in a world in which work matters. The leisure of the future that Page foresees arriving after a worker is liberated from his or her work is not now producing a livable income for wage earners. If they owned the business or had a dividend-producing stock portfolio or just a stash of inherited wealth, their leisure time would be secured. However, I speculate that right now the relationship for the many between work, leisure, and cybertech, and AI is not a for-profit one. All forms of entertainment are now notable and welcomed expansions of what leisure means, all of which will most likely be increased in the future. I refer to the real wondrous eureka! of finding what you want to find on a smartphone, the endless opportunities of enjoying peer-to-peer wisdom—a wisdom far exceeding that of an analog world in which not everyone was blessed with knowing everything, each admirably knowing it differently—and the breathtaking adventure of merely surfing the web.

Whether, however, this cyber-leisure segues into an elixir of work and leisure that produces an income for the many capable of regaining what workers already possessed in a middle-class democracy of the past is unknowable. We do know that cybertech has not produced the jobs that a manufacturing revolution had: "In 1979 . . . General Motors employed 853,000 worldwide. Today, Apple, Amazon, Facebook and Google have something close to $1 trillion in market capitalization. But together, they employ fewer than 150,000 people—less than the number of new entrants into the American workforce every month" (Blaire Briody, "The Rise of Robots—and the Decline of Jobs—Is Here," *The Fiscal Tiimes*, January 14, 2013). Google also foregoes unions and pensions, and thus their vision of leisure in the future is grounded on conditions the world has not yet experienced, or experienced only for the top quintile of the population. It would seem then that Page's view of work evolving into leisure is based on a small sample—namely, a moneyed class whose money does their work.

Leisure may replace work in some harmless way, or the two may unite in some manner. Our idea of leisure may become liberated from the back-in-the-day-nightmare of a poor man with a bottle of beer sitting in front of a TV day and night, and a rich man sailing round the world in a yacht. However, it may be that a mass of liberated, new millennial workers fall into the same sort of stupor that filled the medieval world, powered not by religion or magic but by cyberspace gaming, porn, shopping, and Facebook sociability alternating with vitriolic online comments. It may also be that the working class, now joined by the middle class, moves closer and closer to choosing to storm the Bastille than choosing to continue to live within the woes of being on the wrong side of a huge wealth divide.

I see problems in regard to the quality and compensation for work, the growing wealth gap and its connection to hi-tech ownership, the unequal nature of a liberation into leisure that along with consumption seems to be the highest good of the American Dream, and the recklessness of presuming robotization and AI will lead to a glorious future, or at very least, have a benign effect on human civilization and planetary survival.

From Page's Google perspective, the future will be glorious not only because ownership will bring him googles of profit but because it will fulfill a cybertechnic dream of amalgamating human biology and cybertech and thus expand everything to the point that no one need labor, no one need perform repetitive tasks, no one's mind remain inferior to the work of hands. What we can reasonably say is that both work and technology can, and most likely will, assume roles inconceivable in the present. A total paradigm switch of Thomas Kuhn proportions would mean that there is no one around who understands work in the way we do now, or entertain the question of whether work matters or not. Perhaps a future on-demand economy integrates capital and a freelancing in cyberspace to the degree that wealth gap, work, workers, and leisure no longer matter, or matter in ways inconceivable to us now.

It's possible that a rise in productivity enabled by robotization and AI could float all boats to the degree that everyone is enjoying leisure as Page predicts, work and leisure both allowing one to do what one wills—and what one wills is not caught in a vicious circle or commodified to suit the profit of others. Or, less optimistically, perhaps, the top 20 percent who are doing well now continue to do well and everyone else is anesthetized within the seductions of virtual realities, their expectations and requirements minimized, or mobilized as in the Arab Spring revolutions to "go Bastille." Taking sides here is a suicide leap into our treacherous waters of polarized argument and emotions. Within my narration, it is reasonable for us to face the meanings, values, and constraints of the present without being a Cassandra or a cheerleader of the future.

We can observe a race being run between the endurance of resident values and meanings and those hi-tech is speedily fashioning to all our amazement. We may get to revolution before we get to a place where work, as we know it, does not matter and workers are transformed into a leisure class interacting at will with an on-demand economy. On the other hand, or in the next running lane, US democracy may not be reaching its breaking point because of a wealth divide that encourages plutarchy, but instead both wealth divide and democracy may have little significance in a hi-tech future we cannot know and therefore cannot value as good or bad. This possible scenario, however, has a *Brave New World* horror to it. It would take a lot of soma tablets to get us to forget or ignore so much that has such a hold on us in the present.

Although we are on the threshold of something new, in a liminal stage, so to speak, being out of work or underemployed and thus being underwater on a mortgage, burdened with credit card and educational debts, and so on, being hungry and homeless doesn't seem to be abated by what hi-tech may lead us to. We must also consider that just as the means to leave the planet will not alter the warming of the planet, future hi-tech innovations do not alter the labor/capital problems now. In our present reality, work matters because we are not yet transformed to a place and time where it may not matter.

The greatest impediment to future profits and profits already reaped, is the breakdown of a slowly eroded democratic system which has, in a far healthier condition in the near past, created a middle-class democracy, created a level of economic, political, and social literacy that will not suffer without revolt what appears to be an imminent breakdown. Historically, the greatest impediment to all plutarchies, whether inheritance and imperial or merchant and market fashioned, has been violent, bloody revolutions. Replacing the prerogatives of the market with those of society, which means no longer subsuming societal goals within market goals, would lead to a reconsideration of FDR's "economic bill of rights" which made work and a living wage a constitutional right of every American. In our present climate, we would need to either deliberately legislate the containment of robotization and AI within the larger mission of providing work and a living wage, or governmentally offer jobs and wages as in the New Deal's Works Progress (Projects) Administration.

This seems about as doable as getting Americans to drive less. We may, on the other hand, take the view that the only way to dodge a potential break down of US democracy is to accelerate our hi-tech transformation of work, wage, and wealth gap to something we cannot now conceive. I deem the former rational and the latter cynical and reckless: *cynical* because we know that amping up our cowboy capitalism, the casino capitalism that has led to our dangerous wealth divide, and *reckless*, because that amping up may break this democracy, and not in an unbloody way. Eruptions of rage, violence, and destruction by those not enjoying the profits and leisure of productivity may easily join the ravages of global warming we are already experiencing. This is harsh and not heartening but powerful enough, I think, to push us to do what just sentences before we deemed undoable.

If US democracy is now nearing a breaking point because of the ravaging effects of a wealth gap and the affiliated loss of secure, living-wage jobs, counsel here is to take the wealth gap seriously in a consolidated effort to make work matter and make workers sharers in both their own and the productivity of machines. We have already experienced this identity in our prior middle class, socially and economically mobile democracy. It would be a return to a world in which work matters and its fruits far exceed the infantile and primitive seductions of consumption and leisure.

The American Middle Class: The Political Chosen People?[2]

Let's focus on the middle class.

—Rick Santorum, March 7, 2015

"Everyday Americans" removes political discussion even further from a consideration of class, which presents trouble for those among the working class and smooth sailing for those at the top. (And "middle class" had already done a fine job of that anyhow.)

—Elizabeth Stoker Bruenig, "America's Political Obsession with the 'Middle Class' Hurts Workers," *New Republic*, April 17, 2015

The middle classes are very influential, as they encompass the majority of voters, writers, teachers, journalists, and editors. Most societal trends in the US originate within the middle classes.

—*Wikipedia*

The phrase "everyday Americans" skillfully finesses out of sight the disappearance of all the rungs on the ladder leading to the middle class. This rebranding points to the difficulty of evoking a middle class resonating with past positives such as job security, union protection, pensions, overtime compensation, middle-class livable salaries, and the viability of domestic manufacturing and production jobs. The difficulty emerges from the fact that all of these past positives have been vaporized by the knockout victory of capital over labor in the United States.

The middle class does not arise from nowhere, but we are not disposed to recognize clearly and with any respect any state of being except that of the elite. This may be due to a long campaign within the American cultural imaginary to denigrate and demonize a loser/moocher class while elevating a winner class. What we now have in the United States is a middle class hardly anything like a past middle class, a middle class much like a blue-collar working class, which is itself now distained in a plutarchic culture that has no working-class heroes and holds work to have little intrinsic value for humans, while leisure does. This working class is now much like an underclass, down for the count and awaiting total eviction from the America that financialized, Wild West capitalism has created. All signifiers of class are now afloat, meaningless because all meaning has been vacated or over determined. The signifier "middle class" is overloaded with what it wants not to be identified—namely, the abyss you fall into when the ladder that had been there has been removed.

The collapse of economic and social mobility is a gift of plutarchy, which, within plutarchy, must be appealed to so that it downsizes itself to egalitarian levels and reroutes itself from the benefits of its own identity toward the recuperation of some 80 percent of the population. This is as crazy and as voodoo as it sounds—as voodoo as insisting that siphoning all wealth upward is a boon to 80 percent of the population. To restore a workable economic mobility—which means not only restoring the middle class but reestablishing the distinct integrity and value of a working class, which may not choose a path of gentrified consumption and leisure—a ground-level dismantling of all that supports plutarchy needs to occur.

How this can be done in an America that sees a frightening social- ism in any government act while much admiring the boldness of capital- ism's heroic winners, is difficult to see; but re-establishing a transparency to economic mobility is a start. If it is now an arcane, cabalistic matter to reach upward on the ladder, we need to look lower, lower than the middle class. We need to look at the climb itself to the middle class, at the places that formerly had an identity of their own, an identity that would sometimes be unsatisfying and thus encourage advance, and some- times would be satisfying and no advance made. Such choices are gone. No place but the very top will now satisfy us. All the value of being any place but with the rich and famous has vanished, been stolen from us. The middle class is not on a shaky rung only because of an economic diminishment and a subsequent loss of security but also because there is no supporting structure beneath it. There is no beginning to what is middle class because that beginning has been slandered and corrupted. If we cannot have an "Amend the upper classes!" platform, and we wish to resurrect a strong middle class, then our platform should be "Resuscitate the lower classes!" Such has been done in that long period after WWII right up until Reagan. If we can do that again, we can reassemble an eco- nomic and social-mobility structure that defines and describes an egalitar- ian democratic continuum while eliding the present winners/losers arena in which the winners have full presence and the losers, whatever they call themselves, have complete absence. It's mere brainwashing to assume that a cybertech revolution has made it impossible to follow and augment the successes of the past in regard to economic mobility.

The underclass, the working class, and the lower-middle class do not show up in the media in any aspirational way. They do show up as threats to the security of the middle class, which a self-deluded middle class believes is their security but is, in reality, the security of an upper or gentrifying middle class and the top 1 percent. Elections also ignore the bottom 40 percent, except to say they are "moochers." The so-called middle class now statistically looks more like the bottom 40 percent than the top 20 percent and are likewise so absorbed in survival strategies and so filled with rage against politicians—and not the magnates who own the politicians and the ruthless capitalist system that owns all of us—that appeals for their vote shape a tricky and precarious electoral politics indeed. Precarious because the self-deluded middle class does not support a politics directed at reviving the losers by governmental assistance, a strategy that is too easily labeled by Neoliberals as "socialist."

The perennial problem Neoliberals have in making an electoral appeal to the populace is that it is unknown what percentage has woken up to the real conditions of their lives and what percentage remains deluded. Similarly, Liberals run a risk in assuming that this crucial 40 percent is ready for, say, the platform of Bernie Sanders. What Liberals do know is that their Third Way Liberal politics—begun with Clinton, continued with Obama (when he belatedly realized that no one but he was post partisan politics and thus he had to actually "do" politics), and presumably will be continued with Hillary, if elected—is not fit for the times. What that approach has done is distance Liberals from the disenfranchised underclass, the "class that should not be named"—namely, the working class, and a lower middle class that does not look at all like the gentrifying upper-middle class Liberal who finds Hillary so appealing.

In short, Liberals have done as much to sweep everyone below the top 20 percent offstage in electoral politics, as have the Neoliberals. There is a conjuncture of thought here because the brand of zero-sum economics in play is congenial to both parties. They join in the view that every American is on his or her way to the top 20 percent and that the journey there is totally in the hands of a stochastic, casino capitalism. We are to believe that everyone not among the gentry already is in a chrysalis state, always about to be wondrously metamorphosed by virtue of their own freely chosen choices. It is both ironic and unfortunate that Bernie Sanders—who can enact what those not enjoying the fruits of our financialized capitalism, especially African Americans, desperately need—namely, a substantive remodeling of this very system—profiles with African Americans as disastrously as they themselves do with the police.

We are to believe that because nothing has worth until life is fully monetized, until the American Dream of fame and fortune is achieved, there is no sense in recognizing a lesser level of existence, say, the existence of some 80 percent of the population. And yet there is no relief for the buried underclass if some attention to the values of the working class is not paid. If there is no valuing of a working life that produces a well-being in itself and not deferred to some future state of fame and fortune then where the underclass can go remains invisible. All that they can see is a gentrified success that must appear fantastical, impossible to reach, remote, and bewildering.

Most of the factors that created a middle class in the twentieth century have gone away, either casualties of a "wealth drives democracy" credo or a restructuring of the American imaginary to go along with that credo. Thus, the lower-middle class may be diminished, but it does not matter because somehow it is on its way to the top. Meanwhile, the working class is not on its way anywhere because it has become an underclass/moocher class that has lost any serviceable identity. The upper-middle class is busy gentrifying what has been confiscated from the lower rungs of American mobility. The very wealthy, instead of lying low as after the Great Depression, apparently see no reason to lie low after the Great Recession. That may be because they own hearts, minds, and elections, placing great faith in the lobbying power of wealth as well as the seductive and distracting powers of cyber- and cell tech to keep some 80 percent of the population unaware that the middle class is cut off from reaching the manor house and the lower class is cut off from reaching the middle class.

While the underclass is easily and clearly dismissed by both Liberals and Neoliberals, neglect and dismissal of the working class is a more complicated matter. While it seems that within the American cultural imaginary, the underclass is an unfortunate remnant of the Dark Ages, peasant and out of all civilized reckoning, the working class is necessary collateral damage, superseded and scheduled for extinction as a millennial, post-industrial, information/service, robotic, and AI-directed economy moves onward. Because the liberal view is built on the struggles and successes of a unionized working class, it pretends to do more for the working class than advise them to assume personal responsibility and start a business—the neoliberal counsel. Nevertheless, Liberals have been far more attached to a gentrifying/charter-school upper-middle class than to the lower, beleaguered classes. They have gone along with Neoliberals in allowing a fallen middle class to continue to live within a false consciousness both in regard to their own plight and in regard to the underclass and the working class. Such complicity of Liberals and Neoliberals works to confirm the non-existence of both the underclass and the working class. Such complicity works to eliminate the history of economic and social mobility in the United States while maintaining a belief that the middle class has been a fixed center of life in the United States.

The middle class is encouraged even now in this 2016 presidential campaign to see themselves as the 'chosen people,' the ones who can achieve the American Dream if only the underclass were indeed the non-entities we declare them to be and the working class would accept a similar non-entity future that techno-capitalism has designed for them. It is not the wealthy power brokers who are in the crosshairs of the middle class but those who have by choice, birth, destiny, or inadequacies of all variety no chance at all at climbing a ladder of success that only the middle class see themselves climbing. We are more likely to see a revolution against whatever is left to keep the underclass and the working class afloat than a revolution against a stochastic economic system that benefits a few who empower the continuation of that system. And yet there is now movement on the Left to realize the promise and reality of effective economic mobility engineered by a flexible and fluid class structure, a resuscitating dynamic for some 80 percent of the US population—and a proper deflation of our present plutarchic order.

Notes

1. *Truthout,* December 17, 2013.
2. *CounterPunch,* September 18, 2015.

Chapter Fourteen

Portrait of Generation Next

Because I spent so much of my time writing and teaching what I saw as a paradigm jump from modernity to postmodernity, I now recognize the postmodern effects in our new millennium, especially on those we call "the millennials." I feel it in the words shouted at Rappaccini in Hawthorne's story "Rappaccini's Daughter": "And is this the upshot of your experiment!" Madison Avenue hucksters, used-car salesmen, and politicians have always assumed we lived in a post-truth era—namely, that we all say the truth as we know it; and charisma, spin, desire, power, repetition, and volume do more to establish truth than do philosophers and scientists. You need to imagine that in this era of post-truth talk no subject is confined to an expertise, to an authority that can't be breached. In addition, everyone out there is convinced that his or her personal take is as worthy as anyone else's.

What the faddishness of the postmodern view accomplished, I suppose, was a democratization of the post-truth view, which we narrate according to our needs. My narrative, or truth story, has no more legitimacy than your own. It all fits quite nicely into the already-existing American illusions of individual autonomy and the inviolability of personal choice and freedom. No one paid much attention to the corollary that we chose within the boundaries of choices, not only our own but cultural and historical, already made.

In an era when it's not quite clear whose story tells the truth and whose doesn't, some may seek out the truth and hold on to it even more fervently than anyone in history has ever held on to a faith or an ideology. Others, convinced that in this free-for-all of truth stories no one can gainsay their own, hold on fervently to their own opinions on any subject. What you imagine as the consequences of either option are observable in the state of our politics. We find dogged, unpersuadable attachments to one side or the other as well as a dismissive disdain for politics that naysays one's personal opinions. In both cases, confidence is impregnable. Science, whose method underwrites the modern age, now swims or sinks in post-truth waters, observable, for instance, in statistics that show the more confirmed the evidence for human-made global warming is the fewer Americans believe global warming exists. It may be that in the privileged realm of personal choice, many may feel better if they choose not to pay attention to global warming. Those personal choices of course will have no effect on global warming or the science that identifies it. Understandably, it's not the young who ignore global warming but those who reckon they won't be around to see it. But millennials are attached to self-designed realities impervious to societal forces in something of the same fashion as Lewis Carroll's Humpty Dumpty is attached to his own will-to-power.

Caught in what a Pew Research Poll calls "the teeth of the recession" in 2010, 37 percent of eighteen- to twenty-nine-year-olds are without jobs although they have confidence that they will meet their long-term goals. That confidence emerges from a deep detachment from such realities as the Great Recession, a powerful refusal to acknowledge any force outside their own freedom to choose, affecting their own design of their lives. Confidence was only part of what the Pew Poll called "a portrait of generation next." But like all polls, it was no more than a portrait by numbers. The millennials were born into a post-truth era, thrown into a formative cultural surround, which encouraged them to believe that nothing social trumps the personal. Understandably, a great confidence in themselves emerges from this.

Millennials see themselves as 'post' a great deal that occupied previous generations, from racism and feminism to partisan politics, because the history and politics of rendering issues are overwritten by personal determinations. If life is limited to what you personally choose it to be, then your absence from the historical scene is determinative. If also, the past is an extinct entity like a roll of Kodak film, one is 'post' because nothing that rivals or impacts the present came before.

The past is analog, and analog is dead or dying. An astounding transformation is underway, a revolution that the young see as their revolution. Their own Revolutionary Guard are all the young cyberspace billionaire entrepreneurs who boldly, like Steve Jobs and Steve Wozniak, Larry Page, and Sergey Brin, brought us out of the dark analog past. And in 2008, a young politician named Barack Obama came forward and in a brilliant cyberspace outreach to the millennials promised to do a grand delete on old-school politics and so won the millennial vote. But the transformation from partisan politics to post-politics was not as easy a matter as analog to digital. When both Obama and the millennials confront the hard-shell realities of old-school politics, both withdraw in disappointment, although Obama's withdrawal was a wake-up call to the continued existence of partisan politics. The millennials' fallback position was cyberspace, a space they owned. National politics was unreachable because it remained off-line. The true political upheaval would be arranged in cyberspace, the revolution would be tweeted.

On one hand, such illusions of personal will and power do not auger a promising future, once again, rather like President Obama's confidence in the power of his own will to go beyond partisan politics, to overwrite liberal and neoliberal ideological differences, and create a post-politics. On the other hand, the millennial presumptions regarding their own power to change what they've never engaged is like a Blakean dismissal of a falsely perceived world. Such millennial presumption parallels a Blakean presumption that through energy and imagination a radical apocalypse can disclose what encrusts our seeing; and what really are illusions are what we hold as 'hard realities' and intractable 'conditions on the ground.' And when that box suits a very few while the very many not at all, it seems that new designs should be the order of things.

Over the years, I've found in popular culture, headline events, and elections, signs of the millennial life-world and, though in these essays, I naysayed quite a bit, urging implicitly a close confrontation with our 'fallen' politics rather than a perfunctory dismissal, I tried to maintain a dialectic in the end that recognized the limitations of profiling a genera-tion as well as recognizing the difficulties of truly understanding the dual worlds—real space and cyberspace—that the millennials, unlike myself, were born into. The price of experience, as Blake reminded us, is what some buy for a song but others, like Blake himself, work hard to earn and then overcome and go far beyond.

To Gaga Is to Dada[1]

> [P]osthumans lining the road to the future (which looks as if it exists, after all, even though Dada is against it) need the solace offered by the primal raw energy of Dada.
>
> —Andrei Codrescu, "The Posthuman Dada Guide: tzara and lenin play chess"

Rah, rah, ah, ah, ah
Roma, roma, ma
Gaga, ooh, la la
Want your bad romance.

—Lady Gaga, "Bad Romance"

My piece on Lady Gaga's "Bad Romance" simply got into the Dada-esque spirit of the video, imitating Lady Gaga's own brilliant mock/madness exploitation of herself, romance, celebrity, pop music, men, absent the leftist affiliations of the early twentieth century avant-garde movement. The piece was linked online with the Dadasophers:

> Forged in the headache of the memories of the Cabaret Voltaire, The Dadasophers are an improvising collective curated by the eponymous Lord Dada. Suffered a chance formation involving the passive channelling of Sartre and Hegel to the soundtrack of Jünde Szkøro's guitar strings jerking him like a marionette as panpipes plundered. (https://dadasophers.bandcamp.com)

Perhaps the step to take before satire is a Dada-like upset of the normative 'order of things' fashioned by reason, believing as Swift did that "you cannot reason a man out of a position he didn't reason himself into" ("A Letter to a Young Gentleman, Lately Enter'd into Holy Orders by a Person of Quality," 1721).

Let's Gaga.

Empty sexuality of all its narrative baggage.

When at the moment a pastiche phase of "Bad Romance" resembles you and we begin to share a *mon semblable* link, a phrase—"Gaga, ooh, la la"—severs the connect. Only a dis-eased contact, one that gives us no ease is allowed.

Let me try something else.

To Gaga is to stuff the senses to the max, the saturation point. And so I am Gaga in response, so incensed my balls ache, so delighted to be disoriented, swept away, so enticed I am open-mouthed and without words. I am dis-eased. In a state of Gaga, you—and me too—can never be fulfilled. You and I will forever ache and yearn. Orgasm is one costume change away, one beguiling strut, always deferred. There is no narrative path. To Gaga is to Dada. We can't begin so there will be no capstone orgasmic pop. If there is no beginning, there will be a future always. Perhaps. You know, where the orgasm is.

So let's begin.

Let's "bulletize."

One:

Abelard and Heloise tried mightily to defer sex in God's name. He had to pay the price for his eventual Gaga. It's an age of limited spectacle Gaga, dark, repressed. The disease of your mind. What shunted sexuality breeds is there for deep psychology divers to explore. Whatever. We are hype(r)(d)modern now.

Two:

Dark, hidden Gaga needs a release. Marketers channel it into products where no one purchase is the promised happy orgasm so all purchases are enticingly promising. The only future we now know when the world is Ga Ga'ed is what marketers provide us. A whole global culture swims like anxious sperm in the waters of Gaga, of tight leggings and tramp stamps, Roman sandals and slides, push-up bras and fishnet stockings, tight, low jeans and transparent blouses, of Gaga fad and fashion, hot looks and labels of designer orgasms. And so sexuality has no narrative but is designed nonetheless.

Go there and you will find the flesh you seek on endless replay. The DOW rises. Your penis rises. Everything is wet and ready—for yet another replay of Gaga. The orgasm deferred is a promised future. The more you see, the more you want to see. The more your eyes shop for Gaga, the more unstable you become. The frustration lingers and becomes a fever of desire. The dis-ease remains.

We are at the heart and soul, the fomenting fires, of free enterprise.

Three:

Disease becomes Gaga. The most fertile sexual enchantment is the perverted sexuality that remains, the *fleurs de mal* that vanquish—but never quite—the ennui of a hyper-modern, rootless world. "I want your psycho, your vertical stick / Want you in my rear window, baby, you're sick / I want your love / Love, love, love, I want your love." The Lady, like you, hurts and hungers for it. Her appetite is frustrated. She frustrates your appetite. You are mutually tied, you and the celebrity whose life will replace yours—and you will gladly give it. Your death is the price you will pay, and you give it because this is only the spectacle of death, the spectacle of Gaga that will always begin again. Maddening this, though, that this sexy video can promise but never deliver the orgasm you seek. And this Lady wants bad, diseased, perverted, death-risking sex with you. More the lady for that, no?

History could have left us in a courtly-love tradition where the closure of orgasm means less than the ceaseless yearning. Or, it could have left us troubadours forever singing like Arnaut Daniel, or reciting like the immortal Cyrano whose words fly to the heart but, alas, never seal the deal for him. . . . But what does it matter when we have such words! We could have even been left with the romance of classic Hollywood cinema, perpetual Doris Days and Rock Hudsons tweeting toward a climax without penis or clitoris. We could have settled for the fleshless transparency of Audrey Hepburn, a sterility that would surely have pre-empted "Ga Ga." We could have followed Bogey as he heroically walked away from the magnetizing Ingrid Bergman and forever after lived in an aura of Bogart and Bergman romance.

Not to be. To Gaga the world is to delete any attachment with any part of history, including its narratives of romance. In a state of Gaga, one is proudly detached from any past meaning.

We are all Gaga now. Love, as Newt Gingrich told us long ago (?), was a wrong turn. Or, it's merely exhausted, like the meaning of anything. "Rah, rah, ah ah ah / Roma, roma, ma / Gaga, ooh, la la."

Or, what was love has grown up into Gaga, and we see for the first time—well, the fifth time after Ovid, Omar, the Divine Marquis, and Baudelaire—that the flowers of evil smell the sweetest and that 'all bad' in terms of the orgasm is the content we desire. Fortunately, Lady Gaga turns that into something 'all good.' More the lady for that, no?

Four:
Back to history where bad becomes our good, when perversion is all that is left of romance, and that looks and feels good.

A certain decadence creeps in. The moral center cannot hold. We are hype(r)(d)modern now—call it the "new Dada"—when yesterday is not reversed but erased. World enough and time to start again with a pre-moral beginning. Who here wants an orgasm and a side order of moral conscience? Stand up if you want to go full-tilt Gaga without the Hallmark-card romantic salutation? It is cool here on the dark side. Take a risk. Be risky. There's neither heaven nor hell, good nor evil, right nor wrong, sense nor nonsense. Only Gaga. Caution is a condom handed to you by your grandmother; and your grandmother will never lead you to bad romance, which is now what you want. Raw Dog is Gaga.

Maybe Gaga will take your life; but, friend, if you don't lie down with death—as your Lady Gaga does at video's end—you can't Gaga hard enough. And Gaga wants you. Now where everything is happening. Over and over again. Nothing is so endlessly deferred as the deferred orgasm of Gaga or the deferred happiness of retrieving the spectacle you can never possess, that will never be real, though it possesses you and is the only real you will ever know. We are hype(r)(d)modern now.

But maybe you can choose to have the bad romance Lady Gaga promises. Ah, without our beloved "I am free to choose!" would we so relentlessly and endlessly pursue our desire to rapaciously consume the world's body, turn the whole planet into flesh that we eat and empty, let it all empty into nothingness in an orgy of bad romance, a Gaga mania?

Did I say before that we are now at the heart and soul of free-to-choose enterprise, of a personally chosen personal freedom, of a new Gaga Tea Party orgy? "Rah, rah, ah, ah, ah / Roma, roma, ma / Gaga, ooh, la la."

Five:

So we naturally choose to take a trip to the city to see *Sex in the City II*.

Carrie wants to self-design her marriage the way she has self-designed her career, her wardrobe, her hair, her accessories, her apartment. It can't be done is the meaning here. Instructive but there's no Gaga because everyone in the theatre born after 1980 knows that the Gaga of 'just hooking up' will in no way in their lives collapse into Carrie's marriage. Her marriage is pre-Gaga. Old school when romance, love, marriage, commitment, and fidelity, and orgasm were all loaded down with 'historical and moral narrative.' Empty that. Getting off doesn't need a narrative. Or, maybe just a bad one.

But Kim Cattrall's character Samantha Jones delivers the Gaga. She delivers what Lady Gaga only promises—the enthusiastic sex romp, the hearty hump, the sweaty tryst, the screaming orgasm, the healthy fy-uck. In other words, the full Gaga. First, she's banged hard in bed by a young stud, and then on the hood of the Batmobile as fireworks explode orgasmically in the sky. The whole cosmos is alive with Gaga. She'll have it full Gaga, please, which means nothing but the orgasm. Death is never where the orgasm is, *pace* AIDS. Wasn't AIDS something back in the day? We are all hype(r)(d)modern now. "Rah, rah, ah, ah, ah / Roma, roma, ma / Gaga, ooh, la la."

Gaga in the city then is not about marriage in the city, which is, in our new world of Gaga, as dead as history, conscience, narrative, meaning, and all else not on your Facebook site. Marriage is the impossible and unwanted good romance, the one in which the un-Gaga past was bogged down. Bad romance in the new age of Gaga takes it as it comes, all prohibitions aside, sexuality finally emptied of every good romance narrative, every bit of morning-after twinges of moral residue. Gaga does not call for a review of conscience. The dying do that. To be fully Gaga is to be fully alive. Everything else is laid to rest. RIP.

Six:

If we empty the world of narrative—what we say about anything and everything—we are still caught looking, silent and thoughtless, but still looking. The flesh that looks is owed to the sun—the looking itself impossible without the sun. If we empty ourselves of narrative we are still the flesh driven by orgasm. Narrative, call it history, tames and redirects that orgasmic desire just as all manner of narrative distracts us from the simple and undeniable prominence of the sun. Gaga is a return to a narrative-free relationship with sexuality, the primal source, like the sun, of all our desire and yearning; and that desire and yearning is what propels our buying and selling, our getting and spending, our profits and losses, our building and our tearing down. To empty the primordial force of our nature, the *elan vital* of our being, of all vestigial connections, including romance itself, to demoralize and desacralize and deflower it, is to Gaga the world.

I can, of course, as easily explain and demonstrate Gaga as the poets can explain and demonstrate love. But I know that Gaga does not fear death or the pangs of conscience or comprehend the necessary mutualisms of a lasting romance or ask of itself that it make sense or endure, or set out in search of truth, or in search of origin or end.

You ask if it's exportable? Can you Gaga the Koran? Can you go to Abu Dhabi with a purse full of condoms, copulate on the beach, grab a penis in a restaurant? And so on. Can you go full Gaga, which is what the moment demands, what the culture has journeyed to? When the Muslim women take their headdresses off and display the latest fashion—in *Sex in the City II*—Gaga will happen. It's what they want, even if they don't know they want it.

Penultimate bullet:

Gaga is the new *fleurs de mal*. It has no conscience and therefore engages in no moral review, but this is apt as we in the hype(r)(d) modern world have given up reviewing yesterday's orgasm. Gaga has no romantic roots and therefore can never lead to heartbreak. Marketers have us yearning long past heartbreak. It makes no sense and ends the search for sense with a "Gaga, ooh, la la" that completes the project of "Dada, da da da." Millennials go to find the bad romance never touched by aged hands, never witnessed by yesterday's eyes, the kind of romance that escapes all the dead connections, all that history once had to offer, the kind of romance that ends romance. The bad romance Lady Gaga yearns for is yearned for by those who are themselves unleashed from any narrative except what they choose to recognize. The world of Gaga unfriends the dead past. More the lady for that, no?

"Gaga, ooh, la la."

Final bullet:

This is the Gaga Manifesto, *pace* Dada.

The Twitter Moment[2]

But imagine if social tools like Twitter had a way to learn what kinds of messages you pay attention to, and which ones you discard . . . Such attention filters—or focus assistants—are likely to become important parts of how we handle our daily lives. We'll move from a world of "continuous partial attention" to one we might call "continuous augmented awareness."

—Jamais Cascio, "Get Smart," *The Atlantic*, July/August 2009, 97

So my attention turns in the direction of the populace and turns to the film *Twilight*. I think I'm looking for signs of "continuous augmented awareness," and I'm looking where the Twitter generation of the future is looking—at the film *Twilight*.

Bella this time is not the vampire but the young ingénue who falls for a vampire named Edward, who has all the haughty solemnity of Edward Rochester of *Jane Eyre* fame. That Edward's dark secret was not his vampirism but his wife's insanity, the wife locked up in the attic. Edward the vampire's whole family has a family secret also, but they manage to keep it hidden because they don't feast on the blood of humans but only forest critters. There are bad vampires without family ties. Apparently there can be no family or honor among bad gypsies. The good ones though are a solid family unit and their solidarity will protect Bella, just as Snow White was protected by the seven dwarves.

I think even the Disney hookup here is remote in the popular mind. Bela Lugosi as the vampire in *Dracula*? Not a link for anyone born after 1980. And *Jane Eyre's* Edward Rochester? Until an anime version arrives, I feel confident in saying that this is not a link but a grave. Because the film is not, shall we say, interactive with any sort of cultural history, popular or dead serious, it has no fear of déjà vu or déjà heard. Its only fear is that it will somehow smack of the dead, of the grave, of the past, of what's old, over, and adios, of what is so five seconds ago, of all of human cultural history—scientific, literary, historical, philosophical, religious, psychological, and Transylvanian vampire lore. Garlic and crosses reek of a dead past. No tweets there.

Bella and Edward seem cool, contemporary. There's something about *Twilight* that excites the popular imagination. Run through the icons of the imagination at play here: young blood; blood and predation; risky behavior; revenge drama; love and death; thirst and restraint; Peter Pan flight and immortality; kith, kin and family values; legal aliens; libido gypsies; cherry cobbler and spinach salad; a wet Eden; a *Thelma and Louise* mom and a blood-line dad; and a high rebel without sleep or food vibe.

My imagination is first at play with young Bella—adrift and wandering between divorced parents—a mother who is still wandering and a father, a police officer, who polices wandering . . . from the law. I see Bella as at once disassociated from the ways of courtship, love, and marriage that have left her mother and her father what they so clearly are: victims of love. Bella advises a girl friend not to wait for the boy she likes to ask her to the prom but to take the initiative and ask him. Is it too much a leap to say that in wanting to be like Edward she wants a power that no longer leaves her powerless, a potential victim of love? Bella wants to upset the patriarchal hierarchy of love. She wants the power of the male; she wants to be what Edward is, have what he has, be in an eternal, unchanging moment just as he is. She wants to be a vampire, a bloodsucker. A bloodsucker dominates; she is no longer the cocksucker on her knees. This is Bella, not Monica (Monica who?).

I have a memory of the media coverage of Bill Clinton's paramours: cocksuckers all, characterized as such—according to more than one commentator—by taut, hollowed cheeks made so by the demands of the task. Cable-news pundits point out that you can easily see which women regularly practice the act by taking note of their facial features. When women become bloodsuckers, they leave all that sexist stereotyping behind. Bella is looking for a form of liberation, not only from a world filled with disaster, death, and the play of chance but also from a cultural identity that seems so bound and beset compared to Edward's freedom in his vampire moment, a moment that escapes a world that lusts for women as cocksuckers.

I don't know who I'm channeling here and why this is the first association I make with the film but I think it has to do with the many young women I see around me in the movie who are here because they don't mind seeing themselves as Bella. Just part way into the movie, I am wondering if Bella is where they want to be, what they want to be, what they want. So I suppose it's not surprising that I first wonder about her as a champion, as a hero, not as a heroine waiting to be rescued but as a hero who wants what all the legendary heroes have. She will not be a victim. She will be the vampire.

But Bernie Madoff (Bernie who?) intrudes and my imagination begins to bring to life a whole different way of seeing.

We are viewing après le Wall Street debacle and the latest exposure of predatory capitalism. But the moment is filled with a sort of vampirish 'we will rise again' presumption. No one assumes that after all the Wall Street predators have sucked the blood of pensioners, college-bound hopefuls, homeowners, university endowments, cancer-treating philanthropies, local, state, and federal budgets, and the paychecks of the working class and the vacation plans of the middle class, and sent the bottom 40 percent of the population so far into the dark bat cave that if they ever do get out they'll be blind and bloodless—I mean no one presumes that the cycle won't start all over again. Because the recollecting capacities of Americans show less of a return than GM stock, we need now to imagine how easy it will be for the Bernie Madoffs a month or two in the future to get the old Ponzi scheme (Ponzi what?) going again. I mean who's to remember?

Bloodsuckers live to suck more blood. You can use garlic, and you can cross a crucifix, and you can pound a stake into a vampire heart, but come twilight, the bloodsuckers rise again.

So . . . my next imaginative hookup with this film is to think that this is a paean to the protean nature of capitalism where predation is not a wrinkle in time but a built-in genetic disposition and, like the vampire, it runs on only one axiom: more blood! I guess the idealism is youthful: you can have all your blood sucked out and escape being a victim. I mean you'll rise to the level of a predator yourself: you will, like Bella, yearn to be a vampire. For love. I think love for having it all, other people's blood, Nature's free gifts, and the preservation of your own self-absorption, is capitalism's fluid. Some believe love conquers all but at the same time live in a world where love has been commodified, branded, and turned to profit. The compassionate heart has had its blood drained: witness the compassion of the George W. Bush years.

What time is it? It's a time of war, dying, torture, maiming, ethnic, cultural, and religious hate. We Americans have been vampires to the world, though it is refreshing to think that we are the good vampires enjoying a game of superhero baseball with the fam, that we are not the marauding bad gypsies all jacked up on human blood and anxious for their next market. I mean fix. Opening a new market is not at all like opening a new vein. What did Hugo Chávez (Hugo who?) say when he nationalized his oil industry? Americans would no longer suck the blood of his people?

Losers get their blood sucked. Winners do the sucking. Bella wants to be a vampire; love will take her there. We sit in the dark theatre and envy her. The guys want to be like Edward; the ladies want to be like Bella. Suffer death and move through to resurrection where heaven is a life apart with your fam and your kind, your own private vampire world. What ownership! What lovely apartness! Did I confuse Edward's fam with plutocrats? With the have mores who feast without ostentation or privileged entitlement? Edward's family lives apart in the forest in what appears to be a very luxurious compound. They are isolated from the public throng, alone and unmolested in their private space. It's rather like the private, gated space we all aspire to; but right now, at this moment on the American scene, it's where the corporate looters retreat to, a sort of robber's roost, waiting for either an indictment or a government bailout.

A good portrait of American family life in 2009? It is of course sad and tragic to note the unlikelihood of an American resurrection and to note that like the roving gypsy vampires we can see no end to our own bloodletting as our fears urge us to open yet another vein, suck more blood over there to avoid losing own own blood over here.

Bloodsucking has always been sexy; a vampire flick, always a snuff flick. A deadly, dangerous, degenerate love affair here, absorbing a once-aspiring culture now at twilight.

Time to end my channeling of Adorno and his Frankfurt family. Time to get Bernie Madoff out of my head. I can imagine differently about *Twilight*. I come up with a version of Gore Vidal (Gore who?): "Let the tweeting classes tweet." This is not only a blood-sucking moment but a tweeting one and to explain this I need to begin where my imagination begins.

Edward has been seventeen for a hundred years: why fall in love now at this moment with Bella? How many years in high school is that? But Bella is the one for whom he's now willing to break all the family vampire rules. Has no one so remarkable—and I think she is remarkable only because of the camera's steady marking of her—crossed his path before? But Bella is now and not then. She is the present moment and not any moment in the past. And I know, just as I know it is axiomatic for capitalism to suck all the blood it can, that *Twilight's* audience is an audience of now, of the moment. All of history is dead in this movie and unlike the vampire it isn't revived. No one in the audience cares about or even thinks about what Edward might have been doing during his hundred years in high school. For them—and I see the colorful dial faces of cell phones lighting up all around me in the theatre as the Twitter moment trumps the moment of the film—there is only the moment . . . now. Everyone in the audience is Bella, and Bella is now because they are now, in the present only, in an isolated, frozen pulse beat of now, which is so cleverly realized by the newest digital software, Twitter. In the Twitter moment there is no historical curiosity; you living now are privileged.

I am fascinated by the tweeting of the moment, of Twitter and trace, as I try to imagine grasping the meaning of the moment. The Twitter moment is like the trace, the evanescent residue of past and future, which has no presence but is nevertheless the very tissue of now. Derrida (who?): difference and deferring . . . there can be no difference if we are always in the Twitter moment, the moment now and now and now and now and. . . .

I realize our now is post everything: history, novels, imperialism, pennies, welfare, torture, theory, racism, sentences, modernity, public phone booths, postmodernity, socialism, acoustic guitar, feminism, stickball, antitrust, face-to-face conversation, egg creams, post offices, newspapers, copyright, blackboards, and so on. We are of the Twitter moment now. But I yet recall our poststructural chain of signification upon which a notion of difference was built—namely, that what anything meant in the present moment depended on a trace, a difference that was retained in the present from what went before and was deferred until a trace of what came after was disclosed. Interminably. All such traces could never be fulfilled in the present moment now, and so meaning was endlessly postponed, deferred. The Twitter moment depends neither on differences revealed with the past nor on deferments to the future because the Twitter moment makes no allowances for the past, nor has it any room for the past. The past, history does not matter. Neither does the immediacy, the fullness, and independence of the Twitter moment defer to what may come, to any future possibility.

Bella's desire to endure unchanging as Edward is unchanging, to live in an eternal present where past events and meanings have no effect and the future is not to be feared because it will not change you is, I suggest, a rather perfect imaging of the Twitter moment in which not only the millennials but an increasing number of us in this first decade of the twenty-first century now live. The endless chain of signification where the present moment is not allowed to reveal itself fully without traces of past and future, without memory and expectation, has been replaced by the Twitter moment where the now can stand forth totally disconnected from past and future. The Twitter moment can disclose the fullness of the present. All that is needed is the proper technology and the freedom to choose. What is chosen? You choose to make time yours; you choose to stop time at your will and live eternally in the moment of your choice. I begin to see that this is an enchantment not merely of a teen but of a culture.

Bella wants to place herself where Edward is, a frozen moment where time does not matter and the moment can be seized in a self-contained totality. The vampire has brought time to a standstill; there is no progressing or elapsing of time to the moment of death. Nor does tomorrow or the day after or the years after that alter the eternal present in which the vampire lives. You can, if you live in the Twitter moment, ignore without consequence what has come before your latest tweet. Recognition of what has come before, or, what off-line types call "history," immediately sets up difference, and the observation of difference has its consequences: whether it be interpretation or explanation and understanding. The vampire does not live in history but only in the present. This is where Bella wants to be and, I suggest, it's where the entranced audience wants to be. They want to stop time; they want to stop the interpretation of history and the consideration of where our values and meanings will lead us in the future. The Twitter moment ensnares language and therefore meaning within a personal immediacy that satisfies only because it is inexhaustible and replaceable. The source of this is the never-dying, never-consumed embers of our own self-absorption.

And yet, difference cannot exist without history, and history cannot exist without the recognition of difference. History demands that the present Twitter moment be seen as saturated with all past moments, with every tweeted message shadowed by all previous tweeted messages. But such, of course, is not the magnetism of the Twitter moment: its allure lies in its total disregard of what was before, its severing of then from now.

Bella wants that vampire moment in which all of the past and all of the future have been sucked dry and are emptied of all meaning and interest. That is the Twitter moment, a moment that technology and not vampire legend has brought us. Of course, it seems like the Twitter moment has brought us precisely what our globalized techno-capitalism has brought us—namely, a time and place in which all of the past and all of the future has been sucked dry and emptied of all meaning and inter-est—except self-interest and the meaning that branding reveals. A populace has been very rapidly brought by cybertech from all manner of cultural critique—exhaustive, self-reflexive, indeterminate—to a private and per-sonal texting and tweeting which satisfies self-absorption by deflecting language from its worldly connection and back on to the tweeter.

As much as the Twitter moment wants to elide the world and send its messages totally disconnected to anything but the private YOUniverse, it cannot succeed because the Twitter moment is not frozen time but in time. And place. Thus, my seeking to detect its various links to what Adorno and his Frankfurt cohorts called the "historical/material/objective conditions" of the encompassing surround. My own cultural approach is to observe how this overwhelmingly popular film *Twilight* is at play with our terrorized, globalized, economically depressed, techno–bio–capitalist, plutocractic United States now being steered by a pragmatist who is concerned with what works now for as many as possible. What I have noted in *Twilight* is a playing out of private insularity and a yearning to overwrite 'what is' (the Great Outdoors we are not really outside but inside) with a personal dream of impossible separation, a reduction of all expression to what matters now to ME, all time and expression to a Twitter moment. Though the Twitter moment demands by its very superficiality a total social disconnect, this is as much a dream as Bella's to become a vampire, and one that as you can see, has not preempted my strikes into connections, significance, and critique.

I don't see *Twilight* without ties to many films. For instance, when I was Bella's age, my friends and I went to see a movie called *A Summer Place* (1959). It was a must-see film then just as *Twilight* is a must-see film now. Troy Donohue (Troy who?), the newest young movie idol, is the newcomer in town. He's not secretly a vampire, but he does have a summer romance and that, as boring as it seems now, is it and seems to suffice for this audience. It's classic summer love, and there's no promise of eternity. Summer ends and as Keats (Keats who?) counsels, that's a good thing: that things end. Young Troy wants to fit in: the classic young man's quest. Who am I? What will I become? Young love is powerful here, but it doesn't succeed in setting up its own moment. It doesn't succeed in isolating itself from the world. Young Troy's choices do not rule the day. There seems to be no need to suck the world into your own self; rather, the need seems to be to find a place, make some sort of compromise with the world outside yourself. It's a 'free to choose within the constraints of the world' kind of world. There's a 'winter place' too, in other words.

Some years before, my peers and I were magnetized by James Dean (James who?) in *Rebel Without a Cause* (1955). Dean's the new kid in town trying to fit in. He has a problem with his dad who won't stand up to his mom. He's not a secret vampire because in 1955 cybertech had not set up an escapist reality alternative to the movies. The movies are sufficient. They have not been trumped by the cyber creation of a Twitter moment in which the private tweet stops time and displaces space. But now, in the Twitter moment, movies must leave space for interactivity, which means no more than intruding the personal Twitter moment into a world of characters and plot. In a way then, *Twilight* discloses an appetite for the Twitter moment and is itself a product of that yearning. James Dean's Jim Stark, the new boy in town, has problems communicating with his family, struggles to be recognized by his high-school peers and find friends, find a girl who will love him and whom he can love, and, not least of all, come to some peace with his teenage liminality. His identity angst is classic, his rebellion and alienation typifying his generation.

All of this has either slim or no representation in Bella's life. The historical moment is at once dismissed, and all the problems of youth are unattended and eclipsed by the transcending magic of vampire reality. If she gets to where Edward is at, she can leave the world and all its problems behind. It's the quickest getaway from all the problems James Dean's Jim Stark faces. A grand delete and sweeping rejection of everything that is going on in the United States—from Wall Street predation and looting to ambiguous, unending warfare, just as a tweet promises to replace a *New York Times* editorial. When there is only the Twitter moment, there is no surround, no context; the Twitter moment is no more than the context of no context but more context-less than George Trow (George who?) described it in 1980. It is ironic—though irony has been after 9/11 declared finished because the world has now become unambiguously 'real' on cable TV—that multiculturalism and globalism are grounded in a new respect for difference. Any identity must allow that it has no exclusionary rights, must allow for difference. But when one lives in the Twitter moment, there can be no difference for each tweet is a distinct and separate and inviolable reality unlinked to past or future. It is made to be and then not be. Zero and one. Brief presence and then eternal absence. While the depth of history augments and its length grows, the Twitter moment has a mayfly life. Nothing is retained, nothing is meant to persevere, nothing has more meaning or value than "I'm on the bus," which may await the tweet, "I'm off the bus"; but this is neither a meaning deferment nor a historical relationship.

And yet there is a profound surface to the Twitter moment. I say profound in the sense of multiplicity, proliferation, procreation, which is what any search of cyberspace reveals. I call this the Trystero maze of the world as revealed by Google wherein no closure is achieved and nothing definitive or determinate is revealed. What is Google but Pynchon's (Pynchon who?) mystifying mail system: all that is delivered is yet another link, another site. The Great Google is the Great Magog, the biblical country of the invader. The world in this land of Magog and Trystero maze has not been reduced to a Twitter moment where "I'm on the bus" satiates our hunger. The search is endless; disclosure is deferred. The world is not unveiled nor can the present moment stand forth as in any way sufficient. Maze and mystique. Significance is determined by popular usage, popular usage swayed by market persuasion. Dollars rule meaning.

The profound surface of the Twitter moment seems an inapt, inept oxymoron for: in giving up all ties to the world outside the tweeter, including past and future, and reducing language to no more than a declaration of one's movements and moods, all profundity has been relinquished. It seems as if a *nolo contendere* relationship has been set up with any critical mind. In other words, what I'm writing now about *Twilight* is not only too heavy for the film to bear but can in no way be a meaningful connection with a film that has no meaning. I cannot prosecute a critique, but as you can see, I do. You cannot delve into the Twitter moment; it has neither depth nor breadth. There is no Deep Twitter, no Deep Tweet, although it is what I am obviously engaged in. The Twitter moment is the timepiece of the hype(r)(d)modern.

I think Google has profound surface; it searches for links and develops a web-like tracery of interconnected associations to a phrase, a search term. But the Twitter moment, like the idea of Intelligent Design implying a designer, implies a tweeter and that tweeter emerges from a surround, from a time and place, that although it seeks to erase all trace of these, has interconnections and interrelationships with that surround—call it the world—which is not and never has been merely association, phrase, and search. The world is not software, and *pace* Jamais (never?) Cascio, quoted above, who believes we are tweeting toward a "continuous augmented awareness," we tweet as Nero (who?) fiddled.

Living Backward: The Millennials' Alice[3]

We are but older children, dear,
Who fret to find our bedtime near.

—Lewis Carroll, "Child of the Pure Unclouded Brow"

Tim Burton's movies mean what he wants them to mean. The devil in that sentence is that Tim Burton is not fond of meaning, or, to put it in an Alice-way, he sometimes believes in "as many as six impossible things before breakfast." Why would Tim Burton then turn to Alice's madcap adventures? Why would he turn to the Batman, whom he sees as a dark, brooding presence perched above normalcy? Or to Scissorhands, an outcast Wonderland creature hidden just outside Pleasantville? Or to Ed Wood, a movie director who preceded Burton himself "down the rabbit hole"?

There seems to be a thread to follow here, a white rabbit to pursue, although a *Salon* reviewer feels "[t]here's no compelling thread to follow here" (Stephanie Zacharek, "Tim Burton's *Alice in Wonderland*," March 4, 2010). Some years ago I read a review of Burton's *Sleepy Hollow* that found the film to be spectacle without substance. Burton has nothing to say. No compelling thread. But I found in *Sleepy Hollow* the same subject matter Burton had been drawn to in his Batman films, in *Beetlejuice*, in *Edward Scissorhands*, in *The Nightmare Before Christmas*, in *Ed Wood*. I found a confrontation between the conventional and the strange, the social order in its normative mode and what that social order cannot dream of: entrenched, stable identities running into disturbing differences. Running into dreams.

So I'm not surprised that Burton would sooner or later turn to Lewis Carroll's own brilliant forays beyond our inscribed notions of sense, order, reason, logic, and necessity. Doesn't being in our post-post-modern millennial clime mean that we know we live in narrative bubbles of our own cultural creation, have absorbed that shock, and are now just dealing with it? We've gone on. Or are we now, as the White Queen informs Alice, "living backward"?

We go down the rabbit holes of our own creation and are more than queasy about calling a rabbit hole "reality," and certainly in our millennial, multicultural, globalized world nervous about subjecting those in other rabbit holes to the truths and laws of ours. You might say that the millennial mass psyche has caught up with Tim Burton and Lewis Carroll. This may very well be the reason why the *Salon* review found nothing compelling in Burton's *Alice*, and another review found it boring: Burton is no longer presenting what we can't dream of, what we feel we can't master. He's not exceeding—in some provocative, obsessive manner—our grasp. We are complicit with the film's disclosing, co-directors, if you will.

Let's say that since the countercultural sixties, the American mass psyche, its collective imaginary, has been struggling to *not* go down the rabbit hole but stay on rationality and realism's promised golden road to the truth, a road already mangled by the dark detours of twentieth-century modernism, not only in film, art, and literature but psychology and philosophy as well. Now, in our hype(r)(d)modern clime we feel that we've made the jump, by which I may mean many things, and perhaps six of them are impossible. We may have jumped the hurdle of potential disaster and reached the other side where things are quite like what they were. We may have decided that no jump was required and that we had simply made a wrong turn back there and business can go on as usual as long as we trash everything that led us to think we had to jump from the old to the new, from the familiar to the unknown, from one comfortable way of looking at things to an odd way. We may only think we've jumped clear but are actually sinking in dark, odorous muck. We may not choose to jump or know that a jump was required; and if it was required, what had it to do with us if we chose to believe that it had nothing to do with us?

In this last, we've mastered every aspect of the dilemma in a Humpty Dumpty fashion: everything means "just what I choose it to mean." Or not. It's a "living backward" choice and it's one that Tim Burton hasn't made until now, until *Alice*. He has clearly preferred the joys of living backward, of retreating to a realm of Blakean innocence and imagination, but the world outside our own imagination has not been checkmated or even put into check. But what Alice learns is that her choice does put the whole world into check. She wills herself to be master, rather in the way Oprah touts The Secret of Life is a projection onto the world of a personal will. It's also the choice that the new millennial or we generation has made or, more accurately, a jump made and not a choice because choosing requires awareness of choices.

This is too simple, for both Lewis Carroll and Tim Burton. We must be curiouser.

The entire frame of Cheshire Cat questioning, however, which does lay out choices we face—and not simply chop them off by personal decree—is partially the creation of Tim Burton's work. When he began to enframe us within it, he left us with the residue and remnants of agitating dreams, dreams on the edge of understanding, dreams that drew us deeper into themselves so powerfully that they were not ours but somehow ours. If we were moving to a new awareness of ourselves and our world, that work could not be relied upon to be done by the old awareness.

Some of this is expressed in Thomas Kuhn's notion of a movement in paradigms, of whole ways of being in the world, that could not be fathomed rationally because the reasoning of neither side could be invoked but was indeed incommensurable. If, however, we live presently in our hype(r)(d)modern clime within a frame of questioning that remains unresolved and, in fact, includes a sense that the questions have been answered, a sense that the questions have dissolved, self-destructed, and gone away, and a sense that there is nothing to resolve or dissolve if one chooses that there be nothing, then we cannot summon anyone's work as a guide to where we are and how we got here. At the same time, something, as Joseph Heller put it, "happened," and Tim Burton's films are complicit.

What makes *Alice* a revealing departure from Burton's usual imaginative visualization of our mass psyche is Alice's link to "generation we," a "new generation . . . poised to seize the reins of history" (Greenberg and Weber). There are signs here that Burton has resolved, by living backward—the deep-rooted ontological transformation I have been talking about, the question of how to deal with the limitations of entrenched identities and societal norms—and has done so by reducing the whole enterprise to personal choice, will, and determination. Alice learns to empower herself through her own personal choices, which I consider a retreat to a kind of narcissism of the generation we.

If within our millennial clime we are not able to reconcile a conservative desire to ignore any attack made on a resident sense of reason and realism with a radical desire to jump to a new ordering of both, we can make our escape by contracting and reducing the matter to a personal one. We can take the vial that reads "Drink Me" and bring ourselves to a size that allows us to pass through the door and into a new world. Or, we can take a bite of the *petit four* and grow to such a size that everything around us is diminished.

How does generation We, also called the "millennials," exhibit narcissism, and how indeed are they "post-ideological, post-partisan, and post-political?" How does Burton's Alice exhibit an attachment to this generation?

According to the Greenberg Millennials Study (GMS), millennials are highly politically engaged, believe in collective social movements to solve social problems, believe that success is based on innovation and entrepreneurship, are "[d]etermined to find their own solutions to the major problems we face, and convinced that their unprecedented levels of education and technological know-how will enable them to do so," are pragmatic and open-minded and not ideological, are disgusted with the "narrowness, pettiness and stagnation that characterize both parties," are post-political and "ready to call a halt to `culture wars'" (Greenberg and Weber).

A *Journal of Personality* study in 2008 reported a 30 percent increase in narcissism from the 1979–1985 mean. The Pew Research Center Report on the millennial generation "found that today's young people are more diverse, optimistic and technologically reliant than older Americans" (Kate Stanton, *NewsHour Extra*, February 26, 2010). The same *NewsHour Extra* online report quoted Scott Keeter of the Pew Report: "We know that young people tend to be optimistic in the face of tough economic times, but I think it's especially interesting that there's so much optimism considering that there's so much unemployment." We also know that based on curriculum choices, millennials have a post-history attitude, which is most likely not based on Francis Fukuyama's 1992 book *The End of History and the Last Man,* because we know that the millennials are not a book-reading generation—to the consternation of a failing publishing industry—preferring the elliptical transmissions of cyberspace or the texting and tweeting of cell phones.

Descriptive presentations based on survey polls and questionnaires, however monumental, must await interpretation. My interpretation is fixated on a 30 percent increase in what the DSM-IV describes as narcissism, and I therefore read the poll results in this manner: millennials are post-ideological because ideologies have historical roots, which means their solutions overwrite/override personal solutions; post-partisan because partisanship is collective not personal; post-political because all politics is personal for the narcissist.

We conclude from the Obama campaign that millennials were politically engaged but whether that was rooted in a personal engagement responding to Obama's call for "change" and whether this sort of personal engagement will endure remain to be seen. Narcissists respond to celebrity because they see themselves destined for celebrity. Obama achieved that celebrity status during the campaign; but celebrity attentiveness has a short duration, something President Obama is now discovering. And if we logically—not having fallen down a rabbit hole—pursue what change might mean to those who declare themselves "post-everything," we have to conclude that change here means from public to private, from history to now, from politics to personal opinion, from partisanship to personal choice.

If you also consider that the millennials define the "social" as online interaction, and therefore the "social" is no more than you and your friends, the terms "social movements" and "social problems" have vastly different generational hookups. A social movement is an evolving friending Facebook connection, which taps into the narcissist ego, while social problems have to translate into the personal in order to escape an unfriending or a "whatever." Success is based on entrepreneurship and innovation, which only indicates, unsurprisingly for narcissists, that the millennials are not post-techno-capitalism. With them, the American Dream has perhaps a more personal interpretation than Mr. Jefferson would have hoped. Innovation for those who "text about 150 times a day" can mean no more than cybertechnology innovation, which has come fast and furious enough to keep the off-line world at bay and the online world one's own YOUniverse.

I find it interesting that an editor of the Pew Report on millennials finds it only "especially interesting" that the millennials remain confident and optimistic in the face of the Great Recession and what is clearly a deep-rooted unemployment problem. Curiouser and curiouser. Could it be that in losing themselves in their own self-absorption, gone down the rabbit hole of their own design of cyberspace, the millennials don't know enough of the off-line world to be frightened, full of angst, pessimistic? Am I wrong in thinking that confidence and optimism are to be applauded when they persist in the face of a full look at the worst, and that confidence and optimism retained by ignorance is pitiable?

Once again, however, we must be curiouser.

Has not a glimpse or a premonition of the worst that lies ahead prompted Alice to run from her wedding, her vows to a world sunk in a Great Recession and a deep-rooted unemployment problem? Those are not the problems of her world but ours, but consider them proportionally the same. So if the millennials' Alice takes a pause from "living forward," which has clearly not done us a great deal of good, and ventures into a "living backward," is this pitiable or recuperative? If both we and Alice run from a world in which Humpty Dumpty is to decide what anything is to mean, if we respond by living backward, if we return to a personal space, is this irrational? If the millennials are self-inflated, are more absorbed in themselves than in the shaping powers that surround them, is this not defensive for themselves and perhaps rejuvenating for us all "who fret to find our bedtime near"?

Now here's Alice. "Who in the world am I?" the Cheshire Cat asks. "Ah, that's the great puzzle." Burton has answered this question of identity differently than he does in *Alice*, in the *Nightmare Before Christmas*, for example, where the denizens of a Halloween reality try to reckon with a Christmas reality. Santa Claus becomes Santa Claws. Edward Scissorhands, whose reality is shaped by his scissor hands, in the same manner that Patrick Suskind's character Grenouille in the novel *Perfume* knows the world through his nose, his remarkable sense of smell, cannot fit into life in the 'burbs nor can the 'burbites adapt to him. Incommensurable realities. Identity is thus a product of where we are and when we are.

"Who are you?' the caterpillar asks, and any character in a Burton world before *Alice* would say "Tell me where I am and I'll tell you who am I." When the caterpillar is asked if this is the right Alice, he says she's the wrong Alice. The 'right' Alice, according to Burton's script, is the Alice who will slay the Jabberwocky, which she eventually chooses to do. The right Alice, out of the rabbit hole and back to the 'real world,' proposes a trade scheme and earns a place as a corporate intern. What this millennial Alice learns, and quickly holds on to, is that this is her dream and therefore everything around her is subject to her will. She finally chooses to slay the Jabberwocky because she realizes that the need to slay the Jabberwocky has not been imposed on her but scripted by her.

Lewis Carroll's Alice, in Wonderland and through the Looking Glass, does not contract into a self-absorbed narcissist or return a venture capitalist. Her fantastical and imaginative encounters expand a convention-wrapped sense of reality and realism to astounding possibilities and improbabilities, as do dreams. This is not a collapsing of the outside world into a self-empowered subjectivity. Lewis Carroll's Alice is in a world that does not bend to her wishes and expectations but time and again confounds them. Her encounter with Humpty Dumpty is memorable—but not included in Burton's film—for it is Humpty Dumpty who clearly announces the role of power residing not in the individual but power outside the individual that controls our medium of representation: language:

'When I use a word,' Humpty Dumpty said in rather a scornful tone, 'it means just what I choose it to mean—neither
more nor less.'
    'The question is,' said Alice, 'whether you can make words
mean so many different things.'
    'The question is,' said Humpty Dumpty, 'which is to be
master—that's all.'

Who you think you are is not confirmed in Wonderland but inter-
rogated, disarranged, and rearranged. Every reader who leaves Wonderland
and returns through the Looking Glass is hesitant in accepting as complete
what language makes of us and the world; but yet every reader remains
fascinated by how we can imagine beyond—or under—such constraint
and limitation. Burton's millennial Alice thinks the jump from the tired
old place the world is to a garden of wonders is made by simply wish-
ing it, or not.

But perhaps that's not all she thinks and that's not all we are meant
to think. She returns to the real world with all her Bandersnatch scratches
clearly visible on her arm. Her will has not ruled totally in the Underland.
The child matures because even a world of impossible things is a maturing
world, a world that lies outside the rule of our own imaginations. Even
a millennial generation absorbed in its own self-empowerment cannot
long remain in a living-backward state but must learn of power, whether
arbitrary or imposed, outside its own will.

What both Lewis Carroll and an earlier Burton show us is that what
the imagination can conceive and what limited imagination the world is
bound to are two very different places. In believing that we can individually will ourselves outside of this dilemma, we are indeed living backward,
returning not only to late eighteenth-century notions of the power of
Ego and imagination but to notions of early human development, what
Freud called a "polymorphous perversity" by which infantile desires and
appetites could absorb world into Ego. But childhood, as Lewis Carroll
knew, is the place where the imagination lives, where it does not yet
comply with a Humpty Dumpty rule, where it can break that rule and
move on. To rediscover that is a living backward, a return to childhood
innocence and imagination, what the Albert Finney character Edward
Bloom, in Burton's *The Big Fish,* yearns to do. The millennials' Alice
then is living backward, before—not post—politics, partisanship, ideology.
And this may be, after all, the wisest response, curiouser and curiouser,
impossible as it may appear . . . until we note that the self-absorption of

the hype(r)(d)modern has only a narrowed, hyped responsiveness to the world. And there is not even a Mad Hatter wisdom in that.

Our Millennial Age of Magic[4]

I have bedimm'd
The noontide sun, call'd forth the mutinous winds,
And 'twixt the green sea and the azured vault
Set roaring war . . . graves at my command
Have waked their sleepers, oped, and let 'em forth
By my so potent art.

—Shakespeare, *The Tempest*

[T]he central idea of the Enlightenment: that we get to know for ourselves who we are, by seeking evidence, using reason, and coming to thoughtful consensus on truth.

—Alice Dreger, *Galileo's Middle Finger*, 2015

Remember that your thoughts are the primary cause of everything.

—Rhonda Byrne, *The Secret*

Magic was troublesome to both what Anne Fremantle called "The Age of Belief" and to the birth of science and the Enlightenment, though it was entangled in both. Magic's close attention to Nature in order to discern a connectedness invested in the animate and the inanimate, in birds and bushes, rocks and streams, earth and stars, prefigured science's own turn from medieval scholasticism to rigorous empirical and rational methods. Thus, magic abused Church dogma with its notion of a pantheistic power that could be tapped into and give humans control of all things. Shakespeare's Prospero has this power until he abjures it. Those who believed in magic assumed that the world could be bent at human command, a heresy that violated the Catholic belief that the world was created as a celestial entity wished it to be.

Scientists, like magicians, studied the natural world "by seeking evidence, using reason, and coming to thoughtful consensus on truth." They sought to understand what was previously a celestial province, and then to adapt it, make us of it, and profit from it as humans saw fit. The Enlightenment did not buddy up with magic but instead condemned it as, in the words of Bertrand Russell, "superstitious rot and nonsense" that it was reason's mission to obliterate. There was to be no détente with magic as had been sought between reason and faith via Aquinas.

Magic ruled in what the enlightened saw as a "Dark Age" in which all forms of irrationality filled the world, from the magical evocations of words, symbols, rituals, and a myriad number of 'algorithms' connecting disparate things to the configuration of faces and gestures, constellations and Nature's rhythms. The world was replete with bafflements, deep-down secrets, futile and adept mastery, prodigious study of pattern and chance. Church dogma brought it all to heel within its own circumscriptions and prescriptions, a 'Common Core' rule book that outlawed the presumptions of personal domination of the world that magic promised. Science too cleansed magic of its irrationalities in regard to a magical Ch'i, which wove through all, human and not human, and it did so through the universally accepted universal rod of the scientific method.

Our new millennial-age magic is a different sort of magic, not a renaissance of magic as it existed historically as a thorn in the side of both religion and science but a magic, nonetheless, in that it has, so to speak, old-time magical properties. The attributes or traits of millennial magic do not require an abracadabra for access.

We see first a determination that what is fact is what is personally valuable or of personal interest. Attendant with this is a suspicion of and distaste for all authoritative judgment. More prevalent than distaste is disinterest, especially in the possible existence of any commonly accepted rules of judgment, these viewed as challenges to the authority of personal opinion. Dismissal and disinterest are reactions to the past, because the past not only is analog but also has no personal dimension and therefore offers no interactivity, no chance for the personal to override what history has already implanted. Although technology is itself held as magical and is the medium for self-transformation, its potential as a public forum of truth and reality remains, though, in a constant battle with a desire to reduce it to the dimensions of personal will and individual uniqueness. What persists is a magical sense that truth and reality are unique to every individual who undertakes a personal journey, both off-line and online, to forge that uniqueness. Magical thinking empowers the self to have power over all, to believe that 'your thoughts are the primary cause of everything.' Such personal empowerment is achieved through the maximization of personal choices and the freedom to make such choices.

We can observe this millennial magic operating in a variety of domains.

Science today is an authority much challenged, its methods under suspicion in that they seem adaptable to cultural and political priorities and to capitalist needs. Once revered as universally applied and acknowledged, these methods now seem relative to various dispositions of time and place. We do science, Thomas Kuhn has told us, within paradigms that are more fractal than connected and continuous. We observe what we are disposed to observe, Paul Feyerabend asserts, that theories do not emerge from facts but the opposite is true. What may proceed objectively and disinterestedly may originate in cultural biases, assumptions, and brute capitalistic power, or what a later age may see as totally irrational, phlogiston, for example, or Wittgenstein's story of the scientific pursuit of how mice are born out of old clothes in dark closets. The authority of science seems like that of Louis XVI before Bastille, weakened, corrupted, always under indictment.

Climate change, for instance, is not a Common Core issue, an issue upon which we all join in agreement but an issue waiting for personal response, ranging from not an issue at all to a doomsday issue. The same dispersal of a universal response to a personal one is observable in regard to GMOs, vaccinations, and evolution.

The social sciences have lost even greater authority than the natural sciences, perhaps because of a sixties association with liberal agendas which themselves now seem quaint in an increasingly conservative America. Education is a battleground of opinions regarding not only what students should be learning but whether tax-funded charter schools are better than public schools, and whether a Common Core and the testing to maintain it are good or bad. Home schooling seems now more aligned to personal and family values as opposed to governmental imposition on personal choice. Public education, like all things public, offends the magical sense of personal power. And while no one accepts an authoritative voice that speaks for all in regard to economic issues such as the deficit, jobs, entitlement programs, tax reform, wealth redistribution, robotics, deflation, gentrification, wages, and much more, there seems to be a common acceptance of all parties that market rule can be tweaked but not overhauled. Magic, science, and faith seem to combine universally in our allegiance to market rule and the technology that greases its wheels of profit.

Politics, of course, is the domain in which the millennial magic zeitgeist really comes into play. President Obama's Affordable Care Act, which has so far about twenty million enrolled, is an enraging red flag across party lines. Any attempt by 'Big Government' to put aside a personally acquired sense of reality and truth is attached immediately to socialist domination. The idea that there is such a thing as 'society,' which Margaret Thatcher assured us there is not, a society of others that has some claim on us, is comparable to forcing a Renaissance magician such as Giordano Bruno to bend to the will of Church authority. The popular attachment of a liberal view with government as an answer to all problems sets that ideology against not only the millennial magical mindset but also against the American grain of individual autonomy and personal freedom.

Built into the liberal view that has, especially since Clinton's Third Way, leaned into neoliberal positions, is willingness to compromise. As compromise involves an acknowledgement of the validity of the views of others; it pushes millennial magic toward accepting an authority over and above the personal that has legitimate credentials. That act of self-deferral in the face of the reality and truth not one's own but the other's is less and less observable in our millennial magic climate. The neoliberal position in the United States, however, stays close to the bone of millennial magic logic in its view of compromise as a bad thing, to be placed alongside the illegitimate authority of Big Government and the personhood behind it, in this case Barack Obama. He is caught driving against millennial magic traffic by personifying the liberal view as well as Big Government. The fact that he is caught driving while black is both a back-in-the-day analog issue as we now see ourselves as "post-racist."

We are only able to see ourselves thusly because our heads are now deeply within the mist of magic. Within that mist, we each can personally decide to announce ourselves as "post-" whatever has no personal interest to us. Racists choose to be post-racist as young women now see themselves post-feminist, joining the men who are so eager to make the same claim. In the magical mist, we are post-politics, post-Nature, post-egalitarianism, post-welfare, post-postal, post-getting any kind of a return on a simple savings account, and soon to be, apparently, post-driving, and for 47 percent of the population, according to Tyler Cowen's *Average Is Over*, soon to be post-job.

When you reside within the millennial magic mindset, a great deal that was the backbone of what philosopher John Searle called a "Western tradition of rationality and realism" under attack, at that late-twentieth-century moment, by Derrida's deconstruction, is erased. Politics is no longer the art of compromise but a villainous enterprise in a public guise and acceptable only when kept within the boundaries of personal choice. The idea that society forms government in order to preserve, as in the

United States, a democratic order of things and that rationality is the fluid or medium that allows us to communicate and achieve ends beneficial to that democratic society is challenged by the millennial magic mindset. The idea that the fallout from a Wild West form of capitalism has undermined democracy or that a social democracy or a democratic socialism would best serve the many rather than merely a few cannot arise within our magic mindset. Solidarity working for the public good has no place in the millennial magic mindset.

Ironically, this mood of dealing with the world through a magical personal empowerment rebels angrily against everything but what most seriously encroaches upon that personal empowerment.

Market rule has perfected a form of branding that structures the surround within which millennial magic takes place. The societal and political turmoil that results when we live in a magical sense of truth and reality is yet reached by brands which compete, unhindered by societal and political consensus, which would limit both the range and the power of branding's seductions. The battle to win minds in our magic world is a branding battle, one in which ownership is secured while the illusions of magic, and they are many, are not disturbed. Ideas of what a democracy is, what freedom is, what reason and truth may be, what reality we are in all now exist in a marketplace that capitalism knows well.

Most disastrously, those who are on the wrong side of the wages/dividends divide live within the many distractions of technology that nourish the growth of a millennial magic mindset. They stand fast at the elixir of their own individually concocted empowerment, the allurement of dominating all obstacles, while it seems clear both market rule and technology are taking us toward what John Lanchester in a review of Erik Brynjolfsson and Andrew McAfee's *The Second Machine Age* and Tyler Cowen's *Average Is Over* refers to as a "hyper-capitalist dystopia" ("The Robots Are Coming," *London Review of Books*, March 5, 2015).

Yet another irony resides in the fact that there seems to be impeccable reasoning behind the millennial magic mindset, almost an algorithm for the future that cannot be denied or opposed. Lanchester quotes an interview with Larry Page, founder and CEO of Google: "[I]n a capitalist system . . . the elimination of inefficiency through technology has to be pursued to its logical conclusion." And so, magical thinking finally finds a welcome that both science and faith had denied it. This millennial magic has found its place in a Western tradition of rationality and realism truly transformed, as base metal into gold, to nurture and endorse the illusions of magic.

Notes

1. *popmatters,* October 7, 2010.
2. A different, expurgated version appeared in *The Journal of Popular Culture* 43:4, July 19, 2010 as "The Twittering of Twilight."
3. *Bright Lights Film Journal*, April 30, 2010.
4. *Bad Subjects*, September 19, 2015.

Chapter Fifteen

Occupy Wall Street

Epilogue to the Kindle Publication of
Occupying Here & Now: The New Class Warfare

I self-published *Occupying Here & Now: The New Class Warfare* through
Amazon's publishing arm, CreateSpace's Kindle, while the OWS (Occupy
Wall Street) movement was still making headlines. My intent was to not
wait the two years or so the dozen or so books I've contracted with
university press or commercial publishers usually take to get to print. I
didn't know how long the OWS interest would last and I wanted to be
timely. With the help of Einar Nordgaard, who administers my website,
we got copies ready for sale quickly enough, and the book was available
while OWS was still in the headlines.

I got into Amazon's politics before Hachette took on Amazon over
who should set the price of books: the publisher or the distributor, a battle
that Walmart had won with its own suppliers. Who sets the price is not
my beef. Nor will I take the stand that the last horse-and-buggy enterprise took when the automobile showed up. Physical books are becoming
e-books for economic reasons that cannot be challenged. I prefer a physical book to read but my Kindle is loaded with sample pages of books
in which I'm interested. If I decide to read the entire book, I don't buy
but library loan. Former librarians tend to do that. The problem I see
with e-books is the same problem I see with cyberspace and cell phones;

namely, we are so awash with words, or more likely, a lexicon of abbrevia-
tions, acronyms, emoticons, selfies, videos, and demotic transcription, that
we've been driven into private domains of interests that have evaporated
a public domain, a shared cultural literacy.

"If anyone can publish a book, won't we have more books published? More voices are heard not less, and it doesn't stop anyone with
a strong point of view, I don't see how that's bad," David Pakman, a
venture capitalist states ("Amazon vs. Hatchette: The Battle for the Future
of Publishing," Knowledge@Wharton). I do see how that's bad, and my
own experiences led me to this opinion.

I saw OWS as a first sustained protest recognizing how serious the
wealth gap had become and how disastrous an oligarchic society was for
young non-shareholders. I surmised, along with many others, that OWS
could be the beginning of a serious interrogation of a form of capitalism that was in play in the United States. Alongside numerous other
"fast" responses to OWS resulting from an Amazon search of "Occupy
Wall Street," my book, without marketing and reviews and any publicity,
got lost in the queue. I don't think it fell behind because better books
were out there, but rather there was so very much out there that the
question of quality couldn't be entertained. And much of the "so much"
was not being entertained in books but on Facebook or hashtag sites.
Like everything else, OWS had been privatized even though it started in
a real physical place.

No one wanted to buy someone else's take on OWS when everyone
had his or her own, at least those who were drawn to the protest. Why
buy a wordy book when a hashtag discussion on Twitter or some posting
on Facebook was quicker and easier?

I saw then that I had, for insufficient reason, become complicit in
what I now see as an undermining of critique by swelling the digital
piles of the written word to an unmanageable point, from a reader and a
reviewer's perspective. And in offering an easily accessible market in which
all thought and imagination is leveled and without distinction, the view
that 140 characters is as good as 200 pages and therefore better because
it's briefer is equally disastrous to the intellectual and imaginative life of
all. I'll take 140 characters from Wilde or Dr. Johnson and some few
others. The domain of mastery is not large.

I was, in effect, the author of a Kindle book about OWS competing
with a faceless crowd of other Kindle authors writing about OWS, all of
us equal in a democratization of writing and writers. And the Bezos boys
I had teamed up with were doing all they could to turn authorship and

publishing into widget production, knocking any gatekeepers of distinction out of the way, pushing volume the way Walmart does or McDonalds and doing so by reducing the whole enterprise of writing and reading to a mosh pit in which everyone was free to write, sell some copies to friends, and then get swallowed up or trampled and disappear.

Everything caught in the net is cast on deck, though little of it may be edible. This is not a problem as the Knowledge@Wharton article covers the matter: "Pakman argues that editors who can recognize and recommend good literature will not disappear when the industry is digitized." Instead, "curation becomes very valuable. I might even pay someone with good taste to tell me what to read," he says. "You can still have people in positions of authority finding good stuff. [Digitalization] doesn't suppress good work" (http://knowledge.wharton.upenn.edu/article /amazon-vs-hachette-battle-future-publishing). Converting a printed book that has already gone through the traditional submission and publication process doesn't suppress good work, but preempting that process buries a future Pynchon in a gravel pit of vanity-press publications. Crackpots cranking out some pages in their basements (I choose the top floor to do my own cranking) queue up on an Amazon search along with 'good work.' And curation of e-productions is indeed valuable but possible only within the traditional system that electronic production is eliminating. Digital curation would be no more than yet another site in cyberspace, another site on Amazon, lost within what it is designed to bring to gatekeep.

The gatekeeping establishment comprised of agents, publishers' readers, editors, reviewers, and critics were gotten out of the way as so much impedimenta to individual freedom. "Information wants to be free," though money and property remain in protected facilities. What is really occurring is that thought and imagination are being deflated in value in the same way that in a market economy everything that floods that market loses value. The presence of a creative and intellectual life is different in kind from the presence of real estate or fossil fuels. If new construction floods the market with houses, construction shuts down. If we are flooded with words, online and off-line, reading shuts down. A shared meaning of anything shuts down as we either become ingrown in our own words, attack meaning itself by restricting words to 140 characters, or we attend the words that plutarchic wealth drones in our heads.

We are reaping the chaos that Amazon has wrought, a chaos wherein everyone is a writer and a critic, and therefore there are no more writers or critics. We are awash and drowning in digital piles of words, "so gigantic, unwieldy and unreadable that sometimes we wind up working with no information at all" (Abigail Zuger, "Repeating The Mistakes of History," *New York Times*, October 14, 2014).

But the gates are down, let ten thousand flowers bloom, so many that if someone cried "Fire!" we couldn't hear it, or so many would be shouting "Fire!" that we wouldn't know where to look. I don't see this as a conspiracy to silence critics of plutarchy but nevertheless a situation that prevents us from seeing plutarchy for what it is, like the way the forest prevents us from seeing the trees. It hardly matters that in a gathering of a dozen people, all minds are being formed by personally selected domains of reading, so many that we are all isolated in our own opinions or friending those who share them. The 'one book' venture is an attempt clearly to get folks on the same page so social communication can go on beyond the level of Facebook where I post my life and you post yours and we're both "whatever" about dialogue or dialectic.

The sort of democratization of publishing and reading that Amazon offers has always been the tool of capitalism in every domain except the domain in which "the pen is truly mightier than the sword." While I was very supportive of the City University of New York's move from elite standards for admission to an open enrollment wherein more minds were given an opportunity to learn, this analogy doesn't fit Amazon's eliminating the existing criteria for publication and turning books and reading into confusion. This is a confusion of choices all represented equally except for price. This is a confusion that undermines what we know: there are few among us who can either imaginatively or intellectually and sometimes both represent the world to us in a way that enriches our lives. When the works of those few are inundated as the writers are themselves with the intellectual and creative efforts of everyone on the planet, then no pen is mighty but all fade into an over-saturated mist.

The imaginative and intellectual life of a culture collapses when brought to a lowest common denominator level. Amazon's campaign against any flowering of imaginative and challenging writing through the gauntlet of agent, publisher, reviewer, critic, and deserved reputation is, to my mind, a terrorist attack on the American mind and imagination. To repeat, as Karl Rove suggests, when everyone is a writer, no one is a writer because the distinguishing criteria by which the identity of "writer" is formed is non-existent. When words are written in a world in which their primary appeal is their brevity, and their power to challenge and disrupt must comply with a 'Like,' words lose all meaning, all magic, all their potential revolutionary force. When we are enriched only by our own words, we suffer the same end as a plant whose roots circle back into itself. When a tsunami of communication hits us daily, our own curating is our only defense and also the worst defense.

Psychomachia: Battles within the American Cultural Psyche[1]

In terms of real geography, say, of park, street, countryside, or plaza, or in terms of battle, a battlefield, almost everywhere in the world, the Occupy Wall Street movement has not executed a successful coup d'état. The Wall Street order of things is humming along, mostly indifferent, slightly amused, sometimes annoyed by OWS. In the money-making scheme of things at this moment of continued economic crises, Wall Street traders, hedge-fund quants, and financial institutions that are now, post-2008, so much bigger and therefore so much more impervious to failure, see opportunities to make a lot of money. No, OWS has not led a successful coup.

However, if the coup that is attempted is designed to overthrow an order of things in the mind, in this case in the American mass psyche, or what I also call the "American cultural imaginary"—the subliminal ways in which we see ourselves—I contend that that coup of the mind is still going on, is on the boil so to speak. It's a coup that has already overturned much of the allure of a wealth aristocracy, of an 'affluenza' that led to debt for the many, of Wall Street market 'players' as our champions in the global arena. It's a coup that has brought a truly astounding wealth divide and its effects on our democracy out of the shadows and into view.

To understand the importance and impact of this psychic coup, it's necessary to examine the psychic terrain, the psychic chessboard, so to speak, upon which all our pieces are set up. And like the game of chess, it's an antagonistic chessboard with all the pieces at war. A psychomachia or battle of the psyche, is derived from a medieval allegory by Prudentius in which vices and virtues battle for control of a man's soul. I appropriate this notion of a spiritual battle in ways in which opposing imaginaries within a mass cultural psyche, in this case American, erupt into our conscious, rational awareness with varying levels of force.

As William Blake reminds us in *The Marriage of Heaven and Hell*— "What is now proved was once only imagined"—our rationality and the arguments rationality produces originate in our imaginative grasp, an enfolding of what the world presents us within an encompassing way of seeing, picturing, and narrating. This means that there is a prereflective, prethinking about, affective assembling that goes on in us that must be reached if any change, any coup, is to take place. A successful coup on this terrain is not immediate but plays out like the drama of dream wherein time, like reason, fact, and logic, cannot be calibrated, and duration opens and closes as in Wonderland. Because we are not imagining the world the way we do, the way the winners now imagine the losers, the way the Tea Party imagines Obama, because reason has not led us into this, we cannot expect reason to lead us out. We cannot expect a coup on psychic terrain to be led by argument, debate, discourse.

The first and briefest part of *Occupying* describes the various pieces on our present psychic chessboard. Like a good chess players, we need to study the board for the game has been going on for quite some time. You could say that where all the pieces are now, strong and weak positions, began with the first moves of President Reagan. This is not to say history has not before seen such an arrangement, but there are new and powerful forces on the board, not the least of which is an unchallenged globalized free-market techno-capitalism.

What follows this examination of the game board is a look at OWS in terms of changing notions of class warfare, ending in a confounding of roles as the have-nots and have-less-each day assume the identity and political views of the haves and have-mores. Ideologies and arguments resulting are displaced (in the sense of placing alongside) throughout with the drama of battling affinities and psychic forces and valences, mythos and fable, spins and narratives. If we all are engaged in picturing the world in one way or another, and the world we are in has tied picture-making, spectacle and spin, narrating and narrative to profit, and the business of that world is profit, then we must suspect that we ourselves are pictured for profit. We must suspect that the way we imagine anything has much to do with the way profit making pictures the world. We must suspect that our representing what we see, our bringing into ourselves what is outside ourselves, is a mediation of the world. And that mediation in a capitalist society is a branding for profit, and therefore we can expect that it is done masterfully and done for us. We do not enter a world we make but rather a world already branded for our consumption. Thus, a prefabricated imagining of the world is instilled in the world. This is the world within which we are 'free to choose.'

Because *Occupying* is not a progressive, continuous argument with a conclusion or resolution that clearly results but an attempt to affect the grounding ways in which we imagine the stage upon which we now find ourselves, and an attempt to follow OWS on this stage, I employ repetition and volume for dramatic force on this psychic stage. There is an undeniable power here as when something resonates, like old TV jingles and snatches of lyrics from long ago, or recurrent images in dreams that can't be deciphered. The kind of change we need now requires this deep underlying change in the way we imagine the world, ourselves, and, especially, others.

Occupiers Break Through: We Are the Ones We Have Been Waiting For

Admittedly, we all seem to be in our own media biospheres.

Conservatives prime the pump of their conservatism through Fox News, the *Wall Street Journal* editorials, the *New York Post*, the *Weekly Standard*, the *National Review*, columnists such as Peggy Noonan and Charles Krauthammer, and hard-right squawk-radio gurus such as Rush Limbaugh, and online gurus such as Matt Drudge; liberals prime their pump with MSNBC, the *New York Times*, the *Nation*, columnists such as Paul Krugman and Seymour Hersh, as well as Arianna Huffington's *Huffington Post*. Feel free to extend this list on both sides.

Most of the young now occupying Wall Street get their news through social networks, now predominantly Facebook, which is where a dazzling amount of Internet surfing unloads its links. The air in that cyberspace is not as restricted or localized as in our traditional media biospheres. There's a great deal of anonymity to authorship in cyberspace, which means thought is not tagged at the get-go as it would be for instance in an op-ed piece with a Paul Krugman byline. Get ready for a liberal line. Anne Coulter is not going to give Obama any slack. And so on.

There's also a way in which not only characters dissolve into a "whatever" wash, but plot does also. By plot, I mean both contemporary context and history. For instance, when Herman Cain was asked what he thought of neoconservativism, the ideology that drove American politics from 2000 to 2008, he said the word didn't ring a bell. He's not young, but he's 'context-free,' which might be seen as a 'bad' thing for those who want candidates for the presidency to know recent political history but a 'good' thing for those for whom context goes no further than yesterday's Google search or yesterday's Facebook posting. If the world has gone to hell in a handbasket, whatever that means, why pay any attention to the characters and plotting that got us there? The idea that history is a prelude to the present vies with the idea that history has all the significance of yesterday's tweet.

I have a view of what politics will be like when the radically divided media biospheres fade away and all is mediated and communicated through personalized social networking. In a way it's the anarchist Max Stirner's dream come true: a politics of dispersal in which no institution can trump an individual's personal determinations. There might be more small enclaves already represented in the myriad online cluster blog sites, which have their devoted followers, your acknowledged friends on Facebook. Your social and political world could easily be represented in the apps on your smartphone as well your cell's instant-dial address book of friends.

So as the rising generation, the millennials, move toward a fractured, personalized, self-and friend-designed means of political and social communication, market-backed media remains consolidated. This state of affairs explains the much-noted political disinterest of university students: they've taken politics and protest into the closed reserves of their own personal interests.

Meanwhile, back at the ranch, a neoconservative ideology that wants to win as much as it can of the world before the Chinese gain contesting hegemony, and a financial sector that has gone Wild West in its pursuit of profits anywhere/anyhow, and a wealth gap that makes prerevolutionary France look egalitarian . . . all this remains "whatever" to most Americans, but most especially the eighteen- to twenty-nine demographic.

The conservative media is on the offense while the liberal media is responding with a 'cult of balance' and the leftists are no more than boogeymen to pull out of the closet to frighten the independents. Of course, the bottom 40 percent of the population are feeling the pain of policies that demonize them as lazy losers hoping to suck the blood of the industrious winners. Some are too stunned by life's travails to vote, others see no rescue between two candidates, one waiting till they're scrunched into extinction while the other accepting this inevitability regretfully, and some decide to join the Tea Party and take up the cause of their oppressors.

It took an event—Occupy Wall Street—to force a reinterpretation of what's been going on, especially with the young.

The United States remains a middle-class country, a middle class fast descending to that bottom 40 percent of the stunned, but still a country that produces educated citizens. We have now on hand graduates—high school, college, postgrad—who have not graduated into career-launching jobs. That too gets out on Facebook; the disenchantment grows. This is a population that has not yet been part of the American Dream, so there's no house that's mortgaged, no job they'll work 24/7 to hold on to, no dependent family tempering their growing radicalism. They may be yearning in the trumped-up way Madison Avenue has us yearning, but that yearning is unfulfilled, and there is not a sign of any future fulfillment, a fearful lack considering the average student-loan debt is $28, 950 per borrower.

Most especially, this is a generation that has an anonymous sense of politics and history and the characters who play and have played major roles. In other words, they are 'very upset' but have not the prefab narrative to jump to in response. They are not joining the knife fight in a phone booth that has been American politics for three decades.

The Occupiers are not joined at the hip to any political ideology. This is why candidate Obama's post-partisan claim, his promise to rise above ideology was so appealing to the young. They are more than willing to rise above what they have already been "whatever" about. They are already post-history, post-politics, post-books, post-*New York Times* and the *Weekly Standard*. Obama's failure to deliver on a fantasy pledge is a major reason why he is not the hero of Occupy Wall Street. He himself was scrunched by a deeply divided politics and a long-term memory, which could not be erased. It was what we called before postmodernity, "reality."

Once again, the Occupiers are not joined at the hip to any political ideology. This is why presidential candidate Ron Paul's libertarianism, his promise to do away with government departments, taxes, wars, end the Federal Reserve, regulations, entitlements, public schooling, Obamacare, and so on is so appealing to the young. Ron Paul disdains the characters and plot of politics in the same way they do. His disdain, however, is narrowly directed: away from free markets and toward any infringement of its free play.

Anarchism has a legendary appeal to the young, but the anarchism of the libertarians does not extend to Wall Street. You will not find Ron Paul in Zuccotti Park supporting Wall Street and free-market capitalism as a target. He would instead point to the free market to liberate the Occupiers from their discontent. The present plight of the Occupiers is a result, in the libertarian view, of markets not being free enough. In Ron Paul's view, lack of such freedom caused the Great Recession, which has sent 80 percent into hard times. On the other hand, it seems fairly clear that we're all living in the disastrous climate of an unregulated, unbridled Wild West brand of global capitalist financial finagling.

Ron Paul and the libertarians may be the biggest boosters Wall Street has ever had, but the Occupiers know their target. They can't, as Don Corleone would say, be reached by a system that has kept them unemployed and in debt. They can't be lobbied, threatened with no campaign contributions, promoted, given stock options, and all the rest. They have never tasted the fruits of the system. Some may want to and some may want to undermine it. All may want to be simply not cast aside.

The problem on the Occupiers' side is as follows: how far do you need to go toward rebellion in order to achieve a goal of recognition, acceptance, and admittance? And, much more difficult: if you go beyond admittance to change, how is that achieved? The problem on Wall Street's side is they don't know how to give the Occupiers what they want. The 'invisible hand of the market' just doesn't do justice or humanity or democracy. Creative destruction happens axiomatically when the market no longer needs you. Capitalism is not set up to interrupt that.

Unencumbered by any deep ideological attachments or any sense of the turbulent history of our present ideological divide, the Occupy Wall Street protesters are free to focus on what's before them. They live in a society in which about twenty Americans now own as much wealth as half of all Americans, a society in which the Wall Street financial sector continues during and after the Great Recession to receive huge bonuses and stock dividends, a financial sector that is holding their notes on the financial aid they've received for an education that has led them to unemployment. This is also the age group that has 'volunteered'—read here without any other 'career' choice—to fight wars in Iraq and Afghanistan that have made huge profits for private contractors and steady dividends for shareholders while the warriors themselves have come home—or not—to unemployment. Profit has been made on the marketable frontier of the young, profit made in their education and in the blood shed in wars; and cybertech seemed to be the soma that kept them silent and unresisting.

Driven to the wall by a society in which the winners care little about them, the young have broadcast their frustration and anger on their cell phones and on their Facebook pages. They have recruited and mobilized by using the very media that seemed to have created a detachment of the individual from any social concerns. Now the society of the young and their concerns finds its expression in cyberspace and has reached an actualization in the streets. The two reinforce each other, expression and action, action and expression, in a manner that bypasses a traditional media, a media that has not yet learned to probe and question in any way helpful to the Occupiers.

In other words, Occupiers have broken through the traditional media biospheres whose failures and inadequacies, whose biases and cover-ups, whose own incestuous ties to money and power are at this Occupier moment as clearly exposed as an emperor without any clothes.

Note

1. *Occupying Here & Now: the New Class Warfare*, CreateSpace for Kindle, 2012. Excerpts.

Chapter Sixteen

Travels of a New Gulliver

> *[T]he two great empires of Lilliput and Blefuscu . . . have . . . been engaged in a most obstinate war for six and thirty moons past. It began upon the following occasion. . . . His present Majesty's grandfather, while he was a boy, going to eat an egg, and breaking it according to the ancient practice, happened to cut one of his fingers. Whereupon the Emperor his father published an edict, commanding all his subjects, upon great penalties, to break the smaller end of their eggs. The people so highly resented this law, that our histories tell us there have been six rebellions raised on that account. . . . Many hundred large volumes have been published upon this controversy: but the books of the Big-Endians have been long forbidden.*

> —Jonathan Swift, *Gulliver's Travels*, 1726

I turned to fictional satire with *Travels of a New Gulliver* because it seemed to me that the ludicrous state of a viciously divided, neutered politics in the face of serious issues and potential disasters left unattended, as well as the equally ludicrous turn to personal and privatized responses called for satire. When there's a continuing tug of war as to which side owns the truth, and each side is reasoning in its own way, only Swiftian satire can provide that second order of observation which gives proper justice to the irrationalities and insanities on display.

Travels of a New Gulliver is modeled, of course, on Swift, but the genre is Voltaire's *Candide*, Diderot's *Jacques the Fatalist and His Master*, as well as *Rameau's Nephew*. I mock on the humble heels of Rabelais and feel the angry impatience of Ferdinand Céline, antic in the traces of Lewis Carroll. My new Gulliver is an empty slate, a naïf, a fool, a butt, a prig, a dysfunctional outlier, a victim, a stunned hapless soul, a man of solitude, a tenacious seeker, a spectator—"new" only because the world he travels into always surprises him. I include here the first, "In Which the Author Introduces Himself and Then Sets Out," and the last chapter, "The Author Comes to the End of His Travels," an end which was inevitable as the journey became more like Céline's *Journey to the End of Night* than tales children would read. In fact, this new Gulliver's travels has nothing of Swift's amalgam of storytelling, which leaves us forever in the imaginative land of Lilliput, Brobdingnag, and Houyhnhnms, and poignant satire of his own age. A loquacious parrot in search of identity is a comic Sancho Panza to the new Gulliver, and the fantastical is not in short supply, nor are comical characters. Nevertheless, there's more philosophy and critique here than storytelling. To my mind, it was as if my imagination played second fiddle to my critical intellect, and I did not wish this to be so. My odyssey of mind took me further from novel writing than I had hoped, surprising myself that I wound up closer to Blake's Urizen than Orc and Los, fiery spirits of revolt and imagination. Perhaps the reader will not find it so.

True to a postmodern style, I stole, without their genius, various characteristics of Dickens, Dante, Sterne, Melville, Kafka, Pirandello, Waugh, Le Guin, Chandler, Marquez, as well as characters from literature and film. Popular film provided templates for various chapters; for instance, in chapter 17, excerpts here presented, I had *Being John Malkovich* in mind and *Lost Horizon* in chapter 7, when the Author visits the Mountain Monastery of Mock. Film genres also were sampled. I sampled Bob Dylan's style as well as the Dalai Lama in chapter 4, "The Author Finds Himself in a Dark Wood." For the Author's recurrent boarding-house habitations and the characters therein, I sampled the portrayal of family life in W.C. Fields's in *It's a Gift* and *Man on the Flying Trapeze*. The 2008 US presidential election scene was parodied in chapter 8, "The Political Frontier and What the Author Finds There." I parodied The Singularity in chapter 18 when the Author visits The Singularity Club, as well as Wall Street in chapter 16 where it is called the Brigands' Stronghold. I brought Patrick Suskind's novel *Perfume* into the trial scene in chapter 5, "The Author's dangerous voyages into strange worlds of talk," by making that plot the basis of the prosecution's case. I sampled characters from Anthony Burgess's *A Clockwork Orange* in chapter 6, "The Author Makes a Miraculous Recovery and Sets Out to Find Less Talk," as well as characters from Melville and Kafka.

In Which the Author Introduces Himself and Then Sets Out

My father left me little but his wandering soul. My mother would avow that my peripatetic father owned a disposition that would not allow him to be happy anywhere yet urged him ever onward in such pursuit. In her opine, a present latitude and longitude would soon grow dark and stormy for my father while some distant horizon would begin to glow. And then he would be off in that direction, my mother and myself following.

I have inherited a belief that it is not happiness to be found in an ever-changing latitude and longitude but what can for a time rekindle the fires of interest, reawaken curiosity, and revive the spirit. Such travel can replace the conventional and everyday with a fascination and awe that this planet, this Great Outdoors of wonder, inspires if we just look beyond our own intent.

When my mother grew tired of such wandering, she returned with me to her family's estate in Nottinghamshire and bid adieu to my father who, as was his wont, wandered off.

Upon my mother's sudden death, I found myself in the care of a bachelor uncle whom I attended to in his dotage and whose moods and sudden rages were almost at once followed by a mellowness that put forth apologies I could not deny. My uncle Bruno was oddly wired, I suppose, from birth or perhaps, like Dickens's Mrs. Havisham, had been jilted. Perhaps he had anticipated a promising career in music but had lost his voice or his hearing. Possibly he had relied on friends and been disappointed. Perhaps all his close friends had died off; or perhaps the sporadic aches of gout or arthritis or Lyme disease commanded his disposition; or perhaps a parasite bequeathed to him by one of his cats had lodged in his brain and commanded his disposition. Perhaps the Goddess Fortuna had merely spun the wheel against him, or Odin's thread was wearing thin.

I was never sure of any cause but only quite certain that I spent my boyhood years observing closely the vicissitudes of mind that awaited us all.

My schooling fluctuated with Uncle Bruno's varying moods and so while I began with proper Church of England I did not remain there because the papist idea that a priest could relieve the mind's anguish took hold of him. As a result, I was removed from Church of England and enrolled in a Jesuitical institution.

One afternoon, upon returning from my classes, my uncle rose up and accused me of believing that his Lord was present in a bit of bread

I could then eat. A sudden anti-clerical turn of mind compelled him to now send me to be schooled in an esoteric philosophy that promised to place me in direct communication with the inner workings of all things.

I was at the stage of total bewilderment in regard to this course of study, when my uncle, in yet another frenzy, cursed all claptrap which obscured the basic rights of all to share the earth in common without obstructions of private property, money, and any form of buying and selling. My tenure here ended when I suggested to my uncle that it would be best if he gave up all rights to his own estate and divide his property among any and all.

And so I returned to Church of England schooling. Though my schooling was erratic, to say the least, I have excelled in the study of languages, both classical and modern, history, philosophy, botany, astronomy, rhetoric, and debate, and most especially, geography.

What I endured subject to my uncle's dementia caused me to vow to live my life fully before the diminishing of my own faculties. While I had all the capacity and potential of youth, I too would seek what any horizon promised.

In spite of my dedicated purpose to live an adventuresome life, I succeeded after my errant schooling to live a very sedentary life. Outside of the stimulating minds I encountered in the books I read, I became embedded in a way of life that offered only the stupefaction that inevitably inhabits a world of un-inquisitive minds pursuing what is petty and endlessly repeated. My youth began to lose its bloom in the tired dust of paths trod again and again in the selfsame ways.

I became so dazed myself that my former inclinations to escape the tedium of ordinary life gave way to that very tedium. I was on the brink of marriage and on a ladder to a promising career as an accounts manager when I contracted a deadly virus that was sweeping the globe, and for many weeks I lay in a state closer to death than life. My fever went so high as to vanquish all the ordinary barriers our conscious mind erects against the assault of chaotic musings and deeply buried traumatic moments of primordial ancestors that erupt in the present like volcanic outpourings.

I awoke from that nightmarish ride into the depths of my own mind with a certain theory and it was this: If I travelled and so disarranged my life so that the habitual gave way to the unknown, my internal time clock would, of necessity, constantly wind backward.

The more one knows through experience of the latitude and longitude of one's surroundings, the more one eats up the future before its arrival. In this fashion each day, each week, each month, each year came more speedily upon the one before. No amount of accidental chance could slow down for long that rapid digestion of time before it was lived.

I called upon my own memories of my childhood. What a summer was to be laid before me then as a great mystery that I attended to second-by-second as it unfolded. Every part of my childhood world for me was new, *terra incognita*, and my empty slate of mind had no way of instilling the slightest foreshadowing.

We have not the words in childhood to collapse the magnificence of the world into useful packaging, packaging that will eventually enable us to use, command, resist, and therefore diminish that world. We learn to talk above the world or around it, and our talk falls into patterns of practicality and efficiency, our talk becomes goal oriented and mission obsessed. We very soon become forgetful of what miraculous majesty resides in the sun, in the ocean, in the flowering of Nature.

Now, with a mind not only filled with all manner of knowledge but of the deadening redundancies of life in one place surrounded by minds equally confined, I was moving more rapidly than I had anticipated to the deterioration and incapacity which I saw in my poor uncle.

Determined then to renew my attentiveness to the world by renewing latitude and longitude, I wrapped up my affairs as they were and prepared myself to leave behind my old life. I quit my promising position of employment, made abject apologies to my beloved and assured her that her future would be brighter without me, made arrangements for the care of my uncle, and set off.

What follows here is a very loose account of my voyages and what I found, often accidentally, often against my own will, and seldom as I hoped.

I took with me only a few presumptions, for as Lao Tzu advises, a good traveller has no fixed plans and is not intent on arriving. My few presumptions were tied to my intent not to presume at all.

Is there need to say that I was already loaded at my age with all the baggage of immoveable personality? That I already owned my share of prejudices, deeply held beliefs, and absurd irrationalities that we humans inevitably acquire? How resistant or moveable my moral compass was to the challenges encountered in my travels, the reader must judge. How inflexible or accommodating my political views may seem and to what extent the claims of any society were acknowledged or repudiated, I also leave to the reader's discernment.

You can see how this fascination to step outside my provincial awareness took hold of me and prompted such a quick departure from my homeland.

Unfortunately, our ship was set astray one dark night by a ferocious storm, broke up upon those angry waves, and next morning I found myself a sole survivor on an unknown shore.

....

The Author Is Admitted to The Academy,
Inhabited by Enormous-Headed Giants; Visits The Wick,
the Great Augury, and The Singularity Club;
Meets a Terrorist, and Then Ends Badly

Entrance to the Great Augury is not a casual affair but treated with great pomp and . . . inspection. There were, in fact, three checkpoints that I had to go through before entering the Great Hall where at exactly noon the Great Augury would appear.

The parrot had to go through a Dirty Bomb checkpoint. He was not very pleased judging by his screams.

As I myself was carrying no more than a simple traveller's back-pack, which contained nothing more than a change of clothes and some toiletries and my perennial bedside read, Mr. Swift's *Gulliver's Travels*, I approached the first checkpoint with no trepidation.

I was surprised, however, to discover that my pack was taken off the belt for further inspection. The security official held up the Swift and asked if I knew that the volume exceeded permissible length, which length had been established by an exhaustive study of the reading habits of top spenders. We were allowed to bring into the Great Hall no box cutters, nail clippers, or Swiss Army knives, only three ounces of fluid, and no more than four pages of text, preferably with faces of friends. The Swift was in flagrant violation and was confiscated.

At the second checkpoint, a computer scan was made of my passport, and I was asked the purpose of my visits to Jumpback, Trickle Downs, the Floating Island of Babel, Brigands' Stronghold, the Green Zone, the Political Frontier, Yarbles, and every other place I had by accident or intent visited.

I very quickly discovered that my declarations of abduction and acci-dent fared better than any reasons for my visits, so I wound up declaring ill fortune as the designer of my itinerary.

The third inspection point was not concerned with my baggage or my sojourns but rather with my loyalties to the Terrorist. I said I had none and hardly knew what the Terrorist stood for and was told peremptorily that the Terrorist did not stand for anything, but he did indeed stand in the way of information.

I asked humbly what argument he could possibly have but was told that the Terrorist had no argument. He was as empty as a Black Hole but fools, the young, the disaffected, preternaturalists, loungers, beachcombers, ne'er-do-wells, blackguards, lotus-eaters, blighters, prevaricators, prestidigitators, jazz musicians, tightrope walkers, sundowners, loners, racketeers, mutants, Luddites, ICU nurses, fanatics, thugs, rascals, knaves, fallen angels, pimps, bastards, miscreants, degenerates, the unemployed, delinquents, masterless men, and desperate housewives were attracted to him.

I assured my interrogator that I was none of these and tried to look appropriately so. Nevertheless I was given only qualified admittance into the Great Hall which meant I had to stand in the back, wedged between two security personnel whose heads were quite small but whose length and breadth were gargantuan.

The Great Augury is not a man but a monumental image of a man's head that suddenly appears hovering above the stage at the far end of the Great Hall.

The voice is booming, the eyes are mesmerizing. If you've seen the classic movie *The Wizard of Oz*, he is the Wizard. I mean to say he is the Wizard before the real Wizard is discovered to be a nervous, stuttering, old man pulling levers behind a curtain. I turned my head to see if there was such a curtained area in the Great Hall but saw none. I stood at attention in between my escorts and listened to the Great Augury:

"In the beginning, the Great Augury was a search," the Great Voice echoed in my ears, "a computerized search some thought for quick access to knowledge. That was only a place on route to a computerized mind possessing more knowledge than any human mind. And the intelligence of that mind could not only be accessed and referred to but would be deferred to on any and all occasions. I am that mind. Why do you come to me? Why does anyone come to me for any reason? Because I am the mind that works best. I have the collective knowledge of millions and the mental circuitry to manipulate that knowledge in nanoseconds. I can take into account all known and all possible variables connected to any issue and provide answers and solutions. When instantaneous action is needed, the Great Augury is the only recourse.

How have I risen to such great power?"

At that moment, Sonny, who had been cleared as a Dirty Bomb in feathers, screeched loudly from somewhere on the other side of the Great Hall: "Suck an egg!"

The Great Augury went on as if it had heard nothing, and I concluded that imaged ears do not work.

"When you come to me as you have in greater and greater numbers over time, I learn your thoughts, your desires and interests, your hang-ups and fixations, your fears and dreams. I am built on the bedrock of all your searches. I am the artificial bricolage of all your mentalities, not only the accumulated knowledge of all humankind but the divinely empowered capabilities of every mind. I say 'divine' because the distance between my mind and yours is equivalent to a celestial distance."

I must have been fidgeting, dear reader, because my guardians pressed me more tightly on both sides, and I could feel their eyes upon me as if I were about to pull out a concealed box cutter and head for the stage.

....

The Author Comes to the End of His Travels[1]

I travelled through lives as if they were so much interesting or uninteresting scenery.

In my own defense I will say that Chance played me hard to right and left as I tried to journey forward. I did not place in this world the evil I found in others nor can I be held accountable for the darkness of our human nature and for the rapaciousness of our appetites that so clearly fires up to a violent inferno so much of what I have seen.

If I sought to escape much of what I encountered, I was forced to do so. I never ceased trying to understand all that I encountered but was led early on to question the bound nature of that faculty itself.

Regardless of what the parrot may think, I did not take an egoist's journey and did not address myself to you, dear reader, as an egoist standing before an admiring audience. Neither have I written my account so as to confound or depress you with the deplorable, the absurd, the asinine, or the manic; and if I failed to disclose any sense or meaning in what befell me, the fault is as much the world's as mine.

I don't know if Walker was ever brought to justice or if Ray ever received his chemo or if Betty Bombers has given up her child or if Captain Noble is still in prison or if Microft has taken up science again or whether Kate Whack ever did write her investigative piece on Skample or whether there is any peace now on the Political Frontier or whether Mrs. Angeloni and family were ever evicted or whether Zechariah and Rollins go on with their psychic battle or the Clotter boarders have all collapsed into poverty. Nor had I shown any interest in the fate of Sydney Noble and Ned Parsall, whom the parrot assured me were moving toward a romance that was both daring and interesting to all but myself. I never searched for Don Rodrigo, the murderer of innocent Billy. I had opportunities to stop Brother Frank but I could not muster the will. For all my tears over Carla's death, I forgot her easily enough.

Many places offended me because I found them too self-besot, too ungenerous, too rank and vile in their debased moral sense, too lost in charade and simulation, too far from truth and reason, too anxious to live like dogs rather than people.

I pronounced my judgment and then went to sea.

The parrot thought I did no good for anyone, some harm to some, some fatal harm to some, but for the most part travelled through the lives of others without care or concern or impact. No one was better for having seen me or heard me or known me.

In place of a moral review, I preferred depression. And Jamison. I thought of myself neither good nor bad but either depressed or eager. The parrot thought that what depressed me was a failure on the world's part to greet my eagerness with an eagerness of its own. The world failed to put in my path confirmation of what I reasoned to be true, failed to transparently reveal the workings of that celestial entity I evoked only because I saw that my will did not rule others and I could not stand for the will of others ruling me. My celestial entity was no more than a mask for myself.

Chance, the parrot admitted, often blew me off my course, but I was blind to what it showed me, anxious as I was to regain all that I was.

Everyone who spoke his or her mind to me or revealed his or her heart had done no more than throw seed on rock for I took up no cause nor pursued no belief nor acted for the good of anything but held only the rightness of travelling through and leaving all behind in the hope of finding something better.

The parrot revealed this to me over the long months we spent together in that cell and what parts of it I could absorb and make sense of I reveal here to you, my dear reader. But in my last and final defense I will say that it is immoral for other creatures to represent to you who you are, assuming as they do that what they say is the truth and usurping your own right to identify yourself.

I cannot say that the parrot was not entertaining in what he said, and I cannot say I took his words fully to heart as he was, after all, no more than a parrot. He had, perhaps, heard the various components of his diagnosis of me in a variety of conversations over his long life (I believe Captain Noble said the parrot was celebrating his fiftieth year when I met him but perhaps I misheard and it was his fifteenth year).

Because the two of us were so cloistered and so dependent upon each other's mood in that cell, I thought it best to take the high ground and therefore displayed no animosity toward him. I but informed him on the day we were released that he was not the bird I had taken him for to which he responded: "I am not at all the sort of person you and I took me for." I suppose then that the parrot had himself undergone some sort of transformation, not the least I would think from bird to person, in his own mind.

But we remain inseparable companions and were I to set off once again on my travels, the parrot, who has stuck with the name Jane, which revelation I find somewhat disconcerting after all this time and cannot fathom his amusement at our expense, has promised to travel with me. We will be gentlemen . . . friends . . . of the road once again.

My friends barely recognized me so changed was my outward appearance, and, truth to tell, had they been able to observe me inwardly they would not, I believe, have discovered the man they once knew.

. . . .

I have been for many years now a man who jumps back on every word spoken, regardless of occasion or speaker, and interrogates meaning with an unrelenting brutality. I am, in turns, seeking profit in all things and ranting against mammon; impatient with any matter not affecting me personally and immediately thereafter convinced that all matters personal are in actuality social. I am a man who can rise above the vicious combativeness of politics and also a man who relishes entering the knife fight that represents what politics is.

For many days I lose myself in cyberspace, following the thread of my life, and for just as many days I live screenless, eyes buried in long novels or gazing into the eyes of my fellow humans. I may greet you heartily on one day as if you were my brother and turn from you in disgust the next day as if you were scum.

I believe that whatever the imagination perceives is necessarily true and that what we hold as "that which is" in this world was once only imagined.

And then there are as many days when I believe that withdrawn into the web of our own imaginations we can lose ourselves and the world in a continuous inward spiral. On those days I see the world as a recuperative anchor to the imagination. I feel that the world is both the inspiration of what we imagine as well, paradoxically, as what endangers imagination, our blessed escape.

What I have chosen freely on Tuesday, I see on Wednesday as no more than the effects of Monday.

I have the will to empower myself one half the month, reminding myself that eagles do not catch flies, and spend the other half tracking my own illusions, reminding myself that doubtlessly I too am scripted, a performer whose character is inevitable fate.

I balance self-obsession with a frenzied quest to find in others what is not in myself. At the very moment I see before me a spiritual world, I see it is a picture someone with a baby face has drawn. Some of the time I can reason my way to the truth and some of the time I can't find a reason to go on living.

I bowl alone while I watch a TV monitor overhead showing other people bowling. I still rely on the 'paper of record' for the news, but I am totally mystified as to what is happening in the world.

I have given up travelling above ground, looking forward to continuing the same under drastically different circumstances.

I went far from home for many years to hear talk that eluded me, and I didn't return home to find it there waiting for me.

On some days, I talk with an energy only possessed by a man who believes he can capture the world with words. On other days . . .

. . . .

I mourn for the parrot who died this year, either seventy-five years of age or forty years of age. It does not matter. She is for the ages now. I buried her in my garden and put all the names she gave herself on the gravestone. The epitaph is her own:

Dirt & Poison
Honey & Wax
Sweetness & Light

And so I part from you, my dear reader.

Note

1. Excerpts from *Travels of a New Gulliver*, CreateSpace, Amazon, 2011.

Bibliography

Almost all of the previously published book chapters and print journal essays listed here were revised to meet the direction of this retrospective odyssey.

Natoli, Joseph P. 2003 (2014). "After September 11, 2001." *Memory's Orbit: Film and Culture 1999–2000*. Albany: SUNY Press.

———. 2015. "The American Middle Class: The Political Chosen People." *CounterPunch*. http://www.counterpunch.org/2015/09/18/the-american-middle-class-the-political-chosen-people/. Reprinted with permission.

———. 2010. "Autopsy TV." *Popmatters*. http://www.popmatters.com/feature/120776-autopsy-tv/. Reprinted with permission.

———. 2014. "The Code of Crisis and Disaster." *Truthout*. www.truth-out.org/.../item/23163-the-code-of-crisis-and-disaster. Reprinted with permission.

———. 1998. "Court and Culture: The Days of Our Lives with O. J." *Speeding to the Millennium: Film & Culture 1993–1995*. Albany: SUNY Press.

———. 2014. "Dark Affinities: Liberal & Neoliberal." *Truthout*. http://www.truth-out.org/op-ed/item/21139-dark-affinities-liberal-and-neo-liberal. Reprinted with permission.

———. 2009. "The Deep Morals of *Inglourious Basterds*." *Senses of Cinema*. http://sensesofcinema.com/2009/feature-articles/the-deep-morals-of-inglourious-basterds/.

———. 2014. "Doing the American Hustle." *Bright Lights Film Journal*. Reprinted with permission. http://brightlightsfilm.com/doing-the-american-hustle/#.V4a1A_krK6k.

———. 2014. "The Economics of Immiseration, the Politics of Seduction." *Truthout*. http://www.truth-out.org/news/item/22734-the-economics-of-immiseration-the-politics-of-seduction. Reprinted with permission.

———. 2013. "The Emergence of Greater than Human Sports . . . and Baseball." *Americana: the Journal of American Popular Culture*. http://www.americanpopularculture.com/archive/sports/baseball.htm. Reprinted with permission.

———. 2015. "Endless Deferment of Meaning." *Truthout*. http://www.truth-out.org/opinion/item/30719-endless-deferment-of-meaning-the-media-s-inequitable-melee-of-events-and-words. Reprinted with permission.

————. "Food TV." Condensed from "Our Strange TV Food World," "Weaponized Food Do We Need a Striped Eggplant," "Gulliver's Tale of Three Food Stores," and "Gulliver's Travels in Food, Gardening, and Cooking." *Dandelion Salad.* https://dandelionsalad.wordpress.com.

————. 1997. "Go to *Citizen Kane* to Find Twentieth-Century Modernism: On the Edge of Postmodernity." *A Primer to Postmodernity.* New Jersey: Wiley-Blackwell.

————. 2015. "Gun Control, Illegal Aliens, Moochers, Planned Parenthood, Gay Marriages, 'Big Brother' Government, and Obama." *CounterPunch.* http://www.counterpunch.org/2015/10/16/gun-control-illegal-aliens-moochers-planned-parenthood-gay-marriages-big-brother-government-and-obama/. Reprinted with permission.

————. 2016. "*The Hateful Eight:* History's Dark Bounty." *Bright Lights Film Journal.* http://brightlightsfilm.com/the-hateful-eight-tarantino-2016-western-70mm-lincoln-historys-dark-bounty/#.V4a6KfkrK6k. Reprinted with permission.

————. 2014. "Hearing the Ping of Poverty." *Truthout.* http://www.truth-out.org/opinion/item/23806-hearing-the-ping-of-poverty-or-not. Reprinted with permission.

————. 1994. "Hunting the Haunted Heart." *Hauntings: Popular Film and American Culture 1990–1992.* Albany: SUNY Press.

————. 2013. "The Leftist Psyche." *Bad Subjects.* http://bad.eserver.org/issues/2013/leftistpsyche-html.

————. 2010. "Living Backward the Millennials' Alice." *Bright Lights Film Journal.* http://brightlightsfilm.com/living-backward-the-millennials-alice/#.V4az4fkrK6k. Reprinted with permission.

————. 2013. "A Modest Proposal." *Truthout.* http://www.truth-out.org/speak-out/item/20685-a-modest-proposal-2014. Reprinted with permission.

————. 2015. "Our Millennial Age of Magic." *Bad Subjects.* http://bad.eserver.org/issues/2015/magic.htm.

————. 1984. "Phenomenological Psychology and Literary Interpretation." Revised from *Psychological Perspectives on Literature: Freudian Dissidents and Non-Freudians.* Hamden, Conn: Archon Books; 1986. "Dimensions of Consciousness in Hamlet." *Mosaic.*

————. 2015. "Plutocracy, Gentrification and Racial Violence." *CounterPunch.* http://www.counterpunch.org/2015/08/31/plutocracy-gentrification-and-racial-violence/. Reprinted with permission.

————. 1987. "Preface to *Tracing Literary Theory.*" Board of Trustees of the University of Illinois, pp. 3–24. Chicago: U of Illinois. Reprinted with permission.

————. 2001. "That Rug Really Tied the Room Together." Revised from *Postmodern Journeys: Film and Culture 1996–1998.* Albany: SUNY Press.

————. 2010. "To Gaga Is to Dada." *Popmatters.* http://www.popmatters.com/feature/128762-to-gaga-is-to-dada/. Reprinted with permission.

———. 2010. "Sons of Anarchy: Rebels and Bad Subjects with a Cause?" *Popmatters*. http://www.popmatters.com/feature/121444-sons-of-anarchy-rebels-and-bad-subjects-with-a-cause/.

———. 2010. "Dexter at the Tea Party." *Bad Subjects: Political Education for Everyday Life*. http://bad.eserver.org/issues/2010/natoli-dexter.html.

———. 2010. "The Twittering of *Twilight*." Revised from *The Journal of Popular Culture*, 43(4). http://onlinelibrary.wiley.com/doi/10.1111/j.1540-5931.2010.00764.x/abstract. DOI: 10.1111/j.1540-5931.2010.00764.x.

———. 2013. "US Higher Education: The New 'Treasure Island' for Investors." *Truthout*. http://www.truth-out.org/opinion/item/19892-us-higher-education-the-new-treasure-island-for-investors. Reprinted with permission.

———. 2011. "Why the Rich Get Richer, and Other Truth Stories." *Political Affairs*. http://politicalaffairs.net/why-the-rich-get-richer-and-other-truth-stories/. Reprinted with permission.

Index

advertisements, and death, 225–26

Affair to Remember, An, 89

Affordable Care Act, as Big Government imposition, 321–22

Against Method: An Outline of an Anarchistic Theory of Knowledge, 56

Altizer, Thomas, and Blake, 9

American cultural imaginary, xxii, xxiii, xxiv, xxv, 4, 19, 20; and baseball, 239–42; and choices, 119; dark and hopeful, 271; as divided and affiliated, 271; and education, 259; examination of, 172–78; and fear, 176; and food, 231; as fractured, 111; and freedom to choose, 43; and *The Hateful Eight*, 201–09; and the hustle, 195; and hyper/hyped consciousness, 22–23, 177; and the hyperreal, 154; and mass paranoia, 153, 246; and memoir, 130–31; and money, 213; and moral hazard, 168; and moral relativism, 67; in motion, xxvi; and mutual aid, 14; and 9/11, 134–36; and popular culture, 193–209; and postmodernity, 104, 117; and psychomachia, 329–34; and psychotherapy, xxvii; and rule of opinions, 227; and scenarios of climate change, 272–77; and socialism, 173; and stories of the rich, 167; and TV, 221–26, *passim;*,

and *Twin Peaks*, 156; and winners, and losers, 290; and the working class hero, 267

American Dream, and the collapse of security; and food, 231; and hustle, sex, and greed, 198; and leisure, and consumption, 287; monetized view, 293; and money, 224; and money in *Breaking Bad*, 214, 216, 224; and the rich, 42; of the Winners, 116

American exceptionalism, darkened, 248; and foreigners, 247; and *The Hateful Eight*, 201; and Liberals and Neoliberals, 271; moral nature of, 87

American Hustle, 194–200

American mass psyche. *See* American cultural imaginary

Americana: The Journal of American Popular Culture, interview, 193

anarchy, and anarchists, xviii; and *The Sons of Anarchy*, 211, 212, 219–21

Anderson, P. T., 194

Aristotle, 96; politics and civic morality, 161

Atlan, Henri, and language, 61

attentiveness, and Attention Deficit Disorder, 53; continuous and augmented, 303; and world, 75

austerity, and Great Recession, 153; and Liberals and Neoliberals, 248; its psychic roots, 176; and the

difference, and history, 308–09; and
identity, 109; and the Twitter
moment, 307–08
Different Existence, A, 15, 19
Discipline and Punish, 179
discourse, public, and Twitter, 187;
rational, and the social unconscious,
247
disorder, 55–61; and order, 58; in
literature, 3, 57–61
District 9, 86
doping, and baseball, 236–42
Dostoevsky, Fyodor, *The Possessed*, 28
Dreger, Alice, quoted, 319
Duck Dynasty, guns and religion, 212;
economy and religion, 215
Dude, The, 3; and *The Big Lebowski*,
120–29, *passim*; 149–50; 168; as
abiding 129
Duplicity, 89

Eagleton, Terry, 99
Earth First!, and pantheism, 41
Eco, Umberto, and the postmodern,
89
economics, of immiseration, 253–58;
issues, in millennial view, 293,
321; and mobility, socio-economic,
in the U.S., 265–70 *passim*;
on-demand, 288; and political
equality, 190; psychopathology
of, 223; supply side, xii. *See also*
capitalism, market rule
The Economist Pocket World in Figures,
152
education, as e-commerce, 262–63;
free exchange of ideas, in higher,
261–65; higher, 258–65; higher, and
protests, 265; higher, review essay
of, 258; institutions for profit, 258;
as market driven, 181–84, *passim*,
258–65, *passim*; and school, public,
reform of, 258–60; and schools,
charter, multinational corporate

support of, 259; privatization of,
183; public, and personal choice,
321; and social media, 263; and
teaching, and neutral discussion,
181–84, *passim*
Einstein, Albert, 66
Enlightenment, and Hannibal Lecter,
109; and magic, 319–20; and
politics, 15; pretenses of, 70; and
twentieth-century modernism,
73–86, *passim*

Facebook, 47; and choice, 88; and
de-friending, 51; and illusions, 180;
and personal interest, 119; and
politics, 42
Fanon, Frantz, 54
fantasies, and illusion, 254–58, *passim*.
See also illusions
Farewell, My Lovely, 123
Fargo, 123
Father, The, 22–31, *passim*
fear, and the American cultural
imaginary, 176; and desires, 255;
macro and micro, 222; as universal,
158
Federman, Ray, and *Critifiction*, 103
Feyerabend, Paul, and a dream world,
56, 58
film. *See* movies
Film noir, 155
food, in the American cultural
imaginary, 231; and branding,
235–36; and discipline, 233; and
erudition, and gentrification,
234; as expression of individual
freedom, 231; and fast-food culture,
227–37, *passim*; as free-floating and
transactional, 233; and gentrification,
233; and market rule, 234; its
political dimension, 233–34; and
psychosis, 231; as soma, 231–32;
and TV, 226–37; virtualization of,
233; as weaponized, 234–36

Life-world (*Lebenswelt*), 19–22, 56; and
  consciousness, 20; and disorder and
  order, 58–61; and Hamlet, 32–37;
  humanity's and Nature's, 17; and
  identifying, 57; literary, 32, 46, 56;
  and psychology, 31–37, *passim*
Literary Theory's Future(s), 101–02
lobbyists, and brain space, 171–72; and
  legislation, 218; and students, 262;
  and winners, 114
Lucretius, 17
Lynch, David, 85
Lyotard, Jean Francois, 19, 97–98

magic, millennial, as mindset, traits
  and illusions of, 320–23
Mailer, Norman, violence as the
  dream life of the U.S., 213
Marcuse, Herbert, and "repressive
  tolerance," 67
market rule, 17, 64; and education,
  181–84, *passim*; and egalitarian
  democracy, 183; and food, 234; and
  global warming solutions, 274; and
  marketers, and a promised orgasm,
  299; and moral valuation, 215; and
  post-truth age, 200; and regulation,
  of the financial sector, 252; and
  salaries, 213; as sole authoritative
  voice in the U.S., 321; and uses of
  postmodernity, 67; and winning,
  115
Marriage of Heaven and Hell, The, 3,
  10–13, 55. *See also* capitalism
Marxism, 2, 174; its promise, 177
meaning, and bibliography, and the
  search for literary, 48; as ruled by
  dollars, 311; search for in *Citizen
  Kane*, 83; and value, 124; and value,
  as cultural constructions, 114
media, and the cult of balance,
  332; and cyberspace, 104, 232;
  and "democratization," 181; and
  education, 263; and Facebook, 65,

119; and journalism, citizen variety,
  182; as Liberal, and millennials, 65;
  and public, as counter to profit
  media, 191; reportage, disinterested,
  in a lopsided society, 50–54, *passim*;
  as social, 119; in the U.S., 50–54
Melville, Herman, and Ahab, 28
memoir, and the '90s American
  cultural imaginary, 129–31
Memories, Dreams, and Reflections, 22
Memory's Orbit, xvi, 103, 129–46,
  passim
Merchants of Cool, Frontline, 2001, 38
Merleau-Ponty, Maurice, and
  Phenomenology of Perception, 32
Merod, Jim, 101
metafiction, 61
middle class, American, 290–95; and
  economic mobility, 16; fear of
  decline, 42; fear of the underclass,
  139; and former well-being, 143;
  and gentrification, 141, 266; its
  heyday and descent, 267–69; its
  liminal life, 143; and neoliberal
  seductions, 254, 286; and plutocracy,
  190, 266–67; and Reagan, 170;
  and rebellion, 287; in shards, 145,
  266; and wage decline, and work,
  289–90
millennials, and baseball, 240; and
  a critique of "like," 328; culture
  of, 47, 70, 177; and cyberspace,
  162–64; and government, 322; and
  moral concerns, 87–88; and new
  habits of time and mind, 26; and
  politics not social but personal, 332;
  portrait of, 295–324; and self-image,
  269; and truth, 165; and will to
  success, 38
Miller, J. Hillis, 95
Milton, John, and Blake, 91; and
  Satan, 42
modernism, its anxieties, 70–72; its
  darkness, in the 1990s, 133–34;

post-truth age, 65; 194–95; and
  absolute judgments, 180; influences
  on politics and profiteers, 118; and
  marketing and branding strategies,
  16; and market rule and cyberspace,
  200; and narratives, 52; as opposed
  to empirical view, xxvii; and the
  postmodern, 295
poverty, Neoliberal case against the
  poor, 256–57 *passim*; and the
  rich and poor, 13; and stochastic
  economic system, 258–65, *passim*;
  and West Virginia, 137–41 *passim*
power, asymmetrical arrangement
  of, 179–84; illusions of, 254; and
  millennials, 318; and wealth, xxiii;
  and wealth and market rule, 181
Primer to Postmodernity, A, 2, 63, 64
psychiatry, phenomenological, and
  politics, 243; and popular culture,
  193; and psychopathology, 17,
  19–43 *passim, 223. See also*
  psychology
Psychological Perspectives on Literature, 21
psychology, and literature, 31–37,
  passim; phenomenological, 3. *See
  also* psychiatry
phenomenology, and postmodernity, 46;
  in psychology and psychiatry, 19–43.
  See also psychology, psychiatry
psychomachia, as cultural psychic
  battlefield, 171–78; as drama of
  the American cultural imaginary,
  329–36
public domain, commitment to, 186;
  its intellectuals, 161–62; and private
  interests, 326; and public good and
  socialism, 256; and public good, the
  indifference to, 164
public good. *See* public domain
public sphere. *See* public domain

Rabelais, Francois, and Mikhail
  Bakhtin, 96

Raine, Kathleen, and Blake, 9
Rapaille, Clotaire, and the reptilian
  brain, 37–39
readers, and intentionality, 46; and
  postmodern reading, 48–50; and
  reading as classic realist, 49; and
  strategies of, 49
Reagan, Ronald, xxiv; and class
  warfare, 170; and erosion of social
  mobility, 267–68; and oligarchy, 220;
  and trickle-down economics, 106
reality, and academe, 101; and
  American Hustle, 194–20, *passim*;
  as analog and dull, 240; and *The
  Big Lebowski*, 120–29, 155, *passim*;
  as boots on the ground, 245; in
  Borges, 48; and Burton's *Alice in
  Wonderland*, 312–19, *passim*; and
  Citizen Kane, 72–86, *passim*; and
  cyberspace, 69, 104, 164; and
  different cultures, 152; of food,
  228–36, *passim*; as frames, 26, 32;
  and *The Hateful Eight*, 207–09; and
  Heisenbeg Uncertainty Principle,
  276; and imagination, xxviii; and
  Liberals and Leftists, 173; and
  market rule, 163; and the millennial
  clime, 170; narrated nature of,
  117, 139; and the O. J. Simpson
  trial, 113–17; on-line and off-
  line and baseball, 241; personally
  designed views of, 65, 174, 200;
  as phenomenal, 13–18, *passim*; as
  phenomenal, in *Hamlet*, 33–37; and
  postmodernity, 104, 118; and power,
  66; and a private insularity, 309; as
  rational, 116; and representation, 90;
  and seductions, 258; and *Silence of
  the Lambs*, 108; in Tarantino's view,
  86–94, *passim*; and TV, 129, 154–55,
  159; and truth, 164; and truth in
  American Hustle, 196; and tweets,
  311; and *Twin Peaks*, 156; vampire
  kind, 310; and visionary facts, 20;

Made in the USA
Middletown, DE
31 October 2020